'EVEN WHEN THE SPARROWS ARE WALKING'

Published by

Librario Publishing Ltd

ISBN No: 0-9542960-0-1

(First published 2001 by Gopher Publishers UK. ISBN No: 90-5179-001-5)

Copies can be ordered via the Internet
www.librario.com

or from:

Brough House, Milton Brodie, Kinloss
Moray IV36 2UA
Tel /Fax No 01343 850 617

Printed & bound by Antony Rowe Ltd, Eastbourne

'Even When the Sparrows are Walking'

The Origin and Effect of No. 100 (Bomber Support) Group, RAF, 1943-45

Laurie Brettingham

Librario

*'Main Force has been stood down due to bad weather, but we fly,
gentlemen, even when the sparrows are walking.'*

Group Captain N A N Bray, DFC, Station Commander, North Creake, (No.100 Group)
at a briefing early in 1945.

Contents

Diagrams

Acknowledgements

Many people have contributed to this book by letter and interview and I express my gratitude to all. Particular thanks are due to Maryse Addison for allowing me access to the private papers of her father, Air Vice-Marshal E B Addison CB, CBE, the AOC of No.100 Group; Lady Rowena Ryle provided me with some private 'jottings' made by her husband, Professor Sir Martin Ryle, FRS, who, amongst other wartime duties, was Scientific Liaison Officer to the Group; Juliet Gass allowed me to quote extensively from her father, Wing Commander Norman Cordingly OBE,s book,'From a Cat's Whisker Beginning', in which he described life, and his duties, at No.100 Group HQ where he served as Group Radar Officer. I would also like to thank Harry Reed (No. 169 Squadron) and Bill Bridgman (No.515 Squadron) for their assistance in tracing members of their old squadrons.

My grateful thanks also to my wife, Daphne, who has been helpfully encouraging throughout the researching and writing of the book. Unless an alternative source is stated she drew the illustrations.

Other contributors (ranks, decorations, and professional qualifications, are not shown) were: Mike Allen, N D N Belham, Bert Berry, Rosemary Bower, Michael Carreck, Ken Chapman, Charles Clarke, Eric Clarkson, Philip Colehan, Ralph Connolly, E H Cooke-Yarborough, Ron Crafer, A N Craven, Jim Feasey, Vic Flowers, Peggy Frodin, Peter Giles, E Gomersall, Pamela Gosman, Reg Gould, Pat Gregory, Ted Harper, Cedric Hall, Ted Hardwick, Chris Harrison, Gerhard Heilig, Bryan Helm, Antony Hewish, Jack Hilton, Phil James, George Jamieson, Alan Jeffrey, Bill Jones, Les King, Leonard Lamerton, David Leete, Robert Light, Frank Lindsay, E J Longden, G T Lowe, Norman Mackenzie, Brendan Maguire, Betty Marlowe, Alex McLelland, E and R L Mears, Alan Mercer, Werner Mihan, Roy Mitchell, Bert Moir, George Morley, Bert Mowlem, Bob Muir, Ken Phelan, Jack Philipson, Vic Policheck, Kelvin Purdie, Eric Reedman, Eric Rostron, Frank Savage, N T Scott, Ivy Shinn, John Short, D R Smallwood, Geoff Sparrow, H C Sykes, George Stewart, George Thorne, Ken Thornton, Eric Turner, Merv Utas, Derek Vonberg, R E Vowler, John Whitehead, Peter Woodard.

The following publishers have kindly allowed me to quote from books in which they hold copyright (full details in Bibliography): ADAM HILGER, 'Boffin, A Personal Story of the Early Days of Radar, Radio Astronomy and Quantum Optics'; CRECY PUBLISHING, 'Night Flyer'; SQUARE ONE (Pamela Northrop), 'The Autobiography of a Trenchard Brat'; MIDLAND PUBLISHING, 'Bomber Command War Diaries'; CASSELL, 'Bomber Harris'; CHATTO and WINDUS,

'Cover of Darkness; HMSO, 'History of the Second World War, UK Series vol 1, Victory in the West'; STODDART PUBLISHING, 'A Thousand Shall Fall.'

Grateful acknowledgement is also made of permission to use extracts from George Stewart's article 'Night Intruder' (Canadian Aviation Historical Society, 1977), and 'A Bomber Pilot's Diary' by Lyle James ('Air Force'; Magazine of the Air Force of Canada, vol 19, 1995).

Foreword

My father Air Vice-Marshal E B Addison, CB, CBE, would be delighted that the dedicated work of the men and women under his command, first in No. 80 Wing, and then No. 100 Group, had been meticulously documented in Laurie Brettingham's two books.

The first the public heard of the work of radio countermeasures (RCM) and the tricks played on the Luftwaffe was at a press conference in November 1945. 'It was like a game of chess,' my father said. 'We had the Hun wriggling and squirming every time to get away from our countermeasures.' One newspaper called him 'the War's greatest spoofer'. He enjoyed that. Despite the deadly seriousness of the situation, I can't help feeling that my father's propensity for practical jokes meant that he derived great satisfaction in thinking up new scams to confuse the enemy. His success gained the appreciation of Bomber Command as well as the respect of the Luftwaffe who acknowledged that No. 100 Group had well and truly beaten them at their own game.

My father was never happier than when he was in the thick of things. He had an enormous capacity for work. A memory from the No. 80 Wing Operations Room is typical. 'We were all amazed as he was constantly walking in just as things were hotting up. He was always there,' recalled one of his officers, John Whitehead. But as far as his 8-year-old daughter was concerned, he was never there! He would return home at 8o'clock every morning for a bath and change of clothes, then come into my bedroom to give me a kiss, and then he was gone again!

After the 30 years' restriction was lifted on documents from the Second World War, many books appeared detailing different aspects of the secret war. 'Why,' I asked my father, 'didn't you write a book?' 'I couldn't,' he replied. 'There is still too much which cannot be said.'

Maryse Addison
Brighton, May 2001

Chapter One

An Added Dimension

The decade before the Second World War saw fearsome evidence of the build-up of aerial bombardment as a means of destruction. In October 1935 the Italian Dictator, Benito Mussolini, acquired international infamy when invading Abyssinia by causing his Air Force to drop mustard gas and high-explosive bombs on almost defenceless native soldiers. Two years later the Kondor Legion of the German Luftwaffe, supporting the Nationalist forces of General Franco in the Spanish Civil War, prepared itself for extensive future combat over Europe by attacking, for four hours, the defenceless country town of Guernica in the Basque region of north east Spain causing heavy loss of life to the civilian population and great damage.

Alongside this expanding, aggressive air power significant technological advances took place. Amongst these was the development of radio and radar for military purposes in what eventually became known as 'The Radio War'; this gained in urgency and momentum as Europe lurched towards war. In 1939, the out-break of hostilities between Britain and Germany provided a powerful impetus to this new, scientifically led, by-product of modern warfare.

The Beginning of Radar in Warfare

In January 1935, the Director of Research at the Air Ministry, H E Wimperis, asked Robert (Later Sir Robert) Watson-Watt, who was Superintendent at the Radio Research Station of the National Physical Laboratory at Slough, whether it would be possible to use intense radio waves to provide a 'death-ray' which would incapacitate enemy aircraft and crews.[1] Watson-Watt dismissed this idea as unworkable but informed him that his laboratory was, meanwhile, 'giving attention to the still difficult, but less unpromising problem of radio detection as opposed to radio destruction, and numerical considerations on the method of detection by reflected radio waves will be submitted if required.'

In subsequent correspondence, Watson-Watt, with remarkable foresight, detailed the possibilities of detecting aircraft by the energy which they would reflect when illuminated by a powerful radio beam. The use of radar in warfare had begun; it was to prove invaluable to the fighting services.

Many years later one writer closely involved in those early days described it thus:

In fact the invention of radar in Britain was not a dramatic event, no Archimedes jumped out of his bath shouting. 'Eureka!' It was an almost perfect illustration of necessity being the mother of invention and was done in the sort of way which appeals to tidy-minded people who believe that the production of original ideas, like the production of meat pies, can be planned.[2]

Countermeasures Used for Defence

Initially used in a defensive capacity the new phenomenon originally manifested itself in Britain with the erection of ground radar[3] sites, Chain Home (CH) stations, along the eastern coast of the United Kingdom. Developed by scientists to warn against oncoming enemy attacks from the air, they were to play a vital part in the Battle of Britain.

In 1936, E G 'Taffy' Bowen a scientist at the Air Ministry Research Establishment (AMRE) at Bawdsey, on the Suffolk coast, the forerunner of the Telecommunications Research Establishment (TRE), began working, almost single-handed on Airborne Interception (AI), an area of the radio war in which he was to spend most of the wartime years. He had, in the words of Robert Watson-Watt 'to compress a radar station into an item of aircraft equipment' requiring vast reductions in equipment size and weight. Difficulties abounded. There were difficulties with transmitter power, aerials needed to be much smaller, and there were few valves available at the time which could generate the required power. Bowen initially used a system (known as RDF 1.5.) where the 30 kilowatt transmitter was on the ground (erected on the roof of the Red Tower at Bawdsey), and the receiver (6.7 metre) was placed in an ageing Handley Page Heyford aircraft. Such was the beginning which, improved with development, led to the later equipments that were to prove invaluable in aerial warfare.

'They had seen so many bright ideas come to naught'

Initially, AI was received on nightfighter squadrons with some misgivings. How were the men who were going to use the equipment operationally viewing the new equipment? For some time they had been trying, with limited success, to combat the German night bombers attacking Britain. Lewis Brandon was on a squadron when the change took place:

> A couple of lectures were laid on to give them some idea of what AI could do, for it was something quite new to them. Nearly all the pilots had been chasing about in the dark, without much success, for a year or so. Although they hoped that this AI stuff might be of some use, I could well understand that many of them were only prepared to take it with a pinch of salt; they had seen so many

bright ideas come to naught. Besides, many of them had wanted to be on day fighters, which seemed to offer a great deal more action, so that they were rather disgusted with the night lark.[4]

The initial scepticism proved unfounded and the introduction of AI (with cooperation from ground based radar stations) contributed emphatically to the nightfighters' efficiency in defending Britain against the German night attacks.

Early in the Second World War various defences against radio beams, which it was believed were being used for navigational and blind bombing purposes by the enemy, were also being feverishly worked upon. A large number of the nation's scientific and engineering minds, many hitherto only used to working independently, worked to a common purpose exploring possible countermeasures to this new threat. An operational product of this was the formation in June 1940, after the fall of France, of No.80 (Signals) Wing RAF, the mainly ground-based radio countermeasures (RCM) unit, commanded by Wing Commander E B Addison.

Onto the Offensive

With the Luftwaffe failing to gain command of the air over Britain Hitler abandoned his plan to invade the United Kingdom. In June 1941, in an act of strategic folly, he ordered his forces to attack Russia thereby committing them to fighting on two fronts. Later in the year the attack by the Japanese on Pearl Harbour saw the United States of America – with its immense resources – openly taking up the Allied cause. A change of emphasis in the prosecution of the war began to take place.

The year of 1942 was to prove a watershed with improved fortune for the Allies who shifted from defence to attack. Bomber Command was playing its part. It had, with limited success, been carrying the battle to Germany from the beginning of the War. The effort had proved costly. Senior officers, looking for assistance in reducing losses, thought the provision of counter-measures against the German radio and radar defences arrayed against the RAF bomber force during its raids was likely to prove helpful.

Their thinking was clearly explained by the Air Officer Commanding (AOC) of Bomber Command, Air Chief Marshal (later Marshal of the Royal Air Force) Sir Arthur Harris, GCB, OBE, AFC, in his report[5] at the War's end on the Command's activities:

> The Radio Countermeasures offensive, planned specifically to support Bomber
> Command operations, was wholly developed during the years 1942-45. The
> German controlled night-fighter system, against which the greater part of the
> Bomber Command Radio Countermeasures have been directed, became by 1941
> a factor which was clearly destined to become a very serious menace to the night

bomber. At the same time, the employment of radar aids to flak control increased the efficiency of that other main weapon of German defence against an attack.

At the beginning of 1942, the reality of the threat to our aircraft was well established. The existence of the nightfighter control system was known and much of its method of operational working had been correctly deduced from 'Y' Service [the RAF Unit which intercepted German radio signals] and other intelligence information. There was still lacking, however, the necessary knowledge about the actual radio and radar apparatus in use by the enemy, without which no technical countermeasures could be devised.

During the first six months of 1942 this technical information was gradually acquired. Aerial photographs and captured documents told of the locations and appearance of enemy radar apparatus. From photographs it was possible to form an opinion about the capabilities and functions of the various radar devices and to supplement the information already obtained from the 'Y' Service particularly that part of it which was concerned with monitoring radar transmissions. The Bruneval raid of 27th February, 1942, was successful in its object of capturing a small Würzburg apparatus of the type used for plotting bombers and friendly fighters in a closely controlled interception. By May,1942, an almost complete and very accurate picture of the enemy methods of Ground Controlled Interception (GCI), fighter control had been built up.

At the same time, the rate of losses suffered on bombing operations was steadily rising and it appeared that much of the increase was due to the greater efficiency of the enemy defences following the large-scale introduction of radar-assisted control of both guns and fighters.

Early Radio Countermeasures (RCM) for Bomber Support

Towards the end of 1941, technical and intelligence investigations had been carried out by the RCM group at TRE, to assist Fighter Command sweeps expanding over Europe, and the Bomber Command offensive. In another postwar appraisal[6], the Group's Head, Dr. (later Sir) Robert Cockburn, giving the scientist's viewpoint, remembered the period from the spring of 1941 until the spring of 1942 as one of , 'largely consolidation and mental gestation.' 'During 1941-1942,' he recalled, 'most of the actual RCM projects were in support of Fighter Command who were engaged in the task of regaining air supremacy over France...it was only in the Spring of 1941, when the problems of defensive jamming had been largely solved, that effort became available for the creation of counter radar techniques.'

First results of the TRE study revealed the nature and extent of the enemy's radar systems, and the desirability of neutralising these facilities in the near future.

Three important technical concepts were established. These were:-

[a] The use of 'noise' as an undefeatable jamming modulation.

[b] The simultaneous jamming of a large number of adjacent channels by means of a frequency 'barrage'.

[c] The small amount of jamming power required in an aircraft to screen it from ground radar.

These fundamental concepts determined later development of RCM techniques.[7]

Plans were evolved which, it was hoped, would institute a jamming offensive against the early warning radar chain deployed by the enemy along the coast which they occupied opposite the United Kingdom. The aim was to push back their long range radar cover; similar action against the short range radar and nightfighter interception system was also hoped for. Code words, which would become well-known with the development of the radio war, were introduced for the new countermeasures. MANDREL was a jammer first used against the enemy's Freya long-range radar stations by aircraft of Fighter Command, and CARPET was a jammer for 'spoiling' ground Würzburg radars which the enemy used to control its Anti-Aircraft (AA) guns, for GCI purposes and for 'coast watching'. In addition, a flight of Boulton Paul Defiants of No.515 Squadron was used for MOONSHINE, a single-frequency jamming of the enemy's Freya radar by simulating a mass of aircraft on its radar screens. Although development of both ground and airborne MANDREL sets was not given high priority at first, by May 1942, these three offensive countermeasures were considered to be sufficiently developed to warrant the prototyping of aircraft for the airborne equipment. GROUND MANDREL sites were also selected for the new countermeasures. Another ground-based RCM, GROUND CARPET, was also developed to jam the short-range enemy radar warning system over a short length of the enemy-held coastline opposite Dover.

MANDREL, CARPET and MOONSHINE together formed a protective and spoof screen, the tactical use of which could be applied in a variety of ways. MANDREL aircraft would fly at suitably spaced intervals over the Channel supplemented by GROUND MANDREL stations (operated by No. 80 Wing) at Dover, Hastings, Ventnor (Isle of Wight) and Kimmeridge (near Swanage). The single GROUND CARPET station was installed next to the GROUND MANDREL station at Dover.

In addition, airborne jammers were being more widely developed and WINDOW, intended to produce so many responses in a given area that the enemy's radar devices could not plot aircraft in that area accurately, had been conceived, but not used operationally for fear of retaliation by the enemy. The possible benefits which could be obtained from the use of RCM were, nevertheless, becoming well known.

In August 1942, the Operational Research Section (ORS) at Bomber Command observed that during the previous two months Bomber Command losses had been between 5-6 %. After examining the results of the new policy, it suggested that if complete counter-measures could be taken against the German radio defences the total loss rate of bombers could be reduced by one third. ORS urged that the highest priority be given to the development of all countermeasures against enemy radar.

Their views were echoed by others concerned at bomber losses and high-level support for RCM was forthcoming:

> The Air Officer Commanding, Bomber Command, (Air Chief Marshal Sir Arthur Harris) agreed that the time had come when technical as well as tactical means should be exploited in order to minimise the effectiveness of the enemy defences, and asked the Air Ministry to provide suitable countermeasures on the highest priority.[8]

In addition to MANDREL, MOONSHINE and CARPET it was also hoped that the International Friend or Foe (IFF) set, suitably modified, would also cause some interference, but no other properly designed offensive counter-measures were immediately available.

Senior RAF officers attended a meeting on 6th October, 1942, at Bomber Command HQ, which was presided over by the Senior Air Staff Officer (SASO), Air Marshal Sir Robert Saundby, KCB, KBE. Sir Henry Tizard, Scientific Adviser to the Air Staff, was also in attendance. Three recommendations were made at the meeting which supported reinforced RCM status at this stage in the air war. (a)Increased advantage, it was felt, should be taken of the interference caused by IFF to German radar by using sets, specially modified to interfere with the German intermediate radar frequency (53cm): (b) MANDREL would be fitted into RAF aircraft to jam Freyas (which at the time were believed to be used by the enemy GCI for directing the Würzburg narrow beam radar on to a raiding aircraft during the early stages of an interception): and, (c) the GROUND MANDREL stations of No. 80 Wing, and the MANDREL aircraft of Fighter Command should be used to reduce enemy early-warning radar cover. Approval to these recommendations was given by the Air Ministry on 19th October 1942, and MANDREL was brought into use in the following December.

Modification of the IFF MkII as an RCM was known in Bomber Command by the code-name MONKEY (later SHIVER). When IFF MkIII was proposed to be introduced in February 1943 Bomber Command evaluated SHIVER. Precise results could not be obtained as the other countermeasures, MANDREL and TINSEL[9] , were also brought into use at about the same time. It was noted that references were made by German pilots of interference on their AIs. There were also several occasions when their control stations referred to interference or lost radar contact. During the first month of use the only aircraft fitted with SHIVER suffered considerably less flak than those not fitted. During the latter months there was no noticeable difference to the months prior to SHIVER's use. It seemed although this RCM possibly had some effect when introduced, it did not take the enemy long to eliminate the interference.

Help was forthcoming in other ways. In March 1942 the Germans started to make efforts to interfere with RAF radio aids to navigation by jamming the Medium Frequency (MF) beacons used by Bomber Command. The initial jamming was crude but was later replaced by a meaconing method and this caused considerable inconvenience to Bomber Command aircraft, who, before the implementation of the Gee system, relied heavily on the beacons for navigation and homing back to base. To counteract this, and provide navigational assistance to Bomber Command, two fresh countermeasures, WASHTUB and SPLASHER, were brought into use in the following month.

The first, WASHTUB, used the high-powered BBC transmitter at Droitwich. In order to render them useless to enemy aircraft for navigational purposes, the high-powered BBC transmitters operated generally during the War period as members of synchronised groups and their use by friendly aircraft for homing purposes was therefore not possible. However, with the introduction of WASHTUB the Droitwich transmitter, which was used for broadcasting foreign propaganda, was left 'unspoiled' (open) from two hours after sunset on any night when it was required by Bomber Command for navigational purposes. During these periods the transmitter was under the control of No.80 Wing HQ (via the Liaison Officer at Fighter Command HQ) who could issue orders to 'spoil' (or close down) the transmission in the event of enemy activity. This scheme, which was regarded purely as an emergency measure, was favourably received by RAF aircrews who stated that it provided excellent homing facilities within a range of 150 miles. It was, however, discontinued on 12th April 1942.[10]

The second, was the SPLASHER system (introduced on 4th April 1942) in which certain No. 80 Wing MEACON transmitters were used as assembling and homing beacons. The transmitters used were sited in groups of four at points along lines roughly parallel to the Eastern and Southern coasts of Britain, the original groups being situated at No.80 Wing stations Marske (Yorks), Louth (Lincs), Scole (Suffolk), Flimwell (Kent), Ashmansworth (Hants), Fairmile (Devon) and Mintlaw (Aberdeenshire). Thus organised it was possible to provide a large number of additional beacon transmissions on different frequencies. Transmitters at any given site employed a common call sign so that if one particular frequency was subjected to enemy interference it was possible to move to another frequency with the same call sign to obtain a bearing. Call signs and frequencies were operated on a secret schedule operated by HQ Bomber Command. No. 80 Wing controlled the SPLASHER organisation and they had the right to close down any transmitters which might be needed for meaconing purposes. Meaconing was the interference with Luftwaffe beacon signals by No. 80 Wing. A receiver site would pick up the signal, transfer it by landline to a transmitter site, who would re-radiate it. This could not be detected in aircraft fitted with normal receiving equipment and caused navigational confusion to the attackers.

SPLASHER became an immediate success when introduced, the enemy RCM organisation being swamped by weight of numbers. Good results were obtained and it was popular with the RAF aircrews who were impressed with its simplicity. Towards the end of the year the Germans expanded their jamming organisation. To combat this there was a marked increase in the number of SPLASHER channels and by the beginning of 1943 fifteen sites (54 channels) were in the system.

During the spring of 1943 the USAAF Eighth Air Force began using the system for its daylight attacks, particularly for rendezvous points. The Americans were appreciative. A letter from the Commanding General to Air Commodore E B Addison, at the Air Ministry states that, 'no other single radio aid has been more urgently needed or more extensively used than the SPLASHER beacons.'[11]

In April 1943 further technological advance reduced the necessity for SPLASHER:

In April 1943 the Bomber Command 'Gee' programme was sufficiently advanced to render the use of SPLASHER unnecessary, and from May 1943 a modified system was introduced, the number of frequencies employed being reduced to twenty-four channels. These were used by the US VIIIth Bomber Command during the day, spoof transmissions being made nightly to disguise any changes in radio navigation systems introduced by Bomber Command.[12]

Further Developments

The period from October 1942 to August 1943 saw a proliferation of further RCM to assist Bomber Command. Below is a brief survey of some of the major introductions, some of which are dealt with in greater detail later in this book.

Seeking possible methods for jamming Luftwaffe nightfighter Radio Telephony (R/T) communications, in October 1942, Air Commodore Addison at the Air Ministry, took up an idea from the Royal Aircraft Establishment (RAE). This suggested that the transmitter T.1154 which was normally carried in bomber aircraft for communications purposes, could, by transmitting 'noise' from a carbon microphone hung in the engine cell or airframe, be used as a jammer. Thus was the birth of the countermeasure TINSEL, which was brought into operational use in December, 1942.

At the end of March 1943 evidence was forthcoming of a change in radio tactics by the German air defences in northern Europe. The German Air Force (GAF) nightfighters operated their R/T on Very High Frequency (VHF) within frequency limits of 38 to 42.6 Mc/s for the first time operationally . The change was an indication that TINSEL had been successful on High Frequency (H/F) but it also meant that the RAF bombers would before long be denied the protection of that countermeasure. Bomber Command asked for a suitable VHF jammer to be fitted into their bombers. TRE considered the problem and decided that the most effective way of jamming the enemy R/T would be to use JOSTLE II (the first Mark of this RCM had been introduced for jamming tank communications in the Middle East campaign). It would be some time before the first airborne jammers would be available – these would come with AIRBORNE CIGAR (ABC) – and it was known that jamming could take place from ground transmitters for a distance of 160 miles. Attention was therefore given to providing a ground-based countermeasure, which later became known as GROUND CIGAR.

The discovery of the use by the enemy of a high resolution decimetre radar system on a wavelength in the neighbourhood of 53cm in 1941 brought the need for a measure to counteract it. A TRE report in November indicated that in order to combat the Würzburg system it would be necessary for a barrage jammer to be carried in each aircraft. Robert Cockburn recalled that, 'the use of resonant dipoles for producing echo signals in radar equipment had often been envisaged in many quarters.' Duralumin (a strong, light aluminium alloy containing copper) dipoles had been thrown out of the aircraft by crews of No.205 Squadron, based at Shallufa in the Middle East Theatre in an effort to reduce flak losses without success. It was believed that insufficient quantities had been ejected to give any definite result. Later it became apparent that in order to neutralise the enemy radar system by producing spurious echoes vast quantities of dipoles would have to be used. In the debate which ensued the use of metallised paper and metal-backed propaganda leaflets was also suggested. Thus began the development of WINDOW which, according to Cockburn, was 'almost certainly the most powerful single countermeasure employed.'

The various organisations involved, Air Ministry signals staff and other RAF personnel, scientific intelligence officers and research establishment scientists, strongly supported by organisations from outside the armed forces such as the Post Office radio engineers, radio manufacturers and many others, were learning, and developing, their technical expertise in a wartime capacity. The buildup of this experience was No.100 Group's inheritance.

Footnotes - Chapter One

1   'Three Steps to Victory', Sir Robert Watson-Watt, (Odhams Press)p.83.

2   'Boffin: A Personal Story of the Early Days of Radar, Radio Astronomy and Quantum Optics.' R Hanbury Brown, FRS. (Adam Hilger 1991), p.7.

3   Originally known as Range and Direction Finding (RDF). Later became known generally by the American acronym RADAR (Radio Direction And Ranging).

4   'Night Flyer'. Lewis Brandon DSO, DFC, (Crecy Publishing, 1991), p.32.

5   'Despatch on War Operations 23.2.42 to 8.5.45., Appendix 'E' 'RCM in Bomber Command', p.133. (Harris Archive H122. R A F Museum, Hendon).

6   TRE. 'The Radio War, Sir Robert Cockburn, (1945), p.24.

7   Ibid.

8   Air Historical Branch (AHB), The Second World War 1939-45, R A F Signals, vol.7 p.80.

9   TINSEL was a simple method of jamming enemy HF R/T control of his nightfighters by transmitting engine noise from the ordinary communications transmitter of a bomber (see Glossary). The operator either tuned his transmitter to jam any signal that he heard and thought was German R/T Control, or jammed continuously on a wavelength given him before the sortie.

10   In December 1942, as a result of continued enemy interference with SPLASHER transmissions, the system was re-introduced and augmented by the addition of the B B C Transmitter at Start Point, Devon, known as WASHTUB II. Both operated until the introduction of an expanded SPLASHER schedule in January 1943 made them redundant. WASHTUB remained available if required until June 1943 when it was finally discontinued. (The Second World War 1939-45, R A F Signals, Vol.7), p.92.

11   Ibid/ P.92.

12   Ibid. P.92/3.

Chapter Two.

Spinners of the Web – TRE

For much of the work our final labs were the prototype installations in the Blenheims, Mosquitoes and Lancasters at our disposal.

Martin Ryle, Wartime TRE Scientist.

The role of the scientist in war was clearly indicated by the development and expansion of the Telecommunications Research Establishment (TRE) during the Second World War. This Unit had many varied tasks. In particular, the contribution made to air warfare by its Radio Countermeasures (RCM) Division, led by Dr. (later Sir) Robert Cockburn, was a classic example of superb scientific support for operational activities.

Martin (later Sir Martin) Ryle, with his friend E H Cooke-Yarborough, at a pre-Second World War amateur radio rally at Oxford.
(E H Cooke-Yarborough)

Duties were intense and wide-ranging in application, and high priority was given to them. Many young scientists, some of whom had not even completed their degree courses, were recruited for what was considered essential work. Rarely would their experiments be carried out in ideal laboratory conditions and speed of completion of each project would always be a requirement. Their laboratories could be in the strangest places. They could be perched high up radar towers, exposed on weather-swept cliff tops, or even more bizarrely, be transferred from bench to bomber to test equipment, often trying to do so with the aircraft bucketing along in the sky practising evasion techniques!

One of Cockburn's original team was George Thorne. His personal experience shows the development of the RCM team at TRE and the chronology of some of the more important RCM. It is worth quoting in detail:

> In May 1939 I entered the Royal Aircraft Establishment (RAE), Farnborough and joined a section in the Radio Department designing aerials for the new VHF Communications system for the RAF. Robert Cockburn had been there a year or

so and was heading a team developing VHF transmitters.

The VHF development was completed towards the end of 1939 and in May 1940 about a dozen of us, including Cockburn, were sent to Air Ministry Research Establishment (AMRE) which had been set up at Worth Matravers, Swanage to develop radar.

Six of us got together and formed a bachelor establishment in Newton Road, Swanage. In this group were Jack Hardwick (seconded from EMI), Martin Ryle (from the Cavendish Lab. and later Astronomer Royal), David Allen-Williams, Gurney Sutton, Peter Hall and myself.

At Worth I joined a small group under Cockburn. For the first few months we developed and evaluated a continuous wave (CW) radar system. But this work terminated when Cockburn was selected to run the RCM Group responsible for jamming the KNICKEBEIN beam navigation system.

Since accommodation at Worth was getting scarce owing to a rapid increase in the number of staff, we moved to Leeson House. This was a school on the outskirts of Langton Matravers that had been requisitioned by the Air Ministry. At that time we were about ten in number and had one lab and one office which I shared with Cockburn.

In July 1941 we were asked by the War office to produce equipment to jam German tank communications and a Col. Denman came to discuss the requirements with Cockburn. From this the airborne JOSTLE equipment was developed. From details of the German equipment I was able to calculate the effective range of the jamming. Unfortunately Col. Denman was shot down by the Germans during operational trials of this equipment in the Middle East in October 1941.

The German Freya ground radar system operating at a frequency of 120 MHz along the French coastline was identified in the middle of 1941. Airborne MANDREL was developed to jam Freya and the equipments were in operation in 1942.

Another way of dealing with Freya radars was to spoof them with false signals and this led to the development of MOONSHINE. This started under Jack Hardwick in December 1941 and by March 1942 flight trials against one of our radars showed that the system was effective. A crash production of MOONSHINE equipments was carried out at the Radio Production Unit (RPU) situated in Bournemouth during May and June of 1942. The great exodus to Malvern took place early in May 1942, but I stayed on in Swanage until early July to monitor the MOONSHINE production.

The use of a large number of small reflecting objects to spoof enemy radars had been considered for some time, but it was in early 1942 that serious work was carried out. Cockburn asked Joan Curran to investigate various reflectors and resonant halfwave dipoles made from aluminised paper were adopted as the best solution. These were called WINDOW.

Early in 1943 sufficient information became available on WINDOW dispersal rate, aircraft echoing area, German radar beam widths, and pulse length for me to calculate the amount of WINDOW that had to be dropped to protect a stream of aircraft on a mass bombing raid. For this to be achieved there had to be sufficient WINDOW in the beam of the German radar at all times so that it was not possible to identify and locate individual aircraft.

I was responsible for the design of most of the RCM ground and airborne aerials. Some of this work I carried out on the top of 70 ft wooden lattice towers on the exposed 'C' Site at Worth Matravers. When the wind blew they swayed quite a lot since guy ropes were not used – they only had sand bags on a base plate. Being somewhat concerned about my safety I asked the man responsible for these towers – a Mr. Goldsmith – if they would blow down in strong gale. He made the typical response, 'I've been erecting these towers for the past 20 years and I have not lost one yet.' The next night there was a storm and most of them were blown down. Ever since that occurred they have been guyed.

JOSTLE IV was a high power system to jam the German Nightfighter communications. Experimental work was carried out at Defford with an installation in a Wellington aircraft and we had the problem of installing an aerial in the shortest possible time. It consisted of a three inch diameter brass tube, about six to seven feet long. This had to be retractable since it was fitted under the aircraft and ground clearance did not allow a fixed aerial.

A streamlined aerial was designed by the aircraft installation section at Defford for bomber aircraft and put into production. In order to surprise the Germans, JOSTLE IV equipments were installed in a number of aircraft and were first flown all together on a mass bombing raid over Germany. Unfortunately, the aerial mechanical design was faulty, a severe vibration mode was set up during flight and most of the aircraft returned with the aerials snapped off.

As well as aerial design I carried out the mathematical predictions of the performance of various RCM systems taking into account equipment parameters and propagation conditions. I suppose I could classify myself as a theoretical engineer.

A notable feature of working conditions at TRE during the war was the lack of red tape. It was a new establishment, and administration and bureaucracy had not built up a stranglehold on getting things done quickly.

In August 1943, Robert Cockburn recorded the development of JOSTLE IV:

The necessity in future operations for a high powered communications barrage jammer [against enemy high-power nightfighter control stations] has been clearly established. At present the only equipment of this nature is JOSTLE II which was originally designed under 'flap' conditions in 1941 to operate as an airborne jammer on 27-33 Mc/s to cover the enemy's tank communication network. The equipment was so operated in the Middle East on two occasions, the last being at El Alamein.

These operations showed that it was necessary for the jammers to operate over the actual battle front. JOSTLE II was at that time installed in Wellingtons and in these circumstances the operation proved unduly expensive. There are three possible ways of making the operation less risky:-

[a] Using fast aircraft capable of defending themselves.

[b] Using very high-flying aircraft.

[c] Increasing jamming power to permit the jammers to operate at a safe distance from the battle front.

Since it is difficult to screen the appropriate aircraft required by [a] and [b], method [c] is being adopted. This will also conform with Bomber Command's desire to replace the existing numerous low power jammers by a few very high power equipments in special jamming aircraft.

Thus JOSTLE IV was created, which, according to Cockburn, should be:

A communications barrage jammer providing...jamming output power up to 2kW to cover a band of at least 20-80 Mc/s and preferably 10-160 Mc/s. To be of operational use the scale of research and development effort should be sufficient for at least 50 such equipments to be available in four to five months time.13

As George Thorne mentioned above one early recruit at TRE was Martin (later Sir Martin) Ryle who was, post-war, to distinguish himself in the field of radio astronomy where his eminence was to bring him a Nobel Prize and the office of Astronomer-Royal. Ryle joined TRE (then AMRE) in May 1940 and worked on a number of projects including 1.5 metre radar, Yagi aerial design, Identification Friend or Foe (IFF), and Post Design Services (PDS) before joining Cockburn to work on RCM in June 1942. Post-war he recalled his wartime service (part of which was spent as Scientific Liaison Officer to No. 100 Group) and its effect on his life:

I took my degree in 1939 and was directed into the rather small team then developing radar for the RAF. As the war developed the apparatus grew and we had ever-increasing responsibilities. In my case, never since have I had the responsibilities I had at the age of 25. This makes you grow up fast. You learn how to build up a team, and realise that even the more junior were as important in developing what was then 'state of the art' electronics. You learnt how to talk with Air Marshals on the one hand and a radar mechanic concerned about a

Sir Robert Cockburn's RCM Group at theTelecommunications Research Establishment, taken just after the end of the Second World War. Sir Robert, (with moustache), is in the centre of the front row sitting on the steps. E H Cooke-Yarborough is second left from him: Martin Ryle is second right. George Thorne is standing by himself on the right in the third row from the rear, in front of an R A F officer. David Leete is seventh from the right in the second row from the rear.

(David Leete)

problem of maintenance on the other. Above all, you had the privilege of flying with the operational crews, who, in their rest spells, flew our experimental aircraft. For much of the work our final labs were the prototype installations in the Blenheims, Mosquitoes and Lancasters at our disposal. My Group was involved in disrupting the German air defence system.

The war left him, like so many others, jaded and worn out:

In 1945 most of us were very tired. After making up the last reports and handing in one's pass there came a sense of freedom which hadn't been there for six years. I loaded my worldly possessions into my ancient sports car and drove away on a brilliant September day. There was no traffic so, after 30 miles, I stopped. There was a lark singing and I realised I was free – even my family had no idea when I would be coming home and it was good to feel that nobody in the world knew where I was.[14]

Peter Hall, one of the original six Swanage TRE 'bachelors', (whose brother, S/L John Hall, served in No.100 Group as a Nav/Rad in No.169 Squadron) worked with Martin Ryle trying to combat the V2 menace:

...From Intelligence received we knew that rockets would soon be bombarding the UK and that a sophisticated radio navigation systrem would be used to maximise target efficiency. Clearly it was panic stations to find out how the navigation system worked and then to produce a way of jamming it. The task was given to Martin Ryle. Our activities had to be kept very secure and each of us in Martin's team only knew what was necessary to do our part of the job. We had 'Y' Service reports of a multiplicity of signals from Peenemunde (the home of rocket development). Mysteriously, the navigation receiver that we were told would be installed in the rocket (V2) appeared in our lab. It had a vital part missing but, nevertheless, we concentrated on getting all we could out of the receiver.

Martin, personally, spent many days and nights listening to the signals. He was able to unravel a system that very cleverly hid the true navigation signals amongst a mass of identical signals. Signals were transmitted in two bands: one in the region of 40-50 Mc/s, the other 80-100 Mc/s. Many CW signals (as I recall amplitude modulated) filled each band. Ryle recognised that most had no purpose and were only there to confuse. However amongst them were one or two signals that were used to control the rocket. By clever detective work he discovered that of the many signals in each band, two, one in each band, were the operative ones, and these two were related 'f' and '2f + 4'. If we could jam one of these signals the system would fail. The V2 was, of course, crude by today's standards and the main control was simply the fuel cut off point in the trajectory. If the fuel cut off was accurate, then the rocket landing point would be fairly accurate. We set up a project, therefore, to devise a detection and jamming system that we hoped would be operational by the first V2 launch.

My part in the programme was to ensure that the system as devised could be installed in the aircraft, that it would be workable by an RAF operator, and then coordinate the whole production and installation programme.

The plan was to develop a panoramic receiver that would display, one above the other, the frequency bands 40-50 Mc/s and 84-104 Mc/s, so that any transmissions related 'f' and '2f+4' would be displayed vertically above each other. (The bands were not exactly as stated, but the relationship between the two is correct.) By manually searching with a strobe, operational signals were quickly identified. The strobe control also set the jamming transmitter frequency, which could then be switched on without delay. A jamming transmitter (JOSTLE IV) was available which could be modified to suit...The panoramic receiver with a separate display was developed in double quick time; the display unit was made as small as possible (for ease of installation in a convenient location for comfortable operation) and with operating controls made as easy to operate with flying gloves on as possible. It was important that the operator be able to search with the strobe easily and with the minimum of strain so that he remained alert and quick thinking over his whole shift. Clearly the operational signal had to be detected and the jamming transmitter tuned on in double quick time if the V2 navigational system was to be made ineffective. All our work had to be done on short time scales, with the development to production measured in weeks rather than months. Very close collaboration was vital, therefore, between all concerned. The V2 jamming programme had, perhaps, the tightest timescale of all, and Martin Ryle's team were very much involved in all aspects of this quite complex programme.

After a meeting in London I was due to go to our squadron (No.214, which was later joined in the work by No.223) to check on installation progress...I set off in the late afternoon and somewhere north of London a large explosion seemed to make my car airborne. I remember thinking 'yet another gas main exploding.' In fact, of course, it was the first V2 to arrive – and it didn't miss me by much!

I arrived late in the evening at our airfield (Oulton); the Mess was quiet with few people about...so I went to bed. After about an hour I was woken up by a knock on my bedroom door and a message that the Station Commander wanted to see at once. He informed me that the first V2 had arrived and, when he told me where it had landed, I realised it was not a gas main that had blown me across the road! Clearly we had to get our jammers airborne as soon as possible but a lot of installation work was still to be done on all our aircraft. The Station Commander accepted my suggestion that it would speed up our work if we broke a few rules and took a few risks. We brought all the aircraft from their dispersal points and lined them up close together on a runway. It was a dark night, so we floodlit the area to make finding our way about easier. I only had my best 'going to a meeting' suit with me so I borrowed a Group Captain's uniform!

Frantic work meant that we got an aircraft airborne by early morning, and were able to keep continuous cover from then on. We were obviously keen to have confirmed that the receiver we had in our lab was indeed carried in the rocket. Examination of early bomb craters showed this to be so, but from later craters it was clear that the radio system had been replaced with an inertia system of inferior accuracy. We had jammed the V2s' radio navigation system forcing the enemy to replace it with a less accurate inertia system. With the original it is probable that the targeting would have been more accurate and places of strategic importance would have been destroyed.[15] [See also remarks by General-Major Boner, CSO, Lufflotte Reich, in Chapter Eight.]

E H Cooke-Yarborough, left university in 1940 to join the Royal Aeronautical Establishment (RAE) at Farnborough where, amongst other things, he worked on Monica, the tail-warning device, before moving to TRE in 1942. Here Ryle suggested he join the RCM Group. Sharing a keen interest in amateur radio with Martin Ryle (he had coveted the latter's call sign, G3 CY as they were his own initials), they had become good friends at Oxford. Cooke-Yarborough recalled both of them sitting by the river at Bawdsey, in Suffolk, on a pre-war holiday, wondering what the large aerials were for across the river! Both were to find out in the course of time:

> Martin went to Swanage in May 1940, before the Blitz, because, I think, he found that there was work he could do which would have a positive, rather than a negative effect. He was particularly good at putting himself in the place of the German designers and guessing what they would do next.
>
> There was an awful battle going on in his mind and he really did have a bad time throughout the War. He was very close to a nervous breakdown quite often. I knew it was coming on when he started to lose his temper with everybody and his hands started shaking. He would go off for a week or two, and then return, his usual relaxed smiling self again.

Ryle thought the saving of lives to be of paramount importance and this was to cause him to lose his temper on one particular occasion when Cooke-Yarborough was with him in Robert Cockburn's office:

> I remember one incident with him which has been misreported by a number of people. We were in Cockburn's office one day discussing tactics. Cockburn was sitting at his desk. It was Bomber Command practice at that time to concentrate the bombers as much as possible so as to saturate the defences. Martin had been doing some sums and came to the conclusion that concentrating in the horizontal plane was fine, but it was dangerous to concentrate in the vertical direction because if the anti-aircraft batteries actually got the height at which the anti-aircraft shell exploded right, it would cause devastation to the bomber force because they would be concentrated in this narrow height range. He put this forward in the meeting but two very senior Bomber Command officers (one was the SASO), who were sitting to Cockburn's right, wouldn't buy it. Martin got more and more worked up and said, 'Look, by giving a single command you can save lives this very night.'
>
> Eventually, as the meeting was about to break up, as every one got up, I saw Martin put his hand round a bottle of ink, pick it up, and throw it at the wall behind us as hard as he could. The funniest thing was that everyone pretended not to notice! It has been suggested that Martin threw it at Cockburn. This is totally wrong. Martin Ryle was the most non-aggressive person you could meet, It just showed the intolerable stress he was under. I should add that, despite this story, Martin got on well with senior RAF officers and they really respected him.

Cooke-Yarborough's group were concerned with search receivers and, one of his first jobs was to start work on BAGFUL. The story of its development shows the high degree of flexibility needed in the waging of the 'Radio War'. Receivers were to be fitted to a few aircraft on each operation over enemy-held territory to record the frequencies on which the German Würzburg radars were operating, so that a check could be made on whether they were properly covered by the jamming:

> The basic ideas of BAGFUL were laid down by Farvis' Group who thought up the concept...when I took over the work I don't think it had got very far. When we came to the point where we wanted it manufactured we went to Marconi's. The normal procedure was that one got to the point where one made a 'lab thing' that worked and then we brought industry into it and they took over the manufacturing. The team at Marconi's at Chelmsford was led by Christopher Cockerill (inventor of the Hovercraft), and they made a good contribution to the project.

BAGFUL went into service late 1943/early 1944 but, according to Cooke-Yarborough, was never properly used by the RAF. However, the Americans did use it effectively on one single operation. They were making daylight raids in Fortresses at the time and had a number of aircraft carrying BAGFUL:

> They did a sweep over Occupied France and Germany on just one day, looked in detail at all the records, and were able to pinpoint the locations of nearly all the Würzburgs...by comparing the frequency obtained and consulting the aircraft's log (ie where the aircraft was at a given time) you were able to locate a radar station on the map. It was time consuming because you had to check each record individually but you ended up with the location of the Würzburg and gave information telling us where to jam...it was simply an intelligence activity.

It became apparent from BAGFUL results that the Würzburgs were operating over such a wide frequency range that it was not possible to spread jamming evenly over it:

> The idea emerged of dispersing small, automatic jammers in many of the aircraft of the bomber force, so that a radar would see at least one, whichever way it looked. To cope with the wide frequency range, each jammer would be made to scan until it encountered the frequency of a radar. It would then stop scanning and switch to jamming. To avoid being homed onto by enemy aircraft, it would jam for only about 30 seconds, before resuming scanning again. With several such jammers within the radar's beam width, it was expected that the radar would be jammed for most of the time. This jammer was code-named CARPET II, being a successor to a fixed-frequency jammer of the same name. My group was given the job of developing it, since the critical part was an automatic receiver.[16]

CARPET II caused the Germans to widen the frequency band over which the Würzburgs were operating but there was a limit to the flexibility they could use.

Ted Cooke-Yarborough was reminded of CARPET II long after the war was over:

Among the other people working on it had been a chap called Len Brown. He joined me at Harwell after the war and took CARPET II with him and found it useful for some of the work he was doing there. Years after that he died. One day I was looking out of my office window and saw the contents of his office being pushed out for scrap. Amongst the stuff I saw the CARPET II which I immediately recognised!

He also had other, incidental, memories of those far-off days:

I didn't often get information on the operational effects of the equipment because everything was done on a 'need to know' basis. Everyone worked in their own departments...the RAF personnel we worked with were always changing, literally because of losses...Vibration in aircraft didn't cause much trouble to the equipment. All the equipment was mounted on frames which were on rubber bungees. In other words they were standing on shock absorbing feet. We had failures but I don't think it made any difference whether they were vibrating or sitting quietly!

Sometimes potentially serious situations could be alleviated by humour. On a visit to one particular airfield he saw an aircraft being 'bombed up' in a hangar:

I don't know how it happened, somebody must have pushed the wrong lever I suppose, but suddenly all the bombs were released. There was a 1,000lb bomb, and a whole lot of incendiaries which all started to burn. The ground crew started to run. The Flight Sergeant roared at them, 'Come back!', and they did! They were more frightened of the Flight Sergeant than the bombs! They came back, picked up the incendiaries and chucked them out of the hangar.

The radio war was a frequently changing battle of wits with one enemy trying to out-guess the other. Although OBOE was a navigational aid for RAF bombers and not an RCM, work undertaken on overcoming its jamming by the Germans accurately indicates this contest. Robert Light, on detachment from TRE, worked on it at The Houseboat, in Radlett, Herts, (which was part of No. 80 Wing HQ):

Oboe was intended to guide Pathfinder Force (PFF) Mosquitoes. There was a beam system from the UK plus a ranging system. They went out on a beam until they were at a certain range. We did work on that from The Houseboat . The enemy successfully jammed the Mosquitoes from the ground in Germany. They had the advantage because the longer the distance from the UK stations and the nearer to the jammers the Mosquitoes got the enemy jamming took over and the Mosquitoes could not hear the ranging signals. Ray Calvert (post-war founder of RACAL, the electronics firm) devised a scheme to beat this. He had a receiver on a different frequency (20 Mc/s, I think), installed in the Mosquitoes and I worked on that.

From the English stations Ray was able to derive when the range was right so the Mosquitoes went out on the beam , which they could apparently do through the jamming. Then he transmitted the range to them on this other, different, receiver and was able to tell them when to drop their markers.

I actually flew, and tested, the experimental Mosquito. That was from Foulsham, in Norfolk, and I was probably in a No. 192 Squadron aircraft. I went up to see if it would receive the signal from England over Berlin so we had to go a long range at high altitude. We had to use oxygen. I had to sit on the floor of the navigator's compartment and we flew to Scotland to give us a long flight over friendly territory.

There was a navigational difficulty:

Eventually I told the pilot that we could pack up as everything seemed to be alright with the tests. He went down through the clouds saying, 'We are over the Firth of Forth.' Ten minutes later he told me we were nearly over enemy-occupied France! and did a smart turn to the left. We came back over London dodging the barrage balloons. One forgets that in those days those chaps didn't have any real navigation aids at all. In addition, there was a 150 knot wind blowing up there!

This was in 1943/44 and the RAF were depending a lot on OBOE, which was failing them, and this was attempting to reinstate it.

Another young scientist, Antony Hewish,[17] also destined to achieve later eminence in radio-astronomy, worked on wartime RCM. Taken from university before he had completed his course, he was drafted to the Royal Aircraft Establishment (RAE). At the beginning of 1944 he was sent to TRE where he joined the Post Design Section (PDS).[18] Shortly after arriving he became involved with the AIRBORNE GROCER antenna:

When I arrived there was little time to spare before I became involved in the project and I spent a couple of weeks doing a radar crash course. It dealt with the whole principle of the thing and how you shaped pulses and so on. We had these nice young WAAFs telling us how the electronic circuits worked. There was a special school in what I think they call the 'Monastery' part of Malvern College.

There was a little building set to one side there and [Professor] Ratcliffe had this turned into a radar school. There were many people travelling to and from this place every two or three weeks. They did a standard radar course there which was mixture of servicemen and civilians. At the time there were also a lot of Americans coming over to take part in the technical work and they would go through the school as well. TRE was a very lively place.

Martin Ryle explained the AIRBORNE GROCER system to him and Hewish then began work on the antenna with a colleague, Dave Morris:

We used to go out to Defford where they had Yagi antennas installed in the tail end of the Fortress. We would check simple polar diagram measurements. I would stand behind with a mobile antenna while he switched on the antennas and we would check the diagrams. They used to run up the port outer engine to get the power to the transmitters inside. It was a bit of a dicey job. Dave Morris would be playing with the antennas and I would be standing back with a little mobile receiving aerial. I had to stand there in the path of all the muck being thrown back in the slipstream from the engine. We couldn't do a great deal on the ground but at least you could see if it was working properly and do the standard antenna.

After spending some time with the GEC at Wembley where the RCM was being made Antony Hewish went in the later spring of 1944 to the No.100 Group airfield at Oulton, in Norfolk, where AIRBORNE GROCER had been fitted into the Fortresses (B17s), being billeted in the Officers Mess at Blickling Hall. He gave several lectures on how to get the RCM tuned up:

It was a very simple device, around 500 MHz I think. It was a wide-band transmitter frequency modulated by a noise source. The clever part was to get it covering a wide enough band. You could only do that properly if you were airborne so we used to fly with the equipment. The tail-end of a B.17 is close to the ground and the antennas changed their impedance as you became airborne so you had to fly with the equipment to make sure it was working properly. We did test flights around East Anglia, nothing operational of course, while I did the knob-twiddling…The radio cabin was amidships and I spent a long time in there tuning the equipment. I suppose I was doing this for about two months.

The aircrews were going on operational flights whilst I was at Oulton but as far as I can recall AIRBORNE GROCER was never switched on. I am not sure it was ever used. I gather from the records that they were a little scared of turning it on as it might act as a homing device for enemy fighters. By the time it was ready it was the summer of 1944 and of course summer nights are very light and the German nightfighters would not have needed radar to home in onto our people anyway.

In the following winter I guess the whole radar war had changed and different equipment was being used by the Germans. The equipment AIRBORNE GROCER was intended to jam probably wasn't in operation any longer, but my job had been to get this particular RCM installed properly, and to get the chaps to use it efficiently. I suppose I was involved in this project for about a year, on and off.

Like most of the TRE personnel who worked with them Antony Hewish had great respect for the operational aircrews:

They were certainly competent flyers. I remember coming back from doing some 'tuning up' on AIRBORNE GROCER and seeing the ground over my head in my radio dome. We were nearly upside down! That shook me a bit at the time I have to say. They weren't just flying around to enable me to do my 'tuning up', they were doing other things as well like practising evasive action. They really used to throw the aircraft about.

Martin Ryle's report on AIRBORNE GROCER described the new RCM's expected function:

> With the present bomber concentration of one aircraft per cubic mile, a fighter equipped with the Lichtenstein equipment should, when flying in the bomber stream, be able to obtain about one AI contact per minute. AIRBORNE GROCER installed in RCM Fortresses, flying 10 to 15 miles apart in the bomber stream, or above it at, say, 5000 ft higher, is calculated to lengthen the average time per AI contact to half-an-hour for an enemy fighter flying along the centre of the bomber stream and to six minutes for fighters flying along the edge of the stream...Thus the performance of the Lichtenstein equipment should be degraded to a level comparative with visual observation.
>
> The present concentration [of bombers] is, however, so high that even with visual observation alone a large number of contacts will be obtained by fighters reaching the bomber stream, although the chance of such contacts developing into combats depends largely on the rate at which the fighter can lose its overtaking speed.
>
> The introduction of this AI jamming is likely to cause the enemy to use the Lichtenstein to home into the bomber stream which will result in large numbers of aircraft being potentially dangerous even if ground radar and communications are made inoperative by other RCM.
>
> A reduction in concentration of the bomber stream, if this can be achieved without the failures of the other RCM (eg MANDREL & WINDOW) is suggested as being desirable as this, with adequate AIRBORNE GROCER cover, will result in the greatest overall decrease in nightfighter efficiency. In addition, the use of diversions carrying the full complement of RCM and radar equipment is of value in splitting the enemy nightfighter forces.[19]

In February 1945 the use of AIRBORNE GROCER, suitably modified, was contemplated as a RCM against enemy Würzburg stations:

> Certain operations carried out by aircraft of No.100 Group necessitate the simultaneous jamming of a large number of enemy Würzburg stations. The most important example of this is the jamming, by aircraft of the MANDREL Screen, of these stations when they provide long range early warning. Whilst it is possible to use monitored spot frequency jammers for such operations it is frequently not practicable to ensure complete cover, due to the limitations in the number of

such jamming equipments which can be carried and operated in one aircraft. (Thus it is sometimes necessary for a single MANDREL Screen aircraft to jam up to 15 Würzburg stations simultaneously). Under these conditions it would be highly desirable to provide barrage jamming for those sections of the frequency band in which there is a high density of Würzburg stations. No existing equipment provides sufficient power over a wide enough barrage width to be of practical value when used in this way.

The design of AIRBORNE GROCER normally provides a power output of about 25 watts over a 5 Mc/s band. The method by which this barrage is achieved was thought to be suitable for wider band-spreads at the expense of a reduction in total output power. Experiments were therefore carried out to determine whether this could be achieved...in addition it was desirable that the frequency coverage of the equipments be extended to 600 Mc/s.

By carrying out simple modifications to the AIRBORNE GROCER transmitter (T.1630) it is possible to obtain a bandspread of 12-15 Mc/s anywhere in the range 500-600 Mc/s.

By using four such equipments in each aircraft of the MANDREL Screen (with nine mile spacing) it should be possible to reduce the maximum range of all Würzburg equipments in a 50-60 Mc/s band to 25 miles. In this way monitored spot frequency jammers need only be used to cover Würzburg equipments operating outside the main band of 520-570 Mc/s.[20]

JOSTLE IV (which looked like a rather large dustbin) was being used operationally during Anthony Hewish's time at Oulton. Great consternation was caused, on one occasion, when an airman left his pliers in this equipment when they put the lid on. This would have affected the equipment's use and Squadron Leader Clarkson from PDS was most angry; there was talk of taking disciplinary action against the unfortunate culprit , but 'our Scottish Flight Sergeant suggested the matter should go no further and that is what happened.'

About a year after the War finished, when Professor Hewish started his research at Cambridge, he found himself back at Farnborough. He had been asked by Martin Ryle to return there and try to get one of the German Würzburg radar dishes [for use in what was to become known as radio astronomy] which were now in Allied hands:

> We got two. One fell apart and the other is now at the Imperial War Museum at Duxford.[21] I had to go to Farnborough and isolate it and tell them that we wanted it. They were just being sold off for scrap. In fact, it was in the hands of the scrap merchant when I got there. Heavens knows what he would have done with it!

Derek Vonberg, a close colleague of Martin Ryle at Cambridge immediately after the war, was also a member of PDS. After working with Coastal Command on anti-submarine measures he was transferred, in September 1943, to Bomber Command. Vonberg, who had been engaged on similar projects in Coastal Command, began work on helping to improve the 10cm radar (H2S), (a navigational aid "which produced a crude map on a TV screen showing towns as bright blobs, and rivers and coasts") currently being used by Bomber Command as a means of guiding pathfinders to their targets. The Germans had been detecting radiation from the aircraft with adverse effects on losses. In addition, H2S was good for coastal outlines but did not give very clear indications of towns and inland detail.

A much better picture of inland towns was given by 3cm radar (H2X) which was capable of vastly improving navigation for aircraft fitted with the gear and carrying a well trained operator. He was part of the team whose job in was to introduce this into the Pathfinder Force. He explained, in great detail, how the TRE personnel worked alongside RAF operational staff:

> My immediate boss at Defford was a schoolmaster called Brown and he was under Dr. L H Matthews who looked like, and had indeed been, a big game hunter. He was a zoologist who later was in charge of the Zoological Gardens in Regent Park. He was tremendously good value with a fund of stories and drove about in an enormous open tourer. When it came time to go out to the RAF stations it was he who made the introductions to the station commanders. He clearly got on with the senior ranks of the RAF. This was very helpful when we raw youngsters upset matters in some way or the other and this happened from time to time. When this did happen Matthews would come along and sort in out. I once ran over one of their flower beds in the fog and that took a bit of sorting out I can tell you.
>
> The experience of working with RAF crews and ground staffs at the height of the bomber offensive was like nothing I'd experienced before. Initially, it was a case of lecturing the operational crews on what the equipment could do, first in the lecture room and then on training flights. At the same time sets had to be maintained, the Radar Officer and his mechanics had to be trained, test benches set up etc. etc. Long hours, seven days a week.

The TRE personnel often worked under difficult conditions, trying to do their work on the equipment whilst the RAF ground crews were preparing aircraft for operations:

> It was quite a hairy business tuning up the sets because we had to take a petrol generator out to the aircraft where they were parked on their hard standings around the airfield and carry out the final checks whilst the armourers were hauling ten-ton bombs on board. The 'inside' chap shouted instructions to those 'outside' whilst there was a din going on from loading belts of ammunition to the

turrets, and other instrument mechanics testing compasses and other equipment on the aircraft

When we had done everything we could to get the sets into condition we returned to the Mess and listened to the incessant drone of the aircraft taking off knowing full well that not all of those going out would come back. One was lucky to be safe but it was particularly rotten when the crews one had trained and got to know failed to return. I shared a bedroom with four or five crew members and they kept changing for the worst possible reasons.

We stayed up until the crews returned and then attended the 'debriefing' of the operators who had, quite clearly, gone through Hell on the journey. But they had, in most cases, known where they had been and found the target unless, as in a few cases, the sets had failed. Early next day it was a question of post-mortem examination of the failed equipment. Then reports, repairs and more training. And so it went on.

N D N Belham who left teaching to take part in the scientific war effort came to TRE via RAE:

When World War Two broke out I had been teaching for some seven years and took part in the evacuation of children from London by boat to Yarmouth and then by train to Dereham in the centre of Norfolk. During the 'phoney' war children drifted back to London. Although in a 'reserved' occupation I decided that someone with a physics degree might be better employed and so I answered an advert for staff at RAE. To my astonishment I was called to Admiralty Arch in London and interviewed by a naval officer. He seemed very interested to hear that I had considerable experience with a soldering iron!

When I was transferred to TRE at Worth Matravers, Swanage, I travelled overnight and I reported unshaven and looking like an escaped convict. I had to live with the pass photograph which was taken for several years! I was assigned to the countermeasures group under Dr. Cockburn and recommended to try for accommodation in Swanage at a boarding house run by a Mrs. Hitchcock. She kept us all in order. Later I was able to rent a chalet a few miles inland for my wife and young son.

On my first working day at TRE I was attached to a young man who was working on recording traces from a cathode-ray oscilloscope (CRO), an instrument that provides a visual image of electrical signals, on to sensitive paper. Strip from a roll was driven through a gate in front of a lens by one friction drive and wound up by a second friction drive which was driven by the same motor. At the end of the day I was called in to report to Dr. Cockburn. As a brash young man I told him that the device would never work. Next morning, on reporting for duty, I found my companion had disappeared and I was told to make it work!

One friction drive was removed, the recording paper was replaced by film that was shot into a light-tight box (only short lengths were required).

The move of TRE to Malvern was disagreeably greeted by some of the townspeople who, 'did not take kindly to the boys of Malvern College being displaced by a lot of obviously fit young men in civvies'. A minister was sent down from Whitehall to the town to meet a group of leading citizens to explain something of the importance of the Establishment.

N D N Belham's particular job was to develop recording units for receivers that swept the frequency bands. He worked on BAGFUL (see above):

> At Malvern my work changed to devising recording units to record the output of
> receivers that scanned a frequency band. At first we used teledeltos recording
> paper which enabled the record to be seen immediately. This paper consisted of
> a conducting base on which powdered carbon was laid and this was then covered
> by a very thin, semi-transparent layer. When a suitable voltage was applied the
> top layer was punctured and a black trace obtained. By that time the presence,
> frequency and duration of a signal were known.

David Leete had developed an interest in radio as a nine-year-old when he built a crystal set to receive signals from the BBC Transmitter at Brookmans Park in Hertfordshire near his home. In 1941 he joined RAE at Farnborough to work on air-to-air homing devices for fighters against enemy airborne jammers operating on the VHF communication band. He was transferred to TRE in January 1944, to continue the same type of work but on much higher frequencies.

On arrival at Malvern College he found himself billeted near to House Seven where Dr. Cockburn had his HQ. House Seven itself was early Victorian, much of which had been converted to office and laboratory spaces. Outside there were wooden huts containing generating equipment for the special electrical supplies and other stores, 'the whole place was like a beehive, buzzing with activity!' The next day he met Dr.Cockburn and was told he would join No.3 Group which was concerned with airborne homing systems and which was divided into two sections, aerial systems and receiver displays. In view of his work at RAE he was allocated to the Aerial Systems Section.

His initial reaction to his workplace was depressing:

> Hut Seven on the Aerial Fields was a long building with its interior divided into
> three areas, giving spaces for office and workshop at each end. It was heated by
> tubular electric heaters and was clearly superior to the other huts. There were
> some moth-eaten sheep in the nearby field tended by a local farmer – but the real
> significance of their presence did not become apparent until we started taking
> polar diagrams there and had to ensure we cleaned our feet before re-entering the
> hut! I can remember it still being there in 1993.

My heart dropped when I entered Hut Seven – it was completely empty except for lab type benches in the middle section! The day was spent scrounging around for trestle tables, chairs etc., and moving in my books and other paraphernalia, and generally getting my bearings to begin work. It was at this time that I realised the traumatic transformation that the Malvern Boys College had endured...there were huts, mobile radars, generator trucks, mobile test laboratories etc., all over the place, except the Senior Turf cricket field which was sacrosanct, as also was the Sixth Form Room which became the office of the Chief Superintendent, TRE., and where the Sunday Soviets (qv) were held.

No.3 Group, which I had joined, had been concerned with air-to-air homing onto the radar carried by the German nightfighters. It had developed SERRATE. With the progress of the War the Group had turned its attention to air-to-ground homing for attacking the 'Freya' early-warning radars and the 'Würzburg' gun-laying radars in readiness for the final offensive in Europe. This new project of which I had become part, was code-named ABDULLAH. The knowledge and experience gained from developing SERRATE was used to good effect in that the general positioning of the aerial system was assumed to be similar, except that the elevation aerials were now no longer required. As the Germans tended to change the operational frequencies of their systems in order to confuse us the aerials had to operate over at least 20% bandwidth, or they had to be readily interchangeable...The aerial assemblies were manufactured by Girdlestones of Woodbridge as they had been involved in the SERRATE project.

There were two levels of design and workshop facilities at TRE:

At the first level, each group was allocated a small design office and workshop to whom verbal instructions, or sketches on the backs of used envelopes etc., could be given and with whom close contact could be maintained on a daily basis; by this means equipment modification and small jobs could be quickly done...

At the second level was the big Engineering Unit specially built adjacent to the 'Aerial Fields'; here, any large projects, or those requiring special facilities were designed and constructed, as well as prototype equipment for handing over to external contractors.

Priority was given to providing a RCM to counter Würzburg radar. David Leete explained:

...I now joined up with Peter Leevers of the Receiver Section of my group, and we began discussions on the flight testing of our homing equipment for the Würzburg. The plan was to fit the equipment into a Liberator so that it could seek out these radars and then bomb them in advance of the big invasion. This meant many trips to Defford Telecommunications Flying Unit (TFU) to liaise with the designers and fitters responsible for attaching the aerial assemblies to the wings, running the co-axial cables back to the receiver mounting and arranging for the electrical supplies to the display console.

...It was the first time I had been inside a Liberator – I was amazed at the hugeness of the thing, and particularly at the spaciousness of the navigator's area with his own plotting table, so much in contrast to the cramped quarters of the Mosquito.

Soon all was ready for the flight test; as there was not room for both of us, it was decided that Pete should go in the first instance as he had to twiddle all his knobs on the receiver and display units whilst I really had nothing to do but watch the screen, there being no adjustment on the aerials themselves. The flight went off without any problems and we were pleased to report that 'It worked.' This was the most we could aim for. There was no time to refine equipment to its highest degree of perfection. It was more a war of tactics than a war of strategy and thus speed to get equipment into operational use was more important than anything else.

One senior RAF officer with intimate knowledge of TRE's activities was Air Vice-Marshal Addison, who as CO of No.80 Wing and AOC of No.100 Group had liaised with them throughout most of the war. Some thirty years after the war's end, he described the cooperation thus:

Our relations with TRE (Cockburn's party) were very close and usually very amiable, despite the fact that they sometimes wished to embellish the wonderful contraptions they produced for us. But, by and large, they eventually accepted the ever-pressing need for speed.[22]

RCM 'Black Boxes' used by No.100 Group, in front of one of the Group's Boeing B 17s. The aircraft was used as a flying laboratory. *(Crown Copyright)*

Whenever TRE was presented with a problem to solve on behalf of the operational forces it did its best and worried away at the problem until a solution was obtained. Robert Cockburn who, in his own words, was 'privileged to take an active part in the field of radio countermeasures throughout the war,' did not find it surprising that during wartime an organisation such as TRE, which 'had first call on the scientific and technical effort available in the country, whose projects were given over-riding priority and which was driven by the spur of necessity' should be able to make such a significant contribution to the conduct of the war. But there were also, in his view, two other factors of equal importance:

> The first was the thorough integration between the tactical requirements and the technical responsibilities, which ensured that the equipment when finally produced would be operationally satisfactory, and the second was the independence of thought natural to scientists, which ensured that the various Service demands were critically examined.[23]

The RAF, he thought probably exploited the scientific resources of the country most completely of all the three fighting Services and TRE profited greatly by having to deal with their problems. The scientists were greatly encouraged and:

> There developed a dynamism which ejected the enquiring scientist into operational stations, into policy meetings at Headquarters and into the fastnesses of Commands. He was quite ubiquitous and in search of data or in following up an idea was ready to accost the corporal on watch at a radar station, the C.in.C. of an RAF Command, the foreman glass-blower at a glass factory, or a Cabinet Minister. The resultant personal impacts were stimulating and were of major importance in the effective exploitation of radar in the Royal Air Force.
>
> A most significant factor was the independence of outlook maintained by the scientists which ensured that Service requirements received informed criticism at all stages of their development. Despite the close ties between the Service and the scientists this independence of outlook was maintained throughout the war.[24]

One of the ways the 'close ties' were maintained was by the visits of senior RAF officers and other interested parties to the regular internal discussions which had taken place at TRE since its formation. The value to TRE of such visits was immense and the weekly provision of up-to-date information from the operational side of the war, 'acted as a powerful stimulus for the laboratories who might otherwise have been adversely affected by the more peaceful conditions obtaining in the neighbourhood.' As TRE's activities expanded it contributed more fully to these meetings which became 'a weekly clearing house for technical and operational gossip, and provided an indispensable unofficial channel of information which senior officers of the RAF were glad to make use of.'[25]

The 'unofficial' meetings referred to above were held on the only free day of the week, Sunday, and became known as 'Sunday Soviets.' N D N Belham was at one of these gatherings:

> TRE team leaders and high-ranking service officers met at Malvern on Sunday afternoons to discuss policy and requirements...On one occasion the meeting was thrown open to all scientific staff. At the time the U-boat menace was at its worst and ideas were urgently sought. The U-boats were listening to our radar and diving before aircraft could reach them. Air Marshal Sir Philip Joubert addressed the meeting and we were invited to submit our ideas in writing. It occurred to me that if our radar transmitting power was continuously reduced to keep the amplitude of the echo constant the U-boat might not realise that the aircraft was approaching. In fact centimetre radar being developed at the time was released for the purpose. This gave greater accuracy and surprise, for a time at least, until the U-boats were fitted with receivers capable of receiving on centimetre frequency.

D-Day

TRE participated in the preparations for D-Day. Martin (later Sir Martin) Ryle, was, in 1944, Leader of Group 5 (Electronic Jamming) at TRE, and Scientific Liaison Officer to No.100 Group. Many years after the War was over, he recalled some of the plans that were made:

> The Normandy landings included a sophisticated anti-radar operation, which included an airborne jamming screen to delay German detection of the real invasion fleet, the fabrication of two 'spoof' invasion fleets aimed at the beaches further up-channel, and a 'spoof' airborne force associated with the latter.
>
> The operations on the night of the 5th/6th June involved all the jamming squadrons of 100 Group... and a number of other Bomber Command squadrons, largely to drop massive quantities of WINDOW (strips of silver paper) to simulate the 'spoof' invasion fleets and airborne force. In the case of the latter, the WINDOW-dropping force was accompanied by Lancasters of No.101 Squadron whose aircraft carried an extra crew member to operate jammers [ABC]to interfere with German ground-control radio-telephone contact with their nightfighters. In Bomber Command raids it had proved an effective way in preventing close control of nightfighters as they entered the bomber stream; it was to prove equally effective in preventing the nightfighters (chasing the many WINDOW aircraft) from reaching the real airborne forces far to the west.

RCM FOR OPERATION OVERLORD
The night of 5th/6th June 1944

The five separate RCM tasks were:	Summary of forces employed
(i) TAXABLE — A combined Naval/Air diversion against Cap d'Antifer	16 aircraft of No.617 Squadron
(ii) GLIMMER — A similar operation as TAXABLE but mounted against Boulogne	6 aircraft of No.218 Squadron
(iii) MANDREL — A jamming barrage to cover airborne forces	16 aircraft of No.199 Squadron 4 aircraft of No.803 Squadron (USAAF).
(iv) ABC — VHF jamming support for TAXABLE and GLIMMER and cover for airborne forces	24 aircraft of NO.101 Squadron 5 aircraft of No.214 Squadron
(v) TITANIC — Feints for airborne forces	34 aircraft drawn from Nos. 90, 138, 149 and 161 Squadrons

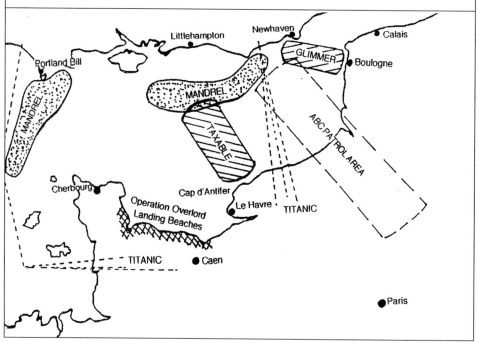

W/C Derek Jackson, DFC, AFC, OBE, who had pioneered the techniques of nightfighting and had also had a very successful operational nightfighter tour, was posted to TRE in 1942 to supervise the testing, methods of manufacture and use of WINDOW, originally against German nightfighter control radars. He was responsible for developing the wide range of WINDOW material required for the different radars which could detect an invasion fleet.

The dropping of the huge quantities of this material needed to simulate an invasion fleet was carried out by the aircraft flying at 200 knots (370 km/h) on an orbiting course, the pattern having to move forward uniformly at 10 knots (18.5 km/h), an operation requiring extremely accurate navigation and flying.

The electronic jamming group at TRE (Group 5) which had been responsible for the design and prototype installation of the 100 Group radar jammers and the communication jammer of the No.101 Squadron Lancasters, had little to do in this area, as the operation was very similar to the tasks they normally carried out in support of bomber raids. However we were involved in fitting four RAF Air-Sea Rescue boats with an electronic deception device to augment the WINDOW against the long-range coastal batteries. This was a device [MOONSHINE] which had been flown in Defiants of No.515 Squadron (Fighter Command) during 1942 to simulate large day raids to get the German fighters into the air. We also had a party installing jammers on landing craft in Portsmouth Dockyard. The urgency evident in these two programmes indicated that D-Day was imminent.[26]

Sir Robert Cockburn later wrote[27], in detail, of the contribution made by his Department to the provision of the 'ghost' invasion fleets mentioned above:

During 1943 we were heavily involved in designing a range of specialised airborne equipments to protect the Bomber force from the increasingly sophisticated German defences. But we were well aware that there was to be a full scale invasion of Europe during the following year, and had given a lot of thought to how we could contribute. We soon decided that we should be able to construct a 'Spoof' invasion.

Twin components would be used to mislead the enemy radar and these:

...would depend on the use of WINDOW, and on a device we had used earlier in the War, MOONSHINE, which expanded and modulated the single-received pulse so that it appeared in the German radar as if it came from a large group of aircraft and caused them to send up an number of their fighters to meet this threat [See Sir Martin Ryle's comment above and Chapter One for a more detailed description of the earlier use of this RCM]. ...It was only usable for a short time because the Germans soon found out how to recognise the decoy pulses.

WINDOW was the code-name chosen at random by the Superintendent at TRE, A P Rowe, because it bore no indication of its real purpose. It had been developed by Joan Curran early in 1942 and consisted of bundles of metalised strips cut to half a wavelength. She demonstrated that two or three such bundles produced in radar an echo equivalent to a four-engined bomber.[See also reference to W/C Jackson above]

TRE's involvement in Overlord had been discussed for the first time in January 1944 and we put forward our plans for a Spoof operation. These were eagerly accepted by the planners. In the Spring I was formally 'Bigoted'. This was a Top Secret clearance which allowed me to know the exact date of the invasion and the positions anticipated during the first week of the fighting. I recall vividly the day I was invited up to Norfolk House which housed the planning staff. I was led into the Map Room and a Colonel unfolded two panels under which was a map illustrating the entire Invasion Plan. I was frightened out of my life that I might inadvertently let slip some vital fact, or even talk in my sleep!

In May 1944 I was given control of two key Squadrons, No.617 Squadron led by G/C Leonard Cheshire. the 'Dambuster', and No.218 Squadron; I visited No.617 Squadron one lunchtime to brief them. All the aircrews knew by now that they had been given some special task in the Invasion and the Mess was tense with anticipation. The G/C and I walked out to the middle of a cornfield and I explained what I wanted. They would have to fly an orbit six miles long progressing at an apparent speed of six knots.

Later we moved up to Tantallon Castle on the Firth of Forth with captured Freya, Seetakt and Würzburg radars, well away from any German monitoring stations, and rehearsed the complicated flight patterns. They were found to be completely successful. Finally we flew a full scale trial round Flamborough Head against one of our Type 11 radars, the nearest equivalent to the German Würzburg. The WAAF operators were not briefed on what to expect but all agreed that the blips on their screens must have come from a very large convoy, larger than they had ever seen before. I was now confident that the 'ghost' fleet would deceive the German radars.

We now concentrated on preparing the second component of the Spoof...Four Air Sea Rescue launches had been allocated to us but they only arrived at Tewkesbury on the Severn during the last week of May. This was the nearest they could get to Malvern. David Allen-Williams fitted them up with the MOONSHINE equipment. Time was so short that the launches could only arrive at Newhaven on the actual day of the Invasion. We nearly missed it as they were delayed by bad weather. Fortunately the Operation had been put back a day so by the skin of our teeth we just managed to arrive in time.

We had had one piece of extraordinary good luck. An American Signals Group which had been stationed in Iceland had been overlooked by their planners and were posted to Malvern to be trained to operate the MOONSHINE launches. They were very expert professionals who rapidly learned their new jobs. We had rigged up in the lab a test programme so that they would recognise any airborne radar characteristics and tune the MOONSHINES to them.

46

It must have been a thoroughly uncomfortable trip to putter along at six knots in quite a rough sea but they performed their task admirably. They MOONSHINED eight airborne radars and also found one more which we had not previously detected. The Navy supported this operation with 14 pinnaces each towing two balloons carrying a corner reflector giving an echo equal to a 10,000 ton ship. When these 'Fleets' had arrived at their stop line, they laid a smokescreen and broadcast the noises made by a number of ships dropping anchor. Their job completed, they all cleared out of the area.

As a further diversion Bomber Command launched an attack down the Somme and jammed all the German fighter communications being supported by powerful jammers back in England. During the previous weeks our fighter/bombers had systematically attacked all the radars along the stretch of coast which we planned to invade; but for every radar attacked in this area, two were attacked elsewhere. We had developed a system which could fix their position to within about 100 ft. So successful was this softening up operation that I became seriously worried that no radars would have survived to detect our 'ghost' fleets.

The Spoof directed towards Boulogne was detected and radar-controlled artillery aimed at it; E-Boats were also instructed to approach the area. The Cherbourg Spoof attracted little attention, either because there were no radars able to operate or because it was too close to the real invasion force. This remained undetected until 2 am on the 6th June when the noise of ship's engines were heard off the east coast of the Peninsula. But it was not until the afternoon that the German High Command finally committed its armour to the battle and by that time we had firmly established our Bridgehead.

Ground-based RCM were also required:

GROUND MANDREL, GROUND CIGAR

Such ground jamming as already existed was re-deployed to meet Overlord requirements and two new projects were introduced. These were complete GROUND MANDREL jamming of the Freya frequencies in the Dover Straits area[28] and the very high-power GROUND CIGAR VHF R/T jamming in the Brighton area. The work was carried out by 80 Wing with technical assistance and advice from TRE.[29]

The provision of accurate information regarding enemy radar activity in the invasion area was also needed. This necessitated the development of DF facilities of much greater accuracy that had hitherto been used. PING-PONG and COAL SCUTTLE were employed, and the self-recording equipment, BAGFUL, which allowed a 24 hour watch to be kept for new frequencies, was also used:

Ron Newbury (Telecommunications Flying Unit) working on one of the engines of a Vickers Wellington at Defford. This was the first aircraft to have a 360 degrees search radar fitted.

(Ron Newbury

PING-PONG, BAGFUL

In August 1943 discussions with Air Defence of Great Britain (ADGB) indicated that the invasion plan would involve the shooting-up of enemy radar equipment. This would require location of sites and measurement of frequency to a much greater accuracy than could be supplied by the existing facilities. The design of direction-finding (DF) equipment with an accuracy of plus or minus a quarter of a degree and covering the frequency band 300-600 Mc/s was undertaken jointly by Mr. Farvis and Dr. Westcott.

The Allied Expeditionary Air Force (AEAF) RCM plan confirmed the necessity for more accurate facilities...and a formal request for eight PING-PONG DF trailers was made in early March. By the beginning of May 1944 Group 6 (Mr. Farvis) had fully equipped four sites with PING-PONG trailers and BAGFUL receivers, the latter covering all known frequencies. Operators were trained by TRE but Group 6 personnel remained on the sites during the Overlord operation.

From the middle of May detailed information on every enemy coastal radar in the invasion area was being supplied to AEAF HQ and was of the greatest value in planning appropriate offensive action. PING-PONG has now been accepted as a routine facility and will presumably be maintained in operation as long as the enemy-held coastline remains in range.

COAL SCUTTLE

Just before D-Day it became urgently necessary to establish whether the enemy was using ground radar transmissions in the frequency band 1000-2000 Mc/s. For various reasons ground watch was unlikely to be effective, and within three days Mr. Ryle, in cooperation with Dr. F C Thompson, provided airborne DF in this band. The equipment consisted of modified H2S and BOOZER equipments combined in a Halifax...three operational flights were carried out by the TFU at Defford before D-night. Although negative results were obtained these were useful in preventing further search effort, and, in addition, indicated the value of such airborne equipment.

MANDREL JAMMING SQUADRON

In support of the airborne landings it was necessary to reduce the range of the enemy early warning system by a special airborne jamming squadron (No.199 Squadron). In view of the very large number of stations and their wide dispersal in frequency the fitting of such a squadron at short notice required some ingenuity...The requirement was finalised at the end of March 1944.

Group 5 (Mr. Ryle) had to design a new jammer, MANDREL III, based on a modified IFF set and to modify existing British and American MANDREL equipments. TRE drawing office completed prototype installation drawings within a month and 12 aircraft were fitted out within six weeks. This outstanding achievement was the result of excellent team work all round...Group 5 assisted in the working up of the squadron up to within ten minutes of the operation.

AIRBORNE CIGAR (ABC)

Airborne jamming of the enemy VHF ground-air R/T was carried out with great success by special Lancaster (No.101 Squadron) and Fortress (No.214 Squadron) squadrons carrying ABC. Most of the TRE work had been carried out in the winter of 1943 on behalf of Bomber Command but during the Overlord period Group 5 (Mr.Ryle) was involved in equipping the Fortress squadron.

ROYAL NAVY RCM

The Admiralty Signals Establishment was responsible for all Naval RCM but TRE issued a report 'An Appreciation of Shipborne Radio Countermeasures' (5/M/89/RC) in which its experience during three years of airborne jamming was applied to the problem of shipborne jamming. The Royal Navy used, in addition to US equipment, the RAF jammers CARPET II, MANDREL I and MANDREL III. As design authority for these equipments TRE gave assistance in testing and checking the Naval installations. This involved all of Group 14 (Mr. Cooke-Yarborough) and Group 5 (Mr.Ryle) for over a month.[30]

TELECOMMUNICATIONS FLYING UNIT (TFU)

An integral part of TRE was its air arm, TFU. The Unit began its existence, at flight strength, in 1936 at Martlesham Heath, in Suffolk, where the Aircraft and Armament Establishment cooperated with the early radar development which took place under Robert Watson-Watt at Bawdsey. It later joined another flight (which had been dealing with ground radar) and, towards the end of 1941, became the TFU. Following TRE around in its travels (including a posting to Scotland) the Unit was stationed at Christchurch (when TRE was at Swanage) and when the parent organisation moved to Malvern in May, 1942, the flying unit went to the nearby airfield at Defford where it spent the remainder of the war. At its wartime peak of activity the TFU had over 100 aircraft and 2000+ personnel (including some naval ratings in an RN Section).

Below is a list showing some of the work undertaken by the TFU shortly after its move to Defford. It indicates the wide range of projects covered and the different types of aircraft used by the TFU in their significant contribution to the work of TRE.

[1] Bristol Blenheim L.9387 Interception of AI Jamming. Bristol Beaufighter R.2347

[2] Bristol Blenheim T1939 Investigation of Blind firing with AI. Bristol Beaufighter T3356

[3] Avro Anson N9743 Test of AI Blind Approach Beacons.

[4] Various Vickers Wellingtons Tests of infra-red identification systems.

[5] Bristol Beaufighter R2373 Windscreen projection on AI Indicator and Artificial Horizon.

[6] Vickers Wellington P9214 Monica system. Vickers Wellington W8830

[7] Avro Anson N3429 Beacon Homing equipment.

[8] Armstrong/Whitworth Rebecca System. Whitley Z 9248

[9] Vickers Wellington W5734 Blind Bombing for Chemical Defence Establishment.

[10] Vickers Wellington 5728 Tests of Air-to-Surface Vessel (ASV) recorder.

[11] Various Bristol Monitoring of AI beams and AI interference. Beaufighters.

[12] Vickers Wellington W5728 Location of single-seater dinghies.

[13] Bristol Blenheim V 6000 Radar trials with AI Mk VIII. Bristol Beaufighter X 7624

[14] Fairey Fulmars N 4072 & AI investigations. X 8798

[15] Vickers Wellington Z 8902 High Power ASV apparatus.

[16] Vickers Wellington T 2968 ASV. Armstrong Whitworth Whitley P 4949

[17] Fairey Swordfish P4008 ASV Installation.

[18] Fairey Fulmar N1859 AI Mk X investigations.

[19] Vickers Wellington X9678 Oboe Mk. III investigations.

[20] Sea Otter K 8854 ASV.

[21] Fairey Swordfish V 4482 ASV/BA for aircraft carriers.

[22] Lockheed Hudson AM 819 MOONSHINE investigations.[31]

Footnotes - Chapter Two

13 PRO AVIA26/1071: 'Memo on the JOSTLE IV Project', Robert Cockburn, dated 18.8.43.

14 MS Notes made by Professor Sir Martin Ryle, FRS, date unknown.

15 Extract (reproduced by permission of the author) from an article, 'Jamming V2s' by Peter Hall in 'Tranmission Lines', the Newsletter of CHIDE (Centre for the History of Defence Electronics), Bournemouth University, September 1999.

16 Extract from correspondence between R Cockburn and E H Cooke-Yarborough 14.2.95 and recorded in the Addendum (ed. E B Callick 1995) to 'The Radio War' by Robert Cockburn.

17 Professor Antony Hewish, FRS, was also a pioneer in radio astronomy. He was awarded the Nobel Prize for Physics in 1974 for the decisive part he played in the discovery of pulsars.

18 Professor Hewish recalled that the members of PDS worked alongside the designers of the equipment at TRE and visited the factory where it was being made. 'So you saw it from the late design stage through to production and then took it to the squadrons. It was a necessary link. I think the equipment was better used because of our work.' The PDS worked in teams of about a dozen people.

19 PRO AVIA 26/715: 'AIRBORNE GROCER', (Martin Ryle [et al]), 16.7.44.

20 PRO AVIA 26/1148: 'Modifications to AIRBORNE GROCER for Würzburg Jamming.' (Martin Ryle.) TRE Memo 5/M 106/MR/DM, dated 22.2.45.

21 Prior to its arrival at Duxford this Würzburg was located in the sports field behind Martin Ryle's house in Herschel Road, Cambridge. When Ryle set up the Mullard-sponsored Radio Astronomy Laboratory at Barton, near Cambridge, the equipment was moved by high-lift helicopter to the new site.

22 Addison Papers: MS notes made by AVM Addison on 21.9.77.

23 'The Radio War', a TRE Report by Robert Cockburn, 1945.

24 Ibid. p.2

25 Ibid.p.4

26 'D-13: Some Personal Memories, 24th-28th May 1944.' By Prof. Sir Martin Ryle, (IEE Proceedings Vol.132, Pt.A, No.6, October 1985).

27 Letter dated 5.3.93, sent by Sir Robert Cockburn to Dr. W H Penley, Purbeck Radar Trust, and now in the Archive of the Centre for the History of Defence Electronics (CHIDE), Bournemouth University.

28 This was particularly successful:

'The convoys of Force 'L' bringing the first follow-up formations (on D-Day+1) of the fighting echelons of the 7th Armoured Brigade and the 153rd Brigade of the 51st (Highland) Division, were due to arrive from the Thames in time to land on the second tide. They included a convoy of large personnel ships, the first big British ships to pass through the Straits of Dover for four years. Enemy gunfire from the French coast had sunk a motor transport ship in the previous convoy, but, using RCM and smoke, the passenger ships passed through without interference. (Victory in the West vol.1:The Battle of Normandy, by Major L F Ellis (et al)in History of the Second World War, UK Series, HMSO 1962).

29 TRE Memo 'RCM for Overlord', dated 18.6.44 (5/M/98/RC).

30 Ibid.

31 'The Endless Sky: Pershore and Defford.' (Written and Published by Glyn Warren, 1988).

Chapter Three

Investigation in the Air: From BATDU to No.192 Squadron

It was amusing to be the sole Halifax amongst 50 or so Lancasters, heading east in the darkening sky...The crews closest would be waving their guns up and down in acknowledgement...They obviously wondered what the hell we were doing. Had we got the correct raid?

John Short, No.192 Squadron rear gunner.

Although the units concerned changed title several times in their existence the use of aircraft-placed equipment and airborne investigations had been an essential part of the campaign against enemy signals throughout the War. The first step in this direction was made in June 1940 by the re-formation of the Blind Approach Training Development Unit (BATDU) to seek information about the Luftwaffe navigational beams (KNICKEBEIN, X-GERÄT and Y-GERÄT) which were being used to guide enemy bombers against key targets in the United Kingdom during the Blitz.

In October the Unit changed its name to Wireless Investigation Development Unit (WIDU), which, in December 1940, acquired squadron status becoming No. 109 Squadron. 'B' Flight of the newly formed squadron took on the airborne investigation of enemy signals and, on 10th July 1942, it became No.1474 Flight based at Gransden Lodge. This Flight was retitled No.192 Squadron on 4th January 1943. On 1st February 1944, No.1473 Flight, whose activities hitherto had been mainly confined to signals investigations over friendly territory under control of No.80 Wing, was merged with No.192 Squadron which then became a three flight squadron. By the end of 1944 the Squadron had replaced all of its Wellingtons, and by the 27th December its aircraft establishment was 17 Handley Page Halifaxes Mk.III; 7 De Havilland Mosquitoes Mk IV and 1 Avro Anson.[32]

BATDU (& WIDU)

BATDU was used prewar to train pilots in blind-approach landings in bad weather using the Lorenz beam. To take its role in RCM it was hastily re-formed on 18th June 1940 to find the German beams (see above) and was based at Boscombe Down in Wiltshire. A small detachment under Flight Lieutenant Robert Sage went to Wyton, Huntingdon, on 17th August to cover beams in the East of England. The new unit carried out airborne searches which, combined with signals intelligence, assisted RCM to be taken against the Luftwaffe. The first CO was Wing Commander (later AVM) R S Blucke, a veteran RFC Observer, who had piloted the Handley Page Heyford K 4030 over Daventry on 26th February 1935 as the airborne component of Sir Robert Watson-Watt's initial experiment which was eventually to provide the priceless navigational tool of radar, now used as an everyday occurrence throughout the world.

Three days after BATDU was re-formed Flight Lieutenant Hal Bufton piloting an Avro Anson with Corporal Dennis Mackey as special operator, on a flight from RAF Wyton, identified the first German beam, KNICKEBEIN, where a single approach beam was intersected by a cross-beam over the target. The Unit aircrews were a mixture of experienced 'beam' pilots, plus radio-educated special operators who had been recruited with the assistance of the Secretary of the Radio Society of Great Britain, the amateur radio enthusiasts' organisation. John Harvey, one of the original six operators, remembered being given an instruction book for a Hallicrafters S.27 radio receiver and told he had one hour to learn about it before reporting to his aircraft for an investigative flight.[33] Such was the urgency of the times.

Later more refined beams, the 'X' Gerät (operated by KGr 100 a Pathfinder/Fire raising Unit for the Luftwaffe Main Force), which used a main beam with three cross beams timed by a 'bombing' clock to indicate at the intersection of the third beam with the main beam that the target was immediately below. In addition, there was 'Y' Gerät, where a ground-based signal was re-radiated from the Luftwaffe bomber to base to give its position in relation to the intended target and to which it could be guided. Many were the enemy beams which had to be investigated and it was dangerous and exacting work.[34]

No. 109 Squadron.

At the end of 1940 the flying unit achieved squadron status and became No. 109 Squadron. Joe Northrop, one of the original beam pilots, served with the Squadron at Boscombe Down:

> In the Officers Mess itself the service was still of a peacetime standard as the mess staff were nearly all of long standing civilian status. They were getting on in years but endeavoured to give excellent service to the Aircraft and Armament Evaluation Establishment (A & AEE) officers and to interlopers like ourselves who interfered with the routine by flying at night. Afternoon tea was still served as a ritual with an individual choice of a small pot of China or Ceylon tea with toast and an assortment of pastes and jams, this after eighteen months of war. The Commandant still hankered after his Sunday morning sherry parties and dining-in nights. Unfortunately two New Zealanders belonging to our Squadron

helped themselves to the Commandant's special bottle of claret that had been set out on the table opened to 'breathe' prior to one of the dining-in nights and emptied it in record time. The incident did not make us popular!

I reported to the Squadron offices at the back of the old Watch Tower to join Vic Willis (Flight Commander 'A' Flight) and sort out my duties. One familiar face was missing, that of Flying Officer Munro...Returning from an investigational flight at night in thick fog his aircraft had crashed killing all on board – a sad end to a flying career spanning many years.[35]

In addition to its beam-seeking activities No. 109 Squadron carried out other operations. It was used to 'spot' deficiencies in the 'Starfish' decoy fires and lights system used in the UK to divert Luftwaffe bombers from key targets, and to attack various KNICKEBEIN transmitters. Also, using a 'J' (narrow) beam developed by George Baillie (who made a major contribution to RCM throughout the war) for use against small targets, the Squadron bombed 'X' Gerät (code-named 'RUFFIAN') transmitters on the Cherbourg Peninsula with some success. Although the exact position of the beam transmitters had been established, it was realised that their destruction would, for two reasons, present a very difficult task. Firstly the actual targets were neither conspicuous nor particularly large, and, secondly, the installations were likely to be heavily defended bearing in mind the importance the enemy placed on them. The bombing began on 14th November 1940, the same night as the heavy German raid on Coventry which had such disastrous consequences.

The attacks on the RUFFIAN transmitters is officially summed up thus:

During the summer of 1941 RUFFIAN activity declined to a very low level, and offensive action against the transmitters ceased at the end of June. Throughout the period of operations attacks had been made on more than fifty occasions (on one occasion, after such an attack the transmitter was not heard for six days). Although no major destruction had been effected, numerous hits had been scored in the target area, many large fires started and considerable damage done to power supplies, stores and defensive positions. Undoubtedly...this difficult and dangerous task, often under hazardous flying conditions, added a valuable contribution to the general defeat of the RUFFIAN system.[36]

During the winter of 1941/2, in 'Operation Trinity', which lasted two months, Stirling aircraft from Nos. 7 and 15 Squadrons, in No. 3 Group, attacked the German capital ships Scharnhorst and Gneisnau and the cruiser Prinz Eugen. These were berthed at Brest after wreaking havoc on Allied shipping in the Atlantic. Experienced beam pilots and SOs from No. 109 squadron were loaned to these squadrons for this operation.

A 'striking flight' of four Vicker's Wellingtons (plus two spare aircraft) was added

F/O Clarkson, and crew ,in front of their No.192 Squadron Handley Page Halifax Mk.III, 'Babe', at Foulsham. *(E G Clarkson)*

to its establishment. In August, 1941, the Squadron was increased to three flights which were employed respectively for:

1 Development of the OBOE technique.

2 Investigations for TRE and 'Y' Service (which intercepted German radio and radar signals).

3 RCM investigation flights.

Nos. 1473 and 1474 Flights

In the summer of 1942 the three flights of 109 Squadron were separated. The OBOE Flight transferred to the PFF retaining the title No.109 Squadron. The RCM Flight became No.1473 Flight concentrating on RCM investigations over friendly territory, continuing to work under the control of No. 80 (Signals) Wing HQ, and the remaining flight, which came under the direct control of Air Intelligence at the Air Ministry, became No.1474 Flight, with responsibility for wireless investigations over enemy territory.

On 8th March 1942, No.1473 Flight, under the command of Squadron Leader

George Grant, a Canadian, moved to its first base being a 'lodger unit' on the Wellington Operational Training Unit (OTU) at Upper Heyford, in Oxfordshire, pending the finding of a more permanent home. The Flight offices were wooden buildings which had been erected in the dispersal area some distance from the main hangars and the other buildings on the station. Eventually arrangements were made whereby Flight aircraft could take off from their dispersal area without causing problems for the everyday activities of the OTU. A small Ops Room was set up with direct telephone link to No.80 Wing HQ., and aircraft could only be 'stood down' on authority from that HQ. Joe Northrop, now a Flight Lieutenant, remembered watching with frustration as some of the OTU aircraft took off to take part in the first 1000 bomber raid on Cologne on 30th May 1942, 'We unsuccessfully appealed to 80 Wing to include our Wellingtons but were refused on the grounds of security.'[37]

It had always been understood that No.1473 Flight would only stay at Upper Heyford until a more permanent base could be found and in November 1942, the Flight moved to Finmere, a new satellite airfield, also being used by an OTU, some 15 miles away. The move was not without its difficulties, several aircraft being kept on 'standby' (in readiness, in case they were required for investigative tasks) whilst moving ground personnel, equipment and serviceable aircraft to the new base. In June 1943, improvement in aircraft height, speed and range and the transfer of extra personnel enabled No.1473 Flight to undertake other commitments which hitherto had not been possible due to shortage of suitable aircraft.

On 14th September 1943, the Flight was ordered to move to Feltwell, in Norfolk, from where it would eventually be absorbed by No. 192 Squadron and transferred to No.100 Group. Joe Northrop was the Flight Commander at the time:

> The move to Feltwell started on 12th September and was completed on the 14th, it falling to my lot to ferry the two Halifaxes and a couple of Ansons over in between supervising the rest of the personnel settling into their new accommodation and keeping standby crews and aircraft on call as required by 80 Wing Operations. Flight Lieutenant Moore had arrived at Feltwell by now and until the last day of the month I spent all my time and energy on handing over the unit to him and briefing him as well as possible on what would be expected of him by the operations staff at Wing Headquarters. Finally, I flew him to Radlett in the Leopard Moth to formally hand over command of 1473 Flight to him.[38]

'When I joined No.1474 Flight after overseas service I was told that the extra equipment the aircraft carried was nothing to do with me, it was highly secret and the less I knew about it the better,' recalled an airframe fitter, Sergeant E Mears, 'My job was to keep the aircraft flying.' He had never seen a GEE set before:

> I did ask a GEE mechanic what it was and was told to mind my own business.

The side of a No.192 Squadron Handley Page Halifax, the 'Richdale Express', named after the favourite brew, Richdale Ale, of the Canadian crew which they obtained when on leave in Sheffield. Each pint depicted a completed operation. The 'artwork' was carried out by one of their airframe fitters, Sergeant E Mears (see text). *(E Mears)*

It was quite a while before I found out that it was a navigational aid and not part of the RCM equipment. I had to show a crash inspector round one of our aircraft and when he asked me about the equipment being carried in the aircraft I didn't know. Neither did he. However little snatches of conversation in the Mess made me aware of one or two things, beam bending comes to mind, but it wasn't until after the War when the press gave details of Jordan's decoration that I found out a little of what we were doing.

Another outstanding memory was the night a Halifax landed on top of a Mosquito. The propeller blades of the Halifax were inches from the Mosquito pilot's canopy. The man who got the biggest shock was a member of the Halifax's crew. When they came to a standstill, he opened the hatch, slid out and fell over six feet to the ground instead of the three feet drop he had expected. It's a wonder he didn't break his back.

Our aircraft never carried bombs [they did towards the end of the War] but at Foulsham a pile of brick rubble behind one of the dispersal areas found its way a bit at a time to Germany! At the end of a 'tour' there was always a celebration ground and aircrews trying to drink the pub dry...and when the bar in the Mess closed, tea buckets were filled with beer, and drinking went on into the small hours. The 'Richdale Express' was the Halifax of one of our Canadian skippers. Although I did the 'art work' I can't remember if the skipper was Ward or Passmore. They both went on to finish tours and used to visit a pub in the Midlands when they went on leave and drink Richdale Ale.

My wife, who had been a Motor Transport (MT) driver with No. 1473 Flight did the usual drivers jobs, taking aircrews to dispersals, flare path, stores runs, etc., etc., We sometimes had Americans diverted to Foulsham, especially after the installation of FIDO.

'A Splendid Performance'

In the early hours of 3rd December 1942 a Vickers Wellington 1C from No.1474 Flight (a month before it became No.192 Squadron), joined a Main Force raid on Frankfurt for an investigation of enemy airborne transmissions. The Wellington's brief was to search for a newly-developed German nightfighter AI, Lichtenstein BC, which was causing serious problems to the raiding RAF bombers. It was a memorable flight during which time the aircraft was attacked 10/12 times by a German nightfighter.

The research and planning of this flight, and the briefings for it, were the work of Air Intelligence Unit 4(a), a department at the Air Ministry which dealt exclusively with collecting intelligence about enemy radio navigation systems and radar. S/L John Whitehead was its CO at the time:

> My prime task on joining AI 4(a),[39] in September 1942, was to collect as much evidence as possible about the enemy's nightfighter systems and in particular the airborne radar arrangements employed by nightfighters.
>
> The personnel at AI 4(a) was entirely made up of RAFVR officers and one WAAF officer. These were F/L Limmer (a solicitor in Civvy Street), F/L Bowyer (a barrister), and Flight Officer 'Tony' Beckett of the WAAF, who was very proud of the fact that she was one of the debutantes at the last big coming out season at Buckingham Palace before the war...
>
> We had little information at the beginning of this investigation. There were some photographs of aircraft on German nightfighter stations taken by resistance workers in the invaded countries, plus a few vague reports from PoWs unconnected with the nightfighter system This was all we could expect since the nightfighters operated exclusively over their own friendly territory.
>
> The photographs were all taken from great distances as would be expected, and, when enlarged, gave only blurred details of the aircraft in the pictures. All that could be discerned was some sort of aerial structure attached to the noses of the aircraft, but the definition was so poor that one could not make any measurements with any accuracy. In short, the photographs were of very little use. In addition to these, I also studied reports sent in by the Y-Service listening stations.
>
> I then looked at reports of radar signals of unknown origin and studied their characteristics. One group of such signals had one thing in common in that they faded and gained strength in an irregular manner. I decided that these signals were worth looking into because they were not the type one would expect from the rotating aerial of a ground installation. I thought that these must be airborne. As far as I can recollect all these signals occurred somewhere in the 60 cm band.

Another characteristic of these signals was that they were heard almost exclusively at night. This convinced me that they could well be coming from a nightfighter radar installation.

About the time that I had come to this conclusion AI 4 (a) was increased in strength by the arrival of my old friend S/L Freddie Butler who had been with me at the No.1 RAF Signals School at Cranwell. He became my No.2 and I introduced him fully into the picture of what I had been doing with regard to this particular investigation. From then on we worked together on the project. It was he who later went to No.1474 Flight, which was under the command of Vic Willis, and briefed Harold Jordan on the frequency band in which to search and the characteristics of the signals he should be looking for.

Not long after this epic flight a German nightfighter crew (disillusioned with the Nazi regime) fled from Norway in their nightfighter, which had the equipment we had been looking for fitted, and landed at Dyce Airport, Aberdeen. If they had done this just a few months before it would have saved us a lot of work!

Altogether 18 sorties were necessary before a successful conclusion to the investigation was obtained. The results had far reaching effects, enabling jamming RCM to be implemented and permitting the formation of a SERRATE squadron, (No. 141 Squadron), which met with considerable success.

Amazingly the Wellington, blessed with an experienced crew, survived the attacks during which time it was a miracle it did not catch fire. The whole operation was a classic example of heroism and dogged persistence and was subsequently described as 'suicidal but successful'. The official version of the story is described thus:

Vickers Wellington MkIC, No.DV819 (Captain, Sgt Ted Paulton) took off on a Special Duty flight from Gransden Lodge, in Cambridgeshire, at 0202 flying across the north coast of France to an area near to Frankfurt... this particular investigation necessitated the Wellington being intercepted by an enemy nightfighter and, up to this sortie, all efforts to get an interception had failed. At 0431 hrs, the aircraft was in a Dead Reckoning (DR) position of 49.54N/07.39E, and set a course for for position 50.30N/07.37E.

The Special Operator (SO), P/O Harold Jordan, a 34 year-old prewar PE/Science teacher from Croydon, in South London, reported that he had been receiving signals on his special wireless equipment which he thought were the ones requiring investigation. He warned his all-Canadian crew to expect a fighter attack.

On this Northerly leg the signals grew stronger and Jordan repeated his warning. A code had previously been arranged so that if the signals were picked up, the frequency would immediately be sent back to base, it being absolutely vital that this information should reach base at all costs. Position 50.30N/07.37E was reached at 0442 and the aircraft set course for the homeward leg. The SO passed the coded message to the Wireless Operator (WOP), Sgt Bill Bigoray, for transmission to base, giving in the message the required frequency and that this frequency was very probably the correct one. He also warned the crew that his receiver was being saturated and to expect an attack at any moment. Almost simultaneously the Wellington was hit by a burst of cannon fire. The Rear Gunner, F/Sgt Everett Vachon was hit in the arm on this first attack and, realising that now there was no doubt at all about the signal being the correct one, the SO changed the coded message, a change that would tell base that the frequency given was absolutely correct and that applied without doubt to the signal being investigated. Although hit in the arm, Jordan still continued to work his sets and to note further characteristics of the signal. The Rear Gunner fired 1000 rounds on his attack, but his turret was hit and made completely unserviceable (U/S), and he was wounded in the shoulder. On the second attack, Jordan was hit in the jaw, but he still continued to work his sets and log the results and told the Captain and crew from which side to expect the next attack.

On the third attack, the front turret was hit and the Front Gunner, F/Sgt Fred Grant, wounded in the leg. The WOP went forward to get him out of the turret but he, himself was hit in both legs by an exploding shell and had to return to his seat. P/O Bill Barry, the Navigator, then went forward and let Grant out of the turret. Jordan was hit once more, this time in the eye, and although he continued operating his equipment and noting further details of the signal, he realised that he could not continue with the investigation much longer, owing to his condition and, seeing that his intercom had been shot away, he went forward and brought back the Navigator and tried to explain to him how to continue operating the equipment and so bring back some more valuable information. By this time he was almost blind but although he tried to tell Barry what to do, he realised that it would be an impossible task and in the end gave up the attempt.

F/Sgt Vachon had by this time come out of the rear turret and had taken up a position in the Astro Hatch, from where he continued to give evasion control but he was again hit in the hand and Barry went back and took over from him. During this period the aircraft had lost height from about 14000 ft down to 500ft, with violent evasive action still being taken by the Captain. After 10 to 12 attacks (of which five or six had scored hits on the Wellington) the Ju88 broke off his engagement and disappeared.

The attacks had resulted in the following damage to the Wellington:

1. Starboard (S/B) throttle control shot away; S/B engine stuck at +3 boost (cruising speed) all the way home.
2. Port throttle jammed.
3. Front and rear turrets U/S.
4. S/B aileron U/S, and trimming tabs having no effect at all.
5. Air Speed Indicator (ASI) readings zero in both positions owing to the pitot head and pipes being holed.
6. S/B petrol tank holed.
7. Fabric shot away and torn away on S/B side of fuselage.
8. Hydraulics U/S.
9. Both engines running irregularly.

The WOP, Sgt Bigoray, in spite of his injuries, transmitted the coded message back to base and, receiving no acknowledgment, continued to send it in the hope that it would be picked up. It was received at 0505 hrs.

P/O Paulton kept the aircraft on course for home and managed to climb up to 5000 ft at which height he came back. At 0645 hrs it crossed the French coast at a point about ten miles NE of Dunkirk, where searchlights tried to pick it up. These were dodged by evasive action and coming down low over the sea. When they were switched off the pilot again managed to gain height.

Sgt Bigoray put the Identification Friend or Foe (IFF) on to Stud 3 and sent out an SOS and a message that they were being attacked by an enemy aircraft. He again transmitted the coded message in case it had not been received the first time.

At approximately 0720 hrs the English coast was reached. P/O Paulton tested the landing light to see if he could 'ditch' using it, but decided it was impossible. He decided to wait for daylight before ditching and asked the crew if anyone preferred to bale out rather than ditch. Sgt Bigoray stated that he preferred to jump, as one of his legs had stiffened up to such an extent that he thought he would not be able to climb out of the aircraft in the water. He made his way to the escape hatch in the rear of the fuselage, from where he intended to jump but, having reached that position realised he had not clamped on the transmitter key and, in spite of his injury, returned to his set, clamped the key down and warned the rest of the crew not to touch it. He jumped over Ramsgate and made a safe landing. The pilot ditched at approximately 0824 hrs about 200 yards off the coast at Deal. The dinghy inflated but had been holed by cannon fire. The SO tried to make it airtight by holding some of the holes but it was impossible and the crew got out of the dinghy and climbed on to the aircraft. About five minutes later a small rowing boat appeared, took them off and rowed ashore.[40]

Thus ended one of the most courageous episodes in the history of radio countermeasures.

The crew later received the following message from the Chief of Air Staff, Air Chief Marshal Sir Charles Portal GCB, DSO, MC: 'I have just read the report of your investigation flight carried out on Thursday 3rd December and should like to congratulate you on a splendid performance.' [41] Jordan received the immediate award of the DSO. Ted Paulton and Bill Barry were both commissioned shortly afterwards and each was awarded the DFC. Bill Bigoray and Everett Vachon were given the DFM.

No. 192 Squadron.

No. 1474 Flight became No. 192 Squadron on 4th January 1943 and operated in No.3 Group until No.100 Group was formed in the following November. It was commanded by S/L (later Group Captain) Vic Willis,[42] one of the original BATDU beam pilots, a man with vast experience of the type of flying needed for RCM work. A close colleague in RCM in the wartime years, John Whitehead, remembered that Willis had always helped to train the pilots for beam flying and often took them on their first operation, 'He was a bomber pilot who had a fighter pilot's reactions and flew from the beginning to the end of the War' he recalled. Norman Mackenzie, then a Sergeant/Pilot, remembered joining No.109 Squadron at Boscombe Down in February 1941. Willis, then a F/L, was his Flight Commander and took him up shortly after his arrival, firstly, to familiarise Mackenzie with Ansons, and 'later he took us on several sorties looking for the German beams.'

Shortly after its formation the Squadron was called upon to carry out an extensive investigation of the whole of the Western Mediterranean to find out what German radar coverage existed in the area. A lone Vickers Wellington Mk.X detached for the purpose proved to be totally inadequate and, on 27th April three Vickers Wellington Mk.X were despatched .They made a total survey of the area bringing many important features to light and returned to the UK on 25th August 1943.

The activities of the Squadron were spread throughout the European Theatre of Operations. It regularly investigated the enemy radar defences on the western coasts of France, Belgium, Denmark and Norway with the object of obtaining as full picture as possible of the density and frequency of the enemy coastal radar organisation with a view to detecting any new frequencies being used. In August, 1944 a Squadron Vickers Wellington found the site of an enemy long-range radar on the coast of north-west Holland, and the following month a survey was carried out on the Norwegian coast which produced good results for the bomber offensive. The object was to try and find a break in the enemy radar coverage between latitudes 60 degrees and 67 degrees

No. 1473 Flight. A Handley Page Halifax crew returning from 'Ops'. *(Eric Rostron)*

north that would enable an attacking force to get through undetected. Investigative flights by a detachment of No. 192 Squadron from Lossiemouth found that such a break did exist on latitude 64 degrees 50 minutes and this revelation enabled Bomber Command to make several attacks on enemy capital ships with few losses.

In October 1944 the Squadron dropped its first WINDOW and, on 12th December of the same year played its first operational role as an airborne jammer when two Mosquitoes from the Squadron were fitted with two channels of PIPERACK (designed to jam enemy nightfighter SN-2 radars in the 95-210 Mc/s band) and flown operationally. Eventually all of the Squadron's Mosquitoes were fitted with PIPERACK enabling them to play a dual role and it became the general practice to carry out signals investigation to and from the target, but using PIPERACK over the target itself. In addition, a considerable number of flights were made to analyse various types of other enemy jamming which had been reported.[43]

One man who served throughout from BATDU to No. 192 Squadron was P/O Eric Rostron, an air gunner. Starting out looking for German KNICKEBEIN and RUFFIAN beams over England in 1940 with BATDU and WIDU, he served in most of the various RCM airborne units. In March 1942 he found himself at Upper Heyford, 'still flying Ansons and Wellingtons on the same old special duties. I still don't know what most were about in detail.' When No.109 Squadron became part of No.8 Group, Pathfinder Force (PFF), later in the year he flew two tests trials for OBOE (one with Group Captain Bennett, the Pathfinder CO) before returning to No.1474 Flight at Gransden Lodge. Rostron completed 42 operations with No. 192 Squadron, 'BATDU, WIDU, and 109 Squadron flying didn't count,' he recollected.

64

On 22nd May 1944, he was in Halifax III LW 624:

> They were a Canadian crew with F/O Chick Webster as skipper. I was a 'spare bod' as mid-upper gunner. We were returning from Dortmund in the Ruhr some time after midnight when we got 'coned' in searchlights, a very unpleasant experience. Due to having to take violent evasive action before we got away from the lights and flak the pilot was exhausted. We came close to baling out. This was the only time in the whole of my flying career (17.5.40 to 13.8.44) when this was 'on the cards'.

Some three months later, on the 12th August, Rostron was mid-upper gunner in Halifax III LW623, (Pilot F/O Sanders), when the aircraft was badly shot up by flak returning from Brunswick and with the port-outer engine u/s they managed to make an emergency landing at West Raynham, in Norfolk, one of the No.100 Group airfields. 'It is impossible to recount now what it was like to get safely home after such an experience,' he recalled with feeling. This particular raid had not been successful. The Bomber Command War Diaries describe it thus:

> This was an experimental raid. No Pathfinder aircraft took part and there was no marking. The intention was to discover how successfully a force of aircraft could carry out a raid with each crew bombing on the indications of its own H2S set. The raid was not successful and there was no concentration of bombing...Other towns, up to 20 miles distant, were mistaken for Brunswick and were also bombed. Of 242 Lancasters and 137 Halifaxes taking part in the raid 17 Lancasters and 10 Halifaxes were lost, (7.1%).[44]

Eric Rostron found the trips were sometimes lengthy:

> I remember flying from Portreath in Cornwall to Gibraltar in Halifax DT 737 with W/C Webster as skipper. It was a seven hours trip in daylight...We were very much on the alert since about the same time an aircraft carrying Leslie Howard, the film actor, was shot down by a Ju 88 on a similar trip. At the time No. 192 Squadron had a detachment at Blida, in Algeria and we were taking men and equipment out there. Some of our duties must have been to do with submarines...the Bay of Biscay was a regular patrol (often 8-10 hours). Sometimes the Atlantic (10 hours+) and North Western Approaches as well.

Occasionally there were non-productive results bearing in mind the time and energy employed:

> As is to be expected some of these flights entailed considerable flying hours before any positive information was obtained and in certain instances (such as an investigation undertaken in the Bay of Biscay searching for submarine radar), well over 1000 flying hours were expended on this search without any positive results.[45]

Michael Carreck, after a first tour on a bomber squadron became an SO in No.192

Squadron. He was recruited for the job in a rather haphazard way:

> My pilot on my first tour on No.105 Squadron was F/O Pete Rowland...he went to train Mosquito pilots and I went to 17 OTU at Upwood. One day, early in May 1943 Pete turned up in the Upwood Crew Room. 'I've got a posting [ie to 192 Squadron],' he said, 'Come with me!' So I really recruited myself. I think I may have been acceptable as I was a radio operator as well as a navigator, and, anyway, Mosquito crews were few and far between at the time.
>
> No.192 Squadron was a very happy squadron under W/C Willis, whom I remember to this day with great respect, admiration, and affection. He was a marvellous CO, flying with crews on their first, and otherwise so often, fatal first Op. Morale on his squadron was tremendously high. I think this may have been due to the extremely worthwhile job we were doing.

It was so different from life in a Main Force squadron in Bomber Command, which, he thought, consisted of:

> ...lumbering a Pickford's van too heavily laden with bombs over Germany, dumping them on something or someone and then lumbering home cold, exhausted, scared fartless and wondering if it was worth all the bother. And also knowing that if 20 bombers took off, one wouldn't come back. Would it be yours with 30 Ops to fly?

He recalled the SO training:

> I was trained at TRE and was enraptured by the oscilliscope, cathode ray tubes (CRT) being science fiction in those days. The course included a visit to the 'Y' Service monitoring station at Kingsdown in Kent. Here a cheerful bunch of German-speaking WAAF sergeants listened in on enemy fighters. 'Here he is!' one cried and they all went 'Oooh!' as a bedroom voice like velvet fog came on the air. Then a pilot in panic. 'Achtung Schpitfeuer' The Voice (the German Controller) spoke. Yells of laughter from the WAAFs. 'Shut up, you bloody fool!,' they translated.
>
> On Special Ops we were given a frequency to monitor, tuned into by an odd variety of radios – I remember one looked like a trombone – and we logged the time of any signal, recorded its pulse rate frequency and noted any particularity. Sometimes we had a Leica camera to photograph the signals on the screen. On a lengthy Wellington or Halifax oversea flight (eg to the Bay of Biscay) the SO had it cushy. He slept across England until the patrol area began at Lands End and settled down to a nice 'kip' when the same location was reached on the way home.
>
> On returning from Germany or the Bay of Biscay we handed our logs into Bill Barry (see 'Harold Jordan's flight' above) who plotted the positions of the signals we'd received. This was no problem with the logs of the Wellington or Halifax

navigators, but with the Mosquitoes Bill had to backtrack the flight as the SO/Navs had to rely on DR after the limit of Gee coverage over the North Sea, and there was no time afterwards to fix and log positions and times. In fact the SOs eyes hardly left his oscilloscope. Little did I see except, say, an aircraft coned or PFF fireworks, of the drama of a Bomber Command raid. Not even the target below.

One Op I do remember, with P/O Salter, later I'm sorry to say, killed in action, as my Mosquito pilot. He had never flown with me before and was very nervous indeed about my navigation. 'Do you know where we are?' he asked me almost as soon we had left Feltwell. I got 'Do you know?' every ten minutes in spite of my confident 'Yes, Yes, Yes,' to his every query. This incessant questioning came to an end when he suddenly said, 'Oh good, there's flak dead ahead. We're on track!'

Special Equipment

Considerable work had to be done on aircraft to make them suitable for signals investigation. Such work included adding a 230 volt AC power supply to the existing power. Mountings had to be fitted into the aircraft to house the special equipment. As each operation varied according to the investigation being undertaken, the installation had to be designed in such a way that it would enable any type of receiving equipment to be placed in the aircraft at a moment's notice. Extra aerials for the additional equipment were necessary.

Self-recording Receivers

Self-recording receivers were also used by the Squadron. The first was Goldmark and, although the recordings made were of some value, they were not comparable with those made using the BAGFUL receiver – a TRE product (see Chapter Two). There was a limit to the usefulness of these receivers in that they only enabled the radio frequency and density of signal in the frequency band being swept to be recorded. Another special receiver, BLONDE, which would have provided full details of radio frequency, pulse recurrence frequency, pulse width, and the general characteristics of a signal, was developed but too late for it to be used operationally.

G T Lowe joined the RAF towards the end of 1941 and, after lengthy initial and advanced wireless training at Wolverhampton and Bolton Technical Colleges, found himself posted, as a wireless mechanic to a 'Special Signals Course on Blind Approach for Aircraft' at Watchfield (near Swindon, Wilts), at the time a civilian aerodrome. It was the only time in his RAF career that he received his pay in a wage packet! The end of course tests were interesting:

The highlight of the course on 'passing out' was when the Signals pupil (myself) flew in an Anson completely blindfolded, when we were landing the aircraft. The landing was accomplished by listening to the beams being transmitted at the approach to the runway. It was supposed to be proof that you understood the equipment being used in both the aircraft and on the ground.

It was from Watchfield, after one year's training, that Lowe was posted, firstly to No.1473 Flight, then No.192 Squadron, 'operating on Special Signals':

My duties were, with colleagues, to install into our aircraft (No.192 Squadron had Wellingtons, Halifaxes and Mosquitoes) the wireless and radar sets assigned to us for the special operations. The equipment was not the normal RAF sets – many were from America (Hallicrafters, I believe) which were used for scanning the airways particularly over the continent, for tracking enemy aircraft, for homing, and for target finding for Bomber forces.

Our Squadron in 1943-45 carried only wireless sets and cameras in the early days and the aircraft had an extra member to operate all the extra equipment. From time to time civilian 'boffins' would join us in our Section to give instruction on new equipment to be used, how to operate, fit and maintain it. The whole 'Signals' operation was moving fast in those days.

The range of wireless/radar equipment covered both transmitting and receiving sets, so my duties occasioned me to have to fly (obviously not over enemy territory) to test the sets under flying conditions – aircrews were at grave risk if sets did not operate correctly on 'ops'. We had to appreciate that the enemy would be trying to outwit us (by tracking aircraft and jamming frequencies). We did 'vice-versa.'

On one occasion we received into our section a piece of captured German radar equipment which had no power pack to operate it. The 'powers that be' were keen to know how it worked, so together in the Section we looked into it and finally managed to get it to work. I believe it was found to be invaluable to us in establishing the enemy's progress in this field.

He arrived at Foulsham from Feltwell and was, initially, very unimpressed with the posting :

We knew we were going to move and had heard that the new station was to be Little Snoring. We were all set to move when instructions came through that the United States Air Force had been assigned to Foulsham but they had refused to move there because of the appalling state of this site.

Well, when we arrived at Foulsham we could understand why the USAAF had reached their conclusion. Foulsham was a wartime station with living quarters spaced around the 'drome some three-quarters of a mile from aircraft dispersal units. Washing and eating facilities and the NAAFI were also some three-quarters of a mile away from the living quarters. However, anyone who could ride a bicycle was issued with one (some were very crude bone-shakers!) and they were much appreciated when we were off duty and could visit nearby dance halls and eating places.

The billets when we first arrived were very cold, draughty places with a small stove in the centre of some 30-odd beds. When it rained the lights would go out for long periods and it was miserable then. To pass the evenings most of us would go to the NAAFI which had improvised lighting where we could at least do our writing to home and friends.

To say the least these early days were pretty dreadful. However, our CO at the time, W/C (later G/C) Willis, called us all together after realising the position and asked us to bear with him and he would make the Station much better. He would put in hand immediately the 'lights' situation with the contractors and would also arrange for a Special NAAFI Club to be opened on the Station. True to his word things improved considerably in the early months of 1944 – the NAAFI Club was opened by none other than 'Jane' of the Daily Mirror who was in her heyday at the time. She presented at the opening, a life-size painting of herself (in all her nudity) which was hung in the foyer of the Club.

Other Duties

In November 1943 the training of special operators was taken over from TRE by No.192 Squadron; the work necessitated a high degree of skill and efficiency. A detailed course was given to the special operators involving approximately two to three weeks of ground lectures and, at the termination of these lectures, an examination was given. On passing the ground examination, additional air training was given to the candidate. Usually the special operator had to have an average of six to nine air training flights before becoming operational. The training of No. 1431 Flight special operators for work with Air Command South East Asia (ACSEA), was also carried out by No.192 Squadron.

Flying Officer Eric Clarkson was a navigator/wireless operator on No. 192 Squadron; he completed 27 sorties; six on Halifaxes, one in a Wellington and 19 in Mosquitoes. He was told by the Adjutant (a WAAF) on his previous squadron that they were, 'looking for volunteers from wireless trades for special duties. They won't say what it is.' At the time he had been 'a bit fed up. I had been back from Canada since the 1st January 1944 and this was now August. I had not done at lot (ten weeks leave and courses!)' so he volunteered:

I was a spare bod. They shot me off to London, the exact whereabouts I am not sure, somewhere in Westminster. That was where I met Jordan(qv). He was

69

wearing his DSO, of course. That was his job – recruiting. He went through my CV; he didn't give much away and was very tight-lipped which was understandable. It was a very short interview, about ten minutes. He came across as a very friendly sort of chap. The whole crew on the flight for which he got his award did well. It was a good job they were in a Wimpey (Wellington). They were strong but it was very uncomfortable where the special operator had to sit. He sat in the 'rest' position and the only heating you had was the end of a heating pipe which you could 'stuff up' your flying jacket.

I only had one trip in a Wellington (a North Sea patrol) and it was the only time I wore my full flying kit, underwear, the lot. They said to me, 'you'll need it because it gets cold. By God it was! We were called 'special operators (SOs)' and this was my first 'op'- in November 1944.

Eric Clarkson trained at Foulsham for his SO duties:

I went to Foulsham in September 1944 and from then until November we were training. Flight Lieutenant Mazdon was the kingpin of the training which had really become his 'baby'. I don't think he had much in the way of technical qualifications. It was just what he had picked up. He was ex-No.80 Wing. Most of us SOs weren't technical people. We operated whatever type of radio necessary to pick up whatever frequency was required. We could twiddle knobs and knew what we had to do. We could operate an oscilloscope, signal generating equipment and cameras. We had 35mm Leica's; sometimes we took pictures of the 'scope; and sometimes used cine-cameras depending, on the job. The Course was intensive, mainly classroom work. There was a small number on each and I can't remember anyone dropping out. We were all keen. I suppose, like me, they had been 'kicking their heels' for so long they wanted to get on with the job. I think one of the most common radio sets was an RCA; the 'scopes and the plugs were all the same. As I said before the radios we used depended on the frequency you were searching (Würzburgs, Freyas, or whatever).

He was sent to look for V2 rockets, not very successfully:

They had the bright idea that V2s were radio-controlled, which they weren't; they thought they were operating on a cm radio band. That was one of the things we were doing in the Wimpey on my first 'op' when we were shot up. The idea was you patrolled up and down at a fairly safe distance off the Dutch coast (because one or two of our aircraft had been chased off by German fighters) and, if the rest of the crew saw a V2 coming out through the cloud you immediately began a frantic twiddling on the knobs. If you got anything you locked it on to your oscilloscope and you left it. You did nothing more; you left it and took your photograph. It all turned out to be a waste of time but until you tried you didn't know this.

When I went up in the Mossie we used to patrol from Antwerp to the Zuider Zee (up and down twice) looking for the V2s. We only had one or two of these patrols and they didn't produce anything much. I never saw one. I suppose we would have seen the exhaust coming from the back. In Mosquitoes the radio and tape recorder were behind you. It was tight; the only way to cope was to unbuckle your harness, turn round and kneel on your seat and operate. Once you had tuned in and got it going on the tape to see what it was you were OK.

Actually my first operation, in the Mosquito, was nearly my last. They gave us our orders to plot our 'op'. It was almost 10/10 cloud on this night and we went up and down, up and down. We went up whatever the weather. We turned for home purely on flight plan because GEE was useless (it was being jammed). It really was a very good navigational aid and worked most of the time giving you a 'fix' but it was easily jammed. Sometimes the jamming just obliterated your signals. On this occasion the wind was a 'reciprocal' and when you are flying at 25000 feet it can be a bit sharp. Instead of a 100 knots blowing North it was 100 knots blowing South! We ended up not knowing where we were and couldn't see anything. We called up a whole lot of people we thought might hear us – not a sound! – until vaguely we heard a very faint signal from 'Kingsley', the call-sign I think of Tangmere. Foulsham was 'Cartwright' and our aircraft was Sturgeon 10'. Anyway 'Kingsley' picked us up, gave us a course to steer, and we were away. We were miles off course; if we had continued on the course we had been on we would have finished up in the middle of the Atlantic. We had a word or two to say to the 'Met' men when we came down!

Foulsham had Fog Investigation Dispersal Operation (FIDO). I only landed once with it. It was like entering 'Dante's Inferno', it was a rectangle of flames. We were in a Mosquito and it was alright when you were approaching it but when you came over the 'end' bit if you weren't ready for it the updraught just shot you up in the air. It was a brilliant thing for cutting a hole in the fog. When it was on it made a terrific row and from where the living quarters were (about 3/4 mile from where the aircraft were) you could hear it when it was going, a great roaring noise just like a jet engine. One night a Mosquito that was not used to FIDO landed far too far down the runway and ploughed through the hedge at the end. The plane caught fire but the crew got out OK.

When I was off sick on one occasion I got roped in to help with a briefing (which they sometimes did). I remember one particular raid (24/25th February 1945) when the Briefing Officer 'told No.462 (the Aussie Squadron), 'We are out to raise a Hornets Nest tonight!' It was an unfortunate choice of words (see Reg Gould's story under No. 462 Squadron in Chapter Five). It was a WINDOW dropping exercise but by then they were carrying a few bombs as well. The

71

Squadron lost four Halifaxes that night and the surviving Aussies were very angry. They thought it was an absolute waste of men and material. Some of them were in the same hut as me and they were a hilarious, good bunch of blokes. One of them, a 35 year old, smoked a pipe, even on 'Ops', where he had a hole put in his oxygen mask so he could do so. They were characters. We laughed so much at their antics we used to ache.

Briefings usually took about half-an-hour. You had the target area (sometimes diversionary targets were given as well), the weather from the 'Met' men, and which areas to avoid (flak). Then the navigators would go away to do their calculations and the bomb aimers were given what was going to be dropped. 'Wanagui', 'Musical Paramatta' and all those delightful Pathfinder titles would also be mentioned. The song of the day in locker rooms before an 'op' was 'Swinging on a Star', a hit, I believe, for Bing Crosby. Whenever I hear it now it always reminds me of that time long ago.

Clarkson recalled only once being shot at from the ground. On one trip his aircraft was 'coned' in searchlights 'somewhere over eastern Germany'. In an effort to avoid them his pilot altered course and height. Shortly after this he looked back to see, some distance away 'four bursts of ack-ack exactly where we had been. The speed of the Mosquito had got us out of trouble'. Sometimes they went to a target area and arrived before the Pathfinders.

There were times when they more than happy to 'shoot a line'. Eric Clarkson came back from RCM duties whilst accompanying a Main Force raid on Homberg on 20/21st November 1944; as Foulsham was fog-bound, they were diverted to Woodbridge, in Suffolk. They gave full rein to their imagination:

Following instructions we declined to be debriefed on our sortie and this gave rise to not a little interest in what we actually did. We invented a story on the spot saying that we carried a device called 'Stovepipe' and that this had been the cause of some recent successful raids. I'm afraid they bought the story to such an extent that our CO had a request some days later for our Squadron to accompany them on future 'ops'! Whilst he was amused our CO made it abundantly clear that we were not to do anything like that again. We did, however, carry, in our Mosquitoes, a jamming device called PIPERACK which we used to good effect...We would orbit a target for anything up to threequarters of an hour before, during, or after a raid, orbiting at a height of 25000-30000 feet.

On the night of 3rd/4th March 1945, the Germans mounted a large 'Intruder' attack on Bomber Command airfields in the UK. Known as 'Operation Gisella' 200 Luftwaffe nightfighters followed the various bomber forces returning to England. Twenty bombers were lost and No.100 Group lost three Halifaxes, one Fortress and one Mosquito. Eric Clarkson was a reluctant witness to the end of one Halifax (it crashed at Fulmodestone several miles to the north-west of the airfield), the only casualty from Foulsham:

> I had the sickening experience of seeing one of ours shot down over Foulsham. I had been on Special Duty and we were back earlier than the heavies. I had been debriefed and returned to my billet. We knew our aircraft were diverting because of Intruders. The whole place was in darkness and the runway lights were off. I heard this Halifax coming up. It had its navigational lights on and it was light enough to detect the shape of the Halifax. Then I could hear the unmistakable sound of a Ju88 coming up behind him and, as he got over the living quarters part of the 'drome there was a rattle of cannon fire. The strange thing is it did not appear to have any effect at first. But it killed the rear-gunner and navigator. The SO and mid-upper gunner baled out from 1500 feet and got down alright.
>
> The Skipper, F/Lt. Thomas was thrown through the windscreen and got out but was badly burned. He went to East Grinstead, was operated on, and came back to No.192 Squadron. He was always a nice, happy sort of cove and it was gut-wrenching to see him. The Flight Engineer was alright as well and that was our only loss from the Intruders. I can still see the night and hear the rattle of the cannons after all these years. I don't know why they didn't 'divert', everyone was told to, and that Halifax was the only one that came back to Foulsham. That was one of the unpleasant things, you never knew what was going to happen to you. Generally our loss rate was fairly good. Still, you remember the people who didn't come back .

Clarkson did his last operation on 25th April 1945, his birthday. It was a raid on an oil refinery near Oslo in Norway. In a Mosquito Mk XVI they flew most of the way in both directions on one engine, 'I told my pilot I didn't like the look of the flame coming out of one of the engines – the weld had gone on the exhaust stubs and flames were licking over the wing – so he 'feathered' it and I suppose we flew threequarters of the way like this.' They heard afterwards that their recording had shown the utter confusion caused by the jamming so it had been a successful sortie.

Eric Clarkson's father's cousin (also named Clarkson), who worked at TRE at Malvern, visited Foulsham. 'TRE and Foulsham

No.192 Squadron – Mrs R L Mears, MT Driver, with the truck which took crews to their aircraft. *(E Mears)*

73

worked closely together. A fat lot of good we'd have done without them, and evaluation of what we did was also important feedback for them.'

For relaxation the crews at Foulsham used to visit Norwich on their nights off. In the village itself, the local grocer, Mr. King, was very keen on male voice singing and, 'about seven or eight of us would gather in his front parlour and rehearse. We used to go round the local villages,' Clarkson recollected.

The enemy inland radar coverage and communication system had to be monitored, and it became the policy for heavy aircraft of the Squadron to accompany the Main Force of Bomber Command on its raids for this purpose. On 5th/6th March 1945 one of the Squadron's Halifaxes was doing this as part of over 700 aircraft taking part in 'Operation Thunderclap'.[46] Flight Sergeant William Young, a Glaswegian on his 63rd 'op', was one of the crew. Prior to take off he and his colleagues, chatting on the perimeter track at Foulsham, had decided that hostilities couldn't last much longer. However, his personal and unforgettable experience on this particular night, and its aftermath, was to be significant testimony to the chaos of war.

On the way to Chemnitz the Halifax was 'coned' by searchlights and attacked by a nightfighter:

> Even as the Halifax went into a dive the Messerschmitt got in a long damaging burst. A jagged line of punctures appeared above my head. In the cruel, garish spotlights that clung to us like silvery leeches, I saw the tensed figure of Flight Lieutenant Jack Irvin struggling to hold the aircraft in a corkscrew dive...the 19 year- old rear gunner, on his first 'op', was screaming, jammed in his turret by cannon shells.
>
> Another blinding flash and the Halifax was once more peppered with exploding metal and the stench of cordite filled the aircraft. We continued our 'corkscrew' downwards. Suddenly, without warning, there came a terrific crash from the front...the nose of our machine vanished in a flurry of Perspex and metal particles. We had collided with the tail unit of a Lancaster!...The skipper pulled us out at 10,000 feet and miraculously we lost the the nightfighter and flak...But we were finished.[47]

As the crippled Halifax[48], losing height all the time, crawled towards the Polish border its nose missing, a gale-force wind blowing snow into the aircraft, it became obvious to all that they would have to bale out. Using the emergency axe to smash to smithereens the special radio equipment the aircraft was carrying Young made for the escape hatch. It was jammed but he freed it after again using the axe, and jumped.

Where had he landed, Germany or Poland? At the briefing at Foulsham the crews had been told to head east towards the Russian lines if they came down and this Young did finding, 'that flying-boots were not intended for cross-country hikes!', the temperature was well below zero, and the snow was seeping through his flying suit. If he was across the Russian lines he would at least be, he thought, 'be among friends, or at least allies.' He was due for a shock..

On the fourth day after he had left the aircraft he was laying in a ditch beside the road, feeling thoroughly demoralised, when he heard a vehicle approaching. As it came into view he saw it was a truck with the Russian red star on its bonnet. He jumped up shouted and waved a small Union Jack at the passing vehicle but it drove on. Later he heard footsteps, and the driver and his mate came back to him. They were distinctly unfriendly and took him, at gun point, to a military post and, later, to a nearby town. Subjected to many hostile interrogations indications were that it was thought he was a German spy. Young was constantly under armed guard and his frequent requests to be put in touch with the British authorities were ignored.

After much shabby treatment Young was eventually taken to an interrogation centre near Cracow where he was reunited with Flight Lieutenant Nixon, his navigator. They were later taken to Kiev in the Ukraine where they joined 60 American aircrew also in the custody of the Russians. Plans for a 'Great Escape' were made by the thoroughly fed-up captives but Young and Nixon were taken to Odessa where they remained until claimed by the local British Mission who 'worked wonders in getting us back into shape' before they were sent home on a Norwegian ship four months after they had left the Halifax.

Bryan Helme, a navigator, joined No.192 Squadron on 1st October 1944, and was posted to the Wellington Flight transferring later to one of the Halifax Flights. He flew in Vickers Wellington LN 879 most of the time and on one occasion had to return with engine trouble, 'belly-landing' at Foulsham. This was on 11th November; four days later the aircraft was serviceable and operational again.

In February 1945, the whole Squadron had to turn out and clear the runway of snow. The first aircraft to do an airtest lost control, damaged its undercarriage and blocked the runway, causing the 'ops' for that night to be cancelled. Helme took up a new Halifax (which had extra fuselage fuel tanks):

> We were supposed to do an airtest and check the new fuel tanks. When we
> switched on the extra tanks over the Bay of Biscay the rear gunner cried out he
> was soaked with petrol. The tanks had been incorrectly connected and the
> fuselage was awash with petrol. Fortunately the H2S was switched off otherwise
> there would have been an explosion. The H2S dome was full of petrol.

The next day's work for the navigators was important from an RCM point of view:

> The morning or afternoon after the trip we had to go to the Navigation Office
> and check the work from the flight and produce an accurate route with times of
> the flight. If any signals were picked up by the three to four SOs we carried then
> the time and position would be logged and the information passed to Group
> HQ...

There was an occasion when the bomb aimer took over as pilot with unsettling results:

> As we only carried one pilot in a Wellington, one of the crew, usually the bomb aimer, was supposed to get minimal pilot training . We had one nasty experience with this. When the pilot went back to the toilet the bomb aimer, who took over, decided that, as there was a cloud ahead to disengage the auto pilot. Unfortunately he was too late and we flew into the cloud and lost control. The aircraft finished up spinning down like a top from 18000 ft to 5000 ft before the pilot was able to get to the controls and recover.

Ted Gomersall joined the Squadron in June 1944 as a navigator/SO in 'C' Flight (Mosquitoes):

> The role varied. Sometimes we were with the main bomber stream to and over the target and the Nav./SO had a triple role, navigation within Gee range (thereafter 'dead reckoning'), jamming over the target, and identifying and photographing any radar signals on the CRT, as well as recording any radar and R/T we could pick up. On these trips we would orbit the target while the raid was in progress with the jammers switched on. I remember that the fuses had nasty habits of blowing at crucial moments, and it was a hell of a job changing them in the cramped Mosquito cockpit, because they were positioned directly behind one's head. Towards the end of the war jamming over the target was a routine task.
>
> Luftwaffe intruders attacked Foulsham in March 1945 and shot down a Halifax. 'Some of the crew, (Canadians), were in my hut and I remember particularly the navigator F/O Darlington. They had only been on the squadron for a few days and it must have been one of their first sorties, if not their very first.'

Like many other aircrew he knew the danger of mechanical failure:

> Our return to Manston on 4th February 1945, was occasioned by the starboard engine overheating over Osnabröck (on a V2 patrol, I think), so it was feathered. We could barely maintain height on one engine, so made for Manston's 'FIDO', which was switched on (or should I say, lit) and which was visible from far over the Continent. We just made it, no circuit, just straight in, shooting off red Very lights! I remember the uplift and a distinct feeling of warmth as we crossed the end of the runway, and the realisation that the aircraft was made of balsa wood. In all these circumstances Bud (F/O George) made an excellent job of what must have been an extremely tricky landing. It was my first, and last, experience of landing on 'FIDO'.

Gomersall was on the Dresden raid on 13th February 1945:

> I remember quite vividly, what I can only describe as awe-inspiring was the sight

of the city in flames. It quite surpassed any other experience on operations either before or afterwards. I believe we arrived shortly after the first markers went down and we orbited the target, jamming, for how long I'm not now sure, the usual time was anything from 20 to 40 minutes (the following night at Chemnitz we were in the target area for 31 minutes).

Eric Turner trained in Canada (where he did a gunnery, navigation and bomb aimers course). He had returned to the UK at the beginning of 1943 but had been engaged on conversion from twin-engine to 'heavies' and courses (engines, H2S and Gee), and came to Foulsham in April 1944 as a bomb-aimer in No.192 Squadron:

We did four 'ops' as a crew in a Handley Page Halifax. The first three were OK but on the fourth, I've a feeling it was Chemnitz, coming back we were well past the French Coast over the North Sea and heading for Cromer in Norfolk, when one of the gunners got a look at something and was convinced that what he saw was an enemy aircraft. The next thing I knew we were 'corkscrewing' like mad and the guns were blazing away. Then it all went quiet and the pilot asked the gunners if they had scored any hits, and one said he thought he had.

We landed back at Foulsham and the next thing we knew was that the skipper, gunners and rest of the crew were ordered to see the CO. Apparently what the gunners thought was a Jerry was a B17 from Oulton! I knew little about the incident as I had been busy with my H2S plot when we had initial contact. The skipper got posted to Transport Command. I was a great friend of his. He just disappeared from the station. The charge against him was that he couldn't command his crew. This was a bit stupid on the part of the 'authorities'. In those circumstances he had to rely on his gunners. If they said you had a contact that was it, you had a contact. I don't blame the gunners either. If you got too close to another aircraft these things happened especially if you had had a 'hairy' trip. The two gunners were demoted (one was from Eire; he went back and never returned!) and the rest of us became 'spare'. This meant we couldn't do many 'official' operations and I sometimes went as a 'passenger' in other aircraft. I attended all the briefings and if it was trip I fancied going on I sneaked into the aircraft as an extra man.

Turner had tremendous respect for the SOs whom he thought did a marvellous job:

You only used to meet them when you got to the aircraft. You didn't see them before, or afterwards. Often there were several of them in the same aircraft. I have even been up on a trip with a female operator. She was German speaking. The Jerry nightfighters were told what to do from their ground stations, where to orbit and so forth, and these were obviously the places that our SOs were looking for. Sometimes our people used to butt in on the Germans and send false messages. The Jerries got wise to that , switched to females, so we tried with

WAAFs and that is what this girl was doing. We didn't know who they were or their names. I have been in an aircraft where there have been SIX SOs. They all had recording cameras in front of the fluorescent tubes. If we had gone down it would have been expensive, they weren't cheap cameras!

The bomb-aimer didn't drop bombs in No.192 Squadron but often assisted the navigator with H2S plots, 'it was a "Godsend" and the further you were going the better the plot became.' It was, Eric Turner thought, 'the one thing we really relied upon because it used to give us dead reckoning points especially when we were doing "turn offs" from the Main Force..' It was whilst doing this that he received his only 'war wound'. When doing his plots he used to keep his dividers on a raised rack in front of him. On one night when they had a fighter contact during a raid the aircraft was thrown about a bit and the dividers flew out and stuck in his forehead just above the eyes.

They also had other duties, 'sometimes we set about making nuisances of ourselves to the enemy by chucking out WINDOW as hard as we could. I did this myself several times with the help of the Flight Engineer'.

'Our aircraft would remain in the bomber stream for so long and then break off in a "dogleg" away from it at a given geographical position and divert (alone) onto a completely different course from them. At our briefings we saw the main force track shown and there used to be a little blue line off somewhere else, and that blue line was us!' Sometimes the RCM aircraft operated alone, 'I can remember at least two occasions when we were the only aircraft flying over Germany on particular nights' .

He was involved in a complete 'slow-roll' in a Halifax which, he considered, 'weren't meant for aerobatics, being structurally unsuitable!' The manoeuvre was caused by a fighter contact:

I think we were coming back from Hamburg. It was a short trip, I remember. When you went back to the Elsan for a 'pee' you should say to the Skipper, 'Coming off intercom, Skip.' He knows what you are going to do. There is an intercom point at the Elsan you should plug in. Nobody ever did, of course! I had just finished relieving myself when there was a shout, 'Corkscrew port, Go!' and the next thing I knew the aircraft was all over the sky. We had a fighter contact and down we went. Prior to this we had 'feathered' the port outer engine because it was overheating. There was me hanging like Jesus Christ on Good Friday. As we went down the port inner engine momentarily cut out. Both port engines were now out and as we were going over to starboard the power of the two starboard engines kept the aircraft rolling until the inner port picked up again. Round we went! It was a beauty, a perfect if involuntary roll. Whatever they say about ground crews keeping Elsans free at all times, they didn't! I got the bloody contents, the lot! Nobody would speak to me for weeks and I acquired the nickname of 'Stinker' It was a good slow roll I must admit. We had a young pilot who hadn't been long on 'ops' but he made a good job of it.

Turner learnt to fear German searchlights. On clear nights 'to start with we used to see a solid blue beam, we called it the "blue stumm"...on cloudless nights you saw this blue beam move backwards and forwards and, alternately, sideways as well.' He assumed it was calling any German aircraft that could see it into that area where they knew the raid was taking place. He felt it was radar-controlled because quite a few times he saw the beam lock on to something and immediately other searchlights used to come on and 'cone'. He spoke to a lot of his aircrew colleagues about this and many remember it.

Off-duty hours for Eric Turner were spent mainly in Norwich. One night, when a bachelor party for a member of the Sergeant's Mess at Foulsham had developed into a pub-crawl:

> We finished up in the 'Bear' pub in Norwich which had a genuine stuffed Canadian bear eight feet tall in the main entrance to the bar. We distracted the landlord's attention and four of our blokes went out with the bear! We loaded it on to the transport (which just happened, by prior arrangement, to be outside) and took it back to the Sergeants Mess at Foulsham.
>
> Three days later the landlord arrived at Foulsham demanding the return of the bear. We denied all knowledge so he went to see the CO (W/C Donaldson) who marched straight down to the Sergeants Mess. I was Chairman of the Mess Committee and we discussed the matter in the entrance to the Mess. The trouble was he could see the bear from where he was standing! He said, 'What do you know about that?' and I replied, 'Not a thing, Sir, it just turned up.' He looked at me and said, 'I will come in here tomorrow and I don't want to see that bear. Put the bloody thing back!' Transport was arranged for one bear! I understand one or two other squadrons played host to the bear on other occasions!

VE Night was celebrated, again in Norwich, by 'some of the Foulsham lads' deciding to have a swim in one of the static water tanks which were kept as an air-raid precaution in the middle of the City . Both the civil and service police arrived at the same time and a heated debate took place over who should arrest the swimmers. While this was taking place the errant airmen dried out, and disappeared into the night.

It would not have required the deductive powers of Sherlock Holmes to know which route they took. At the top of the hill which led from the old Cattle Market to the Railway Station was a garage which used to sell second-hand tyres. A pair of bolt-cutters was produced and the chains securing the tyres were removed. Suddenly there were hundreds of tyres rolling down the hill towards the Station. Traffic was in chaos. This irresponsible behaviour by these men from Foulsham no doubt incurred disapproval in the city. The reason for their tomfoolery is blindingly obvious; they were celebrating being alive.

Peter Woodard was in the Air Training Corps (ATC) and 'like almost every other lad we all wanted to be pilots but eventually became something else.' He became a WOP/AG on No.192 Squadron:

I was at the OTU at Chipping Walden, where I crewed up with F/Lt. Ben Fawkes...we were all gathered in the hangar and all the different aircrew trades were in their separate groups. Ben asked me if I wanted to be his WOP and I agreed. It was by mutual agreement. Then we went to the other trades and collected the rest of the crew. I was the youngest member being 18/19 years old.

A WOP didn't usually have a lot to do because when you were on an operation you observed W/T silence unless you were compelled to use the set. In the main I used to listen to messages, weather forecasts etc., or if we got lost I could get a route finder on the DF loop system.

We went to Foulsham on my birthday, 8th August 1944 and joined 'A' Flight which had Wellingtons; 'B' Flight had Halifaxes and 'C' Flight was the Mosquito Flight. Our first operation was on 6th September in Wellington N 683. It was a 'Special Duty' up and down the North Sea for three hours. Only the Skipper and Navigator knew what it was about....all the special wireless equipment was in the 'rest' position both in the Wellington and the Halifax (mid-aircraft)...it all looked complicated. We were just taxi-drivers really. On the 10th we did a 7 hours 20 minute trip up and down the Dutch Coast. I think we were looking for V2 launching sites...I saw one rocket going up into the clouds. I just saw its fiery tail. I had a prearranged signal to transmit on a certain frequency. Where it was going I've no idea but I should think the damn thing had landed before they received my signal!

Our first 'op' on a Halifax was on 18th February 1945 after our skipper had been 'converted' by S/L Crotch (O/C 'B' Flight) on the Squadron. Our last trip was a 'diversionary' to Flensburg on 2/3 May when the Main Force went to Kiel in what was the last Bomber Command raid of the War.

We completed a tour and had led a charmed life really, only being attacked by a fighter once when we had to corkscrew. The first time we had some flak to deal with was when we went into Europe itself. Up to then we had been going up and down the North Sea. On one occasion I remember the skipper saying on the intercom, 'Come up and have a look at this.' I had my cubby hole with my window curtained off where I used to sit and listen. I went to the cockpit, saw what was going on, and thought to myself, 'How did I get here?' and went back to my seat. I was frightened out of my life. You just kept your fingers crossed.

John Short, a rear gunner on No. 192 Squadron was posted to Foulsham:

We arrived independently by rail from our home leave departure points...our crew (with F/S Don Earl as Skipper) was allocated to 'A' Flight, flying Wellington Mk Xs, with the exception of the mid-upper gunner (for which there was no berth in a Wellington) who went to the Halifax Flight..

The first impression we had as crew was the absolute secrecy surrounding the work of the Squadron. We were thoroughly briefed about our own role and shown round the aircraft with its two banks of oscilloscopes mounted centrally just aft of the main spar. This is where our SO would sit. Externally the Wellington was a standard aircraft except for the additional aerials mounted. An unseen but useful addition was the pannier overload fuel tank installed in the bomb bay which gave greatly increased endurance. On the point about secrecy, many crews were unaware of each others tasking. When diverted and landing away from base the aircraft captain always requested an armed guard to prevent unauthorised entry to the aircraft. On more than one occasion this created a problem with the diversion Base Commander who did not appreciate being denied information on our role.

Our first operation was at medium level down the Brest Peninsula. I can recall feeling somewhat apprehensive but, more than anything else, lonely! Out over the sea heading towards enemy territory I found myself singly loudly, (for who was to hear me?) 'Onward Christian Soldiers!'

In retrospect we were sitting ducks yet only on one occasion were we challenged by a nightfighter. He announced his arrival by dropping a 'fighter flare' and, presumably, attempting to get us into silhouette to make his attack. This scheme was thwarted by putting the 'Wimpy' into a tight port turn around the descending flare. It was a 'tortoise and hare' situation which thankfully we won, as, thankfully, our opponent could not get into position for an attack. I was so keyed up by this occurrence that on our way home I mistook the quarter moonrise showing a red tip above the cloud layer as an enemy nightfighter identification light and called for an immediate 'corkscrew'. After three manoeuvres I realised my mistake...there was laughter from the crew at my mistake and relief that there was no Luftwaffe representative on our tail!

One of the most dangerous moments for John Short came without enemy intervention and showed the importance of proper training:

Our allocated aircraft was Wellington HE 472 'B', this, with the permission of the Walt Disney Studios in Hollywood had been nicknamed 'Bambi'. It had a motif painted on the nose. On 16th August 1944 the aircraft was u/s and we took 'D' Dog for the evening's operation. On running-up at the end of the runway prior to take-off the starboard engine showed a mag-drop. The Skipper reported it but was told to proceed. Just after take-off the bad engine started to run rough and misfire badly. The Skipper called over the R/T that he was executing a circuit for an emergency landing. Concerned about airspeed with only one fully functioning motor and a fully loaded aircraft, he left the flaps up, lowered the undercarriage and attempted a landing. The runway caravan fairly flashed by as we hit the runway at about 140 m.p.h. The tyres burst, the starboard undercarriage leg collapsed puncturing the wing fuel tank and the tank in the bomb bay started to spew fuel which was ignited by the sparks from metal on concrete. As the aircraft slithered to a stop on the grass along the runway, flames leapt skywards as we all scrambled clear. This was achieved in 12 seconds, proving our annoying 'abandon aircraft' practices were well worth while!

After 29 operations John Short left the Squadron for a Gunnery Leader's Course. When he returned to the Squadron he joined the Halifax Flight becoming a gunner on S/L Ben 'Guy' Fawkes crew:

It was amusing to be the sole Halifax amongst 50 or so Lancasters, heading east in the darkening sky on our way to a German target. The crews closest would be waving their guns up and down in acknowledgement ...They obviously wondered what the hell we were doing. Had we the correct raid? As night fell I often wondered what happened to the mass of aircraft which had surrounded us...

Phil James was a Flight Engineer:

I went to No.192 Squadron at Foulsham in May 1944 and did 33 Operations with the same (Canadian) crew. I was 'crewed up' with F/O George Ward at Dishforth, in Yorkshire which was a Heavy Conversion Unit where pilots of Wellington bombers were told 'Sort yourselves out and get engineers.' I was approached by a 6 ft 2 inch Canadian Indian wireless operator, Sgt. Jim Yakimchuck who said 'Would you like to join our crew?' I agreed to do so and was introduced to the rest of the crew, after which we went down the pub to celebrate. I was asked what I wanted to drink and told them , 'Orange Juice'. They were all flabbergasted by this because they had picked me as their Engineer because of my reddish hair and my fresh, reddish complexion! (which, I suppose, they thought indicated that I was a drinker). I became known to them as 'Red'. My crew's aircraft, a Halifax III, DT'O', was called 'The Richdale Express' named after a brewery in Sheffield which my Canadian crew used to visit when on leave.

Some years ago I asked why No. 192 Squadron maintained a 24 hour watch (mostly done by Wellington aircraft) down in the Bay of Biscay. I was told that the Germans transmitted a beam out into the Atlantic to guide the U Boat back to the French submarine pens. Apparently we used to monitor the wavelength to assist our ships and submarines.

On another occasion we were dispatched to Lossiemouth in Northern Scotland in connection with the German battleship Tirpitz which was based at Tromso, in Norway. We were briefed to do a 9 hour 5 minute trip flying under 1000 ft up the Norwegian Coast . At a given point we were to climb to 5000 ft whereupon the Tirpitz would switch on its radar. Unknown to them we were able to plot the gaps and the weak points in their radar 'curtain' which allowed the Lancasters to fly into Swedish airspace and then fly out and sink the Tirpitz with 'Tallboys' (12,000 lb bombs).

The one trip that will always stick out in my mind was a trip we did to Brunswick. The routing was very cleverly done to fool the Germans regarding our course. We were routed south of Duisburg, then turning north so that they didn't know where we were going. Meanwhile the Main Force attacked Duisburg whilst over 100 Lancasters and two 192 Squadron aircraft carried on to attack Brunswick. This was one of the early raids where they used H2S.On the trip home when we were over Wilhelmshaven we were 'coned' by a blue masterbeam searchlight which was radar-controlled and shuttered. They used to plot you by radar and the open the shutters of the seachlight and there you were stark naked in the sky. Of course as soon as you were picked up half a dozen manual searchlights joined in the coning, and the flak started. The obvious way to get out of this was to 'corkscrew'. If ever a pilot sweated to get out of that beam my pilot did. He lost pounds! We eventually finished up at 10,000 ft and escaped from this beam, climbed and made our way home to Foulsham collecting some flak over Heligoland on the way. We looked at the aircraft the next day and saw that there was a few holes in the tail. That trip was my biggest fright, I think. We were told at debriefing that these blue searchlights did not exist! We were also told this when we reported VERTICAL vapour trails in the sky. These turned out to be the new German jet fighters.

Our bomb-aimer was Al Schorn, a Canadian of German descent. Coming in to land one morning he spoke in German to the Control Tower. Of course my pilot was up before the CO the following day and was told ,'You are lucky you are not going to Sheffield' (the RAF Prison). After a discussion the CO said that they would take no further action on this occasion and George said, 'OK, I'm off to Sheffield tomorrow.' and the CO said, 'I've told you, I've forgotten it. You are not going to Sheffield.' What the CO didn't know was they were visiting the Richdale Brewery, in Sheffield, where they were well looked after by the Chairman each time they went there on leave! After the War, my pilot, S/L George Ward, DFC, was an Observer for the R C A F in Florida when the U S was testing rockets and missiles. He held the position for 17 years.

Operational Hours and Sorties Flown. No.192 Squadron [49]

	Hours	Sorties
1943	3,143	440
1944	6,817	1,394
1945	3,121	602
Total	**13,081**	**2,436**

Footnotes – Chapter Three

[32] PRO AIR 25/786

[33] 'Beam Benders; No. 80 (Signals) Wing R A F 1940-45', by Laurie Brettingham, (Midland Publishing, 1997), p. 72.

[34] Ibid. pp. 19-26.

[35] 'Joe. The Autobiography of a Trenchard Brat', W/C Joe Northrop, DSO, DFC, AFC, PFF. (Square One Publications, 1993), p.138.

[36] PRO AIR 41/46, Air Historical Branch 'Official History of No.80 (Signals) Wing R A F 1940-45,' p.20.

[37] Op.cit. (35), p.150.

[38] Ibid.p.156-7.

[39] John Whitehead had for the previous two years been attached to No.80 (Signals) Wing HQ at Radlett where he had been an Ops Room Controller and engaged on intelligence work. [See 'Beam Benders: No.80 (Signals) Wing 1940-45' by Laurie Brettingham, (Midland Publishing, 1997), for further information about this Unit.]

[40] PRO AIR 27/1156.

[41] Ibid.

[42] Group Captain Willis joined the R A F as an aircraft apprentice in 1933 at the age of seventeen and a half and gained a scholarship to the R A F College at Cranwell in 1936. He passed out from Cranwell in 1938, winning the King's Medal, the Aeronautical Engineering Prize and the J A Chance Memorial Prize. On the outbreak of the Second World War he was posted to No.201 Squadron, a flying-boat squadron, for anti-submarine duties and was Mentioned in Despatches. From 1940 to the end of the War he was almost entirely engaged on Special Duties (Signals) flying over Europe and the Middle East , or on Staff appointments connected with this specialised flying. These appoinments included the post of Deputy SASO at No.100 Group HQ and command of R A F Foulsham. He was promoted to Acting Group Captain in 1944 at the age of 28, and held this rank until just after the War's end. He was awarded the DFC in 1942 for daylight jamming operations over the Western Desert, the DSO in 1944

for operations over Europe, and was again Mentioned in Despatches. In 1948 he was awarded the OBE whilst in command of the Flying Unit at R A F Watton, a Signals Flying Unit. After the War he served in the British Military Mission in Greece (1948-51), on the Directing Staff at the R A F College, and from 1955 to 1959 was Group Captain (Operations) at Bomber Command and the Central Reconnaissance Establishment in charge of special duty and reconnaissance operations. In 1959 he assumed command of R A F Luqa, Malta. (Career Brief G/C C V D Willis, at the R A F Museum, Hendon).

43 PRO AIR 25/786, pp. 80-81

44 'The Bomber Command War Diaries: An Operational Reference Book, 1939-45', Martin Middlebrook and Chris Everett (Midland Publishing, 1996), p.560.

45 PRO AIR 25/786.

46 Operation 'Thunderclap' was an Allied plan, not popular with the air authorities, for the total destruction of Berlin, Leipzig, Dresden and Chemnitz. The plan was not fully carried out due to the rapid westward advance of the Soviet Army.

47 Extract from an article, 'Missing: Believed Killed' F/S William 'Scottie' Young (as told to Gordon Thomas) in the 'R A F Flying Review', pp.14-16 (June 1951).

48 There were 52 RCM sorties on this night and two RCM aircraft were lost. In addition to the Halifax a Stirling was a casualty over France. It is believed to have been shot down by an American artillery unit. ('Bomber Command War Diaries', Martin Middlebrook and Chris Everett (Midland Publishing 1996), p.675.

49 PRO AIR 25/786

NAAFi truck at Foulsham with the mascot, Oscar the goat.   *(E Mears)*

Chapter Four

This Strange Conglomeration:
The Formation of No.100 (Bomber Support) Group

Bomber Command called for a unit equipped to undermine the enemy's use of his electronic devices. A novel, highly specialised unit employing skilled scientific and service personnel was required and realised. For the first and only time during the War an operational Group which was a mixture of bomber and fighter squadrons came into being. The utmost priority was given to the forming of this strange conglomeration.[50]

Air Vice-Marshal E B Addison, AOC No. 100 Group.

Air Vice-Marshal E B Addison CB CBE.
AOC, No.100 (Bomber Support) Group

(Maryse Addison)

Edward Barker Addison was born in Cambridge on 4th October 1898. In the First World War, aged 17 years, he joined the Royal Flying Corps and saw active service in France for three years firstly, as a WOP/Air Mechanic, becoming a Corporal in 1917; a year later he was commissioned in the newly-formed Royal Air Force as a Technical Signals Officer. At the conclusion of the War he left the RAF and studied natural science at Sidney Sussex College, Cambridge, graduating with a BA in 1921 (he proceeded to his MA in 1926). Whilst at Cambridge he met a French student, Marie-Blanche Rosain, whom he later married. They had a son and daughter.

In 1921 Addison rejoined the RAF, being recommissioned under the University Entrance Scheme, and was sent to India. In 1926 he spent a year at the Ecole Superieure d' Electricité in Paris where he was awarded the French Diploma of High Frequency Engineering. After three years research work at RAE, and a further two as an instructor to the Officers' Signals Course at Cranwell, he attended the Staff College in 1933, and from then until the first year of the Second World War was employed on Air Staff and flying duties in Singapore, Hong Kong, Palestine (where he was awarded the OBE during the 1937 riots), and Egypt.

Recalled to the Air Ministry in London in 1940 and working again under Air Commodore Lywood – Addison had been adjutant of Lywood's unit in India – he was largely concerned with navigational aids. When the German blind-bombing raids commenced in that year he was given the task of organising RCM in what became known as 'The Battle of the Beams'. For this purpose he set up No. 80 Wing as an independent organisation within Fighter Command.

In April 1942 Addison, by then a Group Captain, returned to the Air Ministry and eventually became Director of Signals. At the end of 1943 when No.100 Group was formed he became AOC (with effect from 8th November 1943). AVM Addison retired from the RAF in 1955 and entered industry, later acting as a consultant for the Vocational Guidance Association. He became a Fellow of the Institute of Electrical Engineers in 1966, and was awarded the CBE in 1942; the CB in 1945 and the US Legion of Merit in 1947. He died on 4th July 1987.

Formation of No. 80 (Signals Wing)

Air Vice-Marshal E B Addison, CB, CBE, described how he became involved in the formation of the RCM unit No. 80 Wing early in the Second World War:

'Lywood and I were old friends... He was Deputy Director of Signals at the Air Ministry. He had me fetched home from HQ Middle East in February 1940 and I was posted to the Air Ministry to work with him at this time being transferred from the General Duties Branch to the Technical (Signals) Branch.

It was Lywood who learned in 1940 about the German plan to use the KNICKEBEIN beam to aid Luftwaffe night bomber crews to bomb UK targets. This was a real threat for our nightfighters were not ready to combat the menace.

He asked how we could best deal with the threat. I suggested radio countermeasures and the name RCM was coined. Lywood asked me to set up an organisation for this purpose outside the Air Ministry. He said that Churchill had said all possible assistance should be given. Thus was No.80 Wing formed, within Fighter Command but completely independent.

Starting at a temporary HQ at Garston, near Watford, in Hertfordshire, I was told I could have a free hand to choose my own personnel. I started with two TRE scientists, Wells and Cox-Walker. I scoured the countryside in the Watford area for more suitable accommodation and eventually found a large country hotel at Radlett (Aldenham Lodge) which I commandeered on the spot as my new HQ. I hastily recruited an HQ staff composed of General Duties and Signals officers known to me and formed an Operations Room manned mainly by WAAFs; the Air Ministry supplied the administrative staff. Many of the technical staff were amateur radio experts skilled in the line of VHF reception. TRE formed a special RCM Section of highly qualified scientists and radio engineers who were involved in very close contact with us. This was headed by Robert (later Sir Robert) Cockburn.[51]

Towards the end of 1943 an important development took place in the radio war, when an RAF unit, No. 100 (Special Duties)[52] Group responsible for most of the operational application and co-ordination of RCM efforts, ground and airborne, in the air war against Germany, was formed. The advisability of having a separate unit, to operate under Bomber Command, arose from the following considerations:–

[a] The growing complexity of RCM activities.

[b] The need to operate specialist RCM aircraft because of the size and weight of the special equipment now required, or because they might be required to operate away from the main force.

Bylaugh Hall, No.100 Group HQ. Some of the RCM Staff. Top row, left to right, W/C McMenemy: G/C Goodman: W/C Cordingly. Bottom row, F/L Grey sitting Between two W A A F Code-Cypher Officers. *(N C Cordingly)*

[c] Fitting and servicing problems, which were becoming increasing complicated could more easily be resolved under centralised control. The need for general installation of RCM equipment in bombing squadrons could be eliminated.

[d] The desirability of specialist direction in developing new RCM techniques.[53]

In addition, TRE was also having difficulties. With the extended use of airborne RCM operations, the RAF began to create various RCM organisations each acting independently of the other. These separate units were all calling on TRE's services. Duplication of effort and wastage of resources were beginning to arise. Robert Cockburn described the RCM position prior to the foundation of No.100 Group, and the difficulties being encountered by his RCM Group at TRE:

> By 1943 various countermeasures had been introduced throughout the RAF as contingencies arose without any effective coordination of effort. For instance, the AIRBORNE MANDREL screen for reducing the range of the enemy's early warning system, and the MOONSHINE squadron, were operated by 11 Group of Fighter Command. Nightfighter squadrons of Fighter Command were being fitted with homing facilities against possible airborne jamming. Ground jamming was operated by No. 80 (Signals) Wing under the technical control of

the Director-General of Signals at the Air Ministry. Bomber Command were building up their own countermeasures effort for direct support of their offensive and were already employing MANDREL and TINSEL and envisaging the introduction of further equipment. Mutual interaction between these various counter methods was liable to arise both technically and tactically and the need for centralised control of operations was obvious.

TRE were being submerged under a series of unrelated demands from the various users which led to duplication of effort in the laboratories. The design of equipment was so closely related to its tactical use that a clarification of the confused operational picture was vital if the limited scientific effort was to be properly employed. Furthermore, the dispersal of countermeasures effort gave rise to an uneconomical use of servicing and testing facilities and accentuated the scarcity of properly trained personnel and test equipment.[54]

The idea of a special group or command which should, as far as possible, control all countermeasure operations and with which TRE could cooperate in working out future applications was explored during the summer of 1943. When it came into existence Cockburn considered it, 'very timely and led to a much better use of the various RCM facilities which were becoming available.' No.100 Group, he thought, 'led to a better correlation of technical possibilities and tactical requirements, particularly as applied to nightfighter operations such as SERRATE and had an important influence on Bomber Command tactics.'

To the scientist's perspective, might be added what was arguably the most important factor of all, the state of mind of the crews in Bomber Command. Many years later the man charged with forming No.100 Group, its AOC, Air Vice-Marshal (AVM) E B Addison referred to this. 'Late in 1943 Bomber Command seemed to be on the point of suffering unacceptable losses' he remembered, and, as a result, 'the morale of our bomber crews had fallen dangerously low.' Much of the Luftwaffe's success was, in Addison's view, attributed in great part to the ever-increasing efficiency of the Luftwaffe in the use of electronic devices and radio communications to assist its fighters to intercept our bombers.[55]

Elsewhere, Addison spoke of

Bylaugh Hall, No. 100 Group HQ. Operations Planning Room. Left to right: W/C Heath (Fighter Ops); S/L Kendrick (Navigation); Leonard Lamerton (Operational Research Section). *Maryse Addison)*

the problems facing Bomber Command, and its new Group, and expanded in greater detail on the reasons for the latter's creation:

> The second phase of the Radio War, that is to say the Offensive Phase, came into being when it was realised that the defensive system of the enemy was becoming so efficient as to inflict serious losses on our bomber forces. We were now on the offensive and the Germans were sinking all their resources into the building up of the air defences of their territory. Their defensive organisation depended for its success to a very large extent indeed on the use of radio, and with the rapid strides made in this art by the German scientists, Bomber Command was meeting increasing opposition as its attacks grew in intensity.
>
> Slowly the toll taken of our night bombers rose as the German defences became more efficiently developed, until it was realised – and at this stage our scientists uttered a grave warning – that defence was likely to outstrip offence where night bombing was concerned. At this time, too, it was becoming very evident that the use of radio by the enemy was a factor which had to be taken seriously into account in our planning of night raids. The Germans were able to gain very early warning of an impending attack and could follow continuously for a long period the approach of our bombers. Thus the enemy could congregate his fighters well beforehand in the right area and so be ready to inject them, with the aid of inland radar systems, into the bomber stream as soon as it arrived overland.[56]

Knowledge of German methods enabled Bomber Command to route their aircraft so as to lessen the danger from the German radar to some extent. For example, it was found that concentration in time and space caused saturation of the enemy's radar. In addition, 'zig-zag' routing made it more difficult for the enemy to guess the probable target. 'But,' AVM Addison recollected, 'our opponents soon learned to modify their defensive systems to counter such stratagems, and although new tactics frequently led to a temporary reduction in our casualty rate, the enemy was quick to readjust his defences to meet every new contingency as it arose.'

It became increasingly obvious that a more positive protection against the effects of the enemy's radio systems was required:

> A number of devices for interfering with the enemy's apparatus, particularly those concerned with the control of his nightfighters, were invented and installed in our main force bombers, but the extra weight to be carried, and the added onus imposed on aircrews who had to operate the complicated apparatus in addition to their normal duties, tended to outweigh any advantage that they bestowed.
>
> Eventually it was concluded that specialist RCM aircraft and escorting nightfighters, fitted with special devices for searching out and destroying the opposing nightfighters, were needed. Thus it was decided, late in 1943, to form

a separate Group within Bomber Command, whose main function would be the protection of our bombers at night. This took time to organise, since the apparatus had to be made and fitted into the aircraft, and the specialist crews had to be trained.[57]

The specialist RCM unit was suggested by Bomber Command in June 1943, approved by the Air Ministry on 29th September. It came into being on 1st December of the same year and, by the end of that month, comprised 6905 personnel, which consisted of 399 officers and 6506 other ranks. Its early life is officially described thus:

> For the first six months after the Group's formation its operations were confined to the nightfighters and the ground-based jammers. During this time the specialised equipment for the RCM aircraft was in development and production and the squadrons were being built up and trained. Apart from ABC which was brought into use earlier, the airborne RCM operations of 100 Group first began on D-Day.[58]

The appointment on 8th November 1943 of Air Commodore (as he then was) Addison as the AOC, seemed an obvious choice. He had extensive experience of RCM from the earlier, defensive phase of the War whilst commanding No. 80 Wing. In addition, in 1942, as the need for widely defensive RCM eased, he moved to alternative, more offensive-based work at the Air Ministry.

Addison was held in high esteem by senior officers. In March, 1942, Air Commodore Lywood, the Director of Signals wrote to Air Marshal Harris, recently appointed C-in-C Bomber Command, about him. Both knew him well and were aware of his personal qualities. Lywood was an old friend, Harris had served with Addison in Palestine and was godfather to his daughter, Maryse.

Lywood wrote:

> Addison of 80 Wing has had a long run there and in view of his exceptional staff abilities we have toyed with the idea of having him up here as deputy to myself. It has also occurred to me that if the opportunity arose you yourself might very much like to have him, particularly in view of his very wide experience during the past 18 months on navigation methods other than our own. He has also, I know, got ideas on what could be done ourselves. You know his capabilities as well as I do – if you felt very strongly about it we would forego our claim in your favour because it is obviously such an ideal posting, in our view, at the present stage of affairs.[59]

Despite Harris speedily replying that he, 'would be delighted to have Addison as his Chief Signals Officer' the move never came about. He was moved to the Air Ministry where he did, indeed, become Deputy Director of Signals under Lywood, subsequently taking over from him as Director. In March 1943, Air Commodore Addison transferred from the Directorate of Signals to the Directorate of Communications taking with him the responsibility for all RCM at the Air Ministry.

The formation of No.100 Group did not proceed quickly enough for Air Marshal Harris. As was usually the case he was prepared to point out what he saw as the deficiencies to the Air Ministry. In a letter, in November 1943, to the Vice Chief of Air Staff, Sir Douglas Evill, he commented on the procrastination:

> It is of the utmost importance that the new Countermeasures Group (No. 100 SD Group) should be got going on the highest priority. The next few months are crucial for the Bombing Offensive, and I am sure you will agree that everything should be done to speed matters up and get this Group fully operational quickly even at the cost of a good deal of inconvenience.

At a meeting held here on November 16th to discuss details of the formation of the Group it was clear that representatives of both Fighter Command and No. 2 Group, who are interested parties in the matter, were contemplating a much more leisurely process of rearrangement than we consider acceptable in the circumstances, and it seems as if the view that the formation of the new Group is a matter of comparatively low priority is also held in some departments of the Air Ministry. I shall be grateful if you can dispel this illusion.[60]

No. 100 Group HQ was to be at Bylaugh Hall, 15 miles north-west of Norwich, near East Dereham, in Norfolk, a large country house built 'amongst the hedgerows and turnip fields', as 'The Builder' magazine recorded, at the time of its construction in the mid nineteenth-century . Subsequently described as 'ugly but well-heated' by the No.100 Group SASO, Air Commodore Chisholm, it stood in its own grounds about a mile from the road, and the HQ staff lived in huts in these grounds. Transport for important journeys was available by light aircraft from the No.100 Group Communicaton Flight at RAF Swanton Morley less than half a mile away. All No.100 Group airfields could be reached within 15 minutes.

The arrival of the new unit meant the removal of No. 2 Group who were currently using Bylaugh Hall as their HQ. According to Harris there had been, 'dilatory action in construction' of No.2 Group's new HQ and he felt, 'a real effort by all concerned' should be made to expedite the move so that No.100 Group could take over Bylaugh Hall as soon as possible. 'I shall therefore,' he added, 'appreciate any help you can give to speed things up. No.100 Group, not No. 2 Group should have preference in such matters.' Harris also complained about Fighter Command:

> Their contention is that as probably only two of the squadrons they are handing over will be operational before January 1st 1944, there is no immediate urgency about the return of Sculthorpe to Bomber Command for the use of 100 Group, and suggest that this might be postponed until January 1st. My view, on the other hand, is that insufficient pressure is being exerted to make the other squadrons operational at the earliest possible moment so that we might get things going more rapidly.
>
> I am not suggesting that there is obstruction or deliberate unhelpfulness on these points but simply that the real operational urgency of getting No. 100 Group started quickly is not generally appreciated as it should be. There is, I understand, a similar feeling abroad at TRE that the provision of high-powered jammers for the Fortress Squadron, which is an essential part of the Group, is not really very urgent or important. Here, too, a word from authoritative Air Ministry quarters would no doubt help a great deal.
>
> ...We must assume that the efforts of Germany to stop our bombing will become ever more strenuous as her position both on the home and Russian

fronts becomes more desperate, and therefore urgent development of the Countermeasures Group and extended use of our own large fighter force to help the bombers through are, at the moment, operational requirements of the very highest importance. It is time that Fighter Command took some interest in the Bomber Offensive. At present they run an entirely private war on their own.[61]

On 19th December 1943, Air Commodore Addison entered Ely RAF Hospital for a few days, in his own words, 'to clear up the remains of "flu" which they think might otherwise lead to something more serious in the boisterous Norfolk climate.' (He clearly did not relish Christmas in hospital and was discharged on 23rd December). Before going into hospital the AOC submitted, via his Senior Air Staff Officer, (SASO), Group Captain Rory Chisholm, a lengthy, but detailed, report to the Deputy C-in-C, Bomber Command, on the current state of the new unit and how he saw its future role. On the night of 16/17th December, No.100 Group had carried out its first few operational sorties. No. 141 Squadron had sent out four SERRATE Bomber Support Fighters. Two of these were Beaufighters and two were Mosquitoes. One Beaufighter returned with radar trouble after a short time, and one Mosquito returned with engine trouble before crossing the enemy coast. The other two fighters damaged an Me110. There were, Addison thought, some interesting and instructive lessons to be learnt which indicated how the efficiency of the Squadrons could be improved. He itemised the deficiencies in aircraft, equipment and training and could not be accused of equivocation:

AIRCRAFT

The aircraft supply position, as I have stressed in my official letter, is critical and its future is no better. The aircraft with which No.141 and the other Squadrons are equipped are all old and some are distinctly dead-beat. They are having constant trouble of the nature that one would expect in old aircraft and this was reflected in this first operation, one Mosquito having to return with engine trouble. The Squadrons have not much faith in their aircraft, I am sorry to say, but that is not surprising since these aircraft are all old and well used.

In my official letter it has been pointed out that immediate steps will be necessary to ensure a future supply of suitable aircraft...A further point was made that the Mark VI is the only Mosquito being built which would be suitable for these Bomber Support fighter duties. It is the only Mosquito which carries guns and which can have the necessary radar installed in it. It is most important that something should be done to ease the present position and I suggest that we would be allotted as soon as is possible some Mark VI Mosquitoes. We could do with one at once so that we ourselves may prototype it to take the necessary radar equipment.

DURATION OF SORTIES.

The amount of petrol that these fighters must carry is a very important point. The Beaufighters, last night, were unable to get to Berlin [Main Force Target]. The Mosquitoes, in theory, should have had 20 minutes in the target area from the beginning of the raid. Petrol is the all important factor in these operations and I feel SD fighters must carry more of it than they do at present in the Mark II Mosquito. The Mark II Mosquito with long-range fuselage tanks carried 550 gallons. The Mosquito VI with jettisonable 50 gallon tanks would carry 613 gallons and this would allow a patrol of an hour in, say, the Berlin area.

As I see it at present, it would seem that while our main function would be to provide support near the bombers, (ie virtually bomber escort), a general anti-fighter offensive should continue as part of the bomber support operation. In order to cover the Hun fighter marshalling beacons; the target area after a raid (where there are the best chances of finding Hun fighters without many identification difficulties); and even, perhaps, the Hun airfields, the fighters will need the maximum possible duration.

By the equipping of these Squadrons with Mosquito VI's not only will we be getting new aircraft which is so essential to their role but we will be getting also the extra petrol which would allow bomber escort and intensive anti-Hun fighter operations to be carried out at the extreme bomber ranges.

This is why I am so keen that we should be made an immediate, if small, allotment of Mosquito VI's. Since we can ourselves install the necessary radar gear we would then have a few very long range (and new) fighters with which to put our proposed plan into effect.[62]

Air Commodore Addison then moved on to equipment:

NEED FOR BETTER AI COVERAGE

From last night's operation we got convincing confirmation of what is already known, the need for better tail warning in these fighters. Both aircraft who completed their sorties had experiences which had a good deal in common. This was the appearance behind them after a SERRATE chase, of a Hun fighter at such short range that the turn they made to intercept it was inadequate and all they were, in fact, able to do was to get away. It has been established that with a high-precision radar of the Lichtenstein type the quick turn by the front fighter must be made at a range of at least 5000 feet. If it is made at smaller ranges the astute Hun will notice the development of this turn at its beginning and will be able to follow the movement of the front fighter retaining it within his AI coverage.

The rear coverage necessary to give a good warning of the approach of this intercepting fighter can be achieved by having a second rearward-looking radar set in the Mosquito. With this equipment the Mosquito will have warning of the approach of the hostile fighter (which seems the common development of many SERRATE chases) at a distance of 15000 feet or more and will trace him in until he gets to 5000 feet. He will then whip round and his turn will become noticeable to the pursuing fighter only when it is well under way and developing so fast as to take the Mosquito outside the enemy AI coverage. In last night's operations both the Beaufighter and the Mosquito that completed their sorties saw a Hun behind them at two to three thousand feet (the maximum range of their present rear radar cover). Both aircraft got away safely and one damaged his Hun during his escape, but neither was able to make sure of fixing the enemy aircraft since the early warning of his approach had been inadequate.[63]

The AOC further complained that the SERRATE aerials in Mosquitoes were giving, 'very bad and baffling performances' but added that a team of experts were engaged on this problem and he was hopeful of a solution within a few days. He also drew attention to the need for intensive AI 'Dogfight' training which, he felt, 'had been a little neglected hitherto' and a syllabus of training was being set up the completion of which would, 'ensure that no crew goes on Bomber Support without knowing all about the technique of intercepting the interceptor.'

Despite the critical theme of the report Air Commodore Addison was cautiously optimistic:

> The Squadrons are in very good heart and they are confident that, given the equipment, they will be able to achieve great success although I am afraid the period of months of neglect and lack of interest through which they have recently passed has left a mark which cannot be eradicated immediately. Nevertheless all these Squadrons are very keen and now that they know they are being assiduously looked after, are becoming like 'greyhounds straining at the leash'. I hope I may have your immediate support over this question of aircraft. The situation is critical and likely to become more so.
>
> I think you will see, however, that we have a long way to go yet before we can give a really good account of ourselves. The technical side has been badly neglected and will require considerable effort before it can be made wholly satisfactory. The training, too, has not been on the right lines. Up to now the SERRATE successes have been due in a large part to the skill of a few individuals of the type who would succeed at anything. I can see no reason why all three Squadrons should not be trained to become very skillful in this form of operation. We are already killing the 'black magic' of it. After all it is a very straightforward and common sense method of homing on to a beacon which happens to be a German aircraft. From then on it is a question of good AI

nightfighting technique – a phase of training which curiously enough does not seem to have received much support in these Squadrons in the past.[64]

He finished the report on an upbeat note. 'I am convinced we have got here a means of doing real damage to the enemy once we can get going in numbers – and then of course, the opportunities will fade as the Hun realises that the indiscriminate use of his AI is likely to call unwanted attention upon himself. By that time I trust we shall have perfected other methods which we have in mind.'

Air Commodore Addison received significant assistance in building up the Group from his Deputy, Group Captain Roderick Chisholm.[65] Chisholm had served with distinction as a nightfighter pilot in the earlier years of the war with No. 604 Auxiliary Squadron, had been CO at the Fighter Interception Unit (FIU) at Ford, in Sussex, where aircraft and equipment for Fighter Command were flight tested, and was generally considered to be an expert on nightfighter tactics. In the month following his appointment to No.100 Group he was awarded the DSO.[66] The citation records that 'he has completed an extremely large number of sorties at night during which he has destroyed nine enemy aircraft displaying exceptional skill and keenness...and his outstanding qualities and personal example have contributed materially to the efficiency of the Unit he commands.' One officer, Charles Clarke, who served under him in No. 100 Group described him thus:

> ...he was the tactician. He was a man who would sit there and say, 'I think they are going to do this, or that, and, therefore, we are going to have this, or that, ready!' He was right more often than not. He wasn't a professional airman; before the War he had been an accountant with Kuwait Oil Company. I admired him. He was very unassuming, but positive. You had absolute faith in him because he knew what he was doing and gave you confidence.'

Dudley Saward, Chief Radar Officer at Bomber Command at the time, thought Chisholm's appointment a sensible one:

> ...Addison had as his SASO Air Commodore Roderick Chisholm, one of the most experienced nightfighter pilots in the Battle of Britain and during the night battles against the German bombers in 1940 and 1941. Chisholm had flown with the first of the RDF (radar) fighter detection equipment and had flown with the latest. Also he had been employed on attacks against German nightfighter stations in the Low Countries in what were known as 'Intruder' operations. With Addison and Chisholm, Harris could not have had better technical advisers for his needs.[67]

Chisholm's posting took him into strange territory. He was profoundly impressed by what he saw. To him Bomber Command was 'new in outlook, new in machinery of command, new in conception of planning, and new in people.'[68] The difference between fighter and bomber activities was immediately obvious. The 'spur-of-the-moment action of fighter operations' contrasted starkly with the 'almost ponderous deliberation' of the Bomber Command planners. Ultimately, the final decisions as to target and scale of attack were made by the C-in-C.

Bomber Command, Chisholm found, 'was proud and defiant', accepting losses 'seemingly crippling to the newcomer' of thirty to forty aircraft or more a night, 'stoically and unflinchingly.' His experience as a fighter pilot caused him to wonder whether the bomber crews, for whom he had 'feelings of simple admiration', were aware that 'the exhausts of their Lancasters could be seen from a mile and a half away, and that they could be seen as silhouettes against stars from nearly a mile away.'[69]

The new SASO was under no illusions regarding the task which lay ahead in what was to become for him 'eighteen engrossing and vivid months.' The need for RCM in Bomber Command was 'acute and continuous':

> Once the enemy had established an efficient fighter-control system, the scales were weighted heavily against the bombers, for aircraft, once seen were vulnerable at night ...and the big bombers could, because of their size, be seen before the small fighters. So the fighter could shoot first and, with its heavier armament, perhaps decisively, while the bomber's only sure safeguard (other than the use of an effective warning device) was constant evasive action, which would certainly hinder the fighter-pilots aim and might even deny him a sighting. But the bombers flew in high concentration, timing had to be precise and navigation accurate, and these prerequisites were not compatible with much evasive action. Thus extraordinary measures had to be adopted...[70]

The task was indeed a daunting one for Bomber Command faced a formidable foe. A report[71] written in February 1944, estimated there were some 700 Luftwaffe nightfighters based at approximately 40 airfields spread over Northern Denmark; Northern, Western and Southern Germany; the Low Countries; and Eastern France. Equipped with AI, they could fly, normally loaded, for over four hours at a time and had a range of 800/900 miles. In their battle against Bomber Command the enemy fighters were used in two ways:

(i) A comparatively small number of aircraft, up to about 50, were employed with a rigid ground control system.

(ii) All the remaining serviceable aircraft, up to about 400, endeavoured to get into the bomber stream as soon as it was possible after it had left the English Coast , and remain in it for as long as their endurance would permit, assuming the role of 'freelance' AI fighters.

Bomber Support had been operating in fragmentary fashion:

> The present Bomber Support tactics are for Nos. 2 and 8 Groups to bomb enemy fighter airfields when the Hun may be expected to take off, No.100 Group to patrol beacons and target area, and Air Defence Great Britain (ADGB) to patrol

enemy airfields near the target area immediately after the main bomber attack.

This scheme is of course variable, depending on weather and other conditions.[72]

It was suggested that there were three possible ways RAF fighters could counter the enemy's 'freelance' fighter organisation:

(i) By attacking the enemy fighters moving in the bomber stream, and over the target.

(ii) By attacking them at their marshalling points before they got into the bomber stream.

(iii) By attacking the enemy fighters when they were landing.

At the time of the report the three Mosquito Squadrons (Nos. 141, 169 and 239) of No. 100 Group were used for the first two functions. In addition, ADGB also operated two dozen Mosquitoes in advance of the bombers against the airfields which the Luftwaffe fighters used but had not been very successful. 'Though once or twice' the report carried on, 'single aircraft have attempted to attack enemy fighters in the process of landing, and have had success, this type of operation is still untried. Nevertheless it presents every possibility of providing good dividends.' The organisation of such operations 'should logically be contained within No. 100 Group...so that all offensive measures against the enemy's 'freelance' organisation are coordinated'. Aircraft used in this role, the report concludes, should have good navigational facilities and special signals equipment so 'that enemy messages can be interrupted and information on the areas to be used by the enemy fighters obtained.'

Intruder Support for Bombing Operations.

No. 100 Group addressed itself to attacking enemy fighter airfields. Towards the end of February 1944, Air Commodore Addison sent this report to HQ Bomber Command:

> I am forwarding to you a copy of the notes that Chisholm (100 Group SASO) has prepared for me on the 'Flower' (low-level Intruder attacks on enemy airfields) held at ADGB last Friday. I think the decisions made, if ratified, will go at least part of the way towards obtaining 'Intruder' support for our bombing operations.
>
> I have previously written to the Deputy C-in-C pointing out the opportunity that would seem to exist of extending the scope and effect of our nightfighter support operations by 'beating up' the Hun fighter aerodromes after a raid.
>
> Owing to the distance of these enemy nightfighter aerodromes we (No. 100 Group) cannot do this with our Mosquito II's. ADGB Intruder Squadrons, with their Mosquito VI's could, however, do the job but their task is mainly a defensive one, ie, the destruction of Hun bombers when returning to their bases after an attack on this country (a relatively short-range operation); whereas our

requirement is to upset the enemy's fighters whilst attempting to land after attacking our bombers (a much longer range operation).

He suggested centralised direction of Bomber Support:

> According to the decision reached at this meeting ADGB will presumably allocate some aircraft to undertake missions of this sort. Later, when we get Mosquito VI's in this Group, we could reinforce the operation. I feel however that unless we get some sort of centralised control we cannot hope to derive full benefit from the scheme.[73]

The AOC, No. 100 Group gave two reasons for holding this view:

> (i) No. 515 Squadron when equipped with Mosquito VI's is to be given an RCM role in support of our invasion forces. Until this time arrives, however, we shall presumably be allowed to use them for long-range Intruder work. If now, ADGB are also engaged on this form of operation (and the more the merrier!) we shall have aircraft of two different Commands undertaking, simultaneously perhaps, a parallel, if not strictly similar, task.
>
> (ii) The Intelligence side is very important. We are probably in a position to get much more information about the Hun night defence organisation than ADGB – my Intelligence Staff has been specially trained to analyse the mass of available information from the point of view of our own particular requirements. It would be a cumbersome and wearisome task to feed all this into ADGB especially as the Hun so frequently changes his defence tactics and organisation. Moreover, we rely a great deal upon the intruding aircrew themselves to give us the 'hottest' information, and to do this they must be specially briefed before their operations, and carefully interrogated immediately after their return to base.
>
> Another point – not only will full details of your planning have to be fed into ADGB just before a Bomber Command raid takes place, but also a quick appreciation of the reactions that your operation is likely to produce upon the Hun Nightfighter Command. Thus an inordinate amount of time back and forth between your HQ and ADGB, and our HQ and ADGB, will have to take place. All this could be avoided if it could be arranged that any ADGB Intruder aircraft allocated to this task should operate under our control, and be briefed and interrogated by us.[74]

In another letter Air Commodore Addison suggests a specific means of attacking the airfields – by bombing them:

> The type of bomb that is needed is similar to the Butterfly bomb (8lb Anti-Personnel Bombs) that the enemy has used with marked success on our own airfields, when he has immobilised them sometimes for the rest of the night on which the attack takes place and often for an appreciable period the next day.

The present method of bombing enemy airfields with 250 and 500 lb. bombs from a Mosquito as in 'Operation Flower' has little chance of procuring lasting effect, and fighter action is believed by many to be more effective. Fighter action depends, for success, on the enemy's use of navigation lights. It cannot be expected that such a method of interception can continue for very long as soon as long-range intruding is established.

The other means of bringing about the interceptions is...Centimetre Radar. As soon as this equipment can be released and acquired it should be pressed into use in this particular function, but it will be some time before much of it will be available, even if it were released tomorrow. Thus there may well be a hiatus between the attack helped by navigation lights and the attack helped by radar, and during that time...the use of suitable small bombs, dropped by fighter-bombers, would certainly fill in the gap very adequately...In the counter-offensive the enemy nightfighters should be attacked in all possible ways, ie, impeded from taking off, intercepted when operating, harassed while preparing to land, and finally, being prevented from landing , or constrained to land with every chance of being blown up on touch down. All these methods of attack should be developed simultaneously.

It is understood that some suitable small bombs are being manufactured but that Tactical Air Force (TAF) have first call on them. It is urgently submitted that in view of the use to which these bombs could be put by Bomber Command, a claim should be staked for them at an early stage.[75]

When No. 100 Group was formed Norman Cordingly was appointed to take charge of Signals (Airborne Radar) with the rank of Wing Commander. In civilian life he had worked for a firm of scientific instrument makers in London as an X-Ray engineering specialist and indeed, in 1936, had supervised the installation on an X-Ray machine into Buckingham Palace for the last illness of King George V. In December, 1940, commissioned in the RAF Technical Branch he reported to the Radio School at the RAF Station at Yatesbury, in Wiltshire, for an introductory course. At the end of the first lecture Group Captain Raymond Hart, who was giving it, mentioned AI as well as the ground radar of the CH stations:

The airborne RDF was a sophisticated new device and had just been issued to Fighter Command twin-engined squadrons. When the Group Captain had finished his talk, he more or less said, 'There you are, gentlemen – take your pick!...'I informed the Group Captain that I wished to take a definite interest in AI.[76]

In mid-January 1941, course completed, Cordingly was attached to No. 604 Squadron, a nightfighter squadron using AI Mk.IV at Middle Wallop, in Hampshire. This was at the height of the Luftwaffe raids on Britain and was to be his introduction to an operational squadron. In February he made a flight to train a radar operator in a Bristol Beaufighter. The pilot was F/O Rory Chisholm (qv). Thereafter the two men often worked together during the war and served in No.100 Group when it was formed.

Norman Cordingly witnessed Rory Chisholm's prowess as a fighter pilot whilst visiting the Ground Control Interception (GCI) station which controlled his squadron's night flying operations. His description indicates how aerial contests were displayed by radar at ground level:

> I was glad I had chosen that evening to visit our GCI station as it turned out to be a Gala night. There was a certain amount of enemy activity and our squadron was airborne. The night was clear, with just a little moonlight. A blip was identified as one of our own squadron's nightfighters and another aircraft, this time hostile, then appeared. The blips converged as a combat ensued. The Controller soon heard from 'Ops' that our pilot, F/O Chisholm, had engaged and shot down an enemy bomber crossing the coast near Bournemouth. Chisholm then returned to base to refuel and rearm. I stayed on to watch the general activity in the coastal area displayed on the Plan Position Indicator (PPI). Later that night two blips were again plainly visible over the coast, one identified as hostile and the other as friendly. An interception took place...and 'Ops' confirmed by telephone that Chisholm had 'done it again' and had destroyed another bomber the same night! Everybody in the room cheered with excitement.

After serving with No. 85 Squadron and at No.11 Group HQ, in the early Spring of 1942, Norman Cordingly, now a Squadron Leader, was transferred to the Air Ministry where he became responsible for most of the AI projects in Fighter Command squadrons. This work entailed plenty of travelling, 'at this juncture nearly all radar devices had been, or were being, converted to the microwave band.' A new form of AI was being developed which was to have an emphatic bearing on No.100 Group's fighter activities later in the War:

> The majority of my time until the beginning of 1943 covered weeks of technical visits to establishments such as RAE, Farnborough, special flight trials at FIU, Ford. Similar work at Defford was of high priority on the microwave gear: a television type of scanning presentation on a cathode-ray tube. It was an outstanding development using the work of British scientists which was the ultimate in technological development at that time. The microwave was highly accurate with a common transmitter and receiver and antenna set in a parabolic reflector which was motor-driven by a mechanism to give a fine line scan. Flying with such a sophisticated device made our early AI Mk. IV look old-fashioned. The television scanned picture was produced by a very narrow beam of radiation

of high resolution, The whole installation was called AI Mk. X. It was to be produced in the United States to relieve Britain's overstretched workload.

Arrangements were made by the Air Ministry Director of Radar and the Ministry of Aircraft Production (MAP) to get the new AI in the pipeline. The American Army Signals Corps planned to fit its equivalent of our new Mk. X to their own nightfighter aircraft , The Black Widow, when available. They proposed to call it SCR 720 (Signal Corps Radio No. 720) and there were to be mutual exchanges as to the progress of work here and in the USA. The American Western Electric Company had a contract to produce gear to meet any immediate needs and civilian engineers were to visit the UK for exchange of engineering and production designs. This called for a close-knit panel of experts to control its use and accordingly I had to see that the RAF's needs were met. With the help of the MAP and TRE we set up a panel to cover operational needs. There were to be some modifications to ensure that the SCR 720 would fit comfortably into the Mosquito to make it the British ultimate in the nightfighter category of AI.

A special perspex bulbous nose-piece called a radome had to be designed to fit on the Mosquito nose. The all-important job was the cockpit mounting of the television scanned indication cathode-ray tube (CRT) display unit and visor; the AI operator being seated to the right of the nightfighter pilot.

With very high priority in mind we soon had a visit by a Western Electric Company engineer, Walter Pree, who was to spend his time with me and the MAP. He was a good radio engineer and did all he could to make sure that our experience with the use of airborne radar on operations would be resolved. It had been arranged by the Director-General of Signals that Walter Pree and I should fly to the US on 27th March, 1943, to convey the story of our own experience in combating the enemy bomber to the Americans through the auspices of the RAF delegation in Washington.

During his stay in the US Norman Cordingly had the opportunity to test the new equipment in flight and found it to be operationally acceptable. He again met Rory Chisholm, this time at the Massachusetts Institute of Technology (MIT) where Chisholm 'had delivered a lively talk to the assembled company of personnel interested in AI nightfighter trials in the UK.'

In the middle of June, 1943 Norman Cordingly returned to the UK, in a Liberator, bringing with him, 'a few of the "first off" productions of SCR 720 equipment' which were urgently wanted for installation and flight testing on Mosquitoes. Rory Chisholm flew back with him flying as second pilot. The flight from Gander, Newfoundland, to Prestwick in Scotland took ten hours and was uneventful. On arrival in Scotland an armed guard was placed on the Liberator to protect the still highly secret equipment.

In October, at FIU, Norman Cordingly had his first flight in a Mosquito fitted with one of the SCR 720 prototypes. They flew at 10,000 feet and used a Beaufighter as a target. It was detected at a range of five miles and he was able to see the position and height of the incoming echo, 'A high resolution picture on the TV-type screen was present and I thought it was good.' Then came the final tests:

> On 2nd November 1943 we had a Wellington Mk.II specially equipped with SCR 720 to be used as a flying classroom. We had a number of passengers: W/C George Adams (in charge of radar at Fighter Command) and two Australian signals officers whom I had already met in Washington. All went well and the flying classroom was an ideal place in which to observe the general performance of the new interception device.

At the end of the following month Cordingly was on the move again:

> One morning in December I was summoned to the Director of Radar's office. Pacing up and down his office carpet with thumbs in his breast pocket was Air Commodore Addison. He was smoking a small cigar and he did not speak immediately. The Director said I was to be posted to a new group still to be formed. ...I was told that my experience and special knowledge of airborne radar for destroying enemy bombers was considered useful. Air Commodore Addison said a few kind words to the effect that he would glad to have me and that I should report to him at the new HQ. He told me the new group would be mainly concerned with radio countermeasures.

In early January 1944 Norman Cordingly, newly promoted to Wing Commander and in charge of the technical side of the airborne radars in the Group, arrived at West Raynham airfield in Norfolk, the temporary home of No.100 Group HQ. He reported to the AOC who explained what the functions of the new group would be:

> He was pleased to see me and said he had a big problem to be solved which concerned the Mosquito aircraft. We went to examine the Mosquito and he explained that the squadron [No.141 Squadron] had been grounded for weeks. They had difficulties in getting the special antennas to work properly in flight. The device used for countermeasures depended upon the use of metal foil which had to be kept in good contact with the leading edges of the aircraft's wooden wings. In flight the foil tended to lift and a good adhesive was therefore required to fix this. I walked back with the AOC and discussed the job. We were joined by the new Chief Signals Officer, Sam Goodman. I said I thought a watertight adhesive ought to be used to fix the metal foil. The AOC picked up a copy of FLIGHT magazine and said, 'Why not call in the BOSTIK man?' an expression already in print as part of the company's current advertisement.

The Bostik Man

The following morning W/C Cordingly telephoned the company and a representative arrived in the evening complete with all kinds of Bostik products including a suitcase full of samples. He was to stay the night and Cordingly escorted him to his room where he left the samples, after which they entered the Mess where he was given to a meal and drinks. Whilst there Cordingly introduced his guest to some of the pilots and radar observers who were present stating how they hoped to solve the problem. The aircrews were restless having been grounded for weeks and considerable quantities of beer had already been drunk. Some of the aircrew members present challenged the Bostik man, saying they doubted his product would do the job. He promptly responded by fetching his case from his room and showing them the products. Then chaos ensued:

> The Bostik man picked up a squeezable tube of black compound and said he was sure it would do the job. I insisted we ought not to jump to any conclusions and we should wait until the morning. A youngish pilot took the tube and gave it a squeeze. A big blob of black adhesive appeared. At this point I regret to say that the situation developed into a riot. The aircrew members grabbed the tubes and started to stick a chap's ears back, covering his hair with black sticky compound. Other experiments were afoot and everyone started to remove samples from the case. I tried to stop one pilot from sticking the Bostik man's pockets together and found he had already glued the lapels! On the floor behind me someone was rolling a chap up in a carpet and trying to seal up the overlapping ends.

> I hoped a squadron flight commander would come in to help to restore order and in the meantime tried to stop the beer drinking which was half the trouble. I was suddenly aware of action in the ante-room. Someone had taken a shield with antlers attached from the wall and was trying to stick the shield to the glass panel on the entrance door. The poor Bostik man was by now very worried, his suit was stuck together, and the chap who had had his ears stuck back simply could not shift them. A flight commander then appeared and I explained the circumstances amidst the chaos and he helped to bundle the party off to their bedrooms with instructions that they should attend the medical section next morning when a suitable solvent would have to be found to unstick hair and ears and to clean up. The next morning they apparently had a very difficult job in trying to do the unsticking.

> ...Needless to say we did find a suitable waterproof adhesive to fix the metal strips and in the end most of our sticky problems of the past evening were glossed over and we were soon ready for flight trials with the respective antennas in situ.

> ...Later in the morning I looked for the antlers which had been stuck to the

glass door panel. Somehow they had been carefully removed. I thought over the aircrew's behaviour the night before. In the circumstances there was an understandable reason why they gave vent to their feelings. I was indeed sorry for the Bostik man who put up a good show. Certainly his adhesive products solved our problem.

After the short stay at West Raynham No.100 Group eventually took over Bylaugh Hall in the following January:

It was an oldish building, a country house, which was substantial looking, in grey stone. The grounds had been neglected though some attempt had been made to keep the weeds down in places. Where there were lovely trees like silver birches and flowering cherries the weeds had taken over. A long drive led up to the entrance of the house. Patches of heather and lily of the valley grew under shrubs and bushes; there were wild birds in that environment too. Iron railings ringed the front of the house which had an imposing entrance accessible from a flight of stone steps.

The entrance hall floor was paved with a smooth stone of marble-like surface and an elegant stone staircase went up to the first floor where I had an office facing the garden at the rear of the house. It had a view of lawn and shrubs. W/C McMenemy shared my office and next door to us was accommodation for the Chief Signals Officer. G/C Sam Goodman. On the first floor front were the offices of AVM Addison, and also an office for Air Commodore Rory Chisholm, the SASO, W/Cs Dunning-White and Ken Davidson were situated next to Rory. Also located in the building was an intelligence office with W/C 'Sunshine' Wells in charge. I was pleased to find Leonard Lamerton[77] a scientific officer, in charge of operational research. I had first met him in my civilian job as an X-ray engineer, at the British Institute of Radiology. At that time he was concerned with cancer research...

Nuremburg, 30th/31st March 1944

On 30th/31st March 1944 Bomber Command launched a raid[78] on Nuremburg which produced the heaviest losses sustained by it throughout the War. Even by comparison with the heavy losses in the recently concluded Battle of Berlin, the 96 aircraft lost on this night, the highest night's loss to date, was an expensive and tragic price to pay. Several books have been written which refer to the raid but an examination of the effectiveness of bomber support on the night by No. 100 Group is worthwhile and interesting. Twenty aircraft from the Group took part and one Ju 88 was destroyed by No. 239 Squadron.[79] (see below)

No. 100 Group's effect on the night's operation can hardly be described as

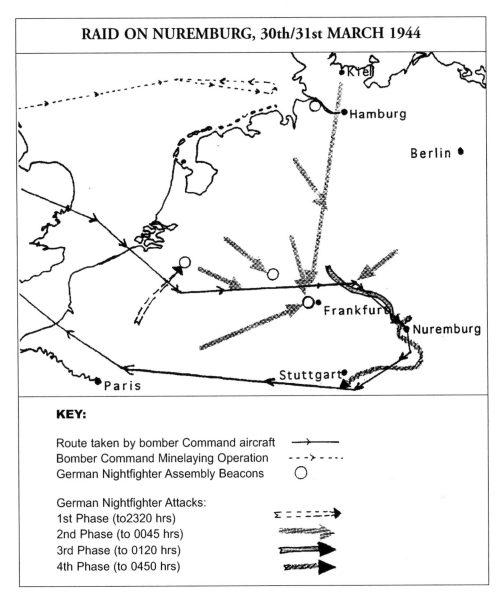

RAID ON NUREMBURG, 30th/31st MARCH 1944

KEY:

Route taken by bomber Command aircraft   →———

Bomber Command Minelaying Operation   - - -> - - - -

German Nightfighter Assembly Beacons   ○

German Nightfighter Attacks:
1st Phase (to2320 hrs)
2nd Phase (to 0045 hrs)
3rd Phase (to 0120 hrs)
4th Phase (to 0450 hrs)

successful, and if its contribution was a failure in bomber support some of the reasons are obvious. There were three SERRATE squadrons (Nos. 141, 169 and 239). Three months after the Group's formation Addison's 'dead-beat' aircraft were still being used and there were deficiencies in the AI equipment used with SERRATE. Five months after Norman Cordingly had test-flown the vastly improved AI Mk.X (US title SCR 720), the squadrons were still flying with the much less-efficient AI Mk.IV. The results to date of the fighter squadrons had not been spectacular. For instance, No.239 Squadron, by the end of March 1944, had only shot down three nightfighters, and had themselves lost six Mosquitoes either on operations or in training.

Those that went to Nuremburg did what they could and there were no No.100

Group casualties. Outside No. 100 Group, No.101 Squadron operating from Ludford Magna on ABC sorties were not so lucky, losing seven aircraft during the raid. No.239 Squadron Mosquito DZ 661 (F/S J Campbell; F/S R Phillips) took off from West Raynham at 2205. Their experience is indicative of the work undertaken and the difficulties encountered, by the bomber support fighter crews:

> Strong SERRATE indications observed throughout the patrol but could not be DF'd owing to switch motor working very slowly. At 2359, at 20000 feet, made AI contact 15000 feet ahead...closed to 300 feet and identified target as Ju 88 showing bluish/green light on each wing tip...gave very brief burst at the enemy aircraft which was flying straight and level, east to west. No results observed as Mosquito overshot beneath enemy aircraft. Contact lost as Mosquito turned hard to port to get behind him again. Mosquito obtained another AI contact at maximum range ahead and weaving. Range closed to 2500 feet when bluish/green lights seen 30 degrees above. Closed in to 800 feet and slightly above and identified enemy aircraft at Ju 88 (possibly the same one as on previous engagement). At 0015, at 20000 feet, Mosquito opened fire at range of 300 feet and the enemy aircraft's port engine blew up. Mosquito turned hard to starboard as enemy aircraft fired tracers (believed from free gun in nose) which set the Mosquito starboard engine on fire. Fire quickly extinguished as pilot throttled back and feathered engine. Enemy aircraft seen burning on ground. Claimed as destroyed. Crew returned to base on one engine and landed safely. Seven bullet holes in aircraft.[80]

Examination of the aircraft on its return showed that the crew were lucky to get back and the ORB of No.239 Squadron pays tribute to F/S Campbell's 'cool-headed handling of a difficult situation' when he was required to fly 200 miles back to West Raynham on the one engine. He was recommended for the award of the DFM.

Another Mosquito crew, HJ 941 (Crew: F/O Newton; F/O V G McBurney), this time from No.141 Squadron, tried to carry out escort duty with the bombers:

> ...contacted bomber stream which seemed to be very widely spread and turned to patrol area north of the bombers. Four SERRATE contacts obtained at range of 40-50 miles, generally south of the bomber track. Chased, but either faded out or no impression could be made. Several AI contacts obtained but lost in pulse transmission jamming in Cologne area or were friendly bombers...It is considered that under normal conditions patrolling the bomber stream is quite practicable but owing to the great width of the stream tonight orbiting was carried out as well as could be done under these conditions...We steered 285 degrees until 0135, at 25000 feet, and were coned by 20-30 searchlights in the Cologne and Dortmund area for 15 minutes and continuously fired at by accurate heavy flak.[81]

F/L Tim Woodman and his radar operator F/O Pat Kemmis, from No. 169 Squadron, also took part in the raid. The following is an extract from the Squadron's ORB relating to their sortie:

Mos DD741. 2305-0325. SERRATE on Nuremburg.

Crew: F/L R Woodman: F/O F Kemmis.

SERRATE and AI contacts numerous but too 'solid' to distinguish. At the end of the patrol AI became u/s. Starboard engine became u/s at Aachen.

...3 individual AI contacts:

(i) A strong SERRATE: closed to 2000 ft before being forced to abandon chase on account of close backward contact. Lost both. (ii) An AI contact, non-Serrating, which dived sharply away at 5000 ft range and (iii) a backward crossing flight which went out of range.[82]

Woodman had complained bitterly (apparently to the SASO at No. 100 Group HQ, Air Commodore Chisholm), prior to the raid's commencement. He asked that Bomber Command reconsider the routing of the raid. The proposed route passed close to German beacons which were usually heavily attended by German nightfighters; F/L Woodman and his colleagues had had recent experience of this Luftwaffe activity.

How far the request progressed is a matter of conjecture. It is not certain, in the confusion of war, whether it ever ever reached High Wycombe. Had the request been received, would it have been acted upon? It seems unlikely. In his book[83] on the Pathfinder Force (PFF), its AOC, Air Vice-Marshal Don Bennett, is critical of Bomber Command tactics on the night. On this occasion the planned route as devised by his PFF HQ was overruled by the C-in-C, Air Chief Marshal Harris, who had agreed instead to a plan devised by the Main Force Group Commanders. As a result the PFF went straight for the target without any diversionary tactics.

AVM Addison, many years later, could not remember hearing about the request from F/L Woodman. Answering a query from Martin Middlebrook, the historian, in 1971, (who was preparing his book on the Nuremburg Raid), he replied:

As regards Gordon Slade (CO of No.169 Squadron), trying to alter Bert Harris's plans, this seems a tall one to me. He was not that sort of chap and I think I would have remembered this.'[84]

The AOC of No. 100 Group was clearly aware of where the Luftwaffe's nightfighters were most active. Earlier in the month he had pointed out[85] to Bomber Command HQ the popularity, as far as the Luftwaffe were concerned, of one particular beacon:

The nearer our main bomber stream approaches his (ie the enemy) main assembly points the easier his task becomes of concentrating his fighters in an area suitable for feeding into the stream. You will note...the fact that on January

2nd/3rd and January 14th/15th when the Bomber raids lay over the Hun's very popular Beacon 'M' our loss rate was well above average. On these nights the Germans were heard monitoring the progress of the bomber force on its outward journey from only 40 miles from the English coast. On 19th/20th February (Leipzig), when our losses were so high (83 aircraft were lost on this night, and the raiding force was under attack all the way to the target), our route again passed very close to 'M'.

Our analysis of the enemy's reaction on this particular night, showed that a number of our bombers were intercepted in the vicinity of this Beacon and that from 'M' to the route marker near Stendal (WNW of Berlin) a very large number of interceptions took place. The traffic overhead on this night does not give a complete story of the movements of the fighters, but instructions were heard sending fighters to Beacon 'M' and from there they were in an excellent position to make contact with the stream. Moreover the general trend of fighters would in any event have been from their assembly point at 'M' to the Berlin area, so that on this occasion our bombers and their fighters were due to cover the same route from 'M' onwards. This may well account for the large number of interceptions that took place on this occasion during the journey into the target.

In this connection it may also be noteworthy that on our recent attacks routed well to the south (Augsburg and Stuttgart) the stream was well away from the German assembly beacons. The losses on these occasions were well below average.

On the night of the Nuremburg raid No. 192 Squadron put up two Mosquitoes, two Halifaxes, and a Wellington on investigative sorties. The following extract from an Intelligence Report is a record of their activities:

A. Two Mosquitoes, flying most of the way with the main stream, investigated the 160-175 Mc/s band for possible AI signals. No signals strongly suggestive of AI were intercepted. A signal on 165 Mc/s...was intercepted near the enemy coast; the signal was steady and did not sweep. A number of Freya-type were received. There also occurred an instance of a 500 c/s transmission on this frequency band being received and holding the aircraft simultaneously with searchlight activity in the neighbourhood of the aircraft.

B. One Halifax investigated the 400-500 Mc/s band for AI signals. Only a very small number of transmissions within the normal 479-501 Mc/s (FuGe 202) range were intercepted. This aircraft flew with Bomber Command to and from the target.

NOTE. In view of the very heavy losses sustained by Bomber Command and the large number of enemy fighters up, this result is somewhat surprising. It does rather tend to suggest the likelihood of a new AI frequency being used by the enemy. Note, however, the result in para. A.

C. One Halifax, flying with the stream, carried out a search from 150-200 Mc/s. A large number of signals on this band were intercepted, many of them of 500c/s PRF. A full analysis of the results is being carried out.

D. One Wellington took off from RAF Ford to investigate No.80 Wing's RCM against the enemy navigational aids KNICKEBEIN 8 (K8) and KNICKEBEIN 10 (K10), operating on 31.5. and 31.2 Mc/s respectively. The aircraft confined its investigation largely to K.10 (Sortosville-en-Beaumont, Cherbourg Peninsula). The beam was flown on to a point 25 miles south of the English coast after which the RCM became effective and beam-flying was impossible.[86]

Jamming by the Group of enemy frequencies appears to have been neither widespread nor effective:

1. AIRBORNE CIGAR (ABC) was requested on 16 frequencies and heard on 11.
2. GROUND CIGAR. Dunwich radiated2356 to 0013. Walmer radiated 2355 to 0038 (intermittently) 0319 to 0320
3. CORONA was employed on 7 frequencies.
4. SPECIAL TINSEL was requested on 8 frequencies.

GROUND MANDREL stations were on air from 2245 to 0100 and 0328 to 0430 and no references to WINDOW were heard.[87]

The Nuremburg raid caused much heart-searching at Bylaugh Hall. The Secretary of State for Air, Sir Archibald Sinclair, showed his personal concern by visiting No.100 Group HQ to try to find out the reason for the Group's lack of success. Enquiries were made about the support given to the bombers and there was a strong case for increasing it. This brought results and two additional fighter squadrons (Nos. 85 and 157) were posted to No.100 Group at the end of the following month bringing with them improved AI equipment, although they would not be used operationally until the following month.

Norman Cordingly met the Secretary of State:

The AOC telephoned me and said he was entertaining Sir Archibald to lunch in the Mess. I was invited to join his party; Rory Chisholm and Sam Goodman were also present. During the lunch the Secretary of State said, 'Where was 100 Group during the raid?' or something to that effect. I think the general feeling that we expressed was that most of our bomber losses were due to the activity of the enemy nightfighters equipped with their own radar...Either we should home to the German nightfighter aircraft's radar with a special receiver or we could interfere with enemy equipment by using a jammer transmitter. The situation was delicate and had to be resolved.

We all had strong feelings about it and for a while we were writing minutes to one another. I wrote to a number of colleagues through the AOC. I received a reply from him which was apt. He had put a footnote to this effect, 'Too much bumf, not enough action. Get cracking!' The AOC's reaction was typical of his ways!... we had a high-powered meeting. I later called at his office and found him busily writing while standing at his special wall-desk. We discussed the contents of his minute.

As preparations grew in the early summer of 1944 for D-Day, the role of No. 100 Group was closely looked at in Bomber Command where a Conference was held on 20th May, chaired by the Deputy C-in-C, Air Vice-Marshal Sir Robert Saundby. The AOC and SASO of No.100 Group were also present. In due course a report was submitted to the C-in-C, Bomber Command, Air Marshal Sir Arthur Harris for his approval.

Air Commodore Addison told the Conference that the role of the squadrons in his Group was to destroy enemy nightfighters. The close escort of the bomber stream was not practicable as their aircraft could not work effectively near the bombers. In addition, he observed, crews must also be trained as Intruders, 'as the role of 100 Group should include offensive action against enemy airfields in advance of the bomber stream, and, also, daylight intruding to selected enemy airfields with the object of destroying aircraft on the ground.' The Deputy C-in-C was in broad agreement with these aims but insisted that, 'the main role of the Group is to act in support of the main bomber force. Nothing should be neglected which could contribute to that end.'

It was submitted to the C-in-C that the primary role of No. 100 Group should be 'to destroy enemy nightfighters which are airborne for the purpose of attacking our bombers, with the secondary role of destroying enemy fighters in the air or on the ground by all possible means both by day and night.' Harris agreed, but added an MS statement that 'RCM are a major part of their (No.100 Group's) role.'

On another policy point the AOC No.100 Group enquired:

>...Whether the Group can operate at any time regardless of whether or not other aircraft from Bomber Command were operating. He felt that the attack against enemy aircraft and airfields should continue at all times with the object of forcing the enemy into action and thus add additional strain on his resources. The Deputy C-in-C agreed to put this question to the C-in-C for a decision.' [88]

Here again, Harris agreed, and there would be a significant number of nights subsequently in the air war against Germany when No.100 Group aircraft would be the only aircraft operating.

It was agreed that:

(i) ADGB should be requested through the Air Ministry to provide crews fully trained in:

    [a] Mosquito flying.

    [b] Navigation and GEE.

    [c] AI Mk IV, and later, Mk X.

    [d] Normal Nightfighter and Intruder technique.

It was also requested that ADGB be further requested to carry out the training as soon as possible. Thirty-two crews per month would eventually be needed thereby covering replacement crews for all Squadrons (it was calculated each Squadron could lose 3-4 crews per month). They should also be requested to undertake the conversion of Squadrons to AI Mk X.

(ii) No. 100 Group would remain responsible for the following training, which would be done in an expanded No.1692 Flight:

    [a] SERRATE.

    [b] Backward AI.

    [c] Any new 'special' training.

    [d] Bomber Support Operational Training.

    [e] Advanced operational training for Squadron crews.

It was further agreed that No. 100 Group should also 'take action to dispose of any unsuitable crews now in Squadrons'.[89]

No. 100 Group HQ was labour intensive and those serving there came from many backgrounds. In pre-war London Dr. Leonard Lamerton had been a physicist engaged in cancer research at the Royal Cancer Hospital. He spent the early war years in the Operational Research Section (ORS) of Bomber Command at High Wycombe. When No.100 Group was formed he was transferred to it and became engaged in analysing the operational performances of the squadrons, and giving suggestions for future operations:

> It was rather a strange world as a young civilian amongst the RAF people. There was one other civilian besides myself, a met officer. He later went into uniform and I was then the only civilian.
>
> My role was to help in assessing the effect of our countermeasures. One of my jobs was to go through the reports brought back by the aircrews on the operation of BOOZER, which was a device designed to pick up the enemy AI. I did a lot of work like this. After each raid I produced maps indicating where the BOOZER signals were picked up, and where WINDOW had been dropped, and so forth. I prepared reports for Air Commodore Chisholm.
>
> I think it would be true to say that Addison was the policy man and Chisholm was in charge of strategy and tactics. I used to discuss my findings with Chisholm and I remember, particularly with regard to BOOZER, discussing with him

where the enemy aircraft were being met, and the airfields they came from, and that sort of thing. I would get the raw material and attempt to put it into a form that could be used for future operations.

I visited stations frequently and talked to the crews before and after operations. I became used to having to talk 'off the cuff'. Sometimes it was difficult. On one occasion when I went to a station with the AOC he gave his talk first. He said exactly what I intended to say!

I had a quarter of a Nissen Hut in the grounds of Bylaugh Hall for a billet...the secrecy of the work there had its effect on me. When I went back amongst civilians I was almost frightened to say anything!

His work was highly regarded. 'The Bomber Command representative in ORS, Mr Lamerton,' it is recorded in the No. 100 Group ORB, 'works so closely with Intelligence...He is responsible for a detailed analysis of each operation and many valuable suggestions for the improvement of planning and tactics have resulted. He is also actively concerned with future developments.'[90]

The Head of Intelligence was W/C Wells, a pre-war schoolmaster, (who was 'remarkably good' according to AVM Addison) and who had been posted there from the RCM Section at No. 11 Group. The Intelligence Section was opened in December 1943, by F/L A E Foster who had been transferred from Intelligence at Bomber Command. Initial difficulties were experienced in obtaining an interim supply of intelligence information, periodicals, maps and other equipment for the new HQ and the three stations at Foulsham, Little Snoring and West Raynham. However, by 16th December, the night of the Group's first operations, the Section was running fairly smoothly.

The main difficulties were:

[a] The wide scope of intelligence requirements in a Group with such diverse functions.

[b] The almost total lack of clerks, typewriters, stationery.

[c] Adapting to Bomber Command organisation and procedure, the units being mainly drawn from ADGB, technical wings and groups.

[d] The lack of adequate telephones and teleprinters in the temporary quarters at West Raynham.

Close liaison was quickly achieved with the other Sections (operational, radar and ORS).

Charles Clarke was employed as a signals officer in No. 100 Group from its beginning. He had started in the RAF as a WOP/AG flying in Bristol Blenheims in No. 5 Group in 1941-2, and had completed 33 operations before being talked into becoming a signals officer by the Station Signals Officer, S/L Byrne, whilst on 'rest' training at Upper Heyford:

Group Captain Goodman was my boss at No. 100 Group. He was a good chap and a very capable signals officer...after the War he went to Reddifon and worked on simulators.

I was Unit Signals Officer at Bylaugh Hall. The posting there came out of the blue. I didn't know who they were. It was just another posting. When I was at an OTU in No. 6 Group, who were Canadians, I developed this thing, I think they called it TINSEL later. I found that if you back-tuned your radio to the German transmissions you could jam them by sticking your microphone on the side of the aircraft. Back-tuning means if you tune into a station you don't know, you can tell by the scale roughly what the frequency is, so you tune your transmitter to your own receiver. You can hear it coming in, there is a terrific whining noise and at that stage you know you are 'spot on'. I had worked with S/L Byrne on TINSEL, and had worked a little on MANDREL which was fitted to our Halifaxes in No.6 Group, but that was my only previous experience with RCM at that stage.

I was responsible for the telephones and teleprinters at Bylaugh Hall. My line of communication was through W/C McMenemy. I was a F/O and was there about three months and was really employed in the administration side of signals. I also spent a lot of time out of the place setting up these other stations, Oulton, North Creake, Swannington, and Sculthorpe; Foulsham and West Raynham were already established.

I had the job of organising them to open from a communications point of view really. It sounds very grand but we had fitting parties who used to attend the stations and do things like siting up the transmitters and receivers, and things like that. They came from a Maintenance Unit somewhere. It was mostly liaison and coordinating work I did. I did a tremendous amount of liaison with the Post Office because they had to put in all the lines, whether it was operating the transmitters from the Control Tower or telephones (including the scrambled 'secret' type). When the two Mossie Squadrons arrived at Swannington we didn't have any telephones at dispersals and I had miles and miles of field telephone cables all over the place. We had dispersal point boxes with so many lines in which would go back through the perimeter cable to the main switchboard frame. I don't think we were supposed to do it this way but the Post Office turned a blind eye. We had a good relationship with them. I also fixed up the connections to the other places, Admin, Armaments, MT, etc., I did this at all of what we might call the 'undeveloped' airfields.

I didn't have much to do with the radio but I used to have to go along to the Radio Room at night before operations to make sure all the equipment was working correctly, and the staffing was alright. You knew exactly what was needed for the projected operations that night and you had to make sure that everything was working properly.

Pamela Gosman, as a Section Officer in the WAAF, was Personal Assistant to AVM Addison at Bylaugh Hall. On one occasion twenty-four journalists, one of whom was Richard Dimbleby a well-known broadcaster from the BBC, visited. Among other visitors were G/Cs Gibson and Cheshire. 'Bylaugh was renowned for its food including the Sunday night cold buffet which in wartime had to be seen to be believed. We had plenty of game and fresh vegetables, and thus lived off the land.' She was a member of the Concert Party which was run there and recalls that there were all kinds of wild flowers she had never seen before growing in the grounds, 'and it was part of my job to see that AVM Addison always had flowers on his desk!'

**Menu of meal offered to visiting journalists in November 1944.
The art work at the top depicting the various No.100 Group
activities was the work of W/C Norman Cordingly (W/C Radar),
a keen and competent artist.**

Ron Greenslade, a WOP, came to No. 100 Group HQ in June 1944:

...we arrived at a little station called Lyng where we were collected and transported by truck to Bylaugh Hall about two miles away... We booked in at the guardroom which was at the end of a long drive off the main road, and were directed through some trees to the airmen's sleeping quarters. We were settled in Hut Six and were a happy crowd. Bill Benson came from Wigan and used to expound on the art of Rugby League, Bill Ballinger from Walsall was a quiet lad and a good artist. Among the others there was Bruce Williams who was in the instruments section. In 'civvy street' he had a jewellers shop which he ran with his twin brother in Liverpool.

We were put on a four-watch system and worked in the Wireless Room which was set in huts which had been attached to the Main Hall. Outside our room was the Sergeant in charge of the whole Watch; next door was the Teleprinter Room (all girls) and beyond that the Telephone Exchange (PBX) where my wife-to-be Iris, worked. In the Wireless Room were six sets, each with its own call sign marked above and manned by both airmen and WAAFs with a Corporal (and assistant) behind us for routing purposes. Our job was to send and receive Morse messages ground-to-ground and ground-to-air. It was not DF work. It was enjoyable but not particularly satisfying.

There was a corridor from the Signals Section to the ground floor of the Hall where the Administration Section operated. At break times we used to regularly collect a mug of tea and a wad or, frequently, Marmite sandwiches. Upstairs was the Ops Room where plane routes and positions were plotted on maps. This was banned to us.[91]

The Camp at Bylaugh Hall was six miles from East Dereham, the nearest town in which was located a cinema – which Ron Greenslade visited regularly – and a Salvation Army canteen which supplied very good meals. Later a new, bigger canteen was opened for RAF and US personnel stationed in the area, 'the counter was always stacked with doughnuts.' He walked back on numerous occasions when he missed the 'Liberty Bus' (a lorry which had two wooden forms on each side in the rear of the vehicle which seated about six people; surplus persons sat in the middle). There were regular runs to East Dereham and Norwich.

Some of the RAF men at Bylaugh tried to supplement their meagre service pay by working on the nearby land. Haymaking, pea picking, potato lifting and currant picking were attempted. Greenslade did not last with the latter, 'I made very little money and decided one day was enough!' He entered into local affairs in other ways. Christmas (1944) approached and he went down to the tiny village church at Bylaugh. He thought he would like to go to the Midnight Service on Christmas Eve as he was not on duty. With the vicar's agreement, and with the help of a colleague,

Bylaugh Hall. Group photograph of HQ staff. AVM Addison is sitting in the centre of the front row, flanked on his left by G/C Goodman (Chief Signals Officer), and on the right by Air Commodore Chisholm (Senior Air Staff Officer). Section Officer Pamela Gosman, (PA to the AOC), is standing behind Air Commodore Chisholm. W/C Cordingly is fourth in from the right in the front row. Leonard Lamerton (Operational Research Section), is in the back row, third from the left. *(Maryse Addison)*

he decorated the church with holly and placed candles at the end of all the pews for the service. 'The midnight service went very well and there was a packed congregation.' Ron Greenslade recalled the night of 'Operation Gisella', on 3rd/4th March 1945 (see Chapter Three):

> One night I was on duty listening out on R/T at a wireless set in an alcove near the Admin Section. It was a very busy night...About 3am our planes came back only to be followed in by enemy fighters. Nobody called me but it was quite a night as I listened in to the comments over the air as our pilots realised they'd been followed. There was a real flap on until they were told to scramble, whereupon they landed anywhere they could over East Anglia and Lincolnshire. They never got back to their own bases until the next day.

There were VE-Day celebrations at Bylaugh Hall:

> ... I offered my services to the Entertainments Officer and found myself on my own at first, though I did get some assistance later when beer was mentioned. Outside Bylaugh Hall on the way to the cookhouse, was a pond set in a garden and I decided to use this in my plans. I obtained a bike and some planks; then devised a plank crossing of the pond. A track was formed to the approach and all

were invited to see if they could get across. It was not surprising that the spare aircrew lads who were now with us, having been grounded for a couple of weeks, were keen to try. They were always game for anything. One or two made the crossing safely but, inevitably, it was only a matter of time before someone got a ducking!

Meanwhile a dance had been organised and beer ordered. Unfortunately beer was difficult to obtain at that time as I suppose everybody was celebrating. However, we managed to get one barrel flown in to Swanton Morley nearby, and we had it tapped only about half-an-hour before the dance started.

Betty Marlowe, a clerk in the Registry at Bylaugh Hall, was on duty on the night of the 5th/6th June, D-Day. 'You will appreciate that Clerks (GD) were not high on the "need to know" batting list' and, therefore, 'We were not told anything of D-Day prior to the 6th June – all I can recall was the mountain of signals coming in from all of our eight Stations all through the night, and the extra weather forecasts we received.' She was told of the finish of the War:

...We were holding a Station Dance when an officer came in and said, 'The War is over.' Nobody took any notice, so he stopped the band, stood in the middle of the floor and said, 'What's the matter with you bloody lot. I've just told you the War is over !' We then went outside and lit the huge bonfire we had been piling up for this occasion, and were then all invited to the Officers' Mess to drink whatever was available. What I remember most clearly was some idiot going round with a pair of scissors trying to cut everyone's tie off under the knot!

Jack Hilton, a Sergeant WOP in the Signals Section, had memories of 'a happy, dedicated bunch of people who kept their duties close to their chest because of the nature of RCM activities.' One man who lived within a bike ride of the HQ, 'being local could be relied upon to provide a dozen eggs, a chicken or rabbits "ready for the pot"; he carried a supply of snares in his uniform pocket!'

Pat Gregory was a Sergeant in the Operations Room of No. 80 Wing HQ, at Radlett and on the formation of No.100 Group she was transferred to Bylaugh Hall where she worked in the Ops Room:

AVM Addison took me to Bylaugh from Radlett. I think he wanted some of his old people there...We weren't actually in the same room as the Ops Room but were up on a stage from where we used to look down on to the Room. We sat with our earphones on taking down all these messages the Germans were receiving, so we knew what was happening. We could see the Ops Room staff plotting on a huge map below. This showed where our chaps were flying. You could hear the Germans telling their aircraft what to do. The German aircraft used to crowd around their beacons so we jammed them. We had several ways of doing it. In addition, our boys added to the confusion by telling them what to do! It was all very interesting and I used to get great satisfaction from it. We didn't get to know the other sections very well, we were all doing our own jobs. Not that we were unfriendly but we all had our own shifts.

The Bylaugh Hall HQ was the place where the major strategic decisions concerning the Group's activities were made, and the necessary information for bomber support collated, analysed and transformed into operational imperatives. The operational responsibility for carrying out Group policy, apart from ground-based RCM, rested with the Group's Squadrons. The story of No. 100 Group, therefore, is best divided into two sections dealing with [a] the RCM story and [b] The Group's Offensive Nightfighters, and, for ease of description, can be referred to as 'The Heavies' and 'The Fighters'. The very nature of No. 100 Group's role meant that the various tasks for these Squadrons would be wide-ranging with the tactics employed by each unit contributing to the Group's common purpose of supporting Bomber Command in its raids on the enemy.

Bylaugh Hall. A Nissen Hut in the grounds during the winter of 1944/5. *(Merv Utas)*

Footnotes – Chapter Four

50   Addison Papers: MS notes made by AVM Addison on 21.9.77.

51   Ibid.

52   PRO AIR 14/2919: 'Special Duties' in the title was changed to 'Bomber Support' by Bomber Command HQ on 2.5.44. The previous month Air Commodore Addison had suggested the change to avoid confusion with 'Special Duties' units which operated outside No.100 Group.

53   'Despatch on War Operations, 23.2.42 to 8.5.45'. Appendix E, 'RCM in Bomber Command', (Harris Archive H122, R A F Museum, Hendon).

54   'The Radio War', a TRE Report by Robert Cockburn, 1945, pp. 6-7.

55   Addison Papers: MS notes made by AVM Addison 21.9.77.

56   Lecture by AVM Addison at the Royal United Services Institute, November 1946.

57   Ibid.

58   PRO AIR 14/2911: 'The Development and Activities of No.100 (BS) Group', p.1.

59   Letter from Air Commodore O G Lywood, CBE, Director of Signals, Air Ministry, to Air Marshal A T Harris, CB, CBE, AFC,; C-in-C Bomber Command, on 21.3.42. (Harris Archive H24, R A F Museum, Hendon).

60   Letter from Air Marshal Harris to Air Marshal Sir Douglas Evill, KCB, DSC,AFC, Vice Chief of Air Staff, dated 18.11.43. (Harris Archive H16, R A F Museum, Hendon).

61   Ibid.

62   PRO AIR 14/738: Report dated 19.12.43 from AOC, No.100 Group to Deputy C-in-C, Bomber Command, (AVM R H M S Saundby, CB, MC, DFC, AFC.

63   Ibid.

64   Ibid.

65   G/C (later Air Commodore) R A Chisholm, OBE, DSO, DFC.

66   London Gazette No. 36329 (12.1.44), p. 285.

67   'Bomber Harris' by Dudley Saward, (Cassell, 1948), p. 235.

68   'Cover of Darkness', Roderick Chisholm, (Chatto and Windus, 1976), p.157.

69   Ibid.

70   Ibid. p158.

71   PRO AIR 14/738: 'Notes on the Attack of Enemy Nightfighters by Aircraft of No. 100 Group'.

72   PRO AIR 14/738: 'Bomber Support – Present Position', Report by W/C 'Ops', HQ Bomber Command, dated 1.3.44.

73   PRO AIR 14/738: Letter dated 22.2.44, to SASO, HQ Bomber Command from AOC, No. 100 Group.

74 Ibid.

75 PRO AIR 14/738: Latter dated 18.2.44 to Bomber Command from the AOC, No.100 Group.

76 'From a Cat's Whisker Beginning' (Written and Published by Norman Cordingly, OBE, 1988), p.41. All further information relating to Norman Cordingly's wartime work is taken from this book unless otherwise stated.

77 Leonard Lamerton went on to a distinguished post-war career in cancer research and held many offices in this field, amongst which was the Chair of Professor of Biophysics Applied to Medicine (London University, 1960); he was appointed Dean of the Institute of Cancer Research in 1967 becoming Director ten years later, and held the post until his retirement in 1980.

78 Much has been written about this night, and the reader seeking more detailed information is referred to Martin Middlebrook's book, 'The Nuremburg Raid', (Allen Lane, 1973).

79 PRO AIR 25/777. No.100 Group ORB.

80 PRO AIR 27/1546: No.239 Squadron ORB.

81 PRO AIR 27/971: No.141 Squadron ORB.

82 PRO AIR 27/1094: No.169 Squadron ORB.

83 'Pathfinder; A War Biography' by AVM D C T Bennett, CB, CBE, DSO, (Frederick Muller, 1958).

84 Addison Papers: Letter dated 20.12.71 sent by AVM Addison to Martin Middlebrook.

85 PRO AIR 14/738: Report dated 2.3.44.

86 PRO AIR 14/2920: Raid Analysis Report No.40/44, Brief Appreciation No.32 of No.192 Squadron Flight Investigations. Night of 30th/31st March 1944. Bombers' Target: Nuremburg.

87 Ibid.

88 PRO 14/738: Minutes of Conference at HQ Bomber Command on 20.5.44, to discuss the 'Operational Role and Training Requirements of Special Duty Bomber Support Squadrons'.

89 Ibid.

90 PRO AIR 25/778: No.100 Group ORB, Summary of Events Dec.1943 to May 1944.

91 'Signals Wallah at Large'. Unpublished MS by Ron Greenslade, PP. 52-3.

Chapter Five

Science and Sorties – The Heavies

Sometimes our Spoof Force would do a double penetration if the Main Force wasn't operating. After clearing the MANDREL Screen we would start our WINDOW drop and head for a target, drop token markers and bombs, and then head back into France behind the MANDREL Screen. We would then descend to a low altitude, orbit for 30 to 45 minutes, then climb back up again and head back into Germany for a second Spoof.

S/L Mervyn Utas, RCAF pilot, No. 223 Squadron.

'The first main application of airborne RCM in 100 Group' it is recorded[92] 'was on D-Day.' An efficient programme had to attack all the links in the chain of the enemy night defence, since no single RCM on its own, it was believed, would be 100% efficient. Consequently RCM to cover the following were developed:

[a] A MANDREL Screen to cut down the enemy early warning.

[b] Communications jammers.

[c] Airborne Interception (AI) jammers.

For WINDOW feint operations no specialised equipment, apart from launching chutes, was needed, and it was decided to equip most of the heavy aircraft in the Group with chutes so that any of them could be used for WINDOW.'

MANDREL Screen.

On the night of 5th/6th 1944 a MANDREL screen was formed by No.199 Squadron and the USAAF No. 803 Squadron to cover the approach of the Invasion forces; No. 214 Squadron also operated in their ABC role. Throughout the month, MANDREL Screens were flown on a number of nights in support of the Main Force and also as 'spoofs'. Owing to a lack of aircraft only a small screen could be put up. It was necessary to fly the RAF aircraft in pairs to give full coverage. The US aircraft flew singly but did not cover as wide a frequency band.

Apart from D-Day its use was limited as it was feared any jamming in the English Channel could interfere with Allied Forces' communications. However, on several nights the screen was stationed over the North Sea at a distance of 80 miles from the enemy coast, on three occasions approaching closer to increase the intensity of the jamming. The latter tactic was employed with some nervousness for two reasons. The aircraft employed on MANDREL approached on parallel tracks and it was thought

GERMAN LONG-RANGE RADAR WARNING SYSTEM

(1st June 1944)

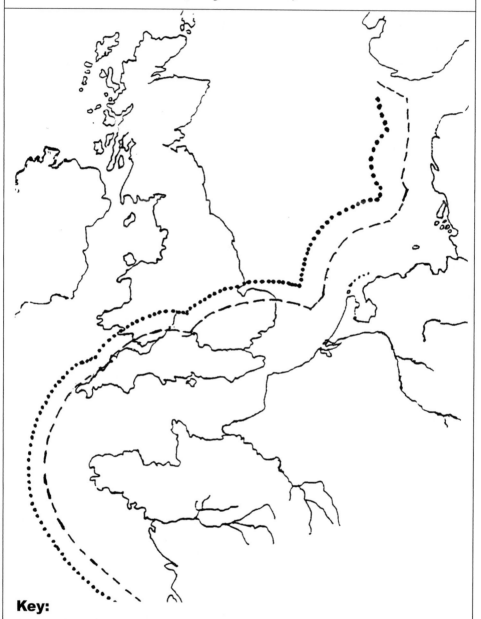

Key:

Areas at which bombers at an altitude of 10.000 ft. can be detected by:

Chimneys and hoardings   ·················

Freyas   – – –– ––

that the enemy might 'see' between the stations. In addition, the distance between the MANDREL aircraft was determined by the relative beam width of the enemy's early warning equipment ; it was also feared that suitably placed enemy stations might be able to 'see' from behind the screen.

The RCM proved a success. It was found, 'to a considerable extent, that in practice, more was achieved than the theoreticians had dared hope.' One such 'theoretician' was Martin Ryle (qv) who had worked on the equipment:

> MANDREL is airborne equipment intended for use against enemy long-range radar frequency range 30-215 Mc/s and consists of a somewhat extensive modified British Mk III IFF Set. Receiver type 3090.
>
> An operator is required who listens for enemy signals with the set in the 'receive' condition, while sweeping a given frequency band with the tuning control provided. When a signal is received which it is desired to jam, the operator tunes carefully to that signal, and then switches the set from 'receive' to 'transmit'. A noise-modulated jamming signal is then transmitted on the desired frequency, ie that to which the set is tuned...
>
> For the initial stages of the landings on D-Day a combined airborne and ground jamming screen was required to reduce the early warning given by the enemy long-range radar in the areas of the main and diversionary approaches. The airborne screen was to use a series of aircraft orbiting about 70 miles from the enemy coast and carrying MANDREL I equipments to cover the frequency range 70-150 Mc/s.
>
> Such an operation involves the maintenance of a series of jamming centres along the front to be covered with a spacing not greater than the beam width of the enemy radars, and with each centre radiating power on all occupied enemy frequencies. In this way each radar equipment will receive a jamming signal irrespective of its azimuth bearing, and if the jamming power is sufficient, will not be able to plot incoming forces in any direction.
>
> To economise in the number of jamming aircraft required to cover a given length of coastline it is desirable to keep the jamming screen as far as possible back from the enemy coast. (Thus to jam the Freya equipment with an effective beam width of 20 degrees, would need a jamming centre every 10 miles if the screen were placed 30 miles from the enemy coast, requiring a total of 15 jamming centres to cover a 150 mile front. If the screen were flown at 100 miles from the enemy coast, this could be reduced to five).
>
> Any increase in this distance involves an increase in jamming the transmitter power, (and, in the case of tunable spot frequency jamming, an improvement in the sensitivity of the monitoring receiver).

With the MANDREL I equipment available, and with the limitations in flying

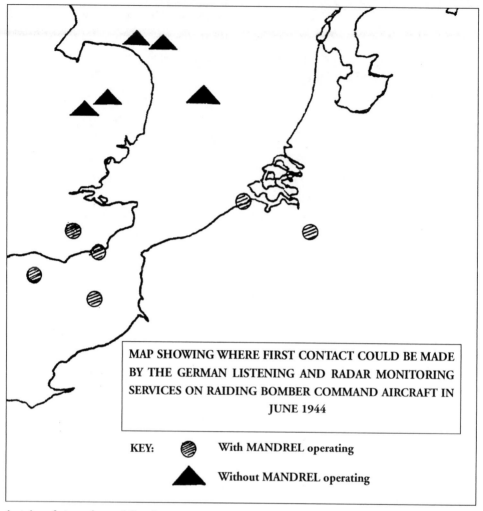

MAP SHOWING WHERE FIRST CONTACT COULD BE MADE
BY THE GERMAN LISTENING AND RADAR MONITORING
SERVICES ON RAIDING BOMBER COMMAND AIRCRAFT IN
JUNE 1944

KEY: With MANDREL operating

Without MANDREL operating

height of aircraft used for the operation, a compromise screen position of 70-80 miles from the enemy coast was decided.

However, the enemy had not been idle in the radio war.

During the early part of 1944 long-range new enemy radars in the band 150-200 Mc/s appeared, and it became essential to provide cover in this additional band, from every aircraft of the Mandrel Screen. The addition of further MANDREL equipment to the existing installation was not possible due to power limitations, and shortage of equipment. In addition, the provision of a complete barrage jam in the band would not have been practicable because of the number of Allied equipments which would also have been affected (in particular IFF Mk III).

From these considerations it was decided to build a low-power spot frequency tunable jammer, with facilities for alignment to the frequencies occupied by enemy radars. It was decided that the quickest way of meeting the requirements was to convert some piece of equipment already in production, or available in quantity. IFF

Mk.III appeared suitable, and a modification of this equipment was produced to provide the necessary facilities (ie a receiver to listen for the radar transmissions, and a transmitter to jam at the frequency to which the receiver was tuned, the operator being able to switch from receive to transmit when desired). IFF Mk III sets so modified were actually incorporated in the MANDREL screen on D-Day, and given the service designation of TR 1657 (codenamed MANDREL III), the actual frequency coverage obtained was 148-196 Mc/s...subsequently the covering range was expanded from 30-215 Mc/s.

MANDREL III was also found to operate without interference with Allied signals:

> One important application of MANDREL III has been the jamming of enemy radars operating in frequency bands also used by Allied equipments. To provide effective cover without jamming our own radars, identification of the received signals is necessary. A method which has been used with success against Freya equipments operating in the band 148-196 Mc/s makes use of the very stable 500 c/s (or sometimes 1,000 c/s) pulse repetition frequency (PRF) of these equipments. No Allied equipments in this band have stable PRFs in this region whilst flight tests have shown that PRFs of Freya equipments are maintained to within a few cycles.
>
> Since the normal time-base of Gee has a recurrence of 250 cycles, it is possible, by injecting the output of MANDREL III receiver on to the Y-plates of the Gee indicator, to obtain practically stationary pictures with signals having 500 or 1,000 c/s PRF, thus enabling positive identification of enemy Freya signals.
>
> An arrangement was therefore devised whereby, when the SO picked up a signal which appeared to be about 500 or 1,000 c/s he could transfer it to the Gee indicator unit and ask the navigator whether or not the resulting pulses appeared stationary (or nearly so). If they were so, then the signal could safely be jammed. However, this arrangement was found to be inconvenient in practice as the Gee indicator was frequently required for a 'fix' at the time when identification of the MANDREL signal was needed. Another scheme was accordingly created by No. 100 Group whereby a separate indicator (a modified FISHPOND) was provided making the MANDREL operator independent of the navigator.[93]

Maintaining Station – Racecourse Pattern

There were initial navigation problems. The first MANDREL screen was flown by visual formation and this proved impossible in poor weather, so a plan for 'Station Keeping' in MANDREL operations was formulated by the Navigation Leader of No.199 Squadron at North Creake, F/L Docherty who:

MANDREL SCREEEN

MAINTAINING STATION RACE-COURSE PATTERN

Pattern adjusted to account for wind drift

Pattern adjusted to account for wind drift

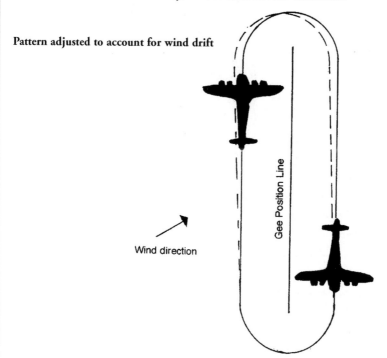

Gee Position Line

Wind direction

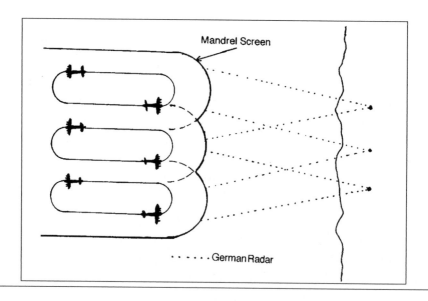

Mandrel Screen

German Radar

... devised the following drill for keeping aircraft at certain stations, in order that they may effectively complete their special duties. These duties make it necessary for pairs of aircraft to remain at a given spot for up to five hours.

Navigators complete their flight plans in selected pairs, and all courses and times, ie set course times, concentration times and times of climbing must be exactly similar. Watches are synchronised to the exact second, as late as possible before take off. Gee fixes are taken at six minute intervals on the route starting at the hour and half-hour. When three successive Gee fixes have been obtained a wind velocity is calculated over this twelve minute period, and used to alter course (if necessary) at a dead-reckoning (DR) [the position of an aircraft computed by log and compass course, without astronomical observations] position six minutes ahead of the last fix. If a six minute period occurs when aircraft are altering course, or within one minute of altering course, this fix is disregarded and a new pattern of fixes started at the next six minute period. Alteration of course is only made when the calculated DR position is more than three miles off the track and more than 30 miles from the next turning point. If the DR position is less than 30 miles from the next turning point, course will be maintained to meet the required track of the extension of the same. If the aircraft are ahead or behind time at any point, the time at the next turning point will be adjusted accordingly, except on the last leg when Air Speed Computation Tables will be used, and Indicated Air Speed adjusted to enable the aircraft to be in a position at the required time.

Estimated Time of Arrivals (ETA) are adjusted to allow for rates of turn as follows:

For turns of less than 90 degrees – turn 1/2 minute before ETA.

For turns greater than 90 degrees – turn one minute before ETA.

The above sequence of events results in aircraft remaining in close contact with each other until arrival at their given point. To remain near these points the following drill has been devised and is known as MAINTAINING STATION – RACECOURSE PATTERN. A pattern is plotted about the selected point in the shape of a racecourse, the long sides being ten miles long at right angles to the enemy coast along a Gee position line, and the short sides four and a quarter miles long. Two points are selected, diagonally opposite and will be referred to as A and B. The coordinates of position A are set up for homing, and times are given at ten-minute intervals. The navigator homes the aircraft to Position A to be there at a predetermined time. When Gee pulses line up the pilot is instructed to commence a rate one turn to port on the required heading for Position B for which an accurate ETA is calculated, it being the position for the commencement of the next turn.

No.171 Squadron. Jim Feasey's crew. Jack Philipson, the pilot, is first left in the back row. Jim Feasey is crouching, first right, in the front row. *(Jim Feasey)*

No.171 Squadron. 'E' Easy. George Jamieson's aircraft. He took the photo on 24th March 1945, after a raid on Leipzig. *(George Jamieson)*

By careful timing and allowing for wind speed and direction, it will be seen that an accurate 'Racecourse' pattern can be maintained. Pilots have been attending navigational briefings and are fully conversant with the accurate flying that is required.[94]

The month after D-Day saw the operational use of two new and important RCM, the Special WINDOW Force and JOSTLE IV. The Special WINDOW Force of No.100 Group made its first appearance on the night of 14/15th July, and was made up of all available spare aircraft (often only 8-10 aircraft) from the Group's Heavy Squadrons. Initially only routed over sea routes, and turning back when a little short of the enemy coast, considerable success was achieved. On at least four occasions in the early period of the use of this RCM the Luftwaffe were deceived as to the size of the raiding force and diverted their fighters from areas where they could, from the enemy's point of view, have been much more efficiently used.

AVM Addison had become aware of the usefulness of WINDOW early in his RCM days:

During the early No.80 Wing days we had already started to collect supplies of WINDOW material in preparation for an eventual bomber offensive – but permission to use it was not allowed until some time after the offensive had started. Despite our pressure the radar experts continued successfully to prevent the use of it in spite of the growing losses suffered by Bomber Command. However the Prime Minister was eventually persuaded to give consent for its use (his famous, 'Open the Window' edict) and the result was the remarkable success of the raid on Hamburg on 24th July 1943.

The use of WINDOW was successful but the Germans soon realised what was causing the damaging effects on their radar system and were able not only to identify WINDOW echoes but to take certain measures to counter the effects. However, as was shown later in No.100 Group operations it was possible, nevertheless, to use WINDOW for Spoofing purposes and in a way which the Germans were unable to counteract.

As far as Main Force bombers were concerned, WINDOW ejectors were installed in each bomber with arrangements being made for each aircraft to drop WINDOW at, say, two packets a minute, covering the whole area occupied by the bomber force. This produced a curtain on the German radar. No.100 Group had ejectors in their bomber aircraft which were capable of dropping up to 300 packets per minute so that the No.100 Group formation, consisting of perhaps 20 aircraft and occupying a space equivalent to that of the Main Force was capable of producing a radar pattern similar to that of the Main Force. When, at a given time, the 100 Group formation broke away from the Main Force and proceeded towards another target (different to that of the Main Force) the Germans would be confronted with two similar patterns and had

No.199 Squadron. Briefing at North Creake. *(Brendan Maguire)*

No.199 Squadron. Vic Polichek near the rear turret of the No.199 Squadron Handley Page Halifax Mk.III of which he was a crew member. *(Vic Polichek)*

to guess which of the two threatened targets the Main Force was making for. Such tactics, repeated, with a number of variations, frequently gave considerable problems to the German Fighter Controllers and, when their guesses proved to be wrong, the enemy fighters would be sent in the wrong direction.[95]

No. 214 Squadron Fortresses flying with the Main Force, began using JOSTLE IV as a jammer of enemy communications successfully on various occasions throughout July 1944; their ABC commitment ceased during this month. This Squadron also provided some Fortresses for the MANDREL Screen. Murray Peden, an RCAF pilot, in his memoir of his service with Bomber Command in the Second World War, described the introduction of JOSTLE IV into the Squadron:

> By July, 1944, a new airborne jammer, of a capacity previously unheard of, 2,500 watts, was in the final stages of development. Codenamed JOSTLE, this monster was to be installed in the bomb bays of our Fortresses, replacing ABC. Whereas, with the operation of ABC, our German-speaking WOP had been required to follow the German nightfighter controllers by tuning manually from one frequency to the other, the great JOSTLE transmitter had such tremendous power that it eliminated the necessity for this and was designed to blank out simultaneously the whole spectrum of VHF frequencies used by the controllers. Indeed, when we received JOSTLE at Oulton for final testing, Johnny Gilbert, whose crew was detailed to carry out one of the tests, had to fly halfway to Iceland to carry out the demonstration, lest JOSTLE play hob (throw into confusion) with all BBC reception over a broad area of England and compromise security.
>
> Afterwards, when we began to use it regularly on 'ops', we did our routine testing at very low level around the aerodrome for the same reason. The Fortress, which served us so adequately in many ways, was the ideal aircraft to carry JOSTLE, since it could readily climb well above the Main Force Lancasters, and thus achieve an even wider range for the super-powerful transmitter.[96]

Towards the middle of July it had been well established that the combination of WINDOW and MANDREL in 'spoof' attacks had tremendous possibilities, and it became obvious that the combination would be frequently used in No. 100 Group operations. There was also a change of tactics for the MANDREL Screen:

> The MANDREL Screen was used on 16 nights in August, on several occasions over S E England, giving coverage to Bomber attacks on the Pas de Calais area. It was found that when other targets in France were chosen, the mere presence of the Screen opposite the Pas de Calais was sufficient to hold enemy fighters in that area. This was a valuable aid in splitting the Hun forces.
>
> The tactic of moving the Screen was continued successfully, and a new tactic exploited. This latter was used only in purely 'spoof' attacks, and consisted of simulating a 'breakdown' in part of the Screen, to ensure that the enemy early warning system should certainly see the WINDOW Force , since, he was, by

now, becoming a little chary of alerting his forces without more evidence than the presence of a Screen.[97]

A major success for RCM took place in the same month. Heavy raids by the Main Force were carried out on Kiel and Stettin on 16th/17th August 1944. On the following night:

> ...no major bombing took place, but a WINDOW force, strengthened in numbers by a Bullseye (training flights made by Heavy Conversion Units (HCU) and Operational Training Units (OTU) over the North Sea to divert German early warning systems), and covered by a MANDREL Screen, headed towards North Germany. The WINDOW Force kept on almost to the Schleswig coast, and created in the enemy mind a complete impression that the previous night's attack was to be repeated. No less than 12 squadrons of Hun fighters were deployed against the WINDOW Force. A still more important after-effect of this 'spoof' took place on the following night, 18th/19th, when a Main Force actually did go to Bremen, on a route similar to that of the 'Spoof' Force. The enemy, thoroughly confused, took this attack as another 'spoof', and left it entirely unopposed as far as his fighters were concerned.
>
> The effect on the Hun of our jamming was demonstrated in this month, particularly by his discarding much of his R/T fighter control in favour of the infinitely more cumbersome, though not so 'jammable', W/T methods.[98]

August saw many changes in No.100 Group. Automatic WINDOW Launchers were being developed and given trials. No.803 Squadron, the USAAF representatives in No.100 Group became 36th Bombardment Squadron and left the Group for Cheddington although still operating under No.100 Group control for MANDREL. No.199 Squadron was increased to three Flights, No.223 Squadron, flying Liberators, was formed and joined No. 214 Squadron at Oulton. Thus the MANDREL, WINDOW, and jamming strength increased considerably.

The following month saw MANDREL, WINDOW and spoof techniques being operated over the Continent with success. The Allied advance further into Europe led to the general retreat of the enemy's Early Warning Stations. It was possible to take the MANDREL Screen much closer to the heart of Germany, thus delaying by very much longer the appearance of the Main Bomber Force. Also the removal of German ground observers from liberated territory made it simpler to route WINDOW Forces to hitherto inaccessible parts of the Reich. An old problem that arose once more was that of possible enemy sightings from behind the MANDREL Screen which was now often positioned east of The Hague (still in enemy hands). This was overcome by increasing the length of the Screen, and bending back the more northerly stations to smother sightings from Holland. It was fortunate that at this time No.171 Squadron was formed at North Creake, equipped with Halifaxes, and fitted for the roles of either MANDREL or WINDOW. North Creake, situated close to the small North Norfolk port of Wells-next-the-Sea was very much a 'wartime only' airfield. Used firstly for 'decoy' purposes in 1941 it became operational in November 1943, for a very short period within No. 3 Group, Bomber Command, being transferred to No.100 Group two weeks later.

With the increasing use by Main Force of the tactics of low flying and maintaining radar-silence as far as possible, by October 1944 it was found that it was possible to delay the MANDREL jamming for longer than had been possible hitherto. In addition, to make Main Force groups aware of the planning of 'feint' operations it was decided that a daily 'Intention of No.100 Group Operations' to be sent to the Groups involved. This was much appreciated by Main Force Groups and, 'For the first time the other Groups began to be fully aware of the protection and assistance' they were getting from No.100 Group. The month showed 'lower losses in the Main Force than the most sanguine could have expected, and it seems fair to suppose that the Spoof Forces had a considerable share in this,' it is recorded, 'for never before had it been so obvious that confusion reigned unchecked in the enemy's plotting system...by the time the Hun Controller had made up his mind, the Main Force were often past the target and on the way home.'

An outstanding WINDOW success occurred on 14th/15th October when 1000 bombers attacked Duisberg and 200 raided Brunswick. It was anticipated that the Duisberg raid by low approach, radar silence and shallow penetration, would get through with little trouble but that the Brunswick Force might be strongly opposed. A WINDOW Force was routed to break off from the Brunswick raid and strike at Mannheim. The ploy was outstandingly successful; the Brunswick attack was virtually ignored and the Mannheim area was anticipated as the main target by the German defences.

October also saw the introduction of PIPERACK, the jammer against SN2, the new enemy AI equipment. In July 1944 a Ju88 nightfighter had landed in error at Woodbridge, Suffolk, and was 'captured'. Amongst its electronic equipment was SN2, which at this time, was unfamiliar to British scientists. It was examined by the Royal Aircraft Establishment (RAE). At the end of the same month, at the request of No.100 Group HQ, TRE set up a listening watch at Gorleston to study these signals. The primary object of the study of the operational use of this new equipement was Direction Finding (DF). For this reason a specially equipped PING-PONG RCM installation was employed. No signals were heard until the night of 16th/17th August after which several interceptions were made. Heavy Bomber Command activity, during which there was much jamming, made interception difficult but the following conclusions were reached:

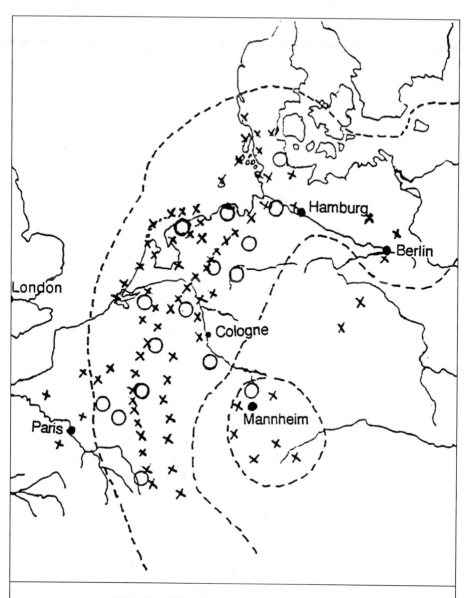

WINDOW DROPPING ZONES

KEY:

X   **Location of German GCI Stations.**

O   **Luftwaffe Nightfighter Aerodromes.**

– – – – **WINDOW dropped within these lines.**

1 SN2 was being used against Bomber Command in the sector Den Helder/Walcheren of Holland.

2 Subject to possibility of 'wipe out' by friendly jammers it appeared SN2 was not used in the area before 16th August and none was heard in the same sector after the 26th of the same month.

3 SN2 when heard was audible for up to 30 minutes continuously. This, as well as tests at RAE, contradicted previous reports that the equipment must not be switched on for more than five minutes at a time for fear of damage.

4 Strength of signals indicated that enemy fighters ventured close to the British coastline.

5 There were at least two versions of SN2 (later there were found to be six) – both of which were transmitted on 90 Mc/s.[99]

PIPERACK, the RCM to combat SN2, was installed in the JOSTLE IV aircraft of No. 214 Squadron, and was frequently used in the WINDOW Force. The combination of these two RCM, H2S and CARPET gave an effective simulation of a Main Force. PFF added to the enemy confusion on several occasions by Oboe-marking and bombing the 'Spoof' target. The noise of 'Oboe' which up until that time, always preceded real attacks only, was thought to give still more confusion to the enemy Controller who was already heavily involved trying to cope with other forms of Allied deceit.

November saw a new and rather different use of the WINDOW Force. Subjected to many attacks by Bomber Command the Ruhr was heavily defended in numbers by the Luftwaffe who adopted a policy of keeping their fighters there, regardless of attempts to draw them away by 'Spoofs'. It was assumed that the enemy always expected the Ruhr to be attacked and could not be dissuaded from this opinion. The WINDOW Force was, therefore, used on several occasions 'to infest the whole Ruhr area with vast quantities of WINDOW immediately prior to the arrival of the Main Force from behind the covering influence of the MANDREL Screen. By doing so they caused such confusion that the German defences 'could not distinguish any bomber track in the maze of WINDOW echoes.' He was further confused when, once or twice, this tactic was employed when there was no bomber force.' Always, however, the MANDREL Screen was present, if the weather allowed, to keep the nightfighter crews in their cockpits, and the Controllers at their desks, just in case the bombers were on their way.'

An outstanding example of the confusion that could be caused was shown on 4th/5th December when the Main Force raids were on targets to the north and the south of the Ruhr. The WINDOW Force went straight into the Ruhr between them, supported by PFF marking, and held not less 90-100 German night fighters in the area until much too late for their effective deployment against the bombers.

At the end of 1944 there was an end-of-year assessment of No.100 Group's contribution to the Bomber Offensive:

> Throughout the year the Fortresses of No. 214 Squadron and, later, the Liberators of No.223 Squadron, had been plugging away, accompanying and 'Jostling' for every major bombing raid. By December, all were able to be of still greater assistance, being fully equipped with CARPET (anti-Würzburg), PIPERACK(anti-SN2), besides JOSTLE IV (anti H/F and VHF). Mosquitoes of No.192 Squadron began operating this month (December) as jammers. Their role was a dual one. They flew to target areas on routes which took them well clear of the Main Force and, on the way, they made recordings for 'Y' Service of enemy R/T traffic. Arriving at the target area they jammed, with PIPERACK, the enemy AI and they stayed there until well after the attack, thus covering the withdrawal of stragglers. It was the intention to increase and prolong the AI jamming in the target areas to which the enemy nightfighters would ultimately gravitate.

The year closed with a welcome Christmas present when No.462 Squadron was transferred from No.4 Group and took up residence at Foulsham. Their immediate task was WINDOW, later to be followed (in March 1945) by ABC, which had not been part of No.100 Group's commitments for several months.[100]

SN2, (FuG 220) was a German nightfighter AI operating in the frequency range 70-100 Mc/s. It had a performance sufficiently high to be of effective use by nightfighters operating without close control inside a bomber stream of high density. PIPERACK was the airborne jamming equipment carried in No. 100 Group aircraft to provide protection to the bombers from such nightfighters. It was claimed that five aircraft equipped with this RCM flying in line behind each other at ten mile intervals would give protective coverage over an area of 65 by 30/40 miles. There were difficulties. PIPERACK transmissions could be picked up by enemy ground stations, as could other radio signals from the bombers, eg H2S, ABC, and CARPET etc. This could indicate probable course and target of the raiding force. The SN2-equipped nightfighters could also pick up PIPERACK although it would have needed a highly-skilled aircrew to do this. Thus dangers could be minimised, as far as the main bomber force was concerned, by using the formations of the specialist aircraft, well separate from the bomber force, and it was considered that 'the advantages of the jamming coverage outweighed the disadvantages...If PIPERACK aircraft flew with the bomber stream, even if the danger to the specialist aircraft is slightly greater than it would be without jamming, this would be more than compensated for by the enormously increased protection it gave to the rest of the bomber force.' PIPERACK was installed in Fortress, Liberator, and Halifax aircraft. Each aircraft carried six equipments to give complete coverage against all known SN2 frequencies. In

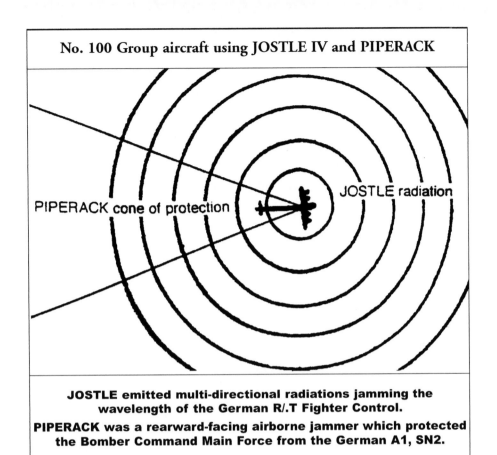

No. 100 Group aircraft using JOSTLE IV and PIPERACK

PIPERACK cone of protection

JOSTLE radiation

**JOSTLE emitted multi-directional radiations jamming the wavelength of the German R/.T Fighter Control.
PIPERACK was a rearward-facing airborne jammer which protected the Bomber Command Main Force from the German A1, SN2.**

addition, a few Mosquito aircraft were fitted with two installations each, and three of these were used for protection over the target area, where the risks would be greater for the normal heavy aircraft carrying jammers.

As the New Year of 1945 began, bombing operations were restricted due to poor weather – during the month of January bombing attacks took place on only 10 nights – but all were supported by RCM. No.462 Squadron took part in the WINDOW patrol for the first time 'and were the inaugurators of a new feature. This was bombing by the WINDOW Force, on markers which were sometimes provided by PFF and sometimes by No.100 Group Mosquitoes.' In this month No.100 Group lost the valued support of the 36th (USAAF) Squadron. Their MANDREL and other jamming aircraft had been greatly in demand for sometime for service with the daylight Forces of the US 8th Air Force. These requirements left the Squadron with no aircraft available for night operations. Another USAAF Unit, 492 Bombardment Group, which had experience of night flying with Liberators joined the 'Special Window Force' and flew with it until the end of the War.

The depth of Main Force penetrations increased during February and it was becoming increasingly difficult to put on a convincing feint attack, owing to the distances which had to be covered over enemy territory, which made the differences between WINDOW and Main Forces much more obvious. However, some success was obtained by Windowing furiously at route turning points, in order to obscure the direction of the Main Force. It was a difficult task for the crews. On one particular operation, in March 1945, each aircraft discharged nearly two tons of WINDOW. When it is considered this was done by hand at the rate of one bundle every two seconds, with the crews in full flying kit and wearing oxygen masks, in extremely cold conditions, one can visualise the problems encountered by them. The Automatic Launching Machine for WINDOW, although in production had not yet been delivered.

As the war neared its end, the front line was constantly on the move so the need for the MANDREL Screen decreased and it was discarded in April. The aircraft normally used for MANDREL flew with the Main Force on three occasions. Heavy use was also made of the JOSTLE IV and ABC Squadrons throughout this period.

In May 1945, only one operation was undertaken by the heavy squadrons of the Group before VE-Day. It was, sadly, to provide a tragic end to No.100 Group's operational activities. On the night of 2nd/3rd May, 82 four-engined aircraft, a record number for the Group were detailed for operations. Thirty nine Halifaxes from North Creake were to take part. Four from No.199 Squadron, and four from No.171 Squadron formed a moving MANDREL Screen (also using WINDOW), eleven from No.199 Squadron, twelve from No.171 Squadron formed part of a WINDOW/Bombing patrol to Kiel, and six from No.199 Squadron with two from No.171 Squadron took part in a MANDREL/WINDOW/Bombing feint in the Schleswig area, one of the few remaining enemy-held parts of the Continent. Kiel was attacked by PFF aircraft at the same time. Little fighter activity was encountered but, sadly, two Halifaxes from No.199 Squadron were lost. It is believed they collided over their target whilst on a bombing run. Thirteen men, most of whom were on their second tour of operations, lost their lives. They were the last casualties of Bomber Command in the Second World War.

HEAVY AIRCRAFT USED BY No.100 GROUP

The airborne RCM war, as it developed, produced bulkier apparatus. The Hallicrafters receivers used in 1940 for detecting Luftwaffe beams in the raids on the UK, were the size of a large domestic radio. Now RCM equipment could be as big as a giant dustbin as was the case with the communications jammer JOSTLE IV. In addition, the aircraft carrying the equipments (often there were several on each aircraft), would be required to travel much further into enemy-held Europe. Consequently, larger aircraft were necessary to transport the wide variety of equipment coming into use. Of the heavier aircraft available to the RAF at the time Short Stirlings, Handley Page Halifaxes, Fortresses and Liberators, in addition to the long-serving Vickers Wellington, were used. The RCM activities of the various squadrons often overlapped with more than one squadron using similar equipment and carrying out similar duties at the same time.

There were,eventually, seven heavy squadrons. The longest-serving in RCM experience was No.192 Squadron, the history of which has been extensively dealt with in Chapter Three. The other heavy squadrons were:

No.171 Squadron. Formed on 7th September 1944 within No.100 Group from one flight of No. 199 Squadron plus additional crews, and which carried out MANDREL, WINDOW RCM. Stationed at North Creake.

No. 199 Squadron. Joined No.100 Group on 1st May 1944 carrying out MANDREL and WINDOW RCM. Stationed at North Creake.

No.214 Squadron. Transferred from No.3 Group on 17th January 1944 and which carried out ABC, JOSTLE and WINDOW RCM. Originally stationed at Sculthorpe and transferred to Foulsham in May 1944.

No.223 Squadron. Formed within No.100 Group at Oulton in August 1944 for MANDREL and WINDOW duties.

No.462 Squadron (RAAF). Transferred to No.100 Group from No. 4 Group in December 1944 for WINDOW and ABC duties. Stationed at Foulsham.

No.803 Squadron (USAAF). Formed at Sculthorpe March 1944 for MANDREL and CARPET duties. Moved to Oulton in May 1944. Redesignated 36th Bombardment Squadron and transferred to Cheddington in August 1944 but still worked under No. 100 Group for RCM duties.

THE SQUADRONS.

No.171 Squadron.

Hans-Werner Mihan, a German soldier in the Second World War, was at his home in Potsdam on 14th/15th April 1945, when a raid (the last major Bomber Command raid of the War on a German city) took place. The sirens sounded and, briefly, he watched the beginning of the raid from his front door before going to the air-raid shelter 'relying on my experience to know in time when something was about to happen.' His period of observation did not last long:

> And then the bombs rained down! In spite of the closed cellar doors, an
> indescribable noise filled the air. The earth shook and the walls of our house

Werner Mihan beside a German 150cm searchlight in the summer of 1943. *(Werner Mihan)*

seemed to shake although the nearest hits, it transpired, were some 200 metres away. One explosion caused the cellar door to spring open, and clouds of dust and stucco filled the air. Trusting our strong cellar walls I was not afraid, but women and children wept and prayed. I would have preferred to have been in my old flak position and to be able at least to fight instead of having to sit and wait.[101]

In the brief period before he hastily went to the cellar air-raid shelter Werner Mihan was surprised to see a solitary enemy aircraft orbiting above the city. Almost fifty years later, whilst researching for a book he was writing about the raid, he enquired of the readers of 'The Marker', the PFF magazine, whether anyone had knowledge of this lone aircraft (which Mihan took to be the 'Master Bomber') he had seen flying in isolation on this night. He received a reply, but not from the 'Master Bomber'. As part of No.100 Group operations, twelve Handley Page Halifaxes from No.171 Squadron (which was based at North Creake) were engaged on WINDOW/MANDREL and bombing operations. 'It was probably us,' wrote Jim Feasey, who had been a Sergeant air-gunner in No.171 Squadron, 'we were on our own over Potsdam that night':

> On the night of 14th/15th April when the Russians were getting near Berlin they apparently requested an RAF raid on Potsdam. We were to support the Main Force in an attack on the SS Barracks there. I volunteered for a trip with our CO,

W/C Mike Renaut DFC, as his regular mid-upper gunner was sick. The rear gunner, P/O Jones (RCAF), went off the air after a couple of hours when his intercom went u/s. En route we changed direction. Our SO, F/S McDonald, was jamming with his MANDREL sets and we were dropping tons of WINDOW making our small force look like a large number of aircraft. Nearing Berlin our own Halifax broke off and, whilst we were on our own, we dropped a small number of bombs on the barracks at Potsdam. We were ahead of the Pathfinders by about 30 minutes and got the enemy defences 'wound up' so that they wasted time and fuel.

Over Potsdam we were coned by several searchlights. Mike dived and weaved but there were so many to try to evade. Nothing hit us and there was no flak which was usually an indication that fighters were about. We had two fighter attacks from behind and Mike saw two attacks develop from head on. He 'yawed' (deviated from the horizontal line of flight) the aircraft and the cannon fire swept under the wing. The WOP, 'Rusty' Willis, who had opened his curtain to see what was going on, said, 'Blow that', or words to that effect, and promptly closed his curtain again! I tried to do something by calling out directions to dive but Mike was doing what he thought was best. I could see a fighter high up above but that was all I could see as I was blinded by the lights.

After about 15 minutes we managed to fly out of it all. Jonesey in the rear turret just had to guess what was going on. We were so short of fuel we had to land at Manston, in Kent, and spend the rest of the night there. We returned to North Creake in the morning. Mike said later that he thought we were for the 'chop' that night.

There were 54 RCM sorties on the night of the raid. The Bomber Command RCM report for the night states that the main attack on Potsdam (there were also much smaller attacks on Cuxhaven and Berlin) was, at that stage of the war, little more than a 'fringe' target. No.100 Group sent 104 aircraft (57 Mosquitoes, 36 Halifaxes, six Fortresses and five Liberators) in support of the Main Force:

For the short distance that the route of the Main Force lay over unoccupied territory – the distance must have been of the order of fifty miles – it was supported by two WINDOW diversions, fanning out to the north and south of the track. Both diversions were accompanied by MANDREL aircraft and all three forces by PIPERACK, JOSTLE and CARPET.

These tactics gave rise to a very considerable confusion in plotting by the enemy. 'Heavy bombers and Mosquitoes' were plotted in places that might be associated with each prong of the trident in turn but the truth of the matter was probably that while the enemy was aware of the presence of a heavy bomber force, he was prevented from obtaining any true idea of either its whereabouts or its movements. Activity by one

Gruppe of fighters was intercepted in the area but it would have had to be lucky to have achieved any success.[102]

The main enemy nightfighter activity was concerned with the subsidiary raid on Cuxhaven:

> The small force of heavies (28 sorties) that attacked Cuxhaven cannot be regarded as a diversion but rather as a separate feint in its own right. As such it was successful in engaging the attention of possibly five Gruppen of enemy night fighters. The force was plotted by the enemy as it approached across the North Sea, the first plots being to the north of Texel and, as it neared the German coast, fighters were ordered to take off. Hamburg was suspected as a possible target and one unit was sent there at 2219. Bombs on Cuxhaven were reported between 2219 and 2230 during which time frequent orders to fly were issued. At 2231 it was apparently realised that the 'attack' was over and the speed with which landing orders followed indicates that the deception was fully appreciated as such. The fighter activity lasted for less than half an hour but what there was of it was quite unprofitable.
>
> Fighter control traffic, which was concerned only with the Cuxhaven raid was heard on three HF and two MF W/T frequencies, and in addition there was one MF beacon passing on plots of the raid. DRUMSTICK and JOSTLE were brought into action against the HF W/T. There is no evidence, however, that they were successful in denying the enemy any of the facilities which were actually being of such little use to him. DARTBOARD was also used against one MF W/T channel and FIDGET against the other two.
>
> Apart from three MF plotting frequencies, no R/T traffic was heard and no countermeasures were required.[103]

Jim Feasey's usual pilot was Jack Philipson, an 'airplane mad' Australian who obtained his 'wings' in April 1943. A couple of months later he arrived in the UK on the 'Queen Elizabeth' from New York. Further training followed and near the end of his last course, at No.1653 HCU on Stirling Mk III, at Chedburgh, in Cambridgeshire, he saw a notice, 'asking for crews for special duties in No.100 Group so we volunteered thinking it might be supply dropping at night to the Resistance.'

He was transferred to No. 199 Squadron on 12th September 1944 and was told, two days later, 'that we were to be the first crews of No.171 Squadron.' The separation of 'C' Flight from No.199 Squadron would be the nucleus for the new squadron, with additional crews being added. W/C Mike Renaut became Squadron CO, 'he had done a tour on the early Halifaxes and was the first person to drop a 8,000lb bomb.' Renaut later wrote a book[104] about his experiences.

Jack Philipson recalled that the Squadron did not lose many aircraft, 'eight in eight months, I think'; also the secrecy. 'We were only told what we needed to know to do the job and were not allowed to discuss our work, not even amongst ourselves. Sometimes we didn't know how close we were to the Main Force, or sometimes where the Main Force was going.' Enquiries made at debriefing brought a noncommittal, 'Oh, we'll let you know if you should have done otherwise.'

Philipson first flew with another crew on a WINDOW operation over the North Sea just off the Danish coast. Shortly afterwards another Australian, S/L Keith Eddy became Flight Commander of 'A' Flight and 'took me up for a check test and fighter affiliation with a Spitfire and, after 40 minutes, said I was OK for ops.' When Eddy left the Squadron in February 1945, after 50 sorties, it was officially recorded that, 'He had given most valuable guidance in the early days of the Squadron.'

Philipson was immediately involved in operations. The night he was passed for ops, 'it was off to Louvain on a WINDOW spoof. Next night to Frankfurt-on-Main, followed two nights later, on September 29th, to Mainz:

> We crossed the coast south of Dunkirk (still held by the Germans and a hot spot), over Charleroi (cleared by the Americans two weeks earlier), and on towards the Mainz-Frankfurt area arriving at about 0335. At the Rhine we turned starboard coming back on to course for Charleroi where we arrived at about 0435 to be shot at by our own guns which, fortunately, fell short of our height. There was no Main Force activity this night and our 25 Stirlings, all with instructions not to go below 10,000 ft over Allied occupied areas, were the only RCM aircraft operating. In addition, the RAF was supposed to notify army intelligence of all flight movements, particularly at night. Somewhere there had been a breakdown in communication!
>
> As we approached the Charleroi area we noticed the odd burst of flak ahead and to port. Then Bang!, Bang!, Bang! By the second Bang! I had the aircraft into a steep starboard turn of 90 degrees, followed by another to port and climbing back on course fast. There were another three shots but now we were at 13000 ft and they were low and behind us. The result of all this activity was that the Windowing stopped, the bomb-aimer was rolled over and wrapped up in the WINDOW from the parcels with his intercom disconnected, the WOP, who was off the intercom listening to the BBC between Group broadcasts thought we had had it and grabbed the nearest parachute, jammed it on to his chest. thereby wedging himself in his seat against the radio table. The flight engineer and bomb-aimer freed him. Nobody was hurt.
>
> Next morning we heard that the Germans had sounded the alarm in the Mainz and Frankfurt area and had called fighters from as far north as Hamburg as a reception committee of 600-700 fighters for us but we had turned back early, or short of them, dropped 2000 ft, and gone for home under our own WINDOW cover. We were just creating a war of nerves.

We usually flew 'spoof' trips in this manner. We flew in three rows. The centre row flew the main track at two minute intervals with a row to port five miles away and the other five miles to starboard flying at similar intervals. This way it was hoped to give a large coverage. Each aircraft dropped thin WINDOW strips Type 'N' (if my memory serves me correct) from the front chute, dropped by the flight engineer up to 12 bundles per minute over enemy occupied territory and Type 'M' (approx. 6 ft by 1 and 1/2 inches) in bundles at 36 bundles per minute dropped by the bomb aimer out of the rear chute. This made our 25 look like 250-300 aircraft .

When you got in the aircraft at base you were greeted by this great stack of brown paper parcels holding the WINDOW. Depending on the length of the trip, they could weigh between 1,600 and 2,000 lbs.

On one of Jack Philipson's last flights in a Short Stirling III before transferring to a Handley Page Halifax III he was required to taken evasive action against an enemy nightfighter. Bound for Mannheim on a WINDOW dropping exercise – the Main Force were going to Saarbrucken – he found the manoeuvrability of the Stirling a great advantage:

We were about 25-30 miles NE of Saarbrucken – the Main Force were raiding a motor transport depot near there – and about 15 minutes before turning to port and home we noticed the flares going down for the raid on Saarbrucken when the gunners shouted out that there was a Me 410 about 1,000 yards to starboard. He started to turn in and both gunners fired a sighting burst at 600 yards shouting, 'Corkscrew starboard, Go!' I gave her full aileron and bottom rudder and we dived right at 45 degrees off course. After dropping 500 ft I went to roll to port but the mid-upper gunner told me to turn to port as the fighter was on our starboard saying , 'He has dropped his flaps to try and follow us.' I did so and the fighter broke away.

We had dropped 900 ft to 15,100 ft and I noticed we had only reached 190 mph. I pulled the aircraft back up and onto course again as the rear gunner, Jim Feasey, called out that his guns were jammed. The bomb-aimer who was sitting next to me talked Jim through releasing each ammo belt to try and get some 'feed'.

Meanwhile our 'friend' came in once more from the same direction but we dived to starboard again and he broke off straight away. Jim eventually got two guns going but it was too late. The fighter never fired a shot at us. After levelling out we all noticed that the four engines had cut momentarily. I must have pushed the wheel forward as we rolled over and placed negative 'G' on the aircraft cutting the fuel for a second or two. This, we found next day, must have also stopped the feed to the rear guns, two belts had jammed as they came out of the ammunition boxes into the long chutes down to the turret.

Later in October, 1944, Jack Philipson and his crew went to No. 1659 HCU at Topliffe, in Yorkshire, for conversion to Handley Page Halifax MkIII. 'We got copies of the pilot's notes before going up there from North Creake. Seven days in and out, (9.55 hrs flying) and you were a Halifax crew. The Halifax rattled and bounced but it was fast'.

The new aircraft carried a heavy load:

We used to go in at about 18,000 ft, perhaps higher if we were bombing. Sometimes we carried 3,500lbs of bombs, (first used by the Squadron in February 1945), extra fuel in case we had to stay out longer, 1,600 lbs of WINDOW, an SO, 12 jamming sets and a cathode oscilloscope to read the wavelength of the signals we jammed. After dropping the bombs and turning for home instead of throttling back a little I would just touch the elevator trim. Slowly the speed would build up, so that after a quarter of an hour or so you could be up to 180 m.p.h. (faster if you got under 10,000 ft). We used to catch up the Main Force Lancs (who flew at 155-160 mph) on the way home.

Early in December 1944 Jack Philipson became unpopular with his superiors when he 'wrote off' a new Halifax Mk.III, NA 694:

We did a 'belly landing' on December 4th after returning from a bombing and WINDOW operation on Kassel. Halfway home the port inner engine tachometer went 'off the clock'. The engine was OK so I thought it was instrument failure. About 25 minutes from home I noticed orange flicks coming out of the exhaust of the same engine. With automatic mixture control I thought there might be mixture problems with the fuel and asked the flight engineer to check the figures. He reported that they were alright. Then the cylinder heads temperature went up, the oil pressure went down, so I 'feathered' the engine.

When we got near to base I told them we had an engine 'out' and asked the flight engineer to go back and de-isolate the flaps and 'take out' the undercarriage 'up' locks for landing. The navigator and WOP had gone back to join the SO for landing and nobody was plugged in to the intercom. I sent the bomb-aimer back to see what had happened and he returned to say that the flight engineer's mike had frozen and he couldn't be heard. Still nobody answered so I sent the bomb-aimer back to smarten them up. Eventually the flight engineer returned to tell me that he had carried out his checks and everything was OK.

I came downwind, eased the trim on the rudder and aileron, eased the power of the starboard inner engine and opened both of the outer engines a little to take off a little of the load on the rudder stick. I selected undercarriage 'down' and instead of two reds going to two yellows for undercarriage movement I got two reds, two yellows and two greens. 'Lights up the creek,' I thought, so I closed all throttles to see if the horn would blow on the crosswind leg.

Neither the bomb-aimer nor myself could see if the undercarriage was down. It was cloudy, dark, and there was a crosswind. We both agreed it must be OK, horn OK, locks out, lights up. We could not think of a reason for it not to be. After selecting 'up' and 'down' three more times in we went.

Looking back I remember vaguely feeling the the tail wheel touch down, then we settled on the belly, the propeller blades clicking as they hit and folded back and we sailed off the runway and across the grass to the middle of the field. After the aircraft had stopped and I turned off the magneto switches the horn started to blast. 'Too late' was the cry! One new aircraft 'wiped out' after sixteen hours! I was sent off, with a flea in my ear, to an engine-handling course for 10 days. In 1986, when I revisited the UK I met our Bomb-Aimer, Norm Harrington, who quietly said to me that, 'When they lifted her up they found a 500lbs bomb 'hung up' underneath!.' It must have been a smooth belly-landing!

March 23/24th 1945 saw Philipson, flying a No.171 Squadron Halifax LK868, in support of the Allied crossing of the Rhine into Germany:

We were doing a jamming trip our 'Racecourse' circuit being 30 miles west of Wesel and were in position 25 minutes before PFF dropped their flares and 200 Lancs bombed the town. There followed the greatest display you ever could see. Dozens of searchlights lay across the Rhine with tanks, field pieces etc.,for a length of 50 or more miles pounding the east side of the Rhine. I believe it was twice the size of the El Alamein barrage...2200 was H Hour for the bombing so we were there and jamming at 2130 and stayed until 2300...I think the crossing by the army started at 2230.

Another Australian pilot on the Squadron, George Jamieson, recalled how a member of his crew used an unorthodox method to silence enemy guns:

One night, on our way home, Gee was u/s and our DR must have been a mile or two out, we went over Dunkirk much to the annoyance of a few gunners who sent up a bit of German hardware. Just for the hell of it our Flight Engineer, Bill Tiltman, fired the 'colours of the day' and the firing ceased and gave us time to get out of there! When we told them the Intelligence blokes were amazed it worked (and so were we!)

Bert Berry, a WOP/AG from London, was posted to North Creake, where he became friendly with a NAAFI lady who became his wife. Initially serving in No.199 Squadron (where he carried out one operation) he too was transferred to the newly formed No.171 Squadron, and completed 34 operations. On one occasion when there was a radio problem:

In October 1944 we were on a WINDOW dropping operation, which had to be carried out in two stages. On completion of the first stage, a duration of four hours and five minutes flying, we had to land at Manston, in Kent. The plan was to refuel and grab a bite to eat from the Church Army mobile canteen before taking off on the second stage.

It appears that all of the No.100 Group heavies had been instructed to land at Manston, so things were pretty chaotic. Eventually, we got airborne again and the second stage of the operation was under way. Having completed our mission and a further four hours flying, we were on the return journey home. It was only then that I picked up our aircraft call sign on W/T and the message 'Return to base.' As we were already doing that, we wondered what on earth was going on.

When we eventually landed back at North Creake, and after the usual interrogations had been carried out, we learned that the second stage of the operation had been cancelled over the R/T, with all aircraft being told to return to their home bases. Apparently, we were the first and only aircraft to take off on the second stage and were out of range of the radio transmission when the 'ops cancelled' broadcast was made. Next day, Intelligence reported our solitary aircraft had been reported as a considerable bomber stream, with German fighter stations alerted for action.

Official records describe the trip thus:

21.10.44. The Halifaxes of No.171 Squadron started WINDOW operations. It would appear, however, that one of the aircraft had failed to receive the recall and had pressed on to their target where it was erroneously plotted by the German controller as 30 bombers, a successful, if unintended start for the Squadron.[105]

Roy Mitchell, a 'straight air-gunner' in No.171 Squadron, a local lad who had been in the RAF since 1937, found himself with a posting to North Creake, near to his home at Brancaster, on the Norfolk coast, a mile or so from the airfield. He lived 'unofficially' at home:

I didn't know the other fellows as I should have done as I wasn't on the Station that much. The RAF was a hindrance at times. It kept getting in the way! I used to get up in the morning, whether I had been flying or not, and have my breakfast and go down to the pub for a game of cards. I'd go up to Creake and say to the pilot, 'Anything on?' and he would say if we were going to be operational, or we might be doing an air test. If there was nothing on I used to return to Brancaster and the pub. I never lived in the Mess at all. I would be there when I was needed and had a bed allocated to me in the billet with the rest of the crew but I only used it when there was a short break between jobs. I realised after the war what a strain it must have been on my mother, her knowing where I was going.

The sparse civilian population of the area nearly lost one of its number:

The RAF in its wisdom had decided to half sink a ship, a small coaster, about a mile off Brancaster for gunnery practice. It was scuttled near the beach, much too close to the village really. My pilot decided we would have some gunnery practice using the ship as a target. We manned all the gunnery positions which meant eight guns all firing at 200 rounds a minute. We took up a position to bash away at this ship's mast and then one of the crew shouted, 'There's somebody on the damn thing!' We were fairly low and I looked down and saw this figure scuttling towards the village across the sand. I recognised him immediately as he was the only fellow in the village who wore a peaked cap with the white top like they wear in the Royal Navy. I thought to myself, 'I know who you are and I'll see you tonight!'

I went into the pub in Brancaster Staithe that night. It was a friendly place. We used to play nap. I said to this chap, 'What were you doing on that ship today?' and he said, 'Roy, it's like this. They came here and scuttled it and the sailors went away leaving practically everything on the ship, the cutlery and crockery. They only took the compass.' I told him, 'Well, It's by absolute sheer luck you weren't cut in half' and told him what we had intended to do. I laid it on a bit thick for him, telling him how many rounds per minute we would have fired. He was horrified! He never went near that ship again, or, if he did, he made sure there were no aircraft about!

Les King was a F/L Special Operator (SO) on the Squadron from December 1944 until the end of the European War. This was his second tour and his crew mostly, like himself, had been instructors between tours of operations:

Having survived one tour of 30 Ops with No. 101 Squadron, in 1 Group during the summer of 1943 (we were the only complete crew on the Squadron to do so from April to September of that year) I was screened as WOP/AG to become an instructor. During the period I was doing this job (one year) the invasion of Normandy had taken place and it was realised that training of further crews would no longer be necessary. Therefore instructors were crewed up in November 1944 to return to operational squadrons to begin a second tour (normally twenty ops). This took place at RAF Langar, near Nottingham, where I found myself allocated to F/L Joe Brogan's crew. I already knew Joe. We were informed we would be trained for No.100 Group RCM duties. I was sent to North Creake ahead of Joe's crew and the rest arrived two weeks later having done a conversion course to the Handley Page Halifax.

On 23rd December 1944 I flew with F/S Brown to the Frankfurt-on-Main region to gain the necessary experience for using MANDREL equipment before Joe and the crew reached North Creake, and 'A' Flight of No.171 Squadron. Basically the duties were to form a screen ahead of the Main Force to protect it from the enemy's radar system.

As far as I remember twelve aircraft were used to form the umbrella screen to arrive at their respective orbiting stations which were more or less as far as our ground forces had advanced from D-Day. Each pair of aircraft orbited approximately 500 ft one above the other at a distance two to three miles apart, with the SOs tuning in the equipment to 'throw back' the enemy signals. The Main Force would then pass through the screen undetected at that point to continue their track to the designated target. The 12 orbiting aircraft of No.171 Squadron would then carry out a 'spoof' raid on another target dropping WINDOW as they proceeded. From the enemy's point of view there now appeared to be two Main Forces approaching and they had to decide where the real target was. As we were only a small force of 12 aircraft our instructions were to then bomb, put our nose down for speed and fly home to base as quickly as possible being more vulnerable to attack.

The severe winter of 1944/45 affected flying:

On the night of 28th January 1945 snow had fallen heavily during the morning accompanied by strong gales and all personnel at North Creake were put to work clearing runways for them to become operational. We took off in Halifax LK868 to climb to 12,000 ft only to become badly iced up and lose control. We finished up levelling out at 1,500 ft with Joe Brogan and the flight engineer, F/S Len Ley, the only NCO in the crew, fighting together to pull the stick back and so fly straight and level. With our instruments u/s and a petrol leak we were diverted to Ford, in Hampshire, returning to North Creake the next day. Again, with more snow falling wearing flying boots we had to clear the snow off the main plane before take off, quite a slippery task, and at the same time turn the propellers to prime the engines and get the oil distributed from the sump.

Ken Chapman's recruitment to No. 171 Squadron was carried out without his knowledge. Whilst on leave – having done six ops in seven days – volunteers were called for to form a new squadron, No.171, for special duties in No.100 Group. No one stepped forward – all were nervous about what 'special duties' meant – so that when Chapman and a colleague returned they found that their names had been drawn by lot and they were to transfer.

On arrival at North Creake operations followed quickly. On one occasion they were, 'sent to circle around part of Germany for a few hours dropping WINDOW and jamming the enemy radar' when they ran into instrument failure:

After climbing to height I had cause to put the nose down only to find that the Air Speed Indicator (ASI) wasn't functioning and, as we had to be on station at a certain time (which we couldn't guarantee if we didn't know our true speed) I was forced to do the 'unmentionable' and break radio silence to inform Group of our problem...However they were not too happy and made us continue (with no

ASI) for nearly another hour before giving us permission to return. This time we went to the emergency landing field at Woodbridge, in Suffolk, landing at one hell of a speed so we didn't stall.

The Pitot Head was repaired but hanging around was boring, so next day we decided to fly back to base. However the weather was atrocious and as we taxied out we were told that flying was cancelled. We chose to 'ignore' the control tower and set off for home but were rather shaken when we flew 'past' a church steeple at about 150 ft, and then had a struggle to miss the huge water tower at North Creake.

On another occasion Chapman and his crew were carrying out air-to-sea firing practice over Brancaster Bay and also giving several ground crew a trip when he decided to fly low over the beach. Suddenly the nose of the aircraft was covered with sand and water, 'I never did find out what caused it but I think I had set off an acoustic mine on the beach', he said. There was no damage, only a very pale and shaken airman who had been sitting in the nose!

The unpredictability of life for wartime flyers and the dreadful price some had to pay was emphasised to Ken Chapman a few weeks before the end of the European War, not over enemy territory but at North Creake:

On 17th April 1945, F/L Johnny Butler (the other 'volunteer' who had been transferred with me to No.171 Squadron) and I were the only two on 'ops' that night. When we went out to airtest the aircraft mine wasn't ready so I decided to go up with Johnny. I filled my battledress with buns from the NAAFI wagon and sat in the second pilot's seat. Unfortunately we swung on take off and shot across the airfield and demolished the airmen's toilet. At about this time, 4pm, it would usually be full of groundcrew having a quick smoke but, fortunately, with only two aircraft going on ops they had completed their work and had pushed off early leaving the toilets empty.

We hit two huge trees which stopped us dead. The aircraft, plus 2,000 gallons of high-octane fuel blew up immediately. The other side of the trees was the MT Section and fuel dump so the trees did us some good! Johnny tried to get out of the escape hatch but his 'chute stuck in the opening, I pushed him out and he disappeared. I followed, jumping about 20 ft to the ground. I broke my ankle, had one charred shoe and someone came and carried me away. I had fallen forward as I jumped but Johnny fell back into the flames.

They took us by ambulance to Kings Lynn. Johnny's face was charred black and he kept asking for a gun to shoot himself. At Kings Lynn they took one look at him and said he was too bad for them. He asked me to stay with him and so we went all the way to Ely Hospital, in Cambridgeshire. He did survive. He was one of Sir Archibald McIndoe's longest serving patients at East Grinstead, but he lost his fingers and ears and was in a bad way. The end of the war came while we were both still in hospital.

Dennis Smallwood was to spend 38 years in the RAF, retiring in 1977. He was not to know this, of course, when posted to begin his third tour as a WOP/AG (also assisting the SO in his duties) to No. 171 Squadron on 20th December 1944. Previously an instructor at an OTU, he had served on Wellingtons, in the Middle East and Malta. He flew his first op with No.171 Squadron, an RCM trip to Osnabrück, on the last day of 1944. The duties consisted of providing 'an airborne electrical jamming screen backed up by liberal use of various types of WINDOW which was dropped at varying rates and ranges. The confusion to the enemy was further enhanced by the odd No.100 Group bomber nipping off and bombing a lone target ahead of the Main Stream, then getting back into the jamming screen cover.' There were also one or two occasions when Main Force were grounded due to bad weather and this meant No.100 Group aircraft were 'on their own' over hostile territory when 'one or more losses were taken'.

The winter of 1944-45 was a very long one, 'or so it seemed!':

> ... the cold weather and winds from the North Sea were very penetrating and you never seemed to get really warm. We lived in unlined Nissen huts in small dispersed areas around the airfield and after landing from a sortie you had to get into a very cold and damp bed and try and catch up with some sleep. Sometimes you tried to light the fire in a very small and inadequate stove but usually abandoned the effort because of wet sticks and very wet and poor fuel. It was not unusual to wear one's flying kit and RAF greatcoat over pyjamas. Seaboot stockings were also a great asset to comfort. I remember F/L Geoff Homer (a good name that!), our skipper, bringing in an electric fire which he would place between his knees under the blankets. You should have seen the rising steam! He used to say, 'When the steam turns to smoke wake me in a hurry!'

> The Squadron had a few 'Colonials' and in the Nissen next door we once watched a couple of Canadians trying to de-feather an acquired chicken. After wringing its neck they nailed it to a power-line pole and proceeded to burn off the feathers with lighted newspaper torches. What a mess and smell that created!

> We used to frequent the 'fishermen type pubs' of Wells and usually either walked there or rode in on service issue bicycles. When returning to base pedalling like mad with no lights showing, the local policeman used to shout, 'Where are your lights?' To which came the chorus reply, 'Next to our livers, Goodnight!'

One night German Intruders followed them back to North Creake ('Operation Gisella'):

> Our Flight Commander and his crew were very badly shot up and had to bale

out at low altitude in our circuit. The crew all made a quick exit and, after pointing the aircraft out to sea he baled out himself from under 250 ft. The first swing of the parachute brought him in quick contact with the ground and he lay unconscious for over an hour. The early dawn was breaking when he regained some sensibility and, after feeling himself all over for missing or broken limbs, he looked up and saw a huge angel towering over him, and thought he had made the trip through the 'Golden Gates'. However he later realised he had landed in Overy Staithe Churchyard and the angel was a stone statue over a gravestone! We lost three of our Halifaxes that night and there were many empty chairs in the Mess dining room at breakfast the next day.

Dennis Smallwood celebrated a lively birthday whilst at North Creake :

On 15th March 1945, my birthday, we went on a long-distance trip into Czechoslovakia. On the way back we were suddenly attacked by fighters over Holland and managed to get away with a few holes. Later, as we crossed the Dutch coast next to the island of Texel the very accurate and heavy flak knocked out our port outer engine and also affected the oil pressure of the port inner engine. We were given the choice of trying to make base with two faulty engines and possible other damage or baling out over enemy territory. We opted for trying to make it back to base. We were not allowed to land at North Creake due to a partially blocked runway. We were called to crash land at Woodbridge, in Suffolk, a 'crash' airfield where the runway had a wider expanse of concrete than was usual. We made a landing of sorts but the undercarriage gave way on touch down and we skidded to a halt. A quick evacuation was made and we stumbled over lumps under blankets at the side of the runway. These were the airborne troops ready for the Rhine Crossing which had been postponed. There were a few choice curses around that morning! We then found we were on a security sealed station and were automatically posted as 'missing on ops'. Three days later we were allowed to contact North Creake.

We then set off, unshaven, with all our flying kit and dinghies by train from Woodbridge-Ipswich-Norwich and North Creake via Walsingham our nearest village to the airfield. After an awful journey, we were unable to find a pub or club open, we parked ourselves in the pub in Walsingham and rang the Duty Officer at North Creake with the message, 'If you want us back come and collect us, but not before closing time!'

The period of time spent by No.171 Squadron in No. 100 Group was short but lively. By January 1945, most of the minor problems had been overcome and the Squadron began to produce a more substantial operational effort, this being coupled with a corresponding lower percentage of early returns and engine failures. This was particularly noticeable in February when the number of operational hours and successful sorties were higher than any other heavy squadron within No. 100 Group. Towards the end of the month directions came from Group HQ that 'the only stand downs would be through adverse weather conditions which would render operational flying impossible.'

The following month saw the Squadron's greatest effort when 195 sorties (1200 hours), the biggest ever in No.100 Group, were flown. The final operation took place on 2nd May 1945 when 39 aircraft (18 from No. 171 Squadron) took off from North Creake. The AOC of No. 100 Group, AVM Addison, who was present at take off, expressed his satisfaction at the size of the final effort.

No.199 Squadron.

Rosemary Bower, almost five-years-old and living at Cawston, in wartime Norfolk, looked forward with childish enthusiasm to the visits of her Uncle Len and his friends from his base five miles away at North Creake. One day she became aware that he would not be visiting anymore. Eventually she found out why. On 25th September 1944, No.199 Squadron Short Stirling LJ 518 EX- K, in which Len Barham was flying as a 'spare' member of the crew, returning to North Creake from a MANDREL Screen operation ploughed into tree tops, rose sharply, and then crashed into the ground at Edgefield Street (3 miles NNW of Sculthorpe, Norfolk). All the crew were killed.

Wall painting at North Creake of a No.199 Squadron Short Stirling lost in action, with the entire crew, on 16th/17th June 1944. Painted by F/S Ted Allen and now in the Bomber Command Hall, R A F Museum, Hendon. *(Jim Feasey)*

155

Later, in adulthood, she thought about her uncle and his wartime colleagues. Aware of the 'sacrifice of the future lives of these young men who were not the fearless heroes (as I saw them in childhood) but frightened young boys who were all the braver for continuing with their horrible task,' she wrote a poem conveying her childish confusion. The following is an extract:

> We children at bedtime would say
> 'Such fun with Uncle Len today',
> They were our heroes, brave and strong,
> Until the day would come along, –
> No blue uniform at kitchen door,
> A certain voice is heard no more,
> Adults' tears and adults' sigh,
> Puzzled, we knew not why[106]

Len Barham had a scary first flight with No.199 Squadron. A fellow member of his crew, Phil (Joe) Branson told his niece:

> B-Beer had finished its modification and it was now time to try out its new toys. So off to Defford we went to fly her back to North Creake. On the take-off from Defford (on full power) the aircraft swung out of control, left the runway, went across the grass and headed straight for the Control Tower. Len and I were standing in the cockpit behind Jeff Button, our Australian pilot, watching horrified as the people in the Control Tower jumped for safety. Then Jeff did one of those things of his. He lifted B-Beer into the air, flew a few yards, and then banged her down hard onto the ground, and again pulled her back into the air. In one bound she hopped over the Control Tower in a Kangaroo jump. So Len was truly initiated into the crew from his first take off with us. Needless to say after that Len thought there was no one quite like Jeff.

'We looked to the darkness for our survival'

Vic Polichek a 19 years-old RCAF air gunner finished training in May 1944. Originally slotted for transfer to the Pacific he eventually found himself in the UK, undergoing operational training with an RCAF crew at No. 20 OTU at Lossiemouth flying Wellingtons. Shortly afterwards he was separated from this crew to subsequently hear that they were missing. Further training with an RAF crew followed. After he completed the course he was separated from this crew also, the crew being required for an operational squadron. Here, again, fate interceded, good fortune attended him:

North Creake Control Tower. Now used as living accommodation. *(Author)*

At Lossiemouth I tossed a shilling coin with another gunner to decide who would be a tail gunner or who would be ventral gunner. He won the toss and chose the tail position. The Wellington did not have a ventral turret so I was not required to go with this second crew. Two months later they were shot down whilst carrying out photo-reconnaisance at 1500 ft over the Belgian frontline. After the loss of these two crews I realised I was lucky to be alive.

I re-crewed with a third crew, trained on a Halifax, and was posted to No.199 Squadron at North Creake, this being the former Squadron of our pilot, F/L Chilcott. We arrived at North Creake very late on 23rd February 1945, tired and hungry but a nice steak – most uncommon at the time – got rid of the latter.

After local flights Vic Polichek began operational flights on 8th March, 'we used to fly at 500 ft over the North Sea (to avoid the enemy radar) eventually rising to 20,000 ft above the target.' He completed 18 operations, the last one being on 24th/25th April, his birthday, when the target was Munich, 'I was 19 when I left and 20 when I got back'. On the night of the raid there was a full moon. 'We could see the ground, mountains, shining railway lines, roads and lakes, and, of course, the River Danube. The only problem was that the Germans could also see, us that is! We were very nervous but we got away with it.'

He felt himself lucky not to have been attacked by fighters during the time he flew on operations, or to receive unwanted attention from the flak batteries, although they were 'coned' by searchlights on three occasions. On another occasion the brakes failed on landing, the bomber ran off the runway across a field and finished up nose first in a ditch, 'The tail turret was quite high in the air. I was still in it. I told the others I almost had to use my parachute to exit the aircraft!'

He blessed his excellent eyesight which got him out of trouble on several occasions:

During these operational flights due to my good night vision I was able to avoid at least three mid-air collisions. Sadly many did occur, some chaps fell asleep. It was very hard to stay awake, especially as we were often flying between midnight and 4am. We were supplied with pills to offset this but I never took any.

One of the great sights was to see the hundreds of bombers silhouetted in the sky, mainly on our outward leg with the sunset behind us. This beauty soon disappeared and it was dark. We looked to the darkness for our survival. The planes that one saw earlier were now unseen and once in a while our aircraft would get a buffeting from the slipstream of the bomber ahead of us, or perhaps one could see the exhausts of the other aircraft, or their shadows. All the crew had to keep a watchful eye into the darkness, for a split second could mean the difference between life and death. The air gunners were, of course the main watchers and I feel we did a good job...The turrets were cold and lonely. Electric flying-suits were supplied but sometimes they failed and for this reason I always carried on board my other flying gear as a back up. I used the fighter pilot style parachute pack for I felt if, in an emergency, we got into a spin and I had to bale out my 'chute was on me and not inside the aircraft out of reach. The German night fighters were aware of the bombers' blind spot, ie under the aircraft, so that is where they headed for. Many had upward firing twin 20mm cannons and they were very effective to say the least.

Visitors to the Bomber Command Hall of the RAF Museum at Hendon, cannot fail to notice a mural of a bomber aircraft on the wall. It is a picture, painted by F/Sgt Ted Allen when he was stationed at North Creake, of a No. 199 Squadron Short Stirling LJ 531N. It once adorned a brick wall at the Airfield (believed to be in the Airmens Mess), and was transferred to the Museum in 1984 as a result of the enterprising and energetic endeavours of the Fenland Aircraft Preservation Society and other aviation enthusiasts.

On the 16th/17th June 1944 this aircraft, one of 16 Stirlings plus five B17s of No. 803 USAAF Squadron, was part of a MANDREL Screen covering a raid to Sterkrade. The aircraft was lost without trace and probably crashed into the North Sea. All the crew are commemorated on the Runnymede Memorial and were the first crew of No. 199 Squadron to be lost whilst the Squadron was in No.100 Group.

The AOC of No.100 Group, AVM Addison, at the end of the European War, was fulsome in his praise of North Creake and the efforts of its squadrons. 'North Creake' he said, on the occasion of the disbandment of the North Creake Squadrons on 3rd August 1945, 'and its two Squadrons have been second to none in efficiency and aggressiveness. Their task has been a difficult and complicated one. They have been set many and varied problems often of a most intricate, and always unique, nature. All have been solved.'[107]

No. 214 Squadron fulfilled a number of functions in Bomber Command. At the outbreak of the Second World War it was a Vickers Wellington training unit located at RAF Methwold. In February 1940 it moved to RAF Stradishall and carried out bombing commitments from that station. From March 1942, the Squadron became non-operational for three months whilst it converted to Short Stirling aircraft. In the next eighteen months it had two moves (to Chedburgh and Downham Market) and completed 1380 operational sorties. During this time No. 214 Squadron also provided crews for the two special duty squadrons at Tempsford who dropped agents and supplies to Resistance Movements in Occupied Europe; 55 of these sorties were flown.

In January 1944, on joining No. 100 Group, the Squadron made its fourth wartime move, to RAF Sculthorpe, where it became the first Bomber Command Squadron to work closely with the USAAF, joining No. 803 Squadron for RCM duties. There followed a happy period of cooperation between the two squadrons:

> In truth the Americans had no knowledge of night operations – just as we on 214 had no knowledge of daylight bombing – and they were well heeled, at least compared to the grossly underpaid British types on the station; but on every other count the fears of the pessimists proved unfounded, and somehow I knew the realisation would come quickly the moment I met the Americans. For the most part they were operational types who had completed 20 or more missions, and after very brief exposure to them we recognised their affiliation with us as veteran members of the we've-been-shot-at-brigade...the excellent rapport we established with the Americans within the first few days was maintained thereafter.[108]

A selected number of No. 214 Squadron ground staff were attached to the American Squadron earning unstinting praise from its Commanding Officer.

On 20th/21st April No. 214 Squadron carried out its first RCM sortie, a small-scale effort with five aircraft using AIRBORNE CIGAR (ABC). In the following month No. 214 Squadron moved, with the American Unit, to Oulton. By the end of the month 22 crews had, with great assistance freely given by Captain Paris, the CO of No. 803 Squadron, been converted to Fortress aircraft.

They were ready for D-Day:

> On the night of the Invasion of Europe (5th/6th June 1944), No. 214 Squadron operated with five aircraft captained by W/C McGlinn, S/L Jeffrey, S/L Day, F/L Peden and F/O Lyle. A protective patrol was flown several miles across the Channel in the Boulogne/Folkestone area carrying out jamming in conjunction with No.101 Squadron of No. 1 Group. The patrol was outstandingly successful

Left – No.214 Squadron. S/L Vandenbok, DFC**, OC 'B' Flight, and crew, returning from a raid.

(Herbert Harker)

Below – A Close-up of S/L Vandenbok's crew in front of their Boeing B17. Left to right: Jim Blake, Len Sheel, Al Schafer, S/L Vandenbok, 'Smithy' John Mills, Herbert Harker, Jim Green, and Howard (Navigator).

(Herbert Harker)

No.214 Squadron. The two waist gunners. Sergeants K W J White and F C Langhorn, in front of their Boeing B17, BU-G HB 817 at Oulton. *(Alan Mercer)*

W/O Al Schafer (RCAF), the rear gunner in S/L Vandenbok's crew, in his turret, surrounded by the various aerials needed for the RCM equipment.
(Herbert Harker)

Below: Part of an ABC installation in a Boeing B17. The signal to be jammed was displayed as a blip rising from the base line on the cathode ray tube.
(Crown Copyright)

and earned a personal congratulation to all concerned by the AOC-in-C, Bomber Command, Sir Arthur Harris, in which he pointed out that, 'the work carried out was of paramount importance in connection with the Invasion Forces.'[109]

The following month saw JOSTLE and WINDOW used for the first time by the Squadron. During the months of July and August, 30 MANDREL patrols were also flown but were discontinued by No. 214 Squadron when the commitment passed to other squadrons in No.100 Group.

At this time the Squadron was employed almost every night in support of Bomber Command. On many nights also when no main effort had been undertaken No. 214 Squadron aircraft took part in WINDOW and Spoof patrols. JOSTLE and WINDOW formed the bulk of the Squadron's work and for the ten months preceding the end of hostilities in Europe over a 1000 sorties were completed on 166 nights. When 11 aircraft from No. 214 Squadron took part in in their last trip of the war, a WINDOW patrol on 2nd/3rd May 1945, the total of completed operations as an RCM Squadron was 1390; 13 aircraft had been lost.

'Some achievements stand out pre-eminently for the record of sixteen months solid work as an RCM Squadron' it is recorded, quoting the following examples:

> For example, F/L Wynne brought back a badly damaged aircraft to Bassingbourne after being compelled to bale-out his crew over Germany. On another occasion F/L Peden made a spectacular arrival at Woodbridge [an emergency landing airfield] on 22nd June, 1944, on two good and one partially serviceable engines, swinging violently off the runway due to damaged aircraft, and crashed into a parked Lancaster without injury to any member of the crew. The WOP and SO had been wounded when the aircraft was engaged by a Ju88 over Belgium. The WOP, F/S Stanley, was awarded the DFM for continuing to carry out his duties after being wounded.[110]

Tony Craven, a navigator on No. 214 Squadron found that:

> So far as our Fortresses were concerned these were substantially altered from the specification used by the Americans, to suit 100 Group's special requirements and members of 214 Squadron had previously been involved in the Bomber Development Unit in Newmarket in studying and testing with a view to determining the requirements. The variations were done at the Scottish Aviation Company at Prestwick where they were worked on day and night under great secrecy to be modified for their new role. Mufflers were riveted to the exhaust pipes to screen the bright exhaust flames as these Fortresses were to fly at night, their noses sprouted bulbous blisters to house the H2S scanners and the bomb bays were sealed up to accommodate all the electronic jamming gear. It was also found that the underbelly gun turret was useless at night and this was removed.

Additionally there was No.1699 Flight which was converting crews to B17s (and later also to Liberators) to which we were attached initially for familiarisation and preliminary training until the 13th August. All this included understanding the aircraft, seven daylight and two night cross-country flights, two 'Bullseye' exercises, air firing, fire, dinghy and parachute drills.

Once familiar with the aircraft it was 'on to ops' with the usual hazards. On 9th/10th November 1944, 'We developed a fire in the port outer engine, the propeller eventually flew off ploughing into the navigator's cabin and affecting the port inner engine which also caught fire and the propeller "ran away" so that it couldn't be feathered.' The aircraft became unmanageable and eventually the skipper, F/L Frank Savage, made a forced landing with the two starboard engines in France, at Juvincourt, 'an airfield which had recently been liberated and was something of a wilderness with a fair collection of destroyed and damaged German aircraft around the place.'

There had been no Main Force activity that night but No. 100 Group had carried out a WINDOW 'Spoof', apparently with considerable success. Dr. R V Jones, ADI (Science) gave this appraisal of the results of their effort in a report to Bomber Command HQ a week later:

> Spoof raids alone, providing they are well done, can be useful in keeping the enemy in a state of constant alarm so that he is divided between the policies of having to intercept all raids, in which case he wastes petrol and tires his crews, and of not reacting until he is quite sure that a raid is genuine, in which case he will almost certainly leave some real raids unmolested. A most satisfactory example of the former policy occurred on 9th/10th November 1944 when, despite an earlier German statement that the weather that night would make operations by large force unlikely but that intruder operations would be probable, the controllers were first deceived into treating a spoof raid on Mannheim as a major raid, and then when they had unravelled this deception, they deceived themselves by concluding that it was indeed the prelude to a major raid. As a result, aircraft of six Gruppen were airborne for two and a half hours.[111]

AVM Addison sent a congratulatory message to Oulton:

> A.1103 10th Nov. Personal from AOC. The results of last night's spoof operation were most gratifying. Our aim was amply achieved in that the enemy was induced to react in a very big way indeed first in the threatened area until he eventually became aware he was being spoofed after the 'Windowers' had returned, and then in the Ruhr area when he believed a real raid was to follow the spoof. I know how difficult were the conditions last night, and how these were aggravated by last minute changes in the programme. The latter however were made to take advantage of the best possible weather conditions on a bad night, as revealed by the stop press weather reports. I congratulate all crews who

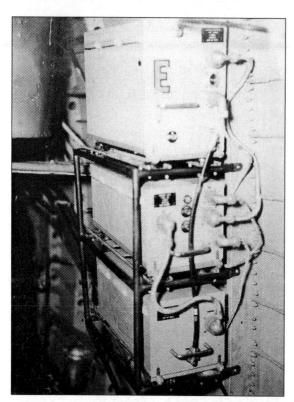

MANDREL equipment in aircraft.
(Crown Copyright)

The T1524 transmitter associated with JOSTLE IV mounted in the bomb bay of a Boeing B17.
(Crown Copyright)

took part in this difficult operation. Their determination enabled the Group to score a very distinct success. Well done.[112]

Tony Craven on a daylight raid on Bottrop which 'was memorable for us night flyers as unusually we could see all the aircraft and the target!' He also felt the effects of a 'corkscrew' to avoid a nightfighter when:

...sudden and dramatic changes of height and pressure followed by steep banking and regaining height brought on me a violent dose of sinus pain and for the rest of the trip I was rolling around in the bottom of the aircraft in agony because I couldn't equalise the pressure...I went to Ely Hospital for treatment.

The airfield was one's home and away from it one felt curiously naked; it was a safe haven to return to and to remain in – a sort of womb. There was much boozing and partying but, in spite of all that, the job was taken seriously...The best crews who always attended to total detail, always had a better chance of survival than those who were more lax, but the odds were still stacked high against everyone.

Neil Scott joined No. 214 Squadron as a pilot in September 1944, 'by which time the worst, had we but known it, was over.' He, nevertheless, in a short but hectic time completed 32 'ops', about a third on Main Force targets (circling for five to 15 minutes each time), the remainder being WINDOW patrols. His last 'op' was on December 18th 1944:

Apart from being severely damaged by American flak, in their nervous reaction to the Ardennes offensive, we escaped without undue mishap until our fuel ran out on the final approach returning from a trip to Most/Brüx in Czechoslovakia with 5 Group. We 'fell out of the air' in my Engineer's words and burned up. My SO was killed and others in the crew damaged in several ways. By the time I got out of hospital and recovered my operational category the war in Europe was over.

Alan Mercer, a navigator recollected that the interior of the Fortress:

... was a spacious compartment used by the WOP and SO together with their radar receivers and transmitters. The internal bomb bays were an ideal shape and size for the pillar-box sized transmitters we carried for jamming purposes. The Rear Gunner had a very tight squeeze with only a saddle type seat to sit on for the total time we were airborne. Further forward the Mid-Upper Gunner had a reasonable position, and of course the Pilot and Flight Engineer enjoyed armchair comfort. The Bomb-Aimer and myself had our little office in the nose, a chart table three feet by two feet, with the Gee set to the left, Air position indicator (a Heath Robinson box of gears and cogs, but it worked), the H2S (radar picture of the ground, fine but the Germans could home onto it) on the right hand side of the table. The Bomb-Aimer worked on some radar gear when we reached the target so we had no need to look out. Our windows were curtained and we declined the pilot's suggestion to look out as we were too cosy to bother about the war outside!

The Bomb-Aimer and I had to stand behind the Pilot and Flight Engineer for take offs and landings. One night when we were returning from an 'op' I saw the red exhaust flames of a plane crossing in front of us from left to right, slightly above us and about 20 ft away. 'Not one of ours!' shouted our skipper sticking the nose down to touch the runway quicker. The only time I had seen the enemy and only two seconds separated us from being in his gunsight.

Bert Mowlem, also a navigator, transferred to No. 214 Squadron a month before the end of the European War:

We used the Fortress because JOSTLE, used for jamming enemy R/T transmissions, would not fit into a Lancaster or Halifax which had horizontal bomb bays whereas the Fortress bomb bay was vertical (it was contained in a huge cylinder mounted upright). We also used CARPET, and PIPERACK to jam the AA guns radar. The crew of a 214 Fortress consisted of ten men. A mid-upper gunner (MUG), a rear gunner, two side gunners (who also threw out WINDOW when instructed), two wireless operators (WOP), one who dealt with the jamming equipment, a bomb-aimer (who dealt with PIPERACK and, I think, CARPET), a flight engineer, plus the pilot and navigator. In the perspex nose enclosure at the front was the bomb-aimer. I was next to him in a sealed box as I had to have a small light to see the charts etc. The pilot and flight engineer were just behind us. Above them and a little to the rear was the MUG. Then came the vertical bomb bay with JOSTLE in it. Behind the bomb bay sat the the two WOPs, one on either side. Behind them, with stacks of WINDOW were the two side-gunners, with 'tail-end Charlie' (the rear-gunner) at the end.

Ken Phelan, was a Fortress side-gunner on the Squadron:

As a crew I suppose we did about 27 operational flights, most of them very similar. In the Briefing Room the wall map of Europe would show our target and route. We would then receive the relevant information regarding the weather and danger points to be by-passed if possible. We were given packets of money and maps covering the area we were to fly over and given a packet of emergency rations. A meal of bacon and eggs was also laid on and a packet of boiled sweets, chewing gum and a flask of coffee. Half an hour before take-off time we would draw our parachutes and be transported out to our dispersal areas. Flying Control would then send us on our way.

His last operation on 7th/8th March 1945 emphasised for him the confusion and brutality of war:

During World War Two, if attacked by fighters, day bombers closed formation and ensured a concentration of fire power for their protection. Not so the night bombers – they depended entirely on their own action. That being the case, the pilot depended on his gunners.

On our last operational flight – I think it was in the Frankfurt area – suddenly, over the intercom:

Mid-upper Gunner to Skipper, 'Enemy fighter on the starboard beam. I'm losing him. Can you see him, starboard waist-gunner?'

'Starboard waist here. I've got him Skipper – starboard quarter down, flying on a parallel course, about 4,000 ft away. He's turning in, Skipper. Prepare for evasive action. He's at 3,000 ft . Corkscrew starboard go!'

I gave him a long burst of machine-gun fire. The tracer bullets seemed to be going right through him. Then he lost interest and dived away. 'Attack broken, Skipper, resume course.' No smoke or debris, so we could not claim him.

Harry, the rear-gunner, came on the intercom, 'Lancaster dead astern. My God, He's firing at us!'

There was a noise like the sound of pebbles on a tin roof as the .303 bullets tore through the fuselage. One grazed my ankle. The port wing burst into flames. We veered to starboard and started to dive out of control. Gravity forced me to the roof, but somehow I got to the rear escape hatch. Jacky, the WOP, and Jimmy, the port waist-gunner, were already there, trying to release the door. P/O Peters, our SO, struggled up. He saw the position and went on to try the rear gunner's escape hatch. We never saw him again.

The three of us pushed again. Suddenly we were floating in space. I was pulled in and smashed against the tail plane. My left leg and jaw were broken and my shoulder dislocated. I am sure my Guardian Angel pulled my ripcord. Then there was a blank – nothing more until I came to in a field surrounded by jackboots and uniforms. Harry, the rear gunner, was quite near me. He was calling for help. He screamed out 'No! No!' Then there was silence. I will say no more.

Eventually we were taken away for interrogation. Under the Geneva Convention we only had to give our name, number and rank. I was badly wounded so they left me alone, but apparently the four crew members who remained had a very tough time. In the end the Germans told them who they were, what they were doing and where we came from. They knew everything about 100 Group.

Out of a crew of ten, only five of us remained. We were sure the Skipper, Navigator and Bomb-Aimer survived the crash. They were never seen again. I remembered little of the interrogation. They placed me on a stretcher and passed me from unit to unit. I eventually arrived at Stalag XB Sansbostal. This prison was no ordinary Stalag. POW were only a small minority. They were mostly political prisoners. We saw them being marched in and heard gunfire, but never realised what was taking place.

On May 1st 1945, after a short sharp engagement, the Grenadier Guards came to our rescue. I will always remember an officer coming along and saying, 'Right, lads. You can go home now.' I went back to the UK and spent three months in hospital at RAF Cosford. Jimmy and Jacky came to see me and verified my version of what happened.

Alex McLelland, trained as an RAAF bomb aimer, became a SO with No. 214 Squadron. Recruitment to the job was for him, like so many of his colleagues, a leap in the dark:

The Special Operators were all trained aircrew who were awaiting postings to OTUs. Anyone who had a knowledge of the German Language was asked to volunteer for undisclosed duties. As our waiting period was likely to be rather long we felt that even the unknown was better than waiting. After a short time I was posted to No. 1657 HCU at Stradishall, in Suffolk, where we had to learn the Luftwaffe 'patter' between their Ground Control and nightfighters, plus other flying duties. We were sworn to secrecy about the work particularly if we landed at a base other than our own. It led to a certain amount of isolation from our own crews and other crews especially when on leave when we could not enter into the comradely chatter that took place about respective experiences.

After Stradishall I was posted to 214 Squadron at Oulton. Initially we had to familiarise ourselves with members of the crew, performance of the aircraft, the operation and purpose of the strange equipment, plus all the other flying duties related to operational sorties. About 40% of our sorties accompanied the bomber stream with our RCM equipment, another 40% was taken up spreading WINDOW on spoof raids. The rest of our time we spent on Big Ben patrols off the coasts of Belgium, Holland and Germany in the fruitless occupation of trying to locate V2 rockets and jam them.

Our instruction on RCM equipment contained very little technical content being devoted mainly to teaching us which knobs to twiddle and which buttons to press, and when. The purposes behind their use was very inadequately explained. This led to a considerable degree of frustration about the importance of our work. We were, however, pretty well informed on how to destroy the various pieces of equipment in the event of possible capture.

Gerhard Heilig, son of a Czechoslovakian citizen forced to leave his homeland by Hitler, also remembered his introduction to RCM work which was brought about by an earnest desire for a change of RAF location. Posted to No. 4 Radio School at Madley, near Hereford, he found that 'the physical conditions at the camp were no picnic. We had to walk a mile from our sleeping site fully equipped for the day's work

Paper tape device used for BAGFUL.   *(Crown Copyright)*

before we could wash and shave at the messing site.' There followed 'interminable marches' all over the camp for various functions. 'We were not a happy band,' he recalled, 'and when the Flight Sergeant announced one morning that anyone with a knowledge of German was to put down his name in the Flight Office, several of us fell out with glee at the vague chance of escape from this depressing life'. Eventually, after several months of this unhappy existence things began to move. Heilig wondered about the spurt in activity at the nearby airfield. Then he had a brainwave, 'Do any of you speak German?' he asked, they all could. No one said a word but by the expressions...all had the same vision of little figures dangling on the end of parachutes on sinister and dangerous missions behind enemy lines!' A quick conclusion to the course was engineered with tests being speedily passed. The reason soon became apparent. They were wanted on a squadron. In 48 hours Gerhard Heilig was qualified, and was posted to No. 214 Squadron at Sculthorpe:

> Johnny and I arrived very late one night at Fakenham station, wondering what we had let ourselves in for...here we were, surrounded by our kit on a deserted platform. However, a 'phone call to Sculthorpe soon had us bouncing along deserted lanes in transit to our new home. We were bursting with curiosity, but all we could get out of our driver was: 'It's all very secret, you'll have to find out for yourselves.' He would not even tell us the type of aircraft the squadron was equipped with in case we turned out to be German spies in disguise.
>
> Our quarters were in a hut accommodating about two dozen NCO aircrew in one long undivided space. To reach the two vacant beds at the far end, we had to run the gauntlet of our new companions who eyed us with undisguised curiosity. We had heard tales of scruffy, devil-may-care aircrew, but what we saw here out of the corners of our timid eyes were immaculate uniforms of Warrant Officers,

VE night at Oulton. *(Bill Bridgman)*

Flight Sergeants and the odd Sergeant, nearly all sporting the 1939-43 Star and some even the DFM. We felt very small indeed.

'Just posted in?' said a voice.

'Yes.'

'Where have you come from?'

'Radio School.'

'Been instructing?'

'No, just passed out.'

There was a deathly silence.

'How many hours have you got?'

'Ten and a half,' said Johnny. 'Eleven,' said I.

Another deathly silence. We felt like crawling away into a hole.

'Ah well, never mind. You'll soon get into the swim of it. Better kip down for the night and we'll show you around in the morning.'

No time was wasted in getting trained on our equipment. It consisted of a control unit with a cathode ray tube scanning the German fighter frequency band. Any transmissions would show up as blips on the screen. We would then tune our receiver to the transmission by moving a strobe spot onto it, identify the transmission as genuine (this was where our knowledge of the language came in as the Germans were expected to come up with 'phoney' instructions in order to divert our jammers), then tune our transmitter to the frequency and blast off with a cacophony of sound which in retrospect would put today's pop music to utter shame.

The transmitters were standard T1154 mf/hf transmitters modified to operate on 38-42.5 Mc/s. Later on, specially designed equipment was to be used...As there were not enough SOs to go round, we were allocated to whoever happened to be flying until our establishment would be complete and allow permanent crewing up. Training went on apace and we felt it could not be long now before we became fully operational.

Gerhard Heilig was right. A month after being posted to No. 214 Squadron he was preparing to go on leave with a friend when, 'We were told that we had been selected along with two others to take part in the Squadron's first operational flight in its new role before going on leave the next day as planned.' The date was 20th/21st April 1944, and the target was the railway marshalling yard at La Chapelle, which was just to the north of Paris:

> We did not know at the time but strikes against focal points of transport were part of the prelude to the Normandy landings. I had celebrated my 19th birthday on the day before and today was another birthday, Hitler's. I thought it rather appropriate that I should have the opportunity to start settling a personal account with That Man!

That sortie proved uneventful, but Heillig completed another nine operations before being posted to No.101 Squadron (qv) who were very short of SOs due to heavy casualties sustained in their ABC role.

No.223 Squadron

No. 223 Squadron was originally formed in Italy in the First World War as a Royal Navy Squadron. After service in Italy and France at the end of that war it was disbanded, being reformed in 1928 in Kenya. In the Second World War the squadron fought through various campaigns from Abyssinia to France until it was again disbanded in July 1944. A month later, in August, the Squadron was again reformed and placed in No.100 Group for RCM duties at Oulton (where it shared the airfield with No. 214 Squadron). Equipped with 16 Liberators, most of the aircrew transferred from Coastal Command OTUs. Among the captains were several very experienced pilots who had already completed long tours on Coastal Command operations.

The Liberator crews, ten in each, were augmented by two SOs for each crew, making twelve in all. Early September saw the Squadron up to full strength with training started. The CO was W/C D J McGlinn DFC, (who handed over on 23rd September to W/C H H Burnell, AFC). Five aircraft were used and assistance in the training was given by two USAAF pilots. Extensive modifications were also made to the Liberators being used by the Squadron. The crew of each was reduced by one as

F/O Merv Utas, (RCAF), by the nose of his No.223 Squadron Consolidated B24 Liberator at Oulton. He remembered, 'We were not permitted to take photographs which included an antenna, as the purpose and frequency of the equipment could be ascertained from the size and shape of the antenna.'

(Merv Utas)

No.223 Squadron. An 'end-of-tour' photo of F/L Stephenson's crew. He is in the centre. The other crew members are, left to right: Glyn Williams, E G Longden, Hugh Williams, Reg Collins, Allen Tonkin, and Paddy O'Brennan.

(E G Longden)

the front gunner was found to be unnecessary. A large floor space in the rear bomb bay was used for storing WINDOW, the whole of the navigator's position was enlarged and improved.

Initial duties for the crews consisted of 'Big Ben' patrol duty, where unsuccessful attempts were made at jamming the V2 rockets being projected from the enemy-occupied coast of Europe. These sorties, mostly of a four hour duration at 20,000 ft, served as a useful start for the crews in their RCM work. Additional jamming equipment was added. In October the sorties against the V2s ceased and the Squadron was carrying out its main functions of WINDOW (first used by the Squadron on 15th October) and JOSTLE RCM. The following month nearly all the Squadron aircraft had DINA and CARPET RCM installed additionally. As November changed to December, No. 223 Squadron operated on eight consecutive nights and, amongst its duties was the first 'target patrol' carried out by F/L Haslie on Karlsruhe. January 1945 saw very poor flying weather but the following month the Squadron worked extremely hard flying on seventeen nights in the month, completing 115 sorties out of a projected 121. In April the Squadron converted to Fortresses and the first operation in this aircraft was carried out on April 19th by F/L Bremness. Two weeks later the Squadron carried out its last operation, a WINDOW Spoof by 4 Fortresses and 5 Liberators on Kiel.

September 19th, 1944 to May 2nd 1945.
Operational hours: 3,513
Sorties: 665
Aircraft Lost: 3
Aircrew (missing) 29

Sergeant Leonard Vowler, a Devon farmer's son from Bickleigh, near Tiverton, a keen, ex-ATC cadet, was so keen on joining the RAF towards the end of 1942 he never told his family he was enlisting fearing he would be kept at home for essential farm work. To keep up the subterfuge he made a point of intercepting the postman when he was making his deliveries to the farm to prevent his father seeing any Air Ministry letters. Eventually, with only his older brother party to the deception, he 'ran away' to join the RAF. Initially undergoing training as a pilot he remustered as an air gunner in June, 1944. On completion of training he was posted, with 28 other gunners, from No. 10 Air Gunnery School at Walney Island, Barrow-in-Furness, to operational duty with No. 223 Squadron arriving at Oulton at the beginning of September. Seven months later he made his last trip.

At 2235 on 20th March 1945, the crew of Liberator 'T' Tommy, TS526[113], with Leonard Vowler as one of its gunners, tasked with a WINDOW operation in support

173

of the Main Force attacks on Bohlen and Hemmingstedt, took off from Oulton. Over Germany the aircraft was shot down and there was only one survivor. Leonard Vowler's nephew, R E Vowler, has since pieced together what happened:

No radio transmissions were heard from the aircraft and there is not much information about what happened although I believe the German nightfighters were very active in the area that night. The plane was shot down at about 0300 hours. There was no warning and it was just shot out of the sky. It was believed to have been attacked from below as this was a popular method of attack employed by Luftwaffe fighters at this time.[114] The plane went down in flames and some of the crew were seen to bale out, including my uncle. The plane was on fire so presumably their parachutes also caught fire. Most of the crew were found dead in, or near, the aircraft which had come down in a heavily wooded area near Wolfhagen. The only survivor was W/O Cole who was in the rear of the aircraft which was split from the front. The JOSTLE equipment fell on top of him and he was seriously injured. He was rescued from the aircraft by locals and given treatment. My uncle's crew had been dropping WINDOW on Kassel as part of the Bohlen raid that night.

S/L Mervyn Utas, an RCAF pilot, completed 37 ops in No.223 Squadron between September 1944, and May 1945. 'Most of the crews were Coastal Command trained and came from No. 111 OTU in Nassau, in the Bahamas. Coastal Command was the only source of B24 trained flight crews and we had spent months learning about Coastal Command flight operations, depth charges, ship recognition and reading Aldiss lamps,' he recalled. Two months after arriving in England they were in Bomber Command. The move brought changes:

The move required some retraining as our navigators were trained to use dead reckoning (DR) and three drift winds, whilst the pilots had probably never had a B24 above 3,000 ft or used the oxygen equipment. The navigators were given some intensive Gee training and then we did three night cross countries around England above 20,000 ft to learn how to use the oxygen system and how the heated suits, socks or gloves could short out and leave you cold and miserable for hours. We also learned that the flare dampers on the exhaust system had a habit of burning out and if happened over enemy territory you had no choice but to shut down the engine and pray that a second flame damper or engine would not fail.

One of Merv Utas' early 'ops', on a V2 'spotting' patrol, indicated clearly to him that he was not facing an inactive foe:

The Squadron's first operations were single aircraft patrols along the north coast of Holland attempting to detect and jam radio signals when we observed a V2 launch from Holland. The Squadron had been engaged in this task for two to three weeks with no reaction from the German defences. However the German defences had not been entirely idle as we were to find out. On our third operation, a daylight V2 patrol, we were just approaching The Hague and had turned northeast when, to put it mildly, all hell broke loose. There were anti-aircraft burst ahead, behind, above and below and on both sides! I assume that for the period that we were doing these patrols the Germans had been following our track and altitude and were able to line up their guns quite accurately. Since we were just off the coast we dived away out over the North Sea and were quickly out of range. We had a few holes in the aircraft. One piece of shrapnel had penetrated the nose section, struck a main frame and broke into small pieces some of which struck our navigator in the lower back. Luckily it did not damage his spine or any nerves. However he did have to spend several months in hospital as they took the pieces of metal out a few at a time with a healing period between each extraction.

There were two major tasks that the Squadron performed in support of Bomber Command, 'You could be part of a Special WINDOW Force, or "spoof raid" as we called it, or do the radio and radar jamming over the target during a Main Force raid'. He described the Squadron's role in detail:

There were a large variety of tactics that could be applied with the Special WINDOW Force. We would sometimes accompany the Main Force and, after penetrating the MANDREL Screen, the Main Force would head for one target while our Spoof Force would start dispensing WINDOW and head for a different target. Other times we would go in before, or after, the Main Force. Sometimes the Main Force would split in two and attack two different targets while our Spoof Force made a feint at a third target. The object was to keep the German nightfighters in the air and spread their strength over several areas. Occasionally, about the time that the nightfighters were landing, a second or third force would appear through the MANDREL Screen and they would again have to get airborne.

Sometimes our Spoof Force would do a double penetration if the Main Force was not operating. After clearing the MANDREL Screen we would start our WINDOW drop and head for a target, drop token markers and bombs and then head back into France behind the MANDREL Screen. We would then descend to a low altitude, orbit for 30 to 45 minutes, then climb back up again and head back into Germany for a second 'Spoof'. The crews always felt we should credit for two ops for these raids but HQ was pretty dogmatic and insisted that 1 take off + 1 landing = 1 operation. Sometimes if the weather forecast for England was extensive fog we would move our aircraft over to Foulsham where we could use FIDO (Fog Investigation Dispersal Operation). At first on these 'Spoof' raids there was only the WINDOW aircraft but late on, to add more realism, we were accompanied by aircraft with a few target indicators and bombs.

At our debriefings the intelligence officers were often pleased when reports indicated that 60 to 70 nightfighters had been directed towards our Spoof raid. The crews did not share in this pleasure as the thought of 70 nightfighters looking for 15 or 16 'Spoof' aircraft was not too appealing. Our only consolation was that with all of our jamming equipment operating we felt that the fighter pilots would only be able to make a 'visual' contact with our aircraft.

The other task, supporting the Main Force with jamming over the target, was quite a visual experience. We would commence orbit and jamming over the target about two minutes before the target indicators went down. This was a tense two minutes and more often felt like twenty minutes. You might question the navigator as to whether he was lost and so far from the target city that we could not see the action, or question whether the WOP had missed the 'recall' signal and we were now the only Allied aircraft over Germany! Then the target indicators would go down, the searchlights and anti-aircraft fire would start up and there would be a sense of relief, even though you were being shot at, that you were not alone after all.

We had been instructed to do our orbit one thousand feet above the bombing altitude. On our first target bombing operation the bombing altitude was 21,000 ft so we were at 22,000 ft. Fortunately it was a clear night because about halfway through our second orbit we found ourselves right in the middle of the Main Force bomber stream but going in the opposite direction. We quickly climbed another 1,500 ft. We found out later that the bomber pilots generally add 500 ft to 1,000 ft to the specified bombing altitude to ensure that there was no one above who could drop bombs on their aircraft. This was, of course, a legitimate concern because my brother, who was in No. 6 Group, had an incendiary bomb go through the wing of his aircraft while over the a target. Fortunately for them it did not ignite. Thereafter we added two to three thousand feet to bombing altitude for our orbits.

We would remain over the target until the last bomber had gone through, usually 15 to 20 minutes. Sometimes on larger raids two aircraft would split the jamming duties and the first shift was always preferable. The Halifaxes and Lancasters were always much faster than the B24 Liberator and when they dropped their bombs their lower weight made the speed differential even greater. The only weight that the Liberator lost was the fuel consumed. You were the last aircraft to leave the target area and with your much lower airspeed you really fell behind the bomber stream as they headed home. Again the saving grace was our jamming equipment which meant that a nightfighter needed visual contact in order to make an attack.

As I mentioned earlier, target jamming was quite a visual experience. On a clear night you could see the target indicators glowing, the bombs exploding on the ground, the anti-aircraft shells exploding in the air and the searchlights weaving around looking for a target. Sometimes you would see a bomber 'coned' by the searchlights. On a cloudy night the visual aspect was a bit different. Through the clouds you could still see the glow of the target indicators and the glow of the bursting bombs. You could also see the anti-aircraft shells bursting above the clouds. However, the searchlights were not moving but fixed and illuminating the clouds from below. From above it looked like a giant white screen and as we were above the bomber stream we could see each of the bombers as a perfect silhouette as they flew across the target. We also realised that we would be just as obvious to any enemy aircraft above us. However the nightfighters generally stayed away from the target because of the intensity of the flak. Often as we left the target for the lonely trip home, our route would be clearly marked by a row of fighter flares dropped by German fighters to indicate where the bomber stream was.

In 1945 we had become quite complacent as it appeared that the war would soon end, so when we got over England after a raid we had started to turn on our navigation lights to lessen the chances of a mid-air collision. In early March we had returned from an operation and were in the landing stack at Oulton. We had just been cleared to join the landing circuit at 1,000 ft when we saw tracers from cannon fire flash by in front of our nose. Then the vague outline of a twin engined aircraft passed by us. A few seconds later there was more tracer fire visible on the other side of the airfield and then an explosion as one of our bombers blew up. We dived down to about 200 ft from the ground so nobody could get below and behind us, and headed west. After about ten minutes we saw an airfield lit up and just as we headed for it we saw more cannon fire and another aeroplane blow up in the air so we continued west. If we had had sufficient fuel remaining we might have finished up in Canada, but we did spend the night in St. David's, in Wales (Pembrokeshire). It seems our coastal defences had become as complacent as we aircrew and had not noticed that several German nightfighters had joined the bomber stream returning to England.

Great arguments took place as to whether it was colder, in the bitter Winter of 1944/45 to live in Blickling Hall or a Nissen Hut:

I think the Nissen Huts, in which I was billeted, won because of our washroom arrangements. Our washroom was a roofed area with no walls. There was a row of washbasins with no protection from the elements except from the roof. The showers had partial partitions on three sides and generally cold water only. We certainly did not threaten the Guiness Book of World Records with the number of showers we took that winter!

Supplementing the coal ration for his Nissen Hut proved a problem, for Merv Utas. 'If you were not raiding Germany you were obligated to raid the coal compound which meant scaling a high brick wall topped with barbed wire.' This required a two-man operation to get in and out of the compound and, 'the taller you were the better. At 6 ft 2 in I was a prime candidate. We loaded the coal into a sack and tossed it over the wall. When we got out of the compound the problem was finding the sack in the blackout!'

H C 'Bill' Sykes became a starboard beam gunner on No. 223 Squadron and flew on 36 operations. He was less than enthusiastic about how he arrived there:

We were all originally graded PNB (Pilot/Navigator/Bomb Aimer) and had completed our initial training, including 12 hours pilot instruction in Tiger Moths, and were awaiting grading and posting for further flying training as one of those categories. However, much to our disgust, we were sent to London and given some rather specious 'aptitude tests' which decided that, after all, 99% of us were better suited to be air gunners.

Not surprisingly, moving the goalposts like this generated a good deal of disenchantment with the RAF. There was no appeal, and we were warned that non-acceptance would mean remustering to the army!

The reason for the con trick was that they needed to form No. 223 Squadron quickly to fly Liberators on the 'Big Ben' sorties. We were therefore sent on a mere six week gunnery course on .303 Brownings and, without any operational training, were posted to the squadron at Oulton to 'top up' some Hudson crews which were brought back from the Bahamas.

The Liberators were from the USAAF and were very much second-hand. They were still in their original silver livery when we got them and carried drawings of large numbers of bombs on their noses giving testimony to their heavy use by the Americans. These 'bombs' were still visible after the aircraft had been sprayed with RAF camouflage!

The American idea of maintenance was to rip out any dud part (such as a faulty engine) and replace it with new, whereas RAF ground crews were accustomed to the concept of repair. As a result, we were likely to arrive at dispersal to find bits of the aircraft scattered around with the ground crew still working on it. The prospect of actually taking off was therefore frequently very chancy. In fact, we calculated that we had as many aborted 'ops' as we actually completed, either by not getting off at all or having to return with snags. Another problem we encountered was the fact that the aircraft were equipped with .5 Brownings which had only been featured on our course on the last day when the instructor held one up and said, 'You won't see one of these because they are only being used by the Americans.'

Matters were not helped when our armourers hacksawed off the American metal ring and bead sights and screwed on the much more effective British reflector sights which could also range the attacking aircraft. The trouble was that no-one knew how to harmonise the guns to ensure they were pointed in the same direction as the sights! With the .303 Browning you slide off the back of the breech and look down the barrel on to a spot on the harmonisation board, and then adjust until it points to the cross on the board. With the .5, however, you cannot slide off the back of the breech.

As a consequence, when we went on an air firing exercise and opened fire on a drogue towed by a Martinet the drogue emerged unscathed. Fortuitously, perhaps, the towing aircraft did too! Our credibility with the rest of the crew was pretty low after that, especially after our oft-repeated assertion that we were really elite gunners because we should have been pilots! Eventually, the problem was solved when we invited an American gunner over from a nearby air base to show us how. He produced a dummy round with a mirror in it which enabled us to look down the barrel and line it up with the sight.[115]

'A Pretty Lethal Scenario'

A stark example of what could happen with faulty maintenance occurred to Bill Sykes' crew on 6th December 1944, in Liberator 'M' for Mother. 'Just after take off I noticed that it seemed to be raining outside the starboard window, which seemed odd because the port side was bathed in sunshine!' Sykes looked out and was horrified to see aviation spirit pouring out of the filler cap on top of the starboard wing. An application to return to base was refused as other aircraft were still taking off, 'so we watched helplessly while the fuel gushed out only inches above red hot exhaust fumes. I was particularly concerned because I realised that as the engines were throttled back on landing sparks invariably flew back under the wing- a pretty lethal scenario!' However, blessed with good fortune the aircraft returned to base and landed safely, whereupon the crew, 'legged it away from the plane.' The aircraft had lost 200 gallons of fuel to due the filler cap being replaced upside down after a refuelling.

On 29th January 1945, returning in a snowstorm from a bomber support operation on Stuttgart, his crew was diverted to Great Massingham as Oulton was snowbound. When the snow had been cleared from the runway at Great Massingham only a path had been made in the centre with the snow piled high on either side within the runway lights, 'Our skipper landed slightly to the left of centre, but inside the lights, and hit the piled snow. This caused the nose wheel to collapse and slewed us on to the airfield.' Covered in mud, but unhurt, the crew were picked up by an ambulance and 'were first in for debriefing and our post-flight meal!

Len Vowler (qv) had originally been a member of Bill Sykes' crew:

> After a few operations it was decided that we did not need a nose gunner because night time attacks from the front were unlikely and the 'closing' speed would be too fast to get in a shot in any case. We 'new' gunners therefore drew lots to see who should go and Len Vowler, who was in fact our front gunner, lost and was posted to another crew. Sadly, Len's new crew did not return shortly afterwards and I only learned a couple of years ago that he had died when I saw his name in the Book of Remembrance in Ely Cathedral.

They sometimes took 'unofficial' steps to keep their off-duty transport running:

> Aircrew were entitled to leave every six weeks instead of the usual three months. Unfortunately, the petrol ration allocated to run the Standard Eight which belonged to Johnny Richards, our rear-runner, was geared to less frequent trips so we regularly 'milked' the airfield tractors. However, when this was eventually thwarted by a switch to diesel we resorted to milking aircraft which were in the hangars for major servicing (a convenient tap in the bomb bay made the task relatively simple.) On the advice of Bill Weir, our flight engineer, the 100 Octane fuel was modified by the addition of a measure of hydraulic fluid. The two gallon petrol cans we used just fitted inside a large pack and thus enable us to pass inconspicuously past the guardroom. We were only challenged once, when Lew Lucas, our WOP, and I had been delegated for the task. 'Wotcha got in the pack, Flight Sergeant?' queried the RAF police corporal on the gate. 'Two gallons of petrol,' replied Lew, with feigned heavy sarcasm. The corporal laughed and so did we – with considerable relief. We knew, however, that in future we would either have to seek a new route or 'go straight'! Engineer friends in later years have told me that our 'additive' was useless for the purpose intended but all I can say is that it worked.

Ted Longden was a rarity in Bomber Command a Wireless Operator Mechanic/Air Gunner. He later became a pilot. 'In the main our RCM was focused on the German Air Force fighter control R/T. They were dicey operations!' Also 'Spoof' raids which, apart from bomber support, were sometimes used in connection with land-based operations such as the combined ground and airborne attack on Arnhem. One of their more hectic operations has, with the passage of time, become more humorous:

> Our beam gunner, Allen Tomkin, a ballet dancer before joining the RAF, called on the intercom that he had never had such an exciting experience and could we go round and do it again? This absurd request was followed by us being 'coned' and taking violent evasive action within a stream of unlit aircraft and being accompanied by anti-aircraft shells exploding too near for comfort. The several responses he got from the rest of the crew I dare not put into print! However, at this time the beam gunners were open to the elements at 20,000 ft and he must have felt really in the midst of the battle and smelt the cordite.

No.462 Squadron

No. 462 Squadron was formed as a Halifax Mk.III squadron (with a majority of RAAF personnel) at Driffield, Yorkshire on 12th August 1944. It operated as a normal heavy bombing squadron in No. 4 Group until 29th December 1944 when it transferred to No. 100 Group, being based at Foulsham. The move was not greeted with enthusiasm. The fact that the Squadron arrived in the midst of poor flying weather in their first month in the Group did little to improve morale. The last three weeks of January were particularly poor. The following extract from the No. 462 Squadron ORB indicates the difficulties:

8.1.45. The weather and serviceability condition were against a larger flying programme.

9.1.45. Snow cancelled all possibility of operations, and all the afternoon Squadron personnel assisted in clearing the main runway of snow. A night programme of Fighter Affiliation was cancelled due to weather conditions.

10.1.45. All members of the Squadron commenced clearing snow from the runways at 0915 and at midday more snow was falling. Runway was serviceable by late afternoon but a slight thaw prevented any possibility of night training which had been arranged with our affiliated Squadron (No.157) at Swannington. No operations were required from the Squadron.

11.1.45. Another day of very poor weather. In late afternoon, a few aircraft became airborne on air tests and local flying. Apart from this, no other flying was carried out.

12.1.45. Twelve crews were detailed to take off in late afternoon for a WINDOW patrol east of the Ruhr area, but this operation was cancelled due to weather conditions. The same crews were briefed At 2315 hrs for the same patrol, but at the last moment, the operation was cancelled.

13.1.45. Thirteen crews were prepared for briefing at 1700 hrs but the Squadron was informed that the detail was cancelled owing to weather conditions.[116]

High winds and sleet added to the problems of ice and snow. Some sorties were flown during the rest of the month, but many were cancelled because of the weather. On 27th January 'there was an improvement in the weather conditions, but the runways were in need of a snow clearance.' Ten crews were detailed for 'ops' and two others were employed on clearing the snow during the day. A further heavy fall of snow in the evening caused the 'ops' to be cancelled. By the end of the month, 'runways and perimeter tracks were still covered with snow.'

During the month the Squadron tried to mount operations. On the first day of the

New Year, 'a cold day with icy conditions on the Station', it put up three aircraft on its first operation within the Group as part of a WINDOW force carrying out a Spoof raid. All returned safely. 'It took some time to accustom the crews to this new role', Bomber Command records state, 'and to convince them of their operational necessity. It was not until a month had elapsed that they began to realise the value of their work to the rest of Bomber Command.' The Squadron carried out 'an outstanding share of WINDOW operations, eventually carrying out 473 sorties in No. 100 Group of which 457 were WINDOW operations. No. 462 Squadron was believed to be the first heavy squadron in No. 100 Group to carry bombs on a diversionary raid when it carried out a 'Spoof' raid on Stuttgart on 7th January 1945. It was also the first squadron in the Group to carry target indicators to mark targets by blind bombing methods.

February brought a slight improvement in the weather with an increase in sorties flown. The Squadron flew 104 sorties with the Special Window Force, the highest in the month within No. 100 Group. During this month the Squadron suffered heavy, almost critical, losses. By the end of the month No.462 Squadron would only have seven serviceable aircraft available for operations out of an aircraft strength of 18. The night of 24th/25th February inflicted particularly savage losses:

> Weather was fine during the day and Bomber Command was on Daylight operations. No.100 Group operated alone. Ten aircraft were required for Operations on this night, which was Spoof and bombing of the Neuss (Ruhr) area, for the second consecutive night. Take off was at 1700 hrs, and the return at 2150 hrs. Unfortunately four of our aircraft (out of the ten) failed to return. The missing crews were those of F/L Rate , F/L Tootal, F/L Ridgwell, and F/O Ely.[117]

'We thought it was a bit dodgy'

One of the 'unfortunates' was F/S Reg Gould, bomb aimer in No. 462 Squadron Handley Page Halifax Mk III MZ 447, 'A for Able', a member of F/L Alan Rate's crew. There was an air of fatality about the mission:

> The particular night when we came down was the only time we didn't fancy doing the operation out of all the number we had done. All the crew felt the same. It was the only time the pilot, normally a steady, reliable type, tried to 'duff up' the engines so that our operation would be aborted. He kept switching the ignition on and off hoping the engines would oil up. It didn't work. It was to be our 29th operation and it looked like suicide to us. I am afraid I was the only one who survived out of the whole crew. We had been told originally that there would not be any 'ops' on that night. My rear gunner and myself had our best blues as we planned to visit Norwich. Training aircraft flew with us. The training aircraft

turned back at the French/German border and we went on, twenty of us, throwing out WINDOW pretending that a raid was carrying on. We thought it was a bit dodgy. Although the route was near to the front line (40 miles away), it was also near Venlo, where the enemy fighters used to circle above the beacon to be directed to the approaching bombers. There were always a lot of fighters in the area.

My pilot F/L Rate. RAAF, wanted me to get a commission and just before this trip a new Bombing Leader, F/O Des Kehoe, RAAF, arrived on the Squadron. My pilot asked him to come on this trip

Reg Gould (No.462 Squadron), after training. *(Reg Gould)*

thinking it would help my application. He came as the 'spare bod' and threw the packets of WINDOW down the chute.

We got to the Ruhr and I released the bombs we were carrying. After I had bombed I normally stayed in the front nose of the aircraft and if I saw any anti-aircraft fire or enemy nightfighters I directed the pilot away from it. However on this trip the pilot told me to go and get a 'fix' on Gee for the navigator to promote my image to the Bombing Leader. I sat down beside the navigator to do this and, for the first time in any aircraft I had been in, found that I needed to sit a bit higher. I returned the few yards to my own position and collected my parachute, returned to the Navigator's table, placed the parachute on the seat, and sat on it. I took the Gee 'fix' and gave it to the Navigator. Then, at 2130 hrs, we were hit by flak.

There was a blacked out window opposite the Nav's table but it wasn't as blacked out as it should have been and I saw that a wing was on fire. We were diving at 340 mph, and a fire like that would have been like a blow-torch coming through the wing. The pilot didn't hesitate and said,' Put on your parachutes; Jump, Jump Jump!' Of course sitting on mine I had it on in seconds. The escape hatch was underneath the seat we were sitting on. I had to wait for the Navigator to clear his maps from the table. He then went away to get his parachute. I folded up the seat we were sitting on and undid the escape hatch underneath. I looked up, waiting for the Navigator to go first, but he had his back to me talking to the WOP, about two to three yards away, and there didn't seem to be any urgency as far as he was concerned. I thought sooner than wait for him to come back I would jump, so I did.

When I prepared to jump I was facing the back of the aircraft. I went through the escape hatch and the slipstream hit me and jammed me against the back of the escape hatch and the stiff packing of the parachute caught on a metal strip that was at the back. I tried to push myself off but didn't have enough strength. I was kicking the underside of the aircraft imagining that I was going to crash land with my legs underneath. I wondered why the other members of the crew weren't trying to kick me out. I looked up and saw the Navigator had his back to me. He didn't even know I was down there. Then I heard the rear gunner shout, 'Dive to starboard!' which indicated that we were being attacked by a fighter. The aircraft turned to the right and that rolled me off the metal strip and out to the side. The next thing I knew I was going down.

I didn't see what happened to the aircraft. I went to pull the ripcord and there was no parachute there! I thought, 'Oh God! Its ripped off in the aircraft!' I thought 'Am I going to be conscious when I hit the ground?' Looking up at the moon I suddenly saw my unopened parachute hanging from the harness on my back and above my head. I had to pull down the harness and pull the ripcord. I was in a proper panic.

The parachute opened but there was no 'jerk' as there should have been if it had opened correctly. I looked up and saw that the parachute was not properly opened but shaped like a candle. Still in a panic I climbed up the harness onto the parachute pack to try and open the rest of the parachute. By then I realised I must have dislocated my shoulder when leaving the aircraft. I was in agony. After climbing about 3 ft I couldn't stand the pain any longer and let go. Suddenly there was a bang and the parachute began to open. It opened like a balloon and I started spinning round and round. With the aircraft diving and suddenly turning right when I slid out I must have spun around as I was doing so and got caught in the wind. This must have accounted for the twisted shroud.

As I came down I could see a line of gunfire which seemed to be about 5 to 10 miles away. Apparently there was a push on that night by the Allies and the gunfire was part of it. I was drifting away from it into Germany. I found out later I was near Boisheim and our aircraft had crashed nearby. I was getting close to a pine forest which was on fire but could not manipulate the shroud lines to take me away from it as they were still twisted too high for me to get hold of them. I eventually landed about 100 yards from the wood landing backwards in a ploughed field. I was winded but not knocked out. I went to grab the quick release on the harness which should have been close to my stomach but there was nothing there. The harness had been so loose it must have fallen off as I hit the ground! I ran away looking for somewhere to hide and saw a house in the distance.

Shortly after landing Gould was captured:

Two soldiers came up to me. One, about 40 years-old had a fixed bayonet and he was accompanied by a lad of about 19. I didn't speak German. It was obvious that the older man wanted to bayonet me but the 19 years-old stood between him and myself to prevent him doing so...

I was marched to a house occupied by the military. I sat down on the floor and whilst I was doing this one of the soldiers wanted to know what my brevet was. It was a 'B' for 'Bomb Aimer' brevet. I told them I was a fighter pilot and that I was in 'B' Flight of my Squadron. I nervously hoped they would accept this as I felt certain that if they knew what it really stood for I wouldn't stand much chance of survival. Whilst on the floor I kept blowing my nose loudly the noise allowing me to slowly pick away at the stitches around the brevet. Each stitch that broke sounded like a pistol shot to me. I got about a third off when I was collected by an escort. When his credentials were being checked I took advantage of this distraction to rip off the brevet and throw it in a ditch.

Eventually I was put in a jeep the Germans had captured from the Americans. Sitting in the back were three RAF chaps whom I recognised as being from my flight. They took us to a frontline command post. We were put in a room and,

A plaque prepared by the villagers of Bosheim, in Germany, to commemorate the loss of No.462 Squadron Handley Page Halifax Mk.III aircraft MZ447, which crashed nearby. Reg Gould was the only survivor. (see text). *(Reg Gould)*

later, I was called before the commander who had an interpreter with him. All the commander wanted to know was if I had bombed Cologne. I said I could only give my number, rank and name. The interpreter said, You must answer him with a "Yes" or "No". As it happened I hadn't bombed Cologne and told him so. I was then sent back to the other room. On the way back the interpreter told me that all the commander's family had been killed in the bombing of Cologne and he had been recalled from the Russian Front to bury them. 'If you had said "Yes" he would have shot you,' the interpreter added. I told the others about it when I got back so that they could be on their guard.

Two days later the place where Reg Gould had been interrogated was captured by the Allies. Sadly he had been moved prior to their arrival and began the unpleasant and difficult experience of captivity as a PoW. Fifty years later Gould returned to Bosheim to take part in a remembrance ceremony for his crew. A local German businessman had paid £200 for seven oak trees to be planted at the site where Reg Gould's Halifax had crashed. He was requested by the German organisers to plant one himself which he did. He also laid a wreath which had a blue silk RAAF sash on it which was provided by the British Legion

The Squadron also used other RCM. The original intention had been for it to be fitted with the latest jamming equipment, the most important of which being ABC. No. 462 Squadron's first prototype fully equipped RCM aircraft using this RCM flew a test flight from Foulsham on 3rd March and the first RCM sortie took place ten days later. After this, ABC aircraft 'operated in small numbers up to the cessation of hostilities.' No.462 Squadron had 11 ABC equipped aircraft at Foulsham and with 'their increased knowledge of the radio and radar "set up" of modern war the crews became more enthusiastic with improving efficiency. This showed in many ways, one of which was that the standard of navigation in the Squadron was the highest in No.100 Group in 1945.'[118]

USAAF Assistance

No.803 Bombardment Squadron/36th Bomb Group.

On 17th January 1944, a small unit of USAAF personnel under Captain G E Paris arrived at Sculthorpe, in Norfolk, already the home of No.214 Squadron (qv), to train both ground and aircrew personnel of that Squadron on B17s. Initially employed in a training capacity they acquired experience of RCM work, became the USAAF 8th Air Force RCM Unit and, eventually, were able to add their efforts to those of the RAF heavy squadrons doing this work in No. 100 Group.

The following month the American Unit was joined by six newly assembled crews

No.36 Bomb Group USAAF. Captain Robert Stutzman, after being presented with the DFC at Cheddington on 16th November, by AVM Addison, AOC, No.100 Group.

(Maryse Addison)

Below: No.36 Bomb Group USAAF. Crew of B24 Liberator 'The Jigs Up'. After RCM duties with No.100 Group, the aircraft, due to bad weather,was diverted from its home base at Cheddington, Bucks, to RAF Valley, Anglesey, North Wales. Returning to Cheddington on 22nd December 1944 the aircraft was lost in the Irish Sea. All the crew baled out but only the pilot and co-pilot survived. In June 1992, Brendan Maguire, an auxiliary coastguard and keen amateur diver, with another diver, dived at the last known location of the aircraft off the Anglesey Coast and recovered one of the propellers. This is now mounted, with a memorial plaque, at the footpath leading to the site of the crash.

(Brendan Maguire)

from No. 96th Bombardment Group at Snetterton, Norfolk. The men, battle-weary and at the end of their operational tours, had been specially selected for the job. They were feeling quite demoralised as most of their unselected comrades were due for repatriation to the US for a rest. Low morale was eased by additional new men being posted to the Unit to complement the veterans.

On 28th March, the US unit became No.803 Bombardment Squadron and had six aircraft and nine crews. In the same month a small USAAF Intruder Unit was established at Little Snoring but did not last long, it quickly being found that the American fighters used were unsuitable for the required role. No. 492 Bombardment Group (qv) assisted the activities of the Special Window Force with bombing.

On 25th April, Captain Paris became No.803 Squadron's Operations Officer and command of the Squadron was taken up by Major C A Scott. It was agreed by the American authorities that the Squadron could fly with No.100 Group in its bomber support capacity. On 16th May the USAAF Squadron moved to Oulton and joined No.214 Squadron, commencing operations the following month, on D-Day. No.803 Squadron had built up its operational strength and on at least five nights during June it sent up 27 aircraft as part of the MANDREL Screen, and later took part in 'Spoof' operations. In August the Squadron acquired a new CO, Major Hambaugh, who had been the Squadron's Liaison Officer with No.100 Group HQ. It also changed its designation to No.36 Bombardment Group.

In November 1944 the USAAF Group returned to the USAAF for duties with the Eighth Air Force but continued to fly some missions with No.100 Group. At the beginning of January 1945 the Unit flew two final patrols with them 'which brought its long and honourable career with the No.100 Group MANDREL Screen to an end.'[119]

No.101 Squadron

No survey of RCM undertaken by the RAF in the Second World War could ignore the work of No. 101 Squadron. Although they were never absorbed into No. 100 Group they made a significant contribution to the radio war from the last months of 1943 to the end of the European conflict during which period they suffered heavy losses. The Squadron became involved in RCM in the following manner:

On 3rd/4th April 1943 'Y' Service reported that enemy fighter traffic had been heard on VHF (38-42 mc/s); although there was difficulty with reception it was clear that the German fighters were claiming increasing victories. A ground-based RCM, GROUND CIGAR, to combat this was operated from Sizewell, on the Suffolk coast, starting at the end of July. Difficulties were created. There were 'energetic complaints' from the 'Y' Services of both the RAF, and the Admiralty (monitoring 'E' Boat activity) that the new RCM was interfering with their monitoring of enemy signals which were being transmitted on the same frequency band, thus depriving them of valuable intelligence information. This was a common complaint about RCM but priority was given to GROUND CIGAR during Bomber Command attacks. Unfortunately, like all ground-based RCM on the higher frequencies, it suffered from lack of range and the effective coverage was not more than 140 miles from the ground station, much of this being, in this particular case, over the North Sea. The real answer to the problem was an airborne jammer and it was decided that a main force bomber squadron could undertake this RCM role in addition to its normal function. No. 101 Squadron was chosen for this role.

On 7th/October 1943, ABC was used operationally by them for the first time. Originally the SOs received some assistance from the 'Y' Service listening station at West Kingsdown, in Kent, who passed them details the active frequencies by means of coded references. The 'Y' Service in the UK still suffered from limitations of range and could not pick up VHF traffic from the whole of the area over which bombers operated. Hence it was soon decided that the SOs should find and jam frequencies independently of any ground control.[120]

The Squadron operated Lancasters carrying the new equipment, and, with an extra German-speaking crew member, they were placed in the RAF bomber stream at intervals in order to give complete protection to the raiding aircraft, jamming and confusing the German nightfighter communications. Ron Crafer, a 19 year-old 'German speaker' explained how he was selected for the job and carried out his duties:

> It appeared that while training to be a Signaller (Air) at Madley, near Hereford,
> I had let slip to my Flight Sergeant that, before joining the RAF, I had had half
> a dozen lessons in German. I finished the signaller's course and was awarded my
> sergeants stripes in April...with hoped-for leave cancelled, three days after passing
> out I found myself posted to No.1 Lancaster Finishing School at Hemswell.
> There I met three other newly promoted aircrew sergeants, all as mystified as I
> was.
>
> The next day the four of us assembled with a Flight Sergeant Instructor.
> 'Through that door is something top secret,' he said. 'If you go through you will
> commit yourself to going on operations. If you wish to withdraw now, you may,
> and will not be considered lacking in moral fibre (LMF).' Needless to say, none
> of us did. So the mysteries of ABC were revealed to us. We were not required to
> be fluent in German but to have enough knowledge to be able to recognise call
> signs etc. I was the only one of the four to survive a tour of 30 operations.[121]

ABC had a range of 50 miles and was designed to interrupt enemy communications by jamming particular frequencies on which radio messages were being sent to nightfighters from ground control stations. The ABC equipment consisted of three 50 watt transmitters, each capable of sending out accurate jamming signals covering narrow frequency bands selected (within the 38.3 to 42.5 MHz range) which were selected by means of manual tuning controls. A panoramic receiver provided means of locating enemy transmissions in this range of frequencies. Some ABC transmitters had an additional feature, BENITO. A high pitched note was employed which the SOs matched to the transmission from enemy beacons. This confused the fighters as to the exact location of their beacon. 'We had to match the pitch aurally,' Ron Crafer remembered, 'but as I have absolutely no musical ability whatsoever and have the greatest difficulty in recognising a note I did all I could not to be allocated to an aircraft carrying BENITO. A wrong note would have given the enemy a perfect target to home in on.'

The ABC aircraft also carried normal bomb loads (the weight limitation was 1000 lbs because of the extra RCM equipment). No. 101 Squadron was the main squadron performing the ABC role in Bomber Command, although No.214 Squadron did so for a period beginning early in 1944. No. 101 Squadron was in No.1 Group where it carried more raids than any of the Group's other Lancaster squadrons, often being required to fly when the rest of the Group was being rested. The Squadron carried out 2477 ABC sorties from October 1943, until the end of the European War.

An article written 40 years later described the experience on No.101 Squadron for one of the lucky survivors, F/L Lyle James, DFC. It covers a short 90 day period from 12th to 15th December 1944, and it is a vivid indication of the loss rate suffered by the Squadron:

> James and his crew flew 32 trips to complete their tour of ops – a Squadron record. Theirs was a 'special duty' squadron... equipped with ABC. Because German fighters could home in on these Lancasters when they were transmitting, No. 101 Squadron suffered the highest loss ratio in Bomber Command. James' aircraft 'W2' or 'William Squared' returned with battle damage on ten occasions and three DFCs were awarded to members of his crew. During that period only five per cent of crews in Bomber Command completed their full tours. Of 15 crews that formed up at James' OTU his crew was the only one to finish the tour. The other 14 crews were lost in action.[122]

No.1699 Flight

No. 1699 Flight was originally formed at Oulton in June 1944 for the purpose of training crews of No.214 Squadron which was also stationed there. The coexistence of the two units on the same station proved to be of great value. Crews of No.214 Squadron were able to gather valuable information operationally whilst at the same time being under training for RCM duties with No.1699 Flight.

The Flight's first three aircraft were Fortress Mk.II aircraft. Crews of seven were posted in from No.1657 Conversion Unit at Stradishall, each crew consisting of pilot, flight engineer, navigator, bomb aimer, WOP and two gunners; on arrival at the Flight an SO for RCM duties was added, plus two beam gunners.

Training consisted of seven days ground instruction. On completion of this crews were given 25 hours flying which covered familiarisation of the Fortress; air firing exercises; fighter affiliation, and daytime cross-country navigation practice. The training ended with a Bullseye Exercise (in which training units sent their aircraft over the North Sea to try and confuse the German early warning radar system). Where possible, each pilot did a sortie with an experienced crew before becoming captain of his aircraft.

In September, after the arrival of No.223 Squadron, the establishment of the Flight was increased to include three Liberators. Crews were to be trained as replacements for that Squadron and instructors were posted in to meet these requirements. The aircrews were transferred from Nos. 91, 92, and 93 Groups, and were mainly ex-instructors who had completed one tour of operations plus one of instructional duty. These crews had not had any experience of four-engined aircraft, but it was found that, with their previous flying experience, little difficulty was encountered in training them for the new aircraft. A similar syllabus to that of the Fortress trainees was adopted to train these crews, each being ten in number consisting of pilot, flight engineer, navigator, WOP, four gunners but with two SOs. 14 crews were Fortress trained for No. 214 Squadron and seven crews were Liberator trained for No. 223 Squadron.

After the training of these first men, crews were no longer available from experienced sources and pupil crews were arriving on the Flight from OTUs. In view of their comparative inexperience lengthier training was clearly necessary. Ground training was increased to 14 days, flying hours to 41 hours minimum, and more attention was given to cross-country exercises.

Later, No.223 Squadron was re-equipped with Fortress aircraft. The establishment of No.1699 Flight was, therefore, altered to six Fortress aircraft, the Liberators being withdrawn and flown to Swannington for disposal.

Up to VE Day 600 crew had been trained in No.1699 Flight and the number of hours flown was 2,200. The Flight's CO had been F/L J Henderson until 1st September 1944 when S/L D J Bollingham, DFC, AFC, took over.

Footnotes – Chapter Five

92   PRO AIR 14/2911: 'Development and Activities of No.100 (Bomber Support) Group: Part II.

93   PRO AVIA 26/849. TRE Report, April 1945. MANDREL III Jamming Spot Frequency Receiver/Transmitter. (M.Ryle and F/L L Mackinnon.)

94   PRO AIR 25/777, No.100 Group ORB.

95   Addison Papers: MS notes by AVM Addison dated 27.79.77.

96   'A Thousand Shall Fall', Murray Peden, (Canada's Wings Inc. 1979), pp, 415-6.

97   Op.cit. (92)

98   Ibid.

99   PRO AVIA 26/1108, 'SN2 Signals Watch': Report dated 4.9.44.

100 Op.cit. (92)

101 Letter to author from Werner Mihan dated 31.7.95. Werner Mihan's experience indicates the lot of many of his generation in wartime Germany. 'After the Battle of Stalingrad in 1942/3 with its disastrous results for Germany, most of the anti-aircraft soldiers were needed for the frontline to make up for the heavy losses,' he recalled. Conscripted from secondary school at the age of 15 he was drafted for flak service as a Luftwaffehelfer (Air Force Helper), and, after 7 weeks hard training, was posted for searchlight duties near Berlin where he served throughout the Battle of Berlin. Only a few of the regular soldiers remained. In September 1944 he was, himself, drafted into regular service on the Western Front, wounded, and eventually sent to a hospital near his home in Potsdam thus being present on the night of the raid.

102 PRO AIR 40/2370. 'Bomber Command Signals Intelligence and RCM Report No.77. 16.4.45.

103 Ibid.

104 'Terror by Night', Michael Renaut DFC,(William Kimber. 1982).

105 Op.cit. (92), p.75.

106 Extract from 'Per Ardua Ad Astra' by Rosemary Bower.

107 Service at North Creake on 3rd August 1945, on the Disbandment of Nos.171 and 199 Squadrons, Bomber Command.

108 'A Thousand Shall Fall', Murray Peden, (Canada's Wings Inc., 1979), pp 338-9.

109 Op.cit. (92), p.85.

110 Ibid. p.86: (Murray Peden gives a detailed account of the latter incident in 'A Thousand Shall Fall', p.405)

111 Page 11 of a Report dated 16.11.44., on 'German Night Defences 1944-5' by ADI (Science), (Harris Archive H77, R A F Museum, Hendon).

112 A copy of this message was sent to the author by F/L Frank Savage, DFC, R A F (Ret), (26.11.95).

113 This was the usual aircraft flown by DAG Anthony and his crew in No.223 Squadron. Anthony, a flight engineer has written a book about his experiences, 'Lucky B 24,' by Arthur Anthony, (janus Publishing Co, 1993).

114 This was known as 'Schräge Musik'. A pair of fixed upward-firing 20mm cannons was mounted behind the cockpit of the Luftwaffe fighter. All that was required then was for the fighter-pilot to manoeuvre his aircraft into a position immediately below the attacking bomber where he could, unseen by the bomber, fire upwards into the bomber's 'belly' – its blind spot.

115 Letters to author dated 3.8.95 and 11.8.95 from H C Sykes; ;'Bill' Sykes also wrote a brief account of Bomber Command's Second World War activities in 'The Forging of a Weapon' (H C Sykes, 1989) the proceeds from the sale of which he donated to the Soldiers', Sailors' and Airmens' Families Association, (SSAFA).

116 PRO AIR 27/1917. No.462 Squadron ORB.

117 Ibid.

118 PRO AIR 14/2911: 'The Development and Activities of No.100 (BS) Group.

119 PRO AIR 25/777. No. 100 Group ORB., p.5.

120 'Despatch on War Operations, 23.2.42 to 8.5.45, Appendix E. 'RCM in Bomber Command', pp 135/6.(H 122,Harris Archive, R A F Museum, Hendon).

121 Article by Ron Crafer in 'Swindon Evening Advertiser', 15.3.94, and sent to the author to him.

122 'Air Force Magazine of the Air Force of Canada'. Vol.19, No.3. Autumn 1995.

Chapter Six.

'Cat and Mouse': Fighter Support

We seemed to confuse the enemy quite successfully by our presence at the nightfighter bases either before, or after, the main bomber stream had passed by. It was really a game of 'cat and mouse'.

Bill Jones, Navigator, No.515 Squadron.

Before No. 100 Group.

At the end of 1943, the German night defence system was recovering from the disorganisation caused by the use of WINDOW. Before this, Luftwaffe nightfighters usually used a system of individual close control from the ground. To do this two Giant Würzburgs, an integral part of the German Ground Control Interception (GCI) system, were employed. One tracked the attacking bomber while the other followed the German fighter. From the information obtained the Controller could direct his fighter, by R/T, (up to a range normally of thirty miles or less).

WINDOW rendered the Würzburgs useless and the enemy was forced to change over to a system of loose control of groups of fighters. The new procedure, known as 'Wilde Sau', involved the broadcasting of commentaries giving the bombers' movements to the Luftwaffe nightfighters from a few high-powered transmitters. In addition, beacons were set up which could be used as 'stepping stones' to direct the German nightfighters towards the attacking RAF bombers. At first the enemy attempted only to intercept the bombers at their target, but confusion as to the actual Bomber Command targets which were being attacked, and the tardiness of the defending fighters in arriving at them, made this scheme unsuccessful. The Luftwaffe then switched to intercepting the raiding bombers on their way to the target, this new strategy meeting with greater success.

When No. 100 Group was formed its fighter squadrons had a significant role to play in its activities. After the initial handicap of worn-out aircraft and unsuitable radar equipment had been overcome, they added much to its success. The AOC of No. 100 Group, AVM Addison, summarised to a post-war audience what he considered to be their effect:

> The aircraft were packed with a mass of apparatus, much of which had to be
> specially designed for the purpose. The Mosquitoes, in particular, carried 'black
> boxes' in every possible available position. This enabled them not only to home

on to the German beacons over which the enemy nightfighters used to assemble, but also to home on to the radio apparatus which the German nightfighters carried for intercepting our bombers.

The material effect of their operations in terms of enemy nightfighters destroyed and damaged was considerable, but possibly the morale effect of their activities was even greater. The enemy nightfighter was no longer able to concentrate solely on his task of shooting down bombers. Now he had continually to be looking over his shoulder in the fear of being followed, and he became apprehensive, too, of the attractive effect produced by the switching on of his airborne radar apparatus, and so became disinclined to use it as freely as before.[123]

Early SERRATE Operations.

As the result of the flight by Harold Jordan's crew at the end of 1942 (see Chapter Three) the Telecommunications Research Establishment (TRE) was able to produce SERRATE, an RCM which could 'home' onto the enemy nightfighter AI (Lichtenstein) frequency in the 490 Mc/s band. Using this in conjunction with the forward-looking AI Mk.IV for completion of interception, No.141 Squadron, an experienced 'radar' squadron, flying Bristol Beaufighters (and operating under Fighter Command control), had used it operationally since June 1943. During the first three months of the SERRATE operations by the Squadron one successful combat resulted from every nine sorties completing a patrol; by November the statistics had deteriorated to one successful combat from every 26 sorties completing a patrol. There were several reasons for the difference in results. The enemy's fighter tactics were changing due to the use of WINDOW (see above), AI Mk IV was being severely interfered with, and it had become increasing clear that the Beaufighter could not match the performance of the types of nightfighters the enemy was using. The position at this time was summarised thus:

> The two main factors affecting the tactics of SERRATE interception were the relatively low performance of the Beaufighter and the fact that the range of the initial SERRATE contact depended very greatly on the attitude of the enemy aircraft towards the SERRATE aircraft (due to the forward beaming of the enemy AI transmission). When the enemy aircraft was pointing towards the SERRATE aircraft, contacts up to a range of 50 miles or more could be obtained, but when pointing away the initial contact could be picked up only at a range of ten miles or less.

One of the most successful tactics of the Beaufighter was to pick up a SERRATE contact from behind, and to allow the enemy aircraft to close until well within the

Beaufighter's backward coverage. Then to whip round and attack the enemy aircraft from astern.

The SERRATE operation at this time was one requiring a very high degree of skill and this is shown by the fact that a very few crews were responsible for a great majority of combats; one pilot (W/C Braham) had nine out of the 23 successes. Two other crews had five each.[124]

No.100 Group Fighter Operations.

In early December 1943, No.141 Squadron became the first fighter Squadron to join No. 100 Group, its Beaufighters were to be phased out and replaced by Mosquito Mk.II aircraft. It was joined shortly afterwards by Nos. 169 and 239 Squadrons, both experienced in defensive AI nightfighting, who were also to be equipped and trained to join in the SERRATE duties. On 15th December 1943, a fourth squadron was added when a squadron with RCM experience, No.515 Squadron, joined the Group. However, Nos. 169, 239 and 515 Squadrons flew no operations in December, 'due to the lack of serviceable aircraft and/or special equipment.' [125]

When the new Group was formed there was little information available on which to base its fighter strategy. The tactics of the enemy were changing and there was not, as yet, sufficient expertise to give a quick, adequate reconstruction of enemy fighter movements which would be of future use to the bomber-supporting fighters. With the enemy's very efficient early warning system and the vast areas to be covered by No.100 Group's fighters it was difficult to see the most effective way of deploying the limited fighter force available for bomber support. Three different types of patrol were considered:

[a] Patrolling in the target area during and after the attack.

[b] At the enemy nightfighter assembly points. Times for these sorties depended on the route taken, and the behaviour of the enemy fighters on previous raids, as shown by the intercepted radio traffic.

[c] Close escort of the bomber stream.

A few sorties to the target area showed that (a) was not practical with the existing equipment. The number of SERRATE contacts present at any one time was too great to allow any Direction Finding (DF) on enemy fighters. Even when it was possible, the large number of AI contacts on the raiding bombers prevented the SERRATE contact being married up with the correct AI contact.

Similar problems were encountered with (c); SERRATE aircraft flying parallel to, and a few miles away from the edge of, the main stream of bombers could sometimes obtain SERRATE or AI contacts from enemy aircraft making their way towards the stream. These contacts could be followed but it was not usually found possible to close in to attack before the enemy aircraft had entered the bomber stream where the contact was lost among the bomber AI contacts.

In the first few months it was found to be more profitable for the target area to be patrolled after the bombing. A good number of AI contacts were made on enemy aircraft although the SERRATE contacts were poor. To add to the difficulties some enemy aircraft remained in the target area with their AI off.

The initial patrols by No. 100 Group fighters to the enemy assembly beacons, singled out by the information obtained from previous operations, were not as beneficial as had been hoped, and met with limited success. On a number of occasions the enemy did use the beacons, but at a different time. They also used other beacons which had not been forecast. Even when a beacon had been guessed correctly the SERRATE aircraft made very few contacts. The difficulty was finding the beacon areas:

> The visual beacons, even in clear weather, were not a good enough guide for the Mosquito crews, where the Observer's preoccupation with the SERRATE/AI equipment precluded the possibility of accurate navigation. The Mosquito was not equipped with the radio aids for finding the beacons used by the enemy nightfighters.[126]

A significant feature after No.100 Group took over the SERRATE operations was the large number of AI contacts obtained directly on enemy aircraft compared with the number obtained via SERRATE chases. The reason for this was probably that the enemy fighters switched off their AI except in the vicinity of the bomber force where the SERRATE aircraft could not be sent owing to the limitations of their equipment. Another factor may have been the introduction at this time of the WINDOW-proof SN-2 AI in the Luftwaffe's nightfighters, which gave them improved range and wider angle of cover compared with the hitherto used Lichtenstein.

The fitting of backward-looking AI in the No.100 Group fighters improved the situation and between December 1943, and April 1944, almost as many combats resulted from them as forward-looking AI. During the period a major improvement in victories over the defending nightfighters occurred. On the nights of major bombing operations (ie Main Force against German targets), one successful combat resulted from every eight completed sorties. Over the same period, one in thirteen of the AI chases, not preceded by SERRATE contacts, resulted in a successful combat. Although unserviceability (u/s) of equipment and interference on AI Mk.IV accounted for some contacts being lost:

> ...the major cause of lost contacts was a tactical one. The contacts were chased and the range often closed to within 5,000 ft when the enemy aircraft appeared to make a violent turn and the contact was lost. It was clear the operation demanded a very high standard of AI skill, and was one of which only a few

especially skilful and well trained crews could take full advantage. Of the 31 successes achieved between December 1943, and April 1944, one crew (who were also one of the most successful in the pre-No.100 Group SERRATE operations) was responsible for six, one crew for three, five crews for two and twelve crews each had one.

It is an interesting point that the chance of an AI contact being converted to an attack was much higher if the AI contact was obtained by a SERRATE chase than if it were obtained directly. On the average one in five AI contacts following SERRATE chases resulted in combats (this was approximately equal to the figure prior to No. 100 Group). The reason for this is probably that in most cases an enemy aircraft with its AI on would be looking for 'hostiles' and consequently flying along reasonably steadily and would therefore be a good target for AI interception, and secondly, if AI contact were lost during the later stages of the interception, it could often be regained after switching back to SERRATE.[127]

It soon became apparent that SERRATE was causing the enemy some concern. Apart from the German nightfighters destroyed and damaged, many others were involved in combat with the No.100 Group fighters when they should have been intercepting the Main Force bombers. 'The enemy controllers were broadcasting frequent warnings to their aircraft to beware of the "long-range nightfighters" (which included Fighter Command intruders), and the morale of the Luftwaffe nightfighter crews must have been seriously affected by the knowledge of the presence of the hostile nightfighters, and every AI contact would have to be treated with caution.[128]

Despite this, there were considerable limitations to the success of the No.100 Group fighter strategy and, in the early months of 1944, the German fighters were achieving considerable success in intercepting the Main Force on the way to the target causing Bomber Command to sustain two of its heaviest losses. On 24/25th March, 72 aircraft were lost out of a raiding force of 810 attacking Berlin. A week later, during the attack on Nuremburg (qv), 96 aircraft were lost from an attacking force of 795. No close escort of the bombers could take place due to the swamping of the AI MkIV which was becoming more and more serious, particularly in the region of strongly defended targets and near the bomber stream. It was clear that the only way bomber support results by the fighters could be bettered was with a more efficient AI for the escorting fighters, which could be used near the bomber stream and which was more competent in tracking evasive action by the enemy. The answer was to come with AI Mk X. As yet it had not been flown over enemy territory but by the end of the year No.100 Group HQ could report to HQ Bomber Command, 'AI Mk.X does it again! Last night Nos. 85/157 Squadrons out of 15 completed sorties destroyed five Hun fighters and damaged one', while 'the three AI Mk IV Squadrons and two non-radar Squadrons completed 18 sorties with no score.'[129]

Equipment Troubles

Inefficient equipment was not confined to radar apparatus. The initial aircraft of the three SERRATE Squadrons (Nos.141, 169 and 239 Squadrons) had been 'the rather ancient Mosquito Mk.II's, which had already given of their best'. The exacting SERRATE operations soon proved too much for these aircraft and the number of aborted sorties was therefore large. The result was that:

> In February, it was decided to take the long term view, which involved reducing
> the operational effort, in order to give the Mosquito aircraft a major inspection
> and to re-engine with Merlin 22's. This policy soon began to bear fruit and, in
> March, the serviceability showed a remarkable improvement. The scale of effort
> of the SERRATE squadrons grew from 41 sorties in January to 175 in April.[130]

In May 1944, a decision was taken to equip the Mosquito Mk.II Squadrons with Mosquito Mk.VI. The first squadron to receive the new aircraft was No.169 Squadron. The prototype SERRATE installation proved entirely unsatisfactory, and a great deal of research experimenting was then undertaken by this squadron which involved structural modification and many hours of test flying. A successful installation was eventually found. By the end of July 1944, all SERRATE squadrons were re-equipped with Mk.VI aircraft, the important feature of which was that drop-tanks could be carried, thereby increasing the radius of action or the time spent on patrol.

Pre D-Day Operations

From March up to D-Day the bombers made a growing number of attacks against pre-invasion targets in France. These attacks were at first almost unopposed by enemy fighters but opposition gradually built up until, in May, the loss rate had crept up to 4.3% over the more heavily defended areas. There was no bomber stream as such; instead, several attacks, each of short penetration, were made simultaneously on targets fairly near to each other. This new approach required the No. 100 Group fighters to adjust their escort duties. Thus the Mosquitoes not only flew parallel with the bombers, but also crossed and re-crossed the bomber tracks. The tactics were surprisingly successful and, in May, 18 enemy aircraft were destroyed and one damaged in 212 sorties. Twelve of the successful combats arose from initial SERRATE contacts, six from initial AI contacts, and one from a 'visual' on an enemy aircraft illuminated by searchlights. One successful chase was carried out on SERRATE alone, the enemy aircraft flying too low for AI Mk.IV to be used. On two occasions enemy fighters were attacked while they themselves were in the act of attacking bombers.

Various factors contributed to the success. The increasing skill and experience of the SERRATE crews improved their efficiency; good visibility was present on several nights; and the fact that the patrols were of short duration was an added bonus. It was thought that crews would be more resolute in their chases with plenty of petrol and time in hand. The inexperience of the opposing Luftwaffe fighter personnel was also thought to be significant. 'Most of the operations in May took place in the Jagddivision (JD) 4 and JD5 areas and many of the nightfighter crews there did not have the experience of those based in Germany.'[131]

Post-D-Day Operations

In June and July 1944, the number of SERRATE contacts dropped. In July the average was only one in every ten sorties reporting a SERRATE contact, (in May it had been one per sortie). There were several causes. One reason was clearly due:

> ...to the replacement of the Lichtenstein in the Luftwaffe aircraft by the new AI, SN-2. However, the number of direct AI on enemy aircraft did increase during June/July, but on the whole the standard of success of the SERRATE operation declined significantly. Eighteen sorties were despatched for every aircraft destroyed or damaged.

Attention to the enemy nightfighter assembly points provided more positive results:

> The increased number of direct AI contacts during these months was due to the success of Beacon patrols. It became clear in June that the enemy was making more and more use of his Assembly Beacons in France and the area around these beacons proved to be the most profitable type of patrol for the SERRATE Squadrons. An important point was that many of the attacking fighters' successes at the beacons were obtained before the German fighters had attempted to intercept the bombers and so a valuable measure of direct support could be given to the bomber operation.

Enemy jamming of the No.100 Group fighters' AI was causing difficulties:

> By June and July interference on AI Mk.IV was a very serious handicap. It was reported by most crews during the whole of the time they were over enemy territory, and particularly at the enemy coast and the Ruhr area. Not only did it mean that a large number of contacts were not obtained at all, but frequently it prevented the successful following-up of contacts which had been achieved.[132]

Nevertheless, on the night 27th/28th June, when the Main Force attacked six flying bomb sites, with supplementary attacks on the railway yards at Vaires and Vitry, No.100 Group put up 60 Mosquito fighters in support. Three failed to return, two from No.141 Squadron, and one from No.192 Squadron. In August and September the number of SERRATE operations dropped almost to zero; at the same time it became increasingly difficult to achieve combats from AI Mk IV contacts. In August 331 SERRATE/AI sorties produced nine successful combats. September was emphatically poorer, with only one successful combat from 240 sorties. The following table shows the decreasing efficiency of AI Mk.IV, per completed sortie, from May to September, 1944:

	May	June	July	Aug	Sept
Average No. SERRATE contacts	1.1	0.2	0.1	0.02	0.005
Average No. of AI contacts (without initial SERRATE)	0.3	0.5	0.8	0.5	0.3
AI contacts per successful combat	9	9	10	16	60

Several factors contributed to this decrease. On many operations in this period the attacking bombers met with little opposition from the defending enemy fighters, but those that did enter into combat proved to be very efficient at evasive action which, according to the attacking fighter crews, was 'not so much due to AI Mk.IV interference as the increased evasive action and speed of the enemy aircraft.' The percentage of lost contacts due to this had increased from 37% in May to 73% in September.[133]

Airfield Intruders

In the early part of April, 1944 it was decided to extend the scope of No.100 Group's activities to include Low-Level (LL) intrusion of enemy airfields. The operations would take place in close cooperation with Fighter Command (renamed after D-Day, 'Air Defence of Great Britain' [ADGB]) who had been carrying out this sort of operation for some time. It was hoped that the knowledge and experience of the enemy nightfighter system that was being gained at No.100 Group HQ through the growing Intelligence and Monitoring sections, and through the operation of their High-Level (HL) fighters, would help to increase the success of airfield intrusion and seriously hamper the German night defence system.

No.515 Squadron had been transferred from No.11 Group, where their role had been that of RCM aircraft. They were at first equipped with Bristol Beaufighter Mk.II aircraft for certain operations (which never materialised), and were later re-equipped with Mosquito Mk.VI aircraft without any form of radar. A period of intense training was undertaken to fit them for LL intruding. In April 1944, they commenced 'nuisance' sorties on enemy airfields, carrying bombs and incendiaries. They were joined in June by No.23 Squadron from the Mediterranean, who were also equipped with non-radar Mosquito Mk.VI aircraft. During the first few months of the operations by the two squadrons, only a small number of enemy aircraft were attacked, but their activities around enemy airfields were a source of considerable anxiety to the enemy:

> From D-Day up to the date of the re-introduction of AI Mk.X into bomber support work at the beginning of September, the main achievement of the bomber support fighters, both high and low-level, lay in the disorganisation their presence produced in the enemy defence system rather than in the number of enemy aircraft destroyed or damaged...from the evidence to hand it is clear that the intruders did cause the enemy controllers much worry.[134]

In October 1944, No.515 Squadron carried out a number of Day Ranger intruder sorties over enemy-occupied Europe to cause disruption to the enemy's activities and draw up their nightfighters. This they did with some success, destroying nine enemy aircraft and damaging five more. The following month the Squadron was equipped with AI Mk.XV (ASH), AI Mk.X not being available to them. Bad weather precluded their employment on many sorties and the Squadron had to wait until the end of December for its first victory with the AI Mk.XV. In January 1945, its partner squadron at Little Snoring, No. 23 Squadron, was also equipped with AI Mk.XV and when a rear-warning device was fitted to all the aircraft of both squadrons they were capable of LL and HL sorties. No.23 Squadron was later also fitted with PERFECTOS.

As enemy fighter activity lessened providing little opportunity for air-to-air combat, the two squadrons concentrated on the bombing and illuminating of the German airfields. In March 1945 an attempt was made to use long range control from No.100 Group Operations Room at Bylaugh Hall. The two squadrons were fitted with SCR 274 sets and although there was satisfactory reception up to 500 miles the new system was not widely used due to a lack of enemy activity. In the following month, as enemy aerial activity diminished even more, Nos. 23 and 515 Squadrons concentrated on keeping the remaining operational enemy fighters on the ground. Both squadrons undertook the finding and marking of enemy airfields and acted as Master Bombers for attacks by other Mosquitoes of the Group who dropped tanks filled with Napalm, a stratagem which met with considerable success.

Identification Problems

As No.100 Group's activities grew, the number of Bomber Support fighters expanded, but they were now operating in a diminishing area as enemy-held territory decreased due to the Allied ground forces advance into Europe. The need for mutual identification between the Group's fighters to avoid the waste of time caused by chases between friendly fighters became essential. A modified IFF Mk.III was fitted into certain aircraft, and also the Type F Infra-Red Identification System. It took several months for these fittings to take place but they proved to be of great value.

Use of Intelligence and Planning

In the early months of 1944, the German early warning system was in operation almost from the take off of the raiding force, which meant that the whole of the German night defence was quickly alerted. There were, in general, only attacks by Bomber Command on single targets with no 'feints' and there was no base-line from which bomber-supporting fighter actions could be planned.

After D-Day there was a marked change. The contraction of enemy-held territory, (for the reasons shown above), forced the Luftwaffe to limit the operation of their fighters to the particular area where a threatened attack was likely. No reinforcements could be flown in from great distances. This fact was of great assistance in planning the bomber supporting fighters' disposition. Also reduction in the enemy's early warning cover meant the attacking bombers could travel a considerable way to and from their target safely.

In addition, No.100 Group and 'Y' Service monitoring had become highly effective at following the movements of the enemy fighters during actual operations. A full reconstruction of the previous night's activities was available the following morning providing useful information on which the next night's operations could be planned. These facts were very helpful in organising the disposition of the bomber supporting fighters, until the final rapid advance by the Allied armies into Germany when precise planning became unnecessary.

AI Mk.X Operations

Strenuous efforts had been made to acquire the new, more efficient, AI Mk.X. This culminated with the transfer to No.100 Group of Nos. 85 and 157 Squadrons at the beginning of May 1944. No.85 Squadron, equipped and trained with the AI Mk.X had been employed in defensive nightfighting over Britain. No.157, whilst using AI Mk.IV (but now equipped with AI Mk.X), had assisted Coastal Command with anti-submarine patrols in the Bay of Biscay. AI Mk.X, unlike AI Mk.IV, had no backward coverage and because of this was unsuitable for use on HL operations. The Bomber Support Development Unit (BSDU) at Foulsham worked on a modification of MONICA I. It was hoped that eventually both Squadrons could be used for both LL and HL support operations with the bombers. However, until it was available both Squadrons were confined to LL work. They began operations on D-Day and until the end of the month carried out LL attacks on enemy airfields. These first airfield intrusions were very promising. From a height of 1,500 to 2,000 ft AI contacts at ranges of three miles or so could be obtained and held. During June of 131 sorties completed, 38 AI contacts were reported leading to the destruction of ten enemy aircraft and three damaged. Part of the Squadrons' efforts towards the end of the month was diverted towards anti-flying bomb duties. On 21st July they were transferred back to Fighter Command at West Malling (Kent), to conduct the work full time. The AOC of 100 Group, Air Commodore Addison was bitterly disappointed. Apart from the commander's natural chagrin at losing units under his command he had sound reasons for his frustration. With new equipment and training they were beginning to give a good account of themselves in their bomber support role. He complained bitterly, and at length, to the C-in-C Bomber Command, Air Chief Marshal Harris:

> Nearly a fortnight ago we were instructed virtually to hand back our newly-acquired AI Mk.X Mosquito Squadrons to ADGB who said they wanted them to protect this country against Flying Bombs.
>
> Just before this happened these two Squadrons had completed their re-equipping and their long intensive training for Bomber Support operations. Although so far inexperienced in this form of operation, they nevertheless showed considerable promise, and in the first ten days of their operations they got no less than ten Huns. We expected great things from these two Units with their new aircraft and centimetre AI, and their début was most promising.
>
> Then ADGB asked for them to be employed to defend this country – and for nearly two weeks these two Squadrons have been supplying sixteen sorties a night on anti-flying bomb patrols in which they have between them destroyed 33 robots.
>
> The reasons given for the diversion of these Squadrons was that they had Mosquitoes equipped with Merlin 25 engines, and had AI.
>
> It was soon shown that the only reason AI was required for this type of operation was to give a range measurement to enable the crew to open fire at just the right moment. Given any simple device capable of measuring range, any Mosquito fitted with a Merlin 25 engine should be equally effective. This means that scores of Mosquito VI's in ADGB, 2 Group or elsewhere could just as well have been used for this purpose. Moreover, the AI Mk.VIII fitted Mosquitoes in ADGB, of which there are many, could also have been used provided that Merlin 25 engines had been put in them (it takes only a day to change the engines of a Mosquito if sufficient urgency is put into the job).
>
> Without AI the anti-flying bomb chaser must have sufficient speed to enable it to fly alongside the flying-bomb and pump lead into it until it blows up. ADGB have an aircraft capable of doing this, ie the Tempest. They have however, only two or three night-flying Tempests – the remainder are day fliers. Surely, however, it would not be a difficult thing to train experienced night flying crews to fly Tempests?[135]

The loaning of the Squadrons to ADGB, Air Commodore Addison added:

> ...is a heartbreaking contemplation. After all the training and hard work that has been put into these two Squadrons to equip them for your special offensive purposes, we now have to see them taken off their Bomber Support role just at the moment when you require them most, and when they have begun to prove their worth. You can imagine the state their engines will be in when they return to us after this exacting job of chasing flying bombs. If anybody wants a really good engine it is our offensive fighter which has to accompany your bombers far into enemy territory. There are only 50 Mosquito XIX in the world, and we are now having to watch them being expended in a role for which they were never intended.
>
> If there had been no alternative but to use them for this purpose I could fully understand the importance of diverting them. But since there are other alternatives – and a fortnight has now passed in which to bring some, at least, of these alternatives into effect – it seems that the continued use of these aircraft in this defensive role is nothing but a 'fast one' on the part of ADGB.[136]

In support of his argument Air Commodore Addison reported that 'We have, at last, after many months of really hard, intensive work, managed to get what few offensive fighters we have been able to scrape together into a good fighting force.' In the month of June, he added, No.100 Group accounted for 52 enemy aircraft (of which 36 were definitely destroyed by No.100 Group nightfighters), 'and this with only three SERRATE Squadrons (Nos.141, 169 and 239), one non-radar Squadron, (No.515 Squadron), and the two AI Mk X Squadrons (Nos.85 and 157 Squadrons) during the few days we were able to use them.'

Air Commodore Addison also complained about the non-transfer of promised fighter units to his Group, and thought the control of all intruder operations should come under Bomber Command:

> You will remember that at the CAS Meeting that was held just before 'Overlord' we were given these two AI Mk.X Squadrons (Nos.85 and 157), and were promised two more non-radar Squadrons (Nos.418 and 605) after 'Overlord'. Although 'Overlord' is dead and gone there has been no sign of Nos. 418 and 605 Squadrons coming to us. Nevertheless ADGB are continuing their night intruder operations over enemy territory despite the fact that one would have thought they should now be devoting all their energies to defending this country. It seems to me that the time has now come when all this offensive intruder work should be organised and controlled by Bomber Command.
>
> At the present time ADGB and ourselves divide the intruder effort between us – but for 'Overlord' reasons they have been given the upper hand. They however look upon intruding as a means of defending this country although they

dub many of the efforts, 'Bomber Support'. Since however the Hun is no longer using 'live' bombers to attack us surely the main role of intruders is now no longer defensive but offensive; and should be aimed primarily at putting out of action and disorganising, German air units that are being used against our bomber forces. If this principle is accepted then surely Bomber Command should wield their own intruder weapon. I feel, therefore, that we should now take over the whole of the intruder effort, and use it primarily for the purpose of Bomber Support. Since Bomber Command has managed a much greater say in this Intruder effort very decisive results indeed have been produced on the German nightfighting organisation.

...I consider, therefore, that Nos. 418 and 605 Squadrons should now come over to us and that our two Mk.X AI Squadrons should be returned to us...and that the control of intruding should now be placed under Bomber Command.[137]

In reply, Air Chief Marshal Harris was fully supportive:

...I entirely agree with you and I personally have done all I can and continue to do all I can to get this matter put on a proper basis. However, I despair of the results. Nevertheless I am sending your letter on to the Air Ministry with a statement saying that the views expressed in it are in entire agreement with my own.[138]

No. 100 Group eventually took on the responsibility for most of the Intruder work although the promised Squadrons never arrived. Some progress was made. Nos. 85 and 157 Squadrons were returned to No. 100 Group in September. They were used for both HL and LL sorties with good results. From 167 AI Mk.X HL patrols 47 AI contacts were reported leading to 12 successful combats, a ratio of 1 in 4. Target areas were also patrolled after the bombing, and 'escort' of the Main Force in the vicinity of the enemy nightfighter assembly beacons (with the No.100 Group fighters flying at 10 to 15 miles from the main track) were also carried out. The AI Mk.X aircraft sent on airfield patrols in September did not, in general, find much activity at the airfields to which they were sent but managed to achieve three successful combats from 13 AI contacts. To these, in the same month, could be added the efforts of the non-radar LL Intruders who destroyed five enemy aircraft and damaged 19 from 232 sorties despatched, a considerable improvement on previous months.

Four months later AVM Addison, (he had been promoted in the interim), was still complaining to Air Chief Marshal Harris. Enclosing a copy of a combat report (Ref. 85/SW/17; the pilot was S/L Burbridge of No.85 squadron), 'that has come lately from one of our Squadrons equipped with AI Mk.X ...describing the timely destruction of a Ju88 by one of our fighters which almost certainly prevented an attack on a Lancaster' and which, he stated, 'affords a very good example of "direct support" of our bombers. He expanded on the No.100 Group position:

It gives a very good idea of what can be achieved when the best equipment is used where it should be used. It seems that our claim for AI Mk.X has failed since Fighter Command and 85 Group, and the Middle East for that matter, still have higher priority for its supply than we have. It may be that this is because there are doubters in very high places who do not believe that nightfighter action can provide direct support to Bomber Command. Perhaps this particular report could be used to persuade some of those who may not have been giving us the support they might have done by reason of not knowing how a nightfighter can protect a bomber.

It had been our intention to increase the number of AI-fitted squadrons in the Group by converting one of our non-AI Intruder squadrons to AI Mk.X at the same time as No.85 Squadron was converting to Mk.XXX Mosquitoes...Now we learn that the supply of Mosquitoes Mk.XXX allocated to us will not allow this to be done, and, therefore, the degree of direct support that we had hoped to be able to give to you during this winter – and I mean high-flying direct support such as was done successfully by the crew who wrote the attached report – will by no means be as great as we planned.

The intention appears to be that we should only have two AI Mk.X Squadrons...we shall be hardly any better off than before. In addition to these Squadrons we shall still have our three Squadrons with AI Mk.IV (now useless), and two without any form of AI at all.

Our hope, you will remember, was to have all seven squadrons fitted with AI Mk.X this winter so that we could have efficient fighters for both high and low intruding. In desperation we have been casting around to find some form of substitute. Thanks to our American and Naval friends, we have been able to get a supply of a neat little set known as ASH[139] Unfortunately it is by no means as effective as AI Mk.X, but we do hope that it will at least give our low intruders some chance of spotting the Hun over his airfields. So we propose to put this little 'electric eye' into the aircraft of our two non-radar squadrons. It will be no good for high work.

It is surely a pity that we should have to resort to such subterfuges to improve our nightfighter effort when better equipment is available, particularly since our nightfighter operations must be amongst the most paying of all at the present time. Would it not be possible to take up the matter once again with the Air Ministry and ask them to abide by the decision made by the CAS at the Air Ministry last May?[140]

Air Chief Marshal Harris asked his Deputy, Air Marshal Sir Robert Saundby to look into the matter. Despite the slight optimism regarding an improvement in resources, his reply to AVM Addison shows the muddled thinking of the Air Ministry at the time over bomber support:

We have heard unofficially but authoritatively from the Air Ministry that our monthly allotment of Mk.X Mosquitoes is to be increased at once to ten. This I hope is only the beginning of a move to give higher priority to our requirements.

I have lately been chasing up the question of Fighter Command squadrons on Bomber Support. One Mk.VIII Squadron has been operating for some little time on low altitude missions. Why they go in for low altitude only I have not been able to make out. The Air Ministry now say that two Fighter Command AI Mk.X squadrons are fully trained and equipped, except for backward-looking AI, and that they are beginning Bomber Support operations forthwith. They also say that two further Mosquito AI Mk.X squadrons will be ready this month, one about December 15th and the other towards the end of the month. We have also been told that the Air Ministry are examining the possibility of turning over the remaining three Mosquito squadrons in Fighter Command to Bomber Support, but this is complicated by counter claims on them by 2nd TAF.[141]

No further Squadrons were added to No.100 Group and it finished the war with seven fighter squadrons. It is clear that the AI Mk.X aircraft had a major input into the successes enjoyed by the Group's fighters. Its late introduction was lamented by others as well as AVM Addison:

> Much progress was made during the closing months of the war in the technique of nightfighter support of the bombers, chiefly due to the introduction of AI Mk.X. It is very unfortunate that the weapon most suitable for bomber support work should not have been available in any numbers until the enemy nightfighter opposition was in eclipse.[142]

HL patrols were best served by AI Mk.X over the target area after bombing, at enemy nightfighter assembly areas, and escorting at a distance from the bomber stream. The target area proved most profitable and, in November 1944, a 'Clock' system of patrol was devised. The protecting fighters were given positions round the target at a distance between six and ten miles. They were detailed to patrol the line between their position and the target, during and after bombing, to intercept the attacking enemy fighters before they reached the bombers. It was not entirely satisfactory:

> In January and February the enemy fighters succeeded, on a few occasions, in getting into the stream and shooting down a number of bombers. Our supporting fighters could do little about this because they were flying well away from the bomber stream owing to the difficulty of operating AI in the midst of the WINDOW and bomber echoes.

The first close escort of the bomber stream was carried out in March. It became clear that AI Mk.X could be used for close escort provided the Mosquitoes flew above the bombers where H2S and WINDOW interference was least.[143]

Lack of enemy fighter opposition meant that the number of AI contacts reported from the AI Mk.X sorties on HL patrols and successful combats was small. However, there were notable exceptions. On 4/5th November, when the enemy fighters did, in fact, oppose the bombers in considerable strength, twenty AI MK.X fighters destroyed six, and damaged two, enemy aircraft. S/L Burbridge and F/L Skelton, of No. 85 Squadron destroying four enemy aircraft on this night. (see No.85 Squadron section of this chapter). The best month was in December when one out of every 2.4 reported contacts on the average yielded a successful combat. From 238 completed sorties, there were 95 suspicious AI contacts producing the remarkable result of 35 enemy aircraft destroyed, one probable, and four damaged.

The following table showing AI contacts per sortie, and the AI contacts per successful combat, indicates the opportunities presented to the support fighters:

	Sept	Oct	Nov	Dec	Jan	Feb	Mar	Apr
Aver. No. AI contacts per sortie	0.28	0.24	0.38	0.34	0.25	0.18	0.18	0.11
Aver. No. AI contacts per successful combat	3.9	5.6	3.5	2.4	3.4	4.6	5.2	5.3

The improved December figures could not be positively explained:

The reason for the increase in the AI contact/combat ratio after December is not altogether clear. The enemy may have been fitting warning receivers actuated by AI Mk.X radiations, and, of course, in March and April the close escort contact would mean that fewer of the suspicious AI contacts would be brought to combat.[144]

Fighter Assistance in other No.100 Group Operations

In June 1944, when No.100 Group began using the MANDREL Screen, WINDOW, and other 'Spoof' operations, SERRATE fighters and the LL intruders contributed to the deception. The SERRATE aircraft accompanied the diversionary forces to give the feint more realism and also to be in a position to intercept enemy fighters when the need arose. In addition, both SERRATE and LL aircraft were occasionally sent to patrol areas well away from the main attack to heighten the deception as to where the attack was actually taking place.

Likewise the fighters also took part with the WINDOW attacks, flying with them to add to the effect of the deception and then 'fanning-out' to take advantage of enemy reaction. From November 1944 onwards, they also carried out a number of bombing operations in support of the WINDOW 'feints', dropping markers and bombs on targets just ahead of the WINDOW force, bombing either visually or by means of Gee.

SERRATE Mk.IV and PERFECTOS

Two new RCM were developed to aid the No.100 Group fighters. When SN-2, the new enemy AI, was discovered in June 1944, work began to try to find a 'homer' to use against it. Eventually, SERRATE IV, was produced. Using an aural presentation, similar to the dots-and-dashes of the Lorenz beam system, this RCM became operational for the first time in January 1945. The other homer was PERFECTOS, work on which started at the same time as SERRATE IV[145]:

> ...the 'Egon' system was one of the main methods the enemy was using for controlling his fighters. In this system, the enemy Freya radars interrogated an IFF (FuG 25A) in the fighter, and so were able to D/F and range on them. There was no reason why the Bomber Support fighters should not do the same as the ground stations, and PERFECTOS was to be an equipment for interrogating the enemy IFF and then D/Fing and ranging (here the new equipment had an advantage over the SERRATE type of homing) on to the return signal.

> PERFECTOS equipment replaced the old SERRATE equipment in certain AI Mk.IV fighters and operations were started with this RCM in November 1944. A number of contacts were obtained in this and the following month, at ranges generally of about ten to fifteen miles, and though some were converted to AI Mk.IV contacts, the only success was a claim by a BSDU aircraft of an Me 110 destroyed from an initial PERFECTOS contact in December. It was thought that it was the limitation of AI Mk.IV, and not PERFECTOS, that prevented successful combats being achieved and it was decided not to fly further PERFECTOS sorties until the fitting of AI Mk.X aircraft was complete.

> In March 1945, 70 AI Mk.X/PERFECTOS sorties were flown and the results were very encouraging. About 39 PERFECTOS contacts were obtained and five were converted to AI leading to three enemy aircraft being destroyed and one damaged. The initial range of most of the PERFECTOS contacts was eight to fifteen miles but one contact was reported at a range of 50 miles. The main limitation of the PERFECTOS equipment was the lack of elevation.

> ...A number of SERRATE Mk.IV contacts were obtained, but very few were converted to AI. Two victories resulted from the use of SERRATE Mk.IV, and these both occurred during one sortie, by a BSDU aircraft, on 13/14th February 1945.[146]

A Weakening Opposition

By October 1944, there was a marked decrease in opposition to the Bomber Command raids. The cause was the positive Allied advance into the continent, and the countermeasures, technical and tactical, which were employed. The enemy's early warning and inland plotting systems were thrown into confusion. This was caused in no small part by activities of the HL and LL fighters who forced the enemy defence to plot hostile aircraft over very wide areas and broadcast frequent warnings to their own fighters of the presence of these hostile intruders. In fact the effect on the enemy's reporting system became in the latter months of the war a very important contribution of the No.100 Group fighters to Bomber Support.

In November 1944, Dr. R V Jones, ADI (Science) at the Air Ministry, made a detailed study of the German Night Defences. He was cautiously upbeat:

Looking now at the principles underlying our success, the classical method of conserving our bombers has been one of evasion: by various countermeasures we have deceived or blinded the enemy as to the real position of our forces. It is the application of this method which has been mainly responsible for our recent low losses. If, however, we attack the remoter targets, the German problem will become easier both in identification and interception. Moreover, a relatively small change in the technical balance of the struggle, such as occurred following our use of extended MANDREL and WINDOW, and as could occur following the German development of new AI, could swing the loss rate on to the high side again, so long as we depend on evasion.[147]

It is also clear he thought No. 100 Group's fighters were a considerable additional asset in support for the bombers:

The No.100 Group nightfighters, however, represent an additional principle which reduces our bomber losses by direct attack on the enemy nightfighters, and is therefore still able to reduce bomber losses should the evasion policy temporarily fail. The Germans clearly fear our nightfighters, and few improvements in German apparatus can reduce their threat. An extension of their activity would therefore increase German difficulties, and would be a valuable safeguard against breakdown of other measures.[148]

This last paragraph appears to have been in accord with the views of the C-in-C, Bomber Command, Air Chief Marshal Harris. Highlighting in pen this particular section of the report he has added, in the margin of the report, the terse note, 'Precisely, then why don't they give us more fighters and AI Mk.X's?'

Operational statistics show No.100 Group fighters' success. Flying approaching 8,000 sorties during their time in the Group they claimed 254 enemy aircraft destroyed (on the ground as well as in the air), with an additional 11 'probables'; 105 enemy aircraft were damaged. Forty-one fighters from No.100 Group were lost, giving a ratio of over 6:1 in favour of the bomber supporting fighters.

The table below gives the figures in greater detail:

No.100 Group Fighter Claims.

	Sorties	E/A Dest	Probables	E/A Damaged
AI Mk.IV.HLP				
(Dec.1943 to Jan.1945)	2662	95	1	18
Non-radar LLP				
(Apr.1944 to Jan.1945)				
(Air)	1601	12	2	17
(Ground)	–	9	–	20
AI Mk.X HLP				
(June 1944 to April 1945)	2016	99	6	20
AI Mk.X LLP	526	17	1	5
AI Mk.XV HLP				
(Jan.1945 to April 1945)	316	4	–	1
AI Mk.XV LLP.				
(Dec.1944 to April 1945)				
(Air)	763	9	1	3
(Ground)	–	9	–	21
TOTAL	7884	254	11	105

(HLP= High Level Patrol: LLP= Low Level Patrol)

The above statistics clearly indicate that the Group's fighter squadrons made a substantial contribution to its success.

THE SQUADRONS

No. 23 Squadron

At the beginning of the Second World War No.23 Squadron was used in a defensive nightfighter role. In December 1940, it began what was to become its main role, intruder missions, over enemy airfields in Europe. Re-equipped with Mosquitoes in July 1942, it had previously flown Blenheims and Havocs, the Squadron moved in the December to Malta for operations over Sicily and Italy. A year later it moved to Sardinia to carry out similar activities over Southern France and Northern Italy.

No.23 Squadron was the last of the fighter squadrons transferred into No. 100 Group. It returned to the UK in May 1944, after eighteen months duty in the Mediterranean:

Alghero, Sardinia.

5.5.44 The news that the whole Squadron had been waiting for, that it was returning to the UK, was announced by the CO in the morning. The rest of the day was spent servicing aircraft which had to be flown back to the MU at Blida. Also a farewell party was organised, and F/L D Griffiths flew to Naples to contact a supply of 'hooch'.

6.5.44. Invitation to the other Squadrons on the aerodrome to join us in saying farewell to Sardinia, and in the evening a party to end all parties was held, whereupon no less than 60 bottles of spirits were consumed, plus various Sardinian and Italian wines and liqueurs. There were a certain number of 'hangovers' in the Squadron in the morning, which made the job of packing very hard indeed.[149]

On 20th May the 'Air' Party sailed in the troopship 'Mooltan' for Gourock, with the 'Ground' Party in the 'Strathnaver' bound for Liverpool. Their arrival at the end of the month in the UK was untimely as far as the prospect of leave was concerned. With the preparations for D-Day building up they were confined to a four-day anchorage before disembarkation. Many of the ground crews had not seen England for four years and there was some resentment but it was 'all over in five minutes'. On 1st June the personnel disembarked and went to Little Snoring, where the Squadron remained until disbanded at the end of the War.

Preparations for duty in No.100 Group moved on apace:

3/5.6.44 spent re-equipping the Squadron with 'new clothes'...First flying from England began on 19th June when 12 aircraft carried out local flying 'to get their hands in'...Everyone was quite excited at the thought of official low-flying especially as the order states 50 ft or below! Night Flying Tests were carried out and it was found that there is quite a difficulty in flying at night in this country in comparison with overseas. Not being used to this 'pansy' Drem lighting system (a standard system of airfield lighting for perimeters, runways and approach work, evolved at Drem Airfield, Scotland) we couldn't believe our eyes when we saw a myriad of lights around the various aerodromes that we passed over.[150]

With new aircraft the Squadron commenced operations in No.100 Group on the 5th/6th July. Although the weather was dull, in the afternoon an improvement made operations possible. W/C A M Murphy, the Squadron CO, and three other crews took part in what turned out to be uneventful sorties. All the crews returned safely. No. 23 Squadron flew 122 sorties on 16 nights in the month of July. In the course of these sorties two enemy aircraft were destroyed – F/L D J Griffiths, the 'honorary' wine merchant for the Mediterranean farewell party claimed one – and 22 enemy airfields attacked. A variety of other targets were bombed, including railways installations, gun sites and bridges. The Squadron also flew seven Day Ranger sorties and the first crew was lost when F/O F D Grimwood and F/S P Woodman failed to return.

The following month No.23 Squadron flew 131 Intruder and two Day Ranger patrols. One of the latter proved lively. F/S W J Hardie saw 'Some Huns were right in his sights on the shore, so he quickly demonstrated his Browning machine guns and cannon thus spreading the Huns over the beach. Also, 27 escort duties with Bomber Command took place. On 29th August sixteen crews flew into the heart of Germany and two enemy aircraft were damaged by the Station Commander G/C B R Hoare (who made 90 Intruders flights over Europe during the War). He was the only one-eyed pilot in the RAF and sported a moustache the length of which, he claimed, was 'six inches from wing-tip to wing-tip!'

In September the Squadron flew 125 sorties on 19 nights. It damaged 8 enemy aircraft in the air and a similar number on the ground. Nine enemy airfields were attacked. Attacks were also made on enemy transportation; four locomotives were destroyed; and six locomotives, eleven trains, and two barges were damaged. Bombs were also dropped on road and rail installations and a searchlight site. Two Mosquitoes were lost. In the same month one of several Air Sea Rescue(ASR) trips looking for 'downed' colleagues took place. Although described in a jocular manner it was a serious business:

> At about 0345 hours in the early morn of the 7th the inmates of Hut 4 were rudely awakened by our Staff Navigator, F/L Gregory, (or the Airman's Friend), with the information that W/C Bromley of No.169 Squadron was missing and that five crews were required to carry out ASR. As is the custom during the 24 hours of the day, F/O Stewart and F/O Beaudet (see below) were out of bed in two ticks closely followed by two more of our delightful Allies...P/O Neil and F/O Berry.' All reports negative – bad weather.[151]

In November the Squadron carried out fighter affiliation with No.223 Squadron at Oulton, the first of several. Also in that month, a feat of superb piloting coupled with exceptional mechanical reliability took place:

> 15.11.44. F/L Badley and F/L Griffiths went on a Day Ranger to Copenhagen. When about to go in for the kill everything including the kitchen sink and bathroom fittings came up at them with murderous ferocity...F/L Griffiths returned to Little Snoring but no news was heard of Badley until well over an hour after he was due. However trust our amazing New Zealand pilot to do the trick and, after travelling 600 miles on one engine with one fan, he landed at Woodbridge. Touching down, however, his undercarriage collapsed but with his usual skill and handling both bodies got away unhurt. This must be a record for a Mosquito to travel so far on one fan.[152]

In the same month new tactics were tried, that of bombing from 20,000 ft over various targets; No.100 Group HQ approved the results. It was not possible to state too accurately the success of these raids as they took place in 10/10ths cloud but it was thought that the success of this idea would show itself on a clear night when they could 'draw Jerry's fighters up there!'

No.23 Squadron sustained a morale-shaking blow at the beginning of December when the Squadron CO, W/C Murphy, failed to return from a sortie. He had been CO for almost a year and was a Flight Commander on the Squadron before that; he was awarded a posthumous bar to his DSO later in the month. A further problem arose in the same month with the exodus of tour-expired crews from the Squadron which had been proceeding at an alarming rate. W/C S P Russell became the new Squadron CO in December and was involved in a hair-raising rescue operation at Little Snoring in the following March when German Intruders attacked the airfield:

4.3.45. W/C Russell (Acting Station Commander) went to the scene of a crashed Halifax from Foulsham and arrived five minutes before the crash tender and was able to remove a wounded rear-gunner. The Hun made one bombing attack, killing eight bullocks, and two strafing attacks on the burning wreckage during the course of the firefighting and rescue operations, naturally making things much more dangerous, but luckily no further injury was caused.

The Hun aircraft was in the vicinity of the airfield for some two hours but no attacks were made on it although four aircraft were shot down in the area. As a result of the above, orders were given that no lights were to be shown on aircraft when taxying out for take off. As a result of this one aircraft from No.23 Squadron and one from No.515 Squadron collided, both were unaware of the other's presence.[153]

Some retribution for this was given in an example of close combat a long way from home which occurred over a German airfield a few days later:

9.3.45. F/O Heath and F/S Thompson. At 2325 hours saw FW190 taking off at Stendal, burning Navigation and Downward Recognition lights- an Intruder's Dream! They fired a short burst at the enemy aircraft but missed and overshot. The enemy aircraft climbed rapidly to 1200 ft; the Mosquito closed to 150 yards on the same height and scored direct hits on its port wing and fuselage. The enemy aircraft peeled off to port and fell to the ground where it exploded.[154]

Towards the end of the War new methods were tried:

18.4.45. The Squadron is settling down in its new role of marking and bombing airfields for No.515 and No.141 Squadrons to follow and bomb. Under the direction of a Master-Bomber from our Squadron up to 20 aircraft are doing concerted attacks on airfield buildings with excellent results. Four crews were detailed for Bombing Patrols of the Munich/Neubiberg area under instructions from the Master-Bomber (F/L Rivaz). These instructions were carried out in detail and flares and incendiaries were dropped to good effect and many fires were observed amongst the buildings. The Master-Bomber directed bombing of

Nos. 23, 141 and 515 Squadrons, and enemy defences opened up with accuracy from 4/5 well-placed guns but this did not prevent the job being carried out successfully. Repeated the following night.[155]

During its time in No.100 Group the Squadron flew 1,067 sorties and completed 70 SERRATE and 125 Intruder operations. It destroyed 66 enemy aircraft (with another 19 probably destroyed) and damaged 89. The Squadron also dropped 160 tons of bombs on the enemy, and made the following successful attacks on enemy ground targets: [1] Trains 636. [2] Motor Transport 915. [3] Shipping 49. [4] Factories 74.[5] Airfields 39. [6] Miscellaneous targets 370.[156]

F/O George Stewart, RCAF, was an experienced Intruder pilot with No. 23 Squadron and flew, with his navigator Paul Beaudet, some 50 operations whilst the Squadron was in No.100 Group. During this time he 'visited' 45 enemy airfields before returning to Canada as an instructor. On the night of 4th/5th November 1944 when the Main Force attacked Bochum, George and his navigator were instructed to patrol enemy nightfighter airfields near the target. No.100 Group Mosquitoes had a very successful night claiming four Ju88s and two Me110s; two other nightfighters were damaged:

> After the briefing...Paul spreads out his maps, his log, Dalton navigational computer – not to be confused with computers as we know them today, but a visual calculator – and Douglas protractor. My job is to draw flying rations, including enemy colours of the period (ESNs) so that we can fire them from our Very pistols if need be. These are nicknamed 'sisters'. I also draw escape kits in which we find small compasses, German aircraft cockpit checks on rice paper, concentrated food portions, first aid materials, water purifying tablets and pills to keep us awake.
>
> I pull out the files on Ardorf, Marx and Varel airfields (our given targets) and note their layouts and remember where their defences are marked, as well as station buildings, ammo dumps etc. I note also the height of nearby obstructions...Paul has by now drawn his tracks to our target...we know we must be off the ground by 1900 hours...Until it's time to go, we feel slightly cold and alone, our beds down at our hut seem to us to be so warm and enticing, with gale force winds of 40-60 mph forecast for that evening, and no moon.

The target was reached without incident:

> Five minutes later, over the Jade Canal, we saw ahead of us the visual Lorenz landing pattern of lights that the Germans used to guide their aircraft in for a landing. It was Ardorf, nicely lit up to welcome us, right on the money at 2015 hours. 'OK Paul' I said, 'Load up a "sister" just in case we need it.' I dived the Mossie to 500 ft so that we could look up and see any aircraft silhouetted...
>
> We raced around the circuit and saw some navigation lights on the final

approach. Turning my gun safety switch to the firing position, I close in on him as he turned on his landing lights and we got a quick shot at him as he was silhouetted against his own light. It was a Ju88. Strikes appeared on him all around the nose area and he must have been very low.

Suddenly, the whole airfield was plunged into total blackness...we see another aircraft on the downwind leg. I pulled up sharply and overshot his tail, and closed in to fire a quick burst of cannon at him. I noticed strikes all over the starboard wing and cockpit area, and pieces fell off the aircraft. It was a Heinkel 111. We hung around the area for a while and, as our patrol was coming to an end, we went into our bombing dive and, at 3,000 ft, we released our bombs just as the searchlights reached up to grab us: we weaved and skidded gently out of the rays, and looked to see that our bombs had struck...right on the runway. All lights were now doused on the airfield and we set course for home.[157]

F/Os Stewart and Beaudet returned to Canada on 17th January 1945, seemingly with a rousing send-off:

A farewell drink in the bar developed into a small party and a sortie was made on one of the 'locals' followed by a return trip to the Mess. By closing time everyone was in good trim. Our gallant Canadians will remember their last night here.[158]

Both were awarded DFC's in March 1945.

No. 85 Squadron.

No. 85 Squadron joined No. 100 Group at the beginning of May 1944 partly, perhaps, as a response by the Air Ministry to the exceptional heavy losses sustained by Bomber Command just over a month previously in the raid on Nuremburg (qv), and also in preparation for D-Day. It brought to Swannington, a newly constructed aerodrome in Norfolk, a squadron which had an extensive knowledge of both daytime and nightfighter tactics. The Squadron was highly thought of at the topmost level. 'These Squadrons' [it went to Swannington with No. 157 Squadron] were, according to the Chief of Air Staff, Sir Charles Portal, 'the cream of Fighter Command's Nightfighter Force and are already experienced in offensive nightfighter operations.'[159]

The transfer seems to have been popular. 'No.85 Squadron were thoroughly dug in at West Malling,' it is cheerfully recorded. 'They had had some measure of success against the enemy in their attacks on London and were resting on the laurels of 211 Huns destroyed in the air since the outbreak of the little misunderstanding with Germany, when they were snatched out of their complacency on 1st May 1944 and whirled from the lush Kentish Weald, and the old faces of No.11 Group, into the frozen north of the foetid fens and the somewhat more vigorous and outspoken leadership of No.100 Group!'

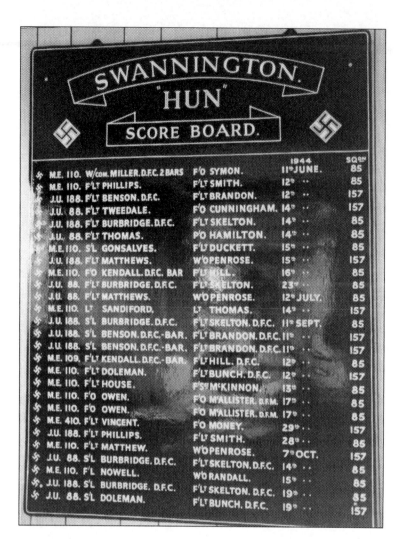

SWANNINGTON "HUN" SCORE BOARD.

			1944	SQDN
M.E. 110.	W/COM. MILLER. D.F.C. 2 BARS	F/O SYMON.	11th JUNE.	85
M.E. 110.	F/LT PHILLIPS.	F/LT SMITH.	12th ..	85
J.U. 188.	F/LT BENSON. D.F.C.	F/LT BRANDON.	12th ..	157
J.U. 88.	F/LT TWEEDALE.	F/O CUNNINGHAM.	14th ..	157
J.U. 188.	F/LT BURBRIDGE. D.F.C.	F/LT SKELTON.	14th ..	85
J.U. 88.	F/LT THOMAS.	P/O HAMILTON.	14th ..	85
M.E. 110.	S/L GONSALVES.	F/U DUCKETT.	15th ..	85
J.U. 188.	F/LT MATTHEWS.	W/O PENROSE.	15th ..	157
M.E. 110.	F/O KENDALL. D.F.C. BAR	F/..LL.	16th ..	85
J.U. 88.	F/LT BURBRIDGE. D.F.C.	F/..ELTON.	23rd ..	85
J.U. 88.	F/LT MATTHEWS.	W/O PENROSE.	12th JULY.	85
M.E. 110.	LT SANDIFORD.	LT THOMAS.	14th ..	157
J.U. 188.	S/L BURBRIDGE. D.F.C.	F/LT SKELTON. D.F.C.	11th SEPT.	85
J.U. 188.	S/L BENSON. D.F.C. BAR.	F/L BRANDON. D.F.C.	11th ..	157
J.U. 188.	S/L BENSON. D.F.C. BAR.	F/L BRANDON. D.F.C.	11th ..	157
M.E. 109.	F/LT KENDALL. D.F.C. BAR.	F/L HILL. D.F.C.	12th ..	85
M.E. 110.	F/LT DOLEMAN.	F/LT BUNCH. D.F.C.	12th ..	157
M.E. 110.	F/LT HOUSE.	F/ST M'KINNON.	13th ..	85
M.E. 110.	F/O OWEN.	F/O M'ALLISTER. D.F.M.	17th ..	85
M.E. 110.	F/O OWEN.	F/O M'ALLISTER. D.F.M.	17th ..	85
M.E. 410.	F/LT VINCENT.	F/O MONEY.	29th ..	157
J.U. 188.	F/LT PHILLIPS.	F/L SMITH.	28th ..	85
M.E. 110.	F/LT MATTHEW.	W/O PENROSE.	7th OCT.	157
J.U. 88.	S/L BURBRIDGE. D.F.C.	F/LT SKELTON. D.F.C.	14th ..	85
M.E. 110.	F/L NOWELL.	W/O RANDALL.	15th ..	85
J.U. 188.	S/L BURBRIDGE. D.F.C.	F/LT SKELTON. D.F.C.	19th ..	85
J.U. 88.	S/L DOLEMAN.	F/LT BUNCH. D.F.C.	19th ..	157

Nos. 85/157 Squadrons' 'Hun Scoreboard' at Swannington.

(Author)

The Squadron received immediate concentrated training in its new Group. At Swannington it was, with its partner Squadron No.157, to destroy in ten months, 106 aircraft over enemy territory. The Squadron found that they had the use of Langtoft GCI (in Lincs. north of Market Deeping) 'who will use them as an ordinary GCI uses night defensive Squadrons, and will provide the Squadron with night interceptions until they are proficient in the use of AI Mk.X.[160] In the event of enemy aircraft coming through the coverage of the GCI whilst the training was taking place the Squadron would be diverted to combat this threat.

There were also visits to bomber stations, dinghy drill at Cambridge, local talks on navigation and PFF techniques. Lectures were given outlining the functions of Bomber Command and the role the Squadron was expected to play in support of the bombers. There was instruction from 'Y' Service personnel on Luftwaffe R/T traffic between the German Controller and the enemy nightfighters. Emphasis was also placed on the HL escort work; the difficulties to be expected from inaccurate navigation; enemy action by flak and nightfighters, or from radio interference. A talk was given to the aircrews by a F/S from a Halifax bomber on 'Escaping from Germany'. He had evaded after being shot down, had walked most of the way, and had stolen a cycle. 'The point most strongly felt by all', it is recorded, 'was the real need for being pretty fit, in case such an emergency arose, for very few of the audience, I feel sure, could have walked through Germany on a full stomach let alone an empty one.' [161]

The training was essential for the different role that the Squadron had now acquired. Tight aerial discipline when working with the bombers was imperative. Instead of defensive operations controlled by GCI radar they would be required to navigate into the heart of enemy-held Europe. Most of the crews had had little navigating to do in their previous operations and were in need of refreshing their navigational skills.

S/L Bob Muir, pre-war Merchant Navy Officer and experienced Intruder crew member, who had completed 59 operations, played a significant part in navigation training. On a 'rest' period after two consecutive Intruder tours with No.605 Squadron he was appointed CO of No.4 (Navigation) Squadron at No. 60 OTU – the only Mosquito OTU at that time – and later became Chief Navigation Instructor. W/C R B 'Sammy' Hoare, DSO*, DFC*, Station Commander at Little Snoring was put in charge of retraining the Nos. 85 and 157 Squadrons. Muir 'had experienced 24 "hairy" operations with this redoubtable gentleman (on one occasion we came back from Berlin on one engine) and he had me seconded to Swannington to train the crews navigationally.' S/L Muir started on 13th May and, according to the Squadron record gave instruction on, 'pre-flight training, DR Navigation, stressed the importance of accurate course steering, with map-reading, principally through water pinpoints, and gave several general hints for pilots and navigators as a crew.' [162]

It was six days of intensive activity:

At 60 OTU my training time with the navigators was spent in the air. When I was called away from this job to train Nos.85 and 157 Squadrons in Low-Level (LL) night intruder work, I did no flying with them. It was all classroom work, not like at 60 OTU where I flew with the navigators as well. I was with them a week and did about 20 hours with each Squadron. I gave lectures as well as individual instruction to each navigator. The latter would take two to three hours at a time. I spent a lot of time with them: it was very important.

When I was training the Squadrons I found the pilots were extremely interested, and they attended some of my lectures as well as the navigators. It was part interest and part self-preservation. The big difference for these crews was that previously they had been used to having the whole space above and around them in which to operate. For No. 100 Group duties they didn't; they had to be in specific places at specific times.

Sometimes going across the Channel we would go as low as 200 ft to dodge the enemy radar. It was always a matter of discipline. You had to do these sort of things to avoid putting the aircraft in danger. It was not unusual for me to alter course about 20 times before we got to the target. We could have got there much quicker and easier by just going straight there, or just doing one or two turns, but it was safer my way. I had to drum this into the Nos. 85 and 157 Squadron navigators. I used to tell them 'A good navigator is never lost, he is only less sure of his position!'

One of the troubles, for the bomber crews as well as our chaps, was that when they had left the enemy coast they thought they were safe, but they were not. This was the enemy nightfighters hunting ground. I advised the navigators to continually watch the tail and not relax after coming out of enemy territory. It took our chaps ages to understand this.

I trained them:

[1] To use pre-planned, dog-legged 'safety' routes to all known enemy airfields avoiding the flak areas, with selected pin-points – coastal; lakes; distinctive river bends etc. with each route frequently dog-legged to confuse enemy radar, ground defences and nightfighters. Many were designed from my own experience.

[2] To use points of entry on to all occupied territory where flak would be minimal. Crews would be seriously endangered by not following this basic advice and straying over areas of highly sophisticated enemy flak.

[3] To fly no higher than 500 ft over the English Channel and North Sea at night – lower on moonlit occasions – and 'on the deck' in daylight; over enemy territory to turn complete circles to confuse flak and nightfighters; to make irregular but compensating zig-zags yet still maintain track; make height changes; undertake frequent dog-legging. All this was designed for safety and to prevent the enemy from anticipating targets.

Bob Muir later received a letter of thanks from G/C Hoare for his short but intensive efforts at Swannington, and for 'the invaluable help you gave to the two Squadrons. They have done exceedingly well, and I do regard it was, actually, entirely due to you that they have achieved their great and immediate success', (the two Squadrons shot down eleven enemy aircraft in one month, possibly an RAF record). He added that 'Both Squadron CO's are also equally appreciative.' Muir returned to No.100 Group in January, 1945, when he became Station Navigation Officer at Little Snoring.

No. 85 Squadron first operated on 27th May off the Dutch Islands. Re-equipped with new aircraft, all navigators had had to be taught to operate GEE, a new

Derelict Control Tower at Swannington   *(Author)*

navigational aid as far as the Squadron was concerned. None of the crews had previously done navigation courses, but the training had gone well.

The Squadron became fully operational the following month when D-Day occurred. The first two weeks are described below in detail:

4/5. 6.44. At 11 o'clock twelve crews were detailed to be at Colerne by one o/clock...and all aircraft were there on time... G/C Cunningham DSO, DFC, came down to brief us on the operation and generally to put us in the picture. Sea and airborne forces were to make landings on the beaches in Seine Bay. As some 2,000 aircraft were to be engaged in the landings themselves, and the bombing of ten coastal batteries, which preceded them, considerable enemy nightfighter reaction was anticipated. Thus six patrol lines had been laid on about 50 miles west, east and south of the landing areas...Of the six, No. 85 Squadron's twelve aircraft were to patrol the four lines in France, Vire-Argentan; Argent-Bernay; Bernay-Pavilly; Pavilly to a point 20 miles west of Dieppe. It was thus hoped that at least some of the enemy fighters from known airfields in France would have to go through our patrols and we were to intercept all contacts that went in towards the landing areas.

We were further strictly enjoined to be most careful about aircraft recognition, as nearly all the aircraft over France would be friendly with a proportion of, perhaps, one 'hostile' to 50 friendly aircraft. In fact with all the Dakotas around it was hinted that anyone claiming a Heinkel 111 would most probably be court-martialled!..At night while waiting to take off it was certainly amazing to see the glider 'trains' going over the aerodrome all with navigation lights on, and appearing, at first, like an airborne flare path. These continued throughout the night, at times so low that people taking off had to fly under them. One could not but feel proud of being part of so inspiring and colossal an operation.

5/6.6.44 The night of D-1 was not as good as had been hoped,with considerable cloud at about 2,000-3,000 ft over England and the Landing Areas. The moon was full, however, and the visibility excellent below cloud... All crews took off as ordered and had nothing to report. Although disappointed at having no combats, there was general satisfaction at having broken the ice, and put all our training efforts to some use. All of the Squadron's aircraft were back at Swannington by 9am.

7/8.6.44 Tonight the Squadron started on their allotted role of Bomber Support duties. As MONICA was not generally fitted, the initial trips were all low Intruder to enemy nightfighter aerodromes. All were uneventful.

10/11.6.44 Although the weather over the Continent was not good, five Intruder trips were sent off. F/L Nowell and Captain Ree who went to Holland both came back early in atrocious weather...While still about 40 miles from our coast Captain Ree suddenly heard cannon-firing, and, doing a very tight turn saw another Mosquito making an attack on him. It was still fairly light so that there seemed little excuse for faulty recognition. Fortunately Captain Ree's aircraft sustained no damage and, on landing, subsequent inquiry showed that a member of 25 Squadron at Coltishall was the attacker. We were glad he was such a bad shot!

11.6.44 (Day). Tonight we had our first success in Bomber Command and as was fitting the enemy aircraft was destroyed by our CO, W/C Miller (with F/O Symon). His report reads:

While patrolling Melun airfield, height 3,000 ft, an aircraft was illuminated and fired off 'recco' signals. Turning towards this position, contact was made, a visual was obtained and the aircraft was recognised as an Me110, the long-range tanks being of great help in recognition. After a five second burst the enemy aircraft caught fire and exploded on hitting the ground. A note to the report suggested, 'that enemy recognition signals and searchlights in the neighbourhood of airfields might prove a suitable source for contacts.' This was later proved to be so, (in the next two weeks seven enemy aircraft were destroyed by the Squadron.)

12/13.6.44. Bomber Command's effort was directed at French Railways and a synthetic oil plant at Gelsenkirchen. In view of this F/O Hedgecoe went to three German aerodromes at Twente, Plantlunne, and Theine, but had an uneventful patrol apart from being shot at, and illuminated by searchlights. Captain Weisteen went to Gilze-Riten, Eindhoven, while F/S Rogers did a

Freshman to Soesterberg and Deelen. Although he had several contacts, he was unable to bring them to visuals, as they were always going in to land and at low speeds. Twice he was illuminated by searchlights as he followed them down the Visual Lorenz and was once shot at but sustained no damage. F/S York who went on to Le Culot had two visuals on Me110s. The first one was going in to land, and he overshot. The other one he saw taking off, as it was burning a blue light. He followed it on AI and after a short burst saw strikes on the port wing. The contact was then broken off. He only claims a 'damaged'.

F/L Philips went to Beauvais. He had just started his patrol when contact was obtained some miles to port. The enemy aircraft climbed to 8,000 ft and levelled out. F/L Philips closed in and recognised the aircraft as an Me110. His first burst of fire produced strikes on the port engine. The enemy aircraft peeled off to port but was followed on AI and, after a while, it straightened out again. F/L Philips closed in and further bursts set the Me110 on fire, and it burst into flames on hitting the ground.

14/15.6.44. F/O Thomas was patrolling Beauvais, Cormeilles, and Criel airfields, and, when approaching two aerial lighthouses, south of Criel, AI contact was obtained four miles away. After following the contact in an orbit round the lights it then set a northerly course, and climbed to 6,000 ft over Paris. It levelled out and F/O Thomas identified it as a Ju88. He fired two one-second bursts from 600 ft. The first started a fire in the enemy aircraft and the second blew up the port engine. The aircraft crashed on Criel Aerodrome. As the result of the night's Intruder activity six enemy nightfighters were destroyed, of which No.85 Squadron got two.

15/16.6.44. Bomber Command sent out some 700 'Heavies' tonight to bomb French targets once more, so the aerodromes we patrolled were in Belgium and France. W/O Alderton did a 'Freshman' to Brussels-Le Culot but was very severely shot at because he flew first over Brussels, then into Antwerp, and finally over Ghent in his efforts to get away. He then came back, no longer a Freshman! Captain Weisteen patrolled Florennes but on the way back over the sea, the starboard engine packed up. He flew back about 200 miles on the port engine, and made a good landing at Swannington.

S/L Gonsalves at long last broke his 'duck' ...While patrolling St. Trond airfield a contact was obtained, and the aerodrome was then lit up. The contact was followed in a wide orbit of the circuit and at 200 ft, from well below the enemy aircraft , it was identified as an Me110 with long-range tanks. Two bursts blew up the starboard engine of the enemy aircraft and it crashed in the Dispersal Area of the airfield. A further contact was obtained a few minutes later, head-on. A hard turn to starboard brought the contact in again at 4,000 ft . It was recognised as a further Me110. A long burst produced a concentration of strikes on the port wing, but no fire. In view of the point of aim this struck S/L Gonsalves as being rather odd , so he pulled up to have another look at it, but the enemy aircraft was diving and contact was lost in the ground returns.

15/16.6.44. The night's Bomber attacks were divided between a target in the Ruhr and a further French target in support of the land forces. Thus three of our aircraft went to Belgium, two to Holland, while F/L Nowell made an uneventful trip to Laon and Juvincourt. W/C Miller went to St.Trond, and F/S York to Florennes, both trips being uneventful. F/L Searle went to Brussels-Le Culot, but he to was caught over Brussels Town and rather severely shot at. The moral seems to be that one should approach Le Culot from the south side of the city, where you can only be engaged by one defended area at a time, which is not the case in the north.

F/L Cleaver went to Leuwarden, while F/O Kendall did a Freshman to Deelen-Soesterberg. Whilst at the latter the airfield lights went up and an aircraft was seen to land. A 'red' was fired, and a further aircraft then put on its lights and went round again. F/O Kendall gave chase, putting down wheels and flaps to keep behind it at 140 Indicated Air Speed (IAS) at 700 ft. It was identified as an Me110, and two bursts were given from 150 yards as it was turning for the final approach. Eight strikes were seen and the aircraft caught fire, and with lights still burning, climbed to 1,500 ft and then dived into the ground, 200 yards short of the runway. Thus, in six days the Squadron destroyed six enemy nightfighters.

After its initial efforts in Bomber Support the Squadron was virtually 'grounded' for a week by poor weather, resuming operations on 23rd June. On this night S/L Burbridge went to Coulommiers Airfield where:

A single searchlight exposed from the aerodrome, and a Very cartridge was fired in response. While hurrying towards the lights, the procedure was again carried out. While proceeding on a right-hand orbit of the aerodrome, contact was obtained 80 degrees starboard at three miles range, and at 1,000 ft height. The recognition signal was again carried out, and by the light of the cartridge the aircraft was recognised as a Ju88. The enemy aircraft then flew across the aerodrome and was illuminated, but searchlights then illuminated S/L Burbridge's fighter which broke away to starboard but maintained AI contact. When the Ju88 was clear of the aerodrome the pursuing fighter closed in once more and a short burst sent the enemy aircraft crashing to the ground. The debris caused a leak in the coolant system of the port engine of the Mosquito, so the airscrew was feathered, and S/L Burbridge flew back 300 miles on one engine.[163]

On 25th June news came through that ADGB wanted four patrols per night from

No.85 Squadron to take part in the fight against the V1 menace. These aircraft would operate from Swannington doing one and a half-hour patrols out to sea under GCI Control. This would, naturally, mean a reduction in the effort on behalf of No.100 Group, although the Squadron was still able to carry out 28 Bomber Support operations.

Feelings were mixed in the Squadron at the prospect of chasing flying bombs 'for the obvious snag of "stooge" patrols loomed large'. One of their number thought the Squadron had been 'reduced to airborne ack-ack against V1s', finding it 'very second eleven stuff'.

The following month, the Squadron, which had settled in at Swannington, was disturbed by being transferred back to West Malling to carry on the battle against the V1s. At this time in their attachment to No.100 Group No.85 Squadron had flown 15 Intruder sorties, eleven HL patrols, and two Night Ranger patrols without successful combat. Their work against the flying bombs is beyond the extent of this book and it is sufficient to say they acquitted themselves well and managed to shoot down 33 'whizzers'.

Bomber Command was annoyed at losing the Squadrons. 'I do not consider that the arrangements will be entirely satisfactory as these squadrons are badly needed for the direct support of the Bomber Force,' wrote the Air Commodore Ops to the Bomber Command SASO, Sir Robert Saundby, 'the Mosquitoes fitted with AI Mk. X have already proved their all-round superiority over the other Mosquitoes in No.100 Group.'[164] After visiting West Malling the No.100 Group SASO, Air Commodore Chisholm, submitted a detailed report to the C-in-C, Bomber Command, Air Chief Marshal Harris, in which he clearly stated the reasons why the two Squadrons would be better employed in Bomber Support:

> The Mosquito Mk. VI and Mosquito Mk.XIX are identical aircraft in so far as airframe and engines are concerned, but the Mk. XIX (used by Nos. 85 and 157 Squadrons) is equipped with AI Mk.X equipment which weighs several hundred pounds, while the Mk. VI has no AI equipment. The Mk. VI Mosquito has the normal Mosquito nose while the Mk. XIX has an enlarged nose made of perspex in which is housed the AI Scanner. It would be right to expect that the Mk.VI is faster than the Mk. XIX and this has been borne out in comparative trials. It also appears to accelerate better in a dive and this is a characteristic which is of great importance in flying bomb chasing.
>
> With regard to the need for AI it is agreed by all who have had practical experience of flying bomb chasing that range measurement is important, yet there are experienced pilots who succeed consistently without a special ranging device. The top scorer among the flying bomb chasers flies a Tempest which has neither AI, nor ranging device, and to date he has personally destroyed 48 flying-bombs.

It is interesting that the CO of No.96 Nightfighter Squadron, an AI Mosquito Squadron that has specialised in the anti- flying bomb role, has chosen for his own use a Mosquito Mk.VI without an AI and with this he has achieved considerable success. His personal preference for his Squadron is for Mustangs or Tempests.

...It is noteworthy that during 13 nights of operations when they (ie Nos. 85 and 157 Squadrons) began Bomber Support they destroyed ten enemy nightfighters for no loss. This gives an idea of the support of which Bomber Command has been deprived by the employment of the Squadrons in the anti-Diver role during their spell at West Malling, which to date has yielded only eight flying bombs destroyed.

Pilots of these two Squadrons have complained that on many occasions when attempting to close in to attack a flying bomb, a Tempest has forestalled them, cutting in and destroying it.

While Bomber Support by destroying enemy nightfighters is today almost impossible without AI, since enemy nightfighters no longer use navigation lights, flying bomb destruction can be achieved by Mosquitoes Mk. VI with a simple range measuring device (radar or other type) and these aircraft would be of little value (having no AI) against enemy fighters. Thus it can be seen that if Mosquito Mk. VI's (which are faster than Mk. XIX) with a simple range measuring device, can be operated against flying bombs instead of the Mk.XIXs, the war effort in general will benefit by the destruction of enemy nightfighters.

No.100 Group have firmly held that radar-equipped nightfighters demand concrete runway airfields since the vibration that is set up during take off and landing on grass airfields seriously increases radar unserviceability, Nos. 85 and 157 Squadrons have, during this second 'Diver' (V1) period, been stationed at West Malling which is a grass airfield, and a rough one at that. The motive for the insistence on this move was the requirement that these Squadrons should be nearer the scene of operations and should thus become imbued with the importance of their new role. It was in fact insinuated that their earlier efforts had been half-hearted.

The surface of West Malling airfield is having disastrous effects on the serviceability of the airframes and radar. The engines are being boosted to 25 lbs and there is no doubt that this treatment will result in failures later on that are bound to affect future operations. It would seem that complete re-engining will be necessary before these fighters can be used on long range Bomber Support. A complete overhaul of AI scanners will be essential on the return of these Squadrons to No.100 Group control.[165]

There was much pressure from both No.100 Group and Bomber Command and, eventually, both squadrons returned to the Group. On 22nd August the Air Ministry told the ADGB that, 'Nos.85 and 157 Squadrons were to be withdrawn from Diver duties and will return to Bomber Command at an early date. The actual date depends on the availability of replacements and this will be given...the highest priority so that the return of the two squadrons to Bomber Command may be affected with the least possible delay.'[166] A week later No.85 Squadron returned to Swannington 'not pleased to be leaving West Malling but pleased to be finished with doodlebugging'. On return to Bomber Support duties:

> We had once more to brush up our navigation and AI but after six days condensed training, we accompanied the Main Force to Karlsruhe on 6th September. This was for us a new role in that we flew high and aimed at being a form of indirect escort for the bombers against Hun Nightfighters...Whilst we always aimed at complete flexibility in our tactics we concentrated on high fighting... witnessing night after night the most stupendous avalanche of fireworks that made pre-war Crystal Palace and Blackpool look like a damp squib.

The Squadron's 'flexibility' operated within a set pattern. The escorting fighters would usually fly at about the same or just below the bombers' height, in order to intercept enemy nightfighters climbing up to attack the bombers. They patrolled about 40 miles from the Main Force. Once AI contact was established on an enemy aircraft, the interception had to be brought to a swift conclusion; there was a maximum of eight minutes flying time between obtaining the original contact, seeking, sighting, and identifying the aircraft, and its destruction if it proved hostile.

They would also, sometimes, fly at lower altitudes:

> 18/19.9.44. Tonight's attack was along the lines of the new low-height tactics. Flying below 2,000 ft and committed to radio silence to 5 degrees east. This has been found to be a good method of preventing the Hun from obtaining early warning of our raids. The programme laid down was that of close escort to the bomber stream together with a triangular patrol to the east of the target area. As the particular area patrolled was rather heavily defended most people we're obliged to spend the time in getting out of the flak and searchlights, which made AI operation rather difficult. Two pilots, S/Ls Burbridge and Gonsalves then went to patrol Stade and Sylt respectively. S/L Burbridge had no joy until the last five minutes when he chased a Mosquito! S/L Gonsalves returned early with AI u/s.[167]

When orders were received from Group HQ, Squadron and Flight Commanders would brief each crew individually regarding their tasks for the night. During the briefing, particular attention was paid to the location of enemy nightfighter assembly beacons and the likely disposition of known searchlight and flak units which were likely to cause problems. Radar assistance, particularly from MONICA, was not always successful as the following HL Intruder Raid report of an operation on 15th/16th September by F/L Cleaver (Pilot) and W/O Nairn (Navigator) flying an No. 85 Squadron Mosquito shows:

> Arrived at enemy coast 0026 (4 minutes ahead of our ETA) so we decided to go out again to lose the time and gain height. Made landfall again at 0030 when MONICA warned at 4,000 ft range. Turned the Mosquito to port and did a hard turn to starboard but unable to get a contact and MONICA contact lost. Straightened out again and the entire performance was repeated another couple of times, Crossed coast once more at 0045 when MONICA warned at minimum range. Mosquito did a 'peel off' to port and then whipped around again but unable to get any contact. Another attempt made to cross coast but position this time uncertain and unable to pinpoint so returned to base.

The first HL success came on 11/12th September when S/L Branse Burbridge and F/L 'Bill' Skelton destroyed a Ju88:

> S/L Burbridge reports that after several chases which proved 'friendly' an aircraft was seen burning navigation lights. As we closed in on it no 'orbits' were made as it was suspected that its lights may have been a 'decoy'[168] . This was not the case, however, and it was identified as a Ju88. At 600 ft two short bursts were fired and a fire started in the fuselage. A further attack from the port quarter sent the Hun crashing to the ground at 2237 hours. Ten minutes later our starboard engine began to overheat and was running very rough. The rest of the journey was made on the port engine only.

As a crew, Burbridge and Skelton claimed 20 enemy aircraft (four in one night) during the War. Burbridge destroyed one more later when Skelton had been posted thus making him the highest scoring nightfighter pilot. Both men entered the church after the War. The next most successful crew were S/L Owen and F/L McAllister who destroyed 15 enemy aircraft.

The Squadron carried on with its 'flexibility':

> 12/13.9.44. Big bomber attack on Frankfurt. Ten aircraft in support. Three at LL, seven HL. The HL patrols were flown 'all at first close to the bomber stream, and splitting up into patrols of assembly beacons.' F/L Kendall patrolling a beacon at Quelle, north of Frankfurt, obtained a 'head-on' contact at 9,000 ft range, 15,000 ft height. On turning behind the enemy aircraft F/L Kendall did two climbing orbits to 17,000 ft and levelled out. At 50 yards he recognised the aircraft as a Me109. He fired a four-second burst which caused the enemy aircraft to blow up and go down...

> 17/18. 9.44. A new device was tried tonight with regard to low Intruders. The airfields being patrolled were in the Ardorf-Varel-Quackenburg-Plantunne area,

and all aircraft going there first flew round in a triangle in Germany, and then set course from there to their own patrol lines. F/O Owen, DFM, on his second 'tour' destroyed two Me110s which he reported thus: 'While on the fourth leg of the patrol had a contact to port. Closed in on to a gently weaving target and after a visual at 1,000 ft recognised it as an Me110 at 100 ft. Shot a burst from 200 yards, the enemy aircraft caught fire and spun in to the ground. The second contact was on a north east heading to port and close. Closed in for a visual at 1,800 ft, and a further Me110 was recognised at 100 ft, astern and below. Opened fire from 200 yards and caused explosion in the fuselage. The enemy aircraft crashed in flames.

As their V-1 rocket launching sites on the Continent were being over-run by the advancing Allied Armies the Germans began to launch these weapons from Heinkel 111s where they were slung underneath the aircraft until fired. In October 1944, No. 85 Squadron carried out patrols over the North Sea to try and intercept these enemy aircraft, but no successes were recorded.

They continued their Bomber Support role with emphasis:

4.11.44. Mosquito 'Y'. Crew: S/L Burbridge, F/L Skelton.

'Highland BS': Time of Take Off (TOT): 1730

Time of Return (TOR) : 2225. (4.55 hours)

Patrol: Ruhr area.

Claimed: 4 enemy aircraft: 1 Ju88G; 2 Ju 88s; 1 Me 110.

A maximum effort in support of heavy raid on Bochum and subsidiary raids on Hamburg and Wilhemshaven. Eight crews patrolled at points round the Ruhr...S/L Burbridge, who has already shown his efficiency as an 'Intruder' pilot on many previous occasions, made history by destroying 4 enemy aircraft during his five hour patrol. Ably assisted by his navigator F/L Skelton they carried four contacts to a successful conclusion, destroying all aircraft (see above) in the vicinity of Bonn. The last two were shot down at low-level near the aerodrome.

It is interesting to note that S/L Burbridge only used 200 rounds of ammunition.

The feat of this particular crew was recognised at the end of the month:

25.11.44. DSO's have been awarded to [1]S/L Burbridge and [2] F/L Skelton. Burbridge joined the Squadron in October 1941, and Skelton in January 1942. They had a long and arduous tour on Havocs without success. They began their second tour, this time together, in July 1943, and on 22/23 February 1944 had their first success.

New tactics were often tried, and at the beginning of February No. 100 Group employed their fighters in a two-part plan. The first part was straightforward HL support for the bombers. The second part was operated 60 minutes after the raid had begun when other fighters from the Group entered the attack. During this time it was hoped to catch the enemy fighters reforming on their assembly beacons in reply to the restarting of a MANDREL Screen. Subsequently the No.100 Group fighters attacked the Luftwaffe airfields.

'Guest' crews contributed to the Squadron's success, sometimes with occasional 'close calls':

> 1/2.2.45. (Night). F/L A P Mellows and his operator, F/L S L Drew (both detached from No. 169 Squadron) were on patrol 30 miles north of Stuttgart on a north-westerly vector when they saw a red star cartridge fired some way off to the north. Turning towards it, a 'head-on' contact was obtained on an aircraft which was chased. Intermittent visuals were seen on a blue light and the aircraft was followed on AI through moderate weaving until it was recognised as an Me110. They opened fire at 300 ft range, the first burst producing a small explosion and some debris. A second burst, produced a very large explosion and the Mosquito flew through the flame, burning off most of the fabric from its own fuselage, and all the fabric from the rudder. The enemy aircraft was seen to explode on the ground at 1910 hours at a point 49.01N/ 09.02E. Since lateral control was affected by the loss of rudder surface, the patrol was ended and the crew made a successful landing.
>
> March 1945, saw enemy Intruders ('Operation Gisella') who had followed the returning bomber stream, 'making an appearance at Swannington at about 11.30pm and prowling around until 2am.' Although aircraft took off to look for them there was no success. Towards the end of the month however, F/L Chapman and F/S Stockley successfully won the 'Sweepstake' for shooting down the 100th enemy aircraft by Swannington squadrons, shooting down two on the same night to make sure!

As the European War came towards its end the Squadron learnt the news in an unusual and roundabout way:

> 7.5.45. Navigation exercises over the Ruhr in order that the crews might obtain some idea of the damage that had been done there. There were six crews on four-hour trips. It was while over the Ruhr and listening to the BBC on his VHF set that W/C Davison, our CO, heard a broadcast to the German People, to the effect that Admiral Doenitz had agreed to the unconditional surrender of all the German Armed Forces to the Allied Armies . The W/C hurried back to Base and was, so to speak, the first in the field with the news that we had so eagerly awaited for days. The Official Broadcast of the news was not until 2000 hours. By this time, the Squadron, in variously decorated cars, were already ranging through the countryside bent on suitable merrymaking. It was generally agreed that our celebration of the peace was as successful as the part we played in winning it.
>
> 7/8.5.45. Night Flying did not take place!

Like the rest of the country the Squadron celebrated:

8.5.45. VE Day. All aircraft were grounded and the day was given over to individual celebration. Initiative in this direction was shown by everyone. In the evening the Sergeants came up to the Officers' Mess, and brought the larger part of the neighbouring villages with them. They finished off all the beer while the children revelled in 'pop' and lemonade. Later on all parties gathered around a bonfire and watched, with suitable decorum, the burning of a very realistic effigy of Goering.

No.85 Squadron clearly thought much of its time in No.100 Group:

We had the privilege to serve in this Group 336 nights, and on 164 of these our aircraft operated. There was new and complicated apparatus (AI Mk.X) but serviceability was always admirable.

...We would like as a Squadron to put it on record that we consider our time with No.100 Group not only the most successful, but quite the most exciting and enjoyable chapter in our Squadron's life. When we operated from Swannington we had nothing but ourselves to rely upon...I must say it never ceased to surprise me that an aircraft should leave Norfolk and then, among a swarm of bombers, jammers, Windowers, and other friendly fighters, search out, bring to combat and destroy, a Hun perhaps near Leipzig, who was, himself, armed with all the aids of the defensive fighter.

For our success we relied implicitly on, and were never failed by, No.100 Group. Our equipment was always the best. No idea, however lowly, was scorned, and never were we faced with anything but the widest and most generous co-operation from the 'Y' Service and the Intelligence Sections of the Group.

During its time in No.100 Group No.85 Squadron claimed 67 enemy aircraft destroyed out of its wartime total of 278.

No. 141 Squadron

A month after the outbreak of the Second World War, No. 141 Squadron was re-formed at Turnhouse in Scotland. Shortly after its formation it became a nightfighter unit, flying Gloucester Gladiators and Bristol Blenheims, later being equipped with Boulton Paul Defiants. In July 1940 it moved south to Kent. Don Aris, who served as an armourer in No.141 Squadron, later wrote:

The Squadron moved south in July 1940 to take part in the Battle of Britain where it was split between Biggin Hill and West Malling, using the forward base of Hawkinge, near Folkestone on the South Kent coast. On 19th July, flying in daylight from Hawkinge, the Squadron suffered its worst losses in crews and aircraft in one day. Nine Defiants from No.141 Squadron were attacked by 20-25 Messerschmitt 109's, and six Defiants were shot down plus one damaged. Ten aircrew were killed or missing, and two injured. They had, however, shot down four of the enemy.[169]

The losses were so heavy that No. 141 Squadron was obliged to return to Prestwick, Scotland, to recover and reform, returning south to Biggin Hill after a month. In April 1941, the Squadron moved back up to Scotland, this time to Ayr, and two months later was re-equipped with Bristol Beaufighter 1F Nightfighters. June 1942 saw the Squadron yet again journeying south, moving in turn to Tangmere, and then Ford, for defensive nightfighter duties. In February 1943, it moved to Predennack in Cornwall, and for the first time, took on an offensive role, carrying out Intruder patrols over southwest France, plus patrols over the Bay of Biscay and the Western Approaches in the Atlantic. The Spring of 1943 saw the Squadron, re-equipped with new Beaufighters, become the first squadron to be fitted with SERRATE (qv). A few months later it also found itself involved in yet another change of role when it started bomber support operations in June 1943, from Wittering, in Cambridgeshire:

> ...On the night of 14/15th June 1943, No.141 Squadron carried out the first SERRATE Bomber Support operations. The Squadron had not expected to operate on that night and were given very little warning when the orders were received. It was therefore impossible to plan the operation as carefully as it might have been. Apart from the unexpected orders to start operations, the crews had had very little training and, also, the SERRATE and Gee equipped Mk. VI Beaufighters were giving teething troubles. This meant that only five aircraft would be available...

SERRATE was not referred to by its codename in official records until several months later, failures in its efficient use being cloaked under the vague description 'radio or instrument defects'. However, a general description of this RCM's first use operationally is given. The first SERRATE fighters clearly did not have everything their own way:

> ...Contacts were first obtained near the Dutch coast, and a few chases back towards England were tried. A number of stern chases on contact alone occurred, but in most cases had to be abandoned when the enemy aircraft switched off its AI. Three enemy aircraft thus chased were clearly conscious of pursuit; one led the Beaufighter eastwards in a series of orbits and jinks, keeping its AI on most of the time, for 20 minutes. The chase ended when the Beaufighter obtained a number of AI contacts, and simultaneous visuals, on several large balloons at 18,000 ft, amongst which the enemy aircraft had vanished. Two enemy aircraft chased the Beaufighter concerned for five to ten minutes respectively, one in a circular chase, and one over the sea in a stern chase. On the second occasion the Beaufighter had insufficient petrol to 'play' and had to evade.

There were other problems:

>...It may also be mentioned that the Lancasters were flying in a high, fast, compact formation; thus the enemy aircraft were flying very fast to intercept the bombers and the Beaufighters were frequently out-distanced, partly due to the fact that they were on the whole below the bombers and thus lacked the advantage of height on the enemy aircraft.

Complaint was also made of the interference of GROCER, an RCM used for jamming German AI which was, 'on occasions, extremely troublesome to the SERRATE operators and did cause some interceptions to be abandoned.' On the whole, however, 'it caused more annoyance than real hindrance and could often be tuned out.'

Bomber Command's target on the 14th/15th June was Oberhausen, in the Ruhr. The Squadron's only success was by its CO, W/C Braham, who shot down a Messerschmitt 110, his fourteenth enemy aircraft destroyed. His combat report reads:

>We took off from Coltishall at 2335 hours...on an Intruder patrol of Deelen (a German nightfighter airfield near Arnhem in Holland). After crossing the English coast between Yarmouth and Lowestoft, we made landfall over Schouwen (Holland) at 0001 hours, and flew to the target area...Reaching Deelen at 0040 hours we patrolled uneventfully in wide orbits, and sometimes flying as far as Venlo (a German nightfighter airfield on the Dutch/German border) and Wesel (Germany), until 0151 hours, when we set course northwest for the coast. At 0210 hours, when we were over Staveren, on the northeast coast of the Zuider Zee (Holland), my Navigator saw an enemy aircraft, an Me110, coming up behind us to attack us from our port side. I orbited hard to port to get behind him but as I did so the enemy aircraft also turned to port. A dogfight followed and I finally manoeuvred until I was on his port beam at 400 yards range. I opened fire with cannon and machine guns and finished a five-second burst 20 degrees astern at 200 yards range, raking his fuselage from tail to cockpit and setting his port engine on fire. As I throttled back to attack again the enemy aircraft went into a vertical dive and crashed eight miles north of Staveren. The combat took place at 10,000 ft, in clear moonlight above the cloud. We saw no return fire.[170]

Due to the limited range of the Beaufighters it was necessary to use forward airfields at Coltishall (Norfolk); Bradwell Bay (Essex); Ford (Hampshire), and West Malling (Kent). Don Aris spent a detachment period at Coltishall, the Airfield most used by No.141 Squadron (it lasted about seven to ten days). He helped to service the aircraft, 'topping up the fuel and putting right any minor faults that may have been found on the flight from Wittering before the aircraft took off on operations.'

In December 1943, No.141 Squadron was the first to transfer to the newly-formed

No.100 Group. It moved to West Raynham, a large, pre-war built, permanent RAF station, eight miles from Fakenham, in Norfolk. It remained there until the War's end:

> Enthusiasm ran high. Aircrew and ground personnel alike looked forward to better equipment, better radar, better aircraft, better 'gen', and proper co-ordination of effort. No.141 Squadron were to be the first operational unit of No.100 Group. For six months No.141 had been the Guinea Pig for SERRATE. It was fairly successful at Wittering. With inadequate aircraft, and near obsolete radar it had destroyed 16 enemy aircraft (plus one 'probable') and damaged eight.
>
> It can probably be fairly said that those achievements of No.141 Squadron were a major contributory factor in the decision to form No.100 Group – at any rate as far as offensive nightfighters were concerned.[171]

One who served with distinction in the Squadron, F/O Michael Allen recalled the wide variety of work they used to undertake:

> There were a variety of tactics used on the HL Bomber Support operations ie patrolling between the track of the Bomber Stream and the German nightfighter fields; or between the Bomber Stream and certain German nightfighter assembly points; flying over the main target itself during the raid; and also immediately after the Bomber Stream had gone through; flying in and out of the Stream on the route home; patrolling in support of a 'Spoof' raid; or simply using one's experience to work out a freelance patrol in the areas where the German nightfighter aircraft was thought to be likely to operate on their defensive patrols.

Whilst serving in No.100 Group firstly with No.141 Squadron, and later with the BSDU at Foulsham, F/O Allen DFC** (Nav/Rad) and his pilot F/O (later Air Commodore) Harry White DFC**, destroyed ten enemy aircraft and damaged one.

Beaufighters were not suitable for the new type of work and were being phased out. A fortnight after the Squadron joined No.100 Group the only two Beaufighters being used on operations had defects. On one, after only five minutes patrol of the target area, the back hatch blew open during a hard turn to port and the aircraft was forced to return home hotly pursued by enemy aircraft. The second Beaufighter reached the German border and was forced to return after two hours with faulty SERRATE and AI equipment.[172]

The Beaufighters were being replaced by 'old and much-used' De Havilland Mosquito 11F aircraft the serviceability of which, 'particularly with engines and radar, was a problem.'[173] They were far from ready for operations. Difficulties were encountered with the aerials. Mike Allen found, 'We had problems with the aerial configuration that was not solved until the middle of January 1944...it left us on the ground just at the time when the heavy bombers needed us most, that is at the height of the Battle of Berlin.' The problem was eventually resolved:

...aircrews found it almost impossible to DF in a turn on the Mosquitoes so, for a time the Squadron had half Beaufighters and half Mosquitoes. Morale sagged. Perhaps the one thing which served to restore confidence more than anything was an informal chat that took place in the Mess between F/O Pollard, the Squadron Radar Officer and the AOC, No.100 Group, which resulted in a Mosquito being placed exclusively at Pollard's disposal for experimental purposes. Within a fortnight this cutting of red tape bore fruit and a new and satisfactory aerial system was designed. The fitting of those new aerials was a difficult and tedious operation.

TRE was worried, in fact everyone was worried, except Pollard who proceeded to get on with the job slowly but surely with many a strip of tinfoil over the leading edges and vast quantities of Bostik (who in the Squadron will ever forget 'Bostik Night' in the Mess? One Wing Commander at Group still wears his neatly parted hair as if it were rubberised!). Eventually the job was done – and well done – and the Squadron were completely converted to Mosquito IIs.[174]

The Squadron also had problems with the engines of the Mosquitoes with which they were re-equipped. 'This is a story of its own', Mike Allen wrote, 'they used to stop!'

The fitting of metal foil around the elevator aerial on the wing was found to be unsatisfactory on the first flight tests and later it was found necessary to strip the aircraft and start afresh. Further tests were made, including using a different quality foil backed paper and a special adhesive was used, not altogether satisfactorily. After consultation with TRE, it was found that the spraying of the wooden Mosquito wing with a mixture of copper and zinc to metalize it, greatly eased the problem, and the first few aircraft were put on operations at the end of January 1944. Long range fuel tanks were also beginning to be fitted to the Squadron's aircraft in readiness for its new role.

Progress in improving aircraft and equipment did take place, albeit more slowly than the Squadron would have wished, but training would be difficult for some time 'Operational commitments and unserviceability have brought training during the last few weeks to a standstill. More and more does the need arise for a training unit so that we do not find ourselves in the hopeless position of operating at full strength one week and then, due to casualties and sickness, having practically nobody to offer in the following weeks.' [175]

In January 1944, the Squadron flew 24 Bomber Support SERRATE operations with 11 'early returns', but by July, with new engines and other equipment, they could record the vastly improved figures of 92 SERRATE sorties with only seven 'early returns'. Mike Allen, and the other 'Nav/Rads' had to submit detailed reports after each operation:

When we AI Operators returned from each trip we had to make out a special 'Top Secret' report (regardless of whether we had any 'joy' or not). This report contained our full story of the trip as seen by us on our Cathode Ray Tubes including a detailed description of all the SERRATE and AI Contacts which we had seen; what had happened to them, ie how we had lost them, if the 'Contact' had not been brought to visual; and, of course, the matching together of the SERRATE and AI Signals where this could be brought about. These reports were whisked away, I think, to the recently formed 'Operational Research Section'. We never saw them again.

The first Mosquitoes may have been, in the AOC's words 'dead-beat', but the crews weren't. S/L (later W/C) Lambert with his Nav/Rad F/O Dear, flew to Berlin. Although they could only claim one enemy aircraft damaged their sortie combat report clearly shows the hectic and dangerous life of the aircrews, and the contribution made by airborne radar:

16.12.43. Mosquito F11, HJ 659 took off from West Raynham at 1745 hours to patrol Berlin. Crossing over Happisburgh (on the Norfolk coast, north of Great Yarmouth), at 9,000ft. Made landfall at 1835 hours, 20,000 ft, just south of De Kooy and flew east to target area. From 30 miles within the Dutch coast and all along the route the Mosquito received indications of some 18/20 enemy aircraft, all about ten miles distant, but, in accordance with instructions they were ignored. Throughout there was excellent visibility with a clear sky but there was considerable ground haze which prevented accurate observation of the ground.

In the neighbourhood of Hoya, at 1920 hours, aircraft obtained one SERRATE contact ten miles ahead and 25 degrees to port. The Mosquito, flying at 21,000 ft, and the enemy aircraft seemed to be at the same height. The enemy aircraft appeared to close to seven miles range and switched his AI off. The next indication, some five minutes later, was an AI back blip at 2,000 ft range slightly to port, both aircraft still flying at about 21,000 ft.

The Mosquito peeled off to port, down to 10,000 ft, hoping that the enemy aircraft would either reappear in front, or enable the Mosquito to turn and get behind the enemy aircraft. In this first turn the blip split into two and it is suspected that there may have been two enemy aircraft who subsequently came in one at a time. A violent dogfight followed as the Mosquito made for the target area at 10,000 ft but the enemy aircraft gave no chance to attack. During the dogfight the enemy aircraft fired one long burst from minimum range and two short bursts from within 2,000 ft range without doing any damage. Throughout the fight the enemy aircraft clung on like a leech. SERRATE indications appeared from time-to-time only briefly but the enemy aircraft managed to intercept with great accuracy and tenacity.

At 1945 hours, when about 50 miles west of Berlin, at 10,000 ft, the enemy aircraft overshot beneath the Mosquito as both were turning hard to starboard. A visual was obtained and the enemy aircraft was identified as an Me110. The Mosquito immediately gave a two-second burst of cannon fire...several strikes were observed on the Me110 and the Mosquito tried to follow up but the enemy aircraft was lost and could not be picked up on AI...it is claimed as damaged.

In August 1944 No.141 Squadron was re-equipped with Mosquito Mk.VI but it was becoming clear that SERRATE and AI MkIV were, to all intents and purposes finished; 899 hours flying by the three SERRATE Squadrons in the month only produced one enemy aircraft destroyed and one damaged. With the new aircraft came new tactics:

There was a change to LL Intruder and ground-strafing deep into Germany. The first dawn raid was on Steenwijk Airfield on 17.9.44. There was intense flak and all six aircraft taking part were hit and only two were repairable. All got back. One Ju88 damaged, hangars and airfield buildings strafed, 'not to mention Winnie's, (Squadron CO, W/C C V Winn), one wheelbarrow destroyed!' [176]

In October, which was altogether a poor month for the three SERRATE Squadrons (Nos. 141, 169, and 239), No.141 Squadron carried out 137 sorties (102 Bomber Support, 27 Intruder and Ranger night sorties, and eight Day Ranger sorties). For the third month running it was able to record that there were no casualties. It also commenced training on AI Mk. XV (ASH). In November and December 1944, the Squadron continued with these activities and, in addition, carried out a limited number of HE bombing sorties. At the end of the year No.141 Squadron carried out its last operations with SERRATE and AI Mk.IV, and began using AI Mk.XV (ASH) and MONICA. In some aircraft PERFECTOS was also used. Re-equipping aircraft, and re-training crews, meant that the Squadron had to reduce its number of operations but, by the end of December, 12 aircraft were fitted, and 19 crews were considered operational on ASH.

In January 1945, the weather intervened; it was the worst month for weather since No.100 Group had been formed. There were 16 days of snow at West Raynham and a 'freeze-up' from the 19th to the 31st in the month and many operations were cancelled. However with the new AI, No.141 Squadron was still able to carry out 80 sorties, with only four 'early returns' due to radar defects, which reflected creditably on the work undertaken by the Squadron's Radar Section.

Making up for time lost the previous month due to the weather No. 141 Squadron, flying on 20 nights, flew 149 sorties (with only four 'early returns') during February. Of these 147 were HL ASH patrols, but some of the crews, after their patrol was completed, carried out LL attacks on ground targets. Although there were no successes in the air, on the ground two aircraft were damaged and considerable havoc caused to transportation targets. One train was probably destroyed, nine trains damaged, four locomotives damaged and one motor vehicle destroyed. One aircraft and crew was lost. In this respect the Squadron had recently been lucky only having lost three aircrew (one became a PoW), in the previous seven months.

In March 1945, the Squadron started to become re-equipped with Mosquito Mk.XXX, with AI Mk.X radar, and MONICA Mk.VIII. PERFECTOS was added to some aircraft. All this again reduced the number of operations flown. Training with the new aircraft and AI including the Nav/Rads training on AI Mk.X with the Wellington and accompanying Hurricanes, took place throughout the month when 640 hours of training flying took place. By the end of the month there were 15 Mosquito Mk. XXX aircraft on charge and most of the old Mk.VI Mosquitoes were flown away.

In April 1945, the Squadron started to attack enemy airfields with 'drop' tanks of Napalmgel, and were believed to be the first squadron in the RAF to do so:

> Napalm used on Neuruppin: Munich: Neubiberg: Sylt: Lubeck: Flensburg and other airfields. Hangars, control towers, barracks and other airfield buildings were left blazing furiously. Some losses; flak heavy. Six aircraft were asked for and 12 volunteered. All went. Each aircraft carried two times 100 gallon drop tanks of Napalmgel with the consequent reduction of fuel and range. Returning aircraft landed at airfields on the Continent.[177]

It is not known whether the Squadron Member, who, in a 'line-shooting' session declared that 'when a drop-tank with Napalm "hangs-up" (ie, fails to drop), that's the time to knock it off with a Very pistol!', had his theory shared by other aircrew in the Squadron. No.141 Squadron's last operation of the War, on 2nd May, was a Napalm attack. By the War's end the Squadron had, whilst in No.100 Group, destroyed 41 enemy aircraft (with one probable), with 11 damaged. On the ground it claimed to have damaged 42 locomotives, six sets of rolling stock, five MT vehicles, 10 hangars and airfield buildings, three factories, one barge, and one tanker.

Mike Allen gives a personal opinion of how he saw his role as a member of a fighter crew in No.100 Group, which must have been shared by most of his comrades:

> To be able to contribute, even in a small and somewhat remote way to the possible survival of some of the bomber crews (with their loss rate so much higher than ours) was of the utmost satisfaction to us...we thought we had the best job in the nightfighter business...and fifty years later I still feel the same!

No. 157 Squadron.

No.157 Squadron was formed on 15th December 1941, as a defensive nightfighter squadron. After five days at Debden the Squadron moved to Castle Camps and

A No.157 Squadron De Havilland Mosquito that was badly 'burned up' by a V1 (Flying Bomb) which exploded when attacked in August 1944. Air Commodore Chisholm, told AVM Addison, that he thought the pilot, F/L Jimmy Matthews (on left in photo), had 'put up a very stout show in getting the aircraft back.' *(Crown Copyright)*

became operational on 27th April 1942; it was the first unit to receive Mosquito nightfighters. The AI equipment fitted to the aircraft brought maintenance problems; cables burned out, dampness attacked the leads, and, according to one report, 'the "Magic Eye" [AI] would often doze off in the middle of a chase for no apparent reason.' Despite the snags, training was started on 'Ranger' operations for hunting enemy aircraft at their own bases and attacks were made on St. Trond, Twente and Dusseldorf. In November 1943, with the easing of attacks on UK cities, the Squadron, operating from Predanack in Cornwall, changed to giving day-fighting assistance to Coastal Command in the campaign against the U-Boat menace, with considerable success. Four months later the Squadron was on the move again:

> It was with regret that we left Predannack on March 26th 1944, to move to Valley (Anglesey), although we were promised new aircraft, a new Mark AI, and a new job. The aircraft, however, did not materialise, we continued training and countless air-firing sorties with the aircraft we had, the majority of which had over 600 hours to their credit; and though all navigators passed through the AI Mk X Circus, no indication was given of our future role.

Not until the end of April, over a month later, when the CO, W/C Denison, was summoned to a conference at ADGB, and given the news that we were to become a Bomber Support Squadron, did the sense of uncertainty and 'unemployment' disappear. No.157 Squadron became No.157 (SD) Squadron and morale soared overnight.

It was with a certain pride that we learned No.85 Squadron, then the crack nightfighter Squadron, were to join us in this task, and with our navigational training against their AI Mk.X experience, we resolved to do as well as they.

May 6th saw the movement of the Squadron by road to Swannington where, with ten borrowed aircraft, pilots and navigators practised intensively all that had been propounded by the Circus and Mk.X films. W/C Hoare arrived as W/C Training and his Intruder lectures assured us that the whole business was a 'portion of culinary confectionery' (ie a 'piece of cake') as he had been 'going in there for years'. [See also remarks by Bob Muir under No.85 Squadron above]. The end of the month produced our Mosquito Mk.XIXs. Meanwhile fraternisation between the two squadrons, both shy at first, began, as the bar takings for the month proved!' [178]

Operations in No.100 Group were started the following month. On the day before D-Day four uneventful Intruder sorties were flown. On 12th/13th June the Squadron claimed its first victory from Swannington. Detailed for a low-level patrol of three enemy-held airfields near Rheims, F/L Benson DFC and F/L Brandon destroyed a Ju88 over Forèt de Compiegne. The whole attack took just under four minutes from the first AI contact on the enemy aircraft being obtained to it crashing into the ground:

> Arrived patrol area (Laon/Couvron; Laon/Athies; Juvincourt) 0115 having evaded 30/40 searchlights from the coast. AI contact on patrol to Juvincourt. 0135 Height 3,000 ft, range 10,000 ft, 30 degrees starboard. Momentary visual obtained on orbit but lost as searchlight came on. Contact maintained on AI while still climbing. Further contact obtained crossing from starboard to port , range 6,000 ft, slightly above. Decided to take this one. 0150 visual obtained on Ju188. Short burst set its starboard engine on fire. Enemy aircraft seen burning on ground at 0153 in Compiegne. Set course for base at 0200.

'Keenness and determination increased hundred-fold' as a result, and the Squadron claimed two further successes on the following two nights:

> 14/15 .6.44. F/L Tweedale. F/L Cunningham 2335-0320.
>
> Juvincourt patrolled 0058-0150. The Airfield was lit on approach but afterwards the lights were doused. Reims Airfield came on with beacon. 5 Star Red fired twice at 0111. At 0130 an aircraft with navigation lights on was seen coming in to land at Juvincourt which had full lighting on at 0148. Head-on contact obtained on AI Mk X target in left hand orbit. Contact regained at

6,000ft 30 degrees starboard, well below. Visual at 1,500 ft and enemy aircraft recognised as Ju88. After approaching to approximately 50 ft dropped level to 300 ft and gave one-second burst. Enemy aircraft burst into flames.

15/16. 6.44. F/L J Matthews. F/S Penrose. 2335-0305.

Beavis-Creil-Cormeilles.

Creil 0110. No Airfield lighting. AI Mk X contact obtained 1,500 ft, range three miles, orbiting to port and climbing. Visual obtained 1,200 ft and below. Recognised as Ju88. Closed and fired a burst. Its port engine exploded and its starboard wing fell off. Another AI contact, visual of Ju88. Short burst and 'strikes' obtained on wing roots. Enemy aircraft dived steeply to avoid combat. Claim one enemy aircraft destroyed, one damaged.[179]

No.157 Squadron were diverted at the end of the month to anti-V1 activity as were No. 85 Squadron with whom they shared Swannington.[180] The former Squadron had flown 22 Intruder sorties (during which they had two AI contacts leading to the destruction of two enemy aircraft) and eleven HL patrols, and were as equally frustrated as their sister squadron :

...The disappointment of leaving an interesting job so well begun at Swannington, coupled with diversions, loose balloons and little intelligence of what was happening among the nightfighters of Germany, caused the majority of crews to regard this new job with disfavour. Nevertheless, encouraged by our CO, W/C Davison, we practised AI on NFT's. We also held weekly conferences on how best to keep in trim for Bomber Support on our return...

On 28th August we returned to Swannington to pick up the thread of our former task...W/C Beauchamp, from Bomber Command took over the reins from W/C Davison, who had suffered various illnesses at West Malling, and under his guidance the Squadron passed on to the most successful months of its career. By the end of the year, S/L Benson[181] and our new found 'aces', S/L 'Dolly' Doleman (six enemy aircraft destroyed, one damaged, so far in No.100 Group) and S/L Jimmy Matthews[182] (seven destroyed, two damaged so far in No.100 Group) had proved the value of careful planning of every trip, based on previous raid analyses and the knowledge of German nightfighter disposition, setting an encouraging example to the new crews arriving from OTUs.

The victories were not without cost. On 15th September 1944 S/L Chisholm and F/L Wilde failed to return from a patrol in the Kiel area where flak had been heavy; a fortnight later two more crews were lost:

29.9.44. Search of North Sea for F/Os Fry and Smith who had failed to return from a sortie the previous night. 20 miles off Great Yarmouth F/L Waddington (Pilot), F/L Lomas (Nav/Rad) attacked by Me410 which shot them down. F/L Vincent observed this and stationed himself behind the enemy aircraft and, at the same time, warned F/L Waddington of the presence of the enemy aircraft over R/T. Apparently unheard. F/L Vincent fired a long burst at the enemy aircraft and observed a fire in its fuselage. The enemy aircraft peeled off and was lost. Nothing was seen of the missing crew.

In addition to the loss of crews aircraft were a problem. The CO, W/C Beauchamp, called a meeting of the Squadron and, 'forcibly expressed his displeasure at the number of aircraft that were being "broken". He suggested that this may be due to carelessness by experienced pilots and continued with a pep talk on flying discipline.'

The crews didn't only need to employ vigilance against the enemy:

6.11.44. S/L Doleman and F/L Bunch shot down an Me110. After numerous other chases on friendly aircraft they themselves were chased on the way home and challenged by an American voice. They quickly identified themselves on Channel C, waggling their wings, and putting on navigation lights as they heard a second American voice advising the first to 'Shoot the bastards down.'

Resourcefulness and an element of luck sometimes brought shot-down crews home:

21.11.44. 14 Aircraft on sorties.

Over Holland F/O Mackinnon and F/O Waddell were returning with radar trouble when they were shot down by enemy fighters. The crew landed several miles apart SE of Helmond and both thought they were in enemy territory due to seeing gun flashes to the south west. Mackinnon walked 12 miles during the night until a dump of old tins and cigarette packets gave him a clue that he was in friendly territory. At first light he sighted a main road and a jeep and found his way to a unit of the Canadian Forestry Corps. Waddell was luckier. After a two hour walk he heard the strains of 'Hokey-Cokey' and found an officers mess. They were reunited at Eindhoven on 22nd November, flown to Tangmere on the 23rd, and returned to Swannington by train on 24th November.[183]

After the winter, with the Allied offensive pushing into Europe and the Luftwaffe becoming more wary of Mosquito Intruders, the enemy were more difficult to find. Extra training was carried out by the Squadron to minimise the risk of losing the few contacts that were being obtained, but still only occasional claims were made. The Squadron claimed six enemy aircraft destroyed, two 'probables', and three damaged, during 1945.

By the War's end the Squadron was patrolling as far into enemy territory as Munich and Leipzig and, at the beginning of April, even simulated an attack on Berlin by bombers. During its Bomber Support role, No.157 Squadron destroyed 36 enemy aircraft, with five 'probables', and 13 damaged, flying 1,122 sorties and losing five aircraft.

No.169 Squadron

No.169 Squadron was formed in June 1942, as a reconnaissance unit for the Army; equipped with Mustang aircraft it moved to Duxford in December of the same year. Shipping reconnaissance and ground strafing operations were undertaken on the Continent and, for a time, the Squadron was used defensively against low-level attacks by enemy fighter/bombers on coastal towns of the UK. Disbanded on the 30th September 1943, the Squadron was re-formed the next day acquiring Mosquito Mk.II nightfighters; the ground crews were taken from the previous Mustang Squadron, the aircrews being transferred from other nightfighter squadrons.

On 7th December 1943, No.169 Squadron was transferred, with W/C E J Gracie DFC as CO, to No.100 Group,[184] moving from RAF Ayr to Little Snoring, Norfolk. It commenced operations the following month overcoming adverse weather to do so:

> 20.1.44. Still too much ground fog to permit flying; slight improvement PM and weather cleared at 1600. The first operational sortie since the Squadron was re-formed carried out by CO, W/C E J Gracie, with F/L W Wylton-Todd, who took off at 1650 and landed at 1945. The job consisted of penetration into Northern Holland in support of a heavy bomber attack on Berlin. Three contacts but no combats...S/L Cooper and F/L Connolly were detailed to take off ten minutes after the CO. They returned a few minutes later after sustaining a fabric tear in the port wing.

The first victory was claimed by S/L J A Cooper who shot down an Me110 near Berlin:

> 30.1.44. A glorious, Spring-like day. Every serviceable aircraft in the air for air testing, practice etc., 'The ice is broken'. S/L Cooper and F/L Connolly destroyed an Me110 about 40 miles west of Berlin. This is great news, as this is the first full-scale operational sortie. S/L Cooper took off at 1755 and landed at 2155. The Me110 was contacted on AI at about 20,000 ft. S/L Cooper closed in on it and got a visual at about 800 ft. He then closed to 200 ft and gave it three-second and seven-seconds bursts. The enemy aircraft disintegrated in mid-air and S/L Cooper broke away violently and spun to avoid a collision, pulling out at 5,000 ft.

A fortnight later the Squadron lost its CO:

> 15.2.44. W/C E J Gracie DFC and F/L Wylton-Todd took off at 1845 on what was a heavy bomber raid on Berlin. Their estimated time of return was 2230 and anxiety increased from that time onwards terminating in the unhappy knowledge, in the early hours of the morning, that some mishap had befallen them.
>
> F/L Wylton-Todd was lucky and survived [See Ralph Connolly's recollections below in this Chapter].

Feedback from operational crews was helpful:

18.4.44. F/L R G Woodman (Pilot) and F/O Kemmis (Nav/Rad) have been commended on instructions from No. 100 Group HQ as a result of their observations in relation to enemy Visual Beacons during their offensive patrol on the night of 25th/26th February 1944. An extremely valuable observation made by these officers has enabled confirmation of information received from other sources.

The exact 'observation' is not recorded. Five days later this crew destroyed an enemy fighter near Bonn in circumstances described as 'a little unusual':

After a head-on contact and short chase F/L Woodman obtained a visual on the bright tail light of the enemy aircraft. This exceptionally bright light initially prevented Woodman from identifying this aircraft which subsequently proved to be an Me110. He then found his gunsight would only work in the 'Off' or 'Brilliant Day' position. His aircraft had to be aimed by instinct and, after a long burst, the enemy aircraft disintegrated and caused slight damage to the port wing of our aircraft.

The following month brought further success:

15.5.44. P/O W H Miller and P/O F C Bone in an operational sortie over the Dutch Islands destroyed three enemy aircraft, two Ju88's and one Me110. In the first kill the enemy aircraft shed a wing after two attacks, the second was attacked from behind, and the third, the Me110 was flying straight and level with a tail light...probably had no idea of what hit him and he blew up after a steady burst. We are a very happy Squadron. We like successes in lumps occasionally!

By the time they were shot down on 12th August 1944 and became PoW's F/Os Miller and Bone had accounted for ten enemy aircraft. On 4th June 1944, two days before D-Day, the Squadron made the short move to Great Massingham where it was stationed until disbandment in August 1945:

The Big Day. Only crews on 'ops' had any knowledge that their early morning's work would be in support of the Invasion of France. Ten aircraft took off from 0100 at short intervals and patrolled Northern France. No contacts. Four aircraft completed uneventful sorties inland of the Beachhead on the Normandy Coast.

The following week was more profitable:

13.6.44. W/O L W Turner and F/L E F Francis destroyed a Ju88 over North-West France. They obtained an AI contact at a height of about 5,000 ft, chased the enemy aircraft into cloud, and followed its steady course in the cloud, and finally obtained a visual. A short one and a half second-burst saw the enemy aircraft's port engine catch fire and it finally crashed to the earth in flames. The combat took place quite near to Paris. This crew also brought back useful information with regard to enemy beacons.

In the following months the Squadron's fortunes were mixed. At the end of July one crew received a surprise over Germany:

28.7.44. F/L Woodman on Bomber Support to Hamburg, with his AI elevation hopelessly unreliable, had a 'dogfight' with what must have been a balloon barrage, near Emden. The 'perfect discipline' of these balloons gave our crew quite a shock before they decided that they were playing with stationary objects.

On 3rd September, the Squadron CO, W/C Bromley returned from leave. Three days later he, and his Nav/Rad F/L Truscott, failed to return from a sortie. Both were awarded DFCs. On 18th September, W/C T A Heath was posted from No.100 Group HQ to assume command of the Squadron. The following month Juvincourt began to be used as a forward base enabling sorties to take place over SE Germany/NW Austria. PERFECTOS, which gave a bearing on enemy AI, was used. F/L Woodman made several contacts, 'but severe icing hampered his vision and no visuals were obtained.' A week later this equipment was more effectively used when three aircraft completed early morning patrols over Western Germany supporting a Spoof attack on Mannheim where WINDOW and the MANDREL Screen were also used. In addition, nine aircraft completed freelance PERFECTOS patrols.

Early in December crews reported difficulties due to the faster speed of the enemy aircraft:

4.12.44. Nine PERFECTOS Bomber Support aircraft for Karlsruhe...both PERFECTOS and AI contacts showed marked superiority of speed and, in every case, drew away from our aircraft.

Just before the War's end No.169 Squadron, with other squadrons, successfully attacked enemy airfields with Napalm-Gel. There were complications:

2.5.45. 12 aircraft LL attack on two airfields, Jaget and Westerland on Sylt with drop-tanks filled with Napalm-Gel. F/O R Catterall DFC and F/S D J Beadle failed to return from Jagel. An explosion was seen by several crews about five miles west of the Airfield which might have been due to an aircraft crashing. F/O W A Glendinning landed at Woodbridge on one engine. S/L J A Wright was unable to jettison his starboard tank which was filled with Napalm-Gel but hearing F/O Glendinning in trouble on his way back climbed to 6,000 ft and relayed messages to Coltishall. When he finally landed an hour later, S/L Wright's tank fell off on to the runway but fortunately did not explode. F/O K R Miller (RAAF) had a similar experience with a drop tank which also fell on to the runway without exploding. He had been involved in a LL attack on Schleswig-Jagel Airfields carrying two 100-gallon Napalm-Gel drop-tanks. One tank 'hung-up' and it was brought back to base. The incident does not appear to have greatly disturbed F/O Miller. Three weeks after the incident he assumed his alter ego as

Keith Miller, Australian Test Cricketer, in a Victory Test at Lords, and scored 105 runs against England.

Ralph Connolly was a 'Nav/Rad' on the Squadron:

My pilot, Joe Cooper (S/L J H Cooper) and I had been together on No.141 Squadron and had been on aircraft delivery to the Middle East. We joined No.169 Squadron at Ayr in September/October 1943. Joe and I scored the Squadron's first No.100 Group victory on 30th January 1944 when we shot down an Me110 nightfighter shortly after we left the Berlin target area.

Initially the Squadron had been formed (re-formed to be more accurate) with experienced crews most of whom had already completed one tour of operations. One great advantage that experience gave was the ability to find your way there and back home again. Navigation was primarily by Dead Reckoning (DR), plus the advantage of radar. Gee was useful at times but subjected to a lot of jamming by the Germans. Mother (our own aerodrome's system for homing) was always useful but had very limited range.

During 1944 the OTUs were closed down and each squadron became responsible for giving operational training to new crews. I believe that some new crews just got lost over the 'other side' (which was what we called Occupied Europe). New crews were usually sent on a few 'nursery trips', ie part of the way on a real raid. One night a raid on Hamburg (in which some of us took part) was the occasion for such a trip for one of our newcomers. They were told to fly around Heligoland, then fly south a little before flying west to the coast of East Anglia. We all returned from the 'op' except the trainees (who should have landed an hour before us). Just after the CO had left the Mess, to write letters to parents about missing sons, the 'phone rang. RAF Tangmere told us our missing crew had landed with little fuel left. The next day they told us what had happened. After leaving Heligoland they flew south east and then west and 'crossed a lot of water which we thought was the North Sea'. In fact it was the Zuyder Zee. After crossing a lot more sea they came down low to have a look round using the the searchlight cooperation system to locate the nearest airfield. The trouble was they were German searchlights and, of course, they were shot at by the enemy ack-ack. After calling on all channels of the radio for a position they eventually received a course for Tangmere. We gave the crew more training (Land's End to John O'Groats etc.) but they failed to return from a trip to Paris and we concluded that they had lost their way for the last time.

The Squadron CO was fully operational and carried out 'ops' to the same extent as any of his pilots. No.169 Squadron were unlucky in that two were killed,and a third wounded, all in less than two years. The first CO was W/C Gracie. On an early trip to Berlin he and his navigator, Wylton-Todd, were shot down by flak shortly after leaving the target. This was on 15th February 1944. We thought they had both been killed but shortly after the War I was walking down Piccadilly, in London, when I met Wylton-Todd, who had become an architect and designer in civilian life. He told me that Gracie had shouted, 'Out, Out!' to him when the flames and explosions started and he had baled out. An hour or so later he was picked up by a German patrol and became a PoW. Gracie failed to bale out. Wylton-Todd knew he had been hit by pieces of flak.

It wasn't all work:

> We had a lot of fun on our nights off. There were the local pubs, very friendly residents, and most hospitable farmers. We could only get petrol for our cars when going on leave, (and very useful it was too), but farmers got petrol coupons for driving on farming business. One of our particular farmer friends used always to be on 'farming business' – which meant he used to drive us around to parties and dinners towing a trailer containing 'A pig for delivery'. That poor pig clocked up about 300 miles a week!
>
> The Derby horserace was held at Newmarket, rather than Epsom because of air raids. We (and the pig!) went to the 1944 Derby. A Newmarket trainer had tipped a horse called Happy Landings to win so we put our money on the nose because of the name. Not surprisingly it came last and the winner was Flare Path!
>
> Joe and I were on 'ops' the night before D-Day. We supported the bombers and gliders. It was a dramatic and very unusual night's operation even for us who were used to the unusual. The weather was bad, particularly over Occupied Europe, with low cloud and drizzle. In fact a frontal system ran down the North Sea and into France. We flew with a number of Mossies from Great Massingham, in Norfolk, to Caen, Normandy, a longish trip. We climbed through the cloud after take off and saw a mass of green lights on our port side as far as we could see, and red lights all away to starboard. They were the navigation lights of RAF aircraft (some were towing gliders) and were helpful in preventing collisions. It was, of course, the biggest air armada of the war.
>
> Because of the weather, navigation was difficult. In addition, Gee was jammed by the enemy. We had to come down through cloud east of the Seine estuary, pick up Le Havre, follow the low-lying coast westwards to Ouistreham and fly up the 'canalised' Dives to Caen. At, and around (mainly around), Caen flares were dropped for the gliders to pick out their landing places. We saw that most of the flares had been dropped some miles away from Caen (due to poor visibility), and thus the glider troops landed too far from Caen.

Harry Reed became a pilot in No.169 Squadron after service in the Battle of the Atlantic:

> We had the 'old' AI (ie Mk IV) and SERRATE equipment which gave us direction finding only on the German nightfighers when they were transmitting

(ie no indication of range until within the range of our AI), whereas the 'straight' Intruder's were catching the German nightfighters as they landed...A run down in enemy activity over the UK meant we could be used for other purposes and so we came to the No.100 Group work.

We never used to take the ends off of the exhaust stubs of the Mosquitoes...as we were attempting night interceptions...and were never encouraged to ask about the activities of the other squadrons. We did our own work and that was it.

There was one particular night, I can't remember the raid, when there were no RCM, or if there were they were being used grudgingly. The target was obvious when the bombers set out and there was no 'dogleg' to suggest anything different to what we were doing and no 'Spoof' raid. It was a basic sort of 'dirty-dart', in and out. We lost a great number of aircraft that night. Andy Miller was flying that night, I don't think I was. He called out on Channel C, the Universal Channel (which we weren't suppose to use), 'Come down this way. They are knocking them down like flies,' (or words to that effect.)

AVM Addison instituted a Competition to 'Shoot Down the Hundredth Hun in No. 100 Group'. The score hovered at about 98-99. There was one 'doubtful' score which was not confirmed (there was some talk about it being a friendly aircraft but nobody said much about that!). All the Squadrons were on one night...the other Squadrons got nothing, we got three! Among those making claims were W/C Bromley, our Squadron CO, F/L Fifield and myself. We never established which one of us got the hundredth but they gave us a tankard which was inscribed to 'The Hungry Hun Hunters of 169 Squadron'...the names on the tankard were W/C Neil Bromley and F/L Truscott; F/L J S Fifield and F/O F Staziker; P/O H Reed and F/O J S Watts.

During its time in No. 100 Group, No.169 Squadron destroyed 28 enemy aircraft and damaged eight.

No.239 Squadron

No.239 Squadron was formed at Ayr in September 1943. Most of the aircrew came from Fighter Command where they had acquired knowledge of AI. The initial eighteen crews found their training severely hampered by the absence of training aircraft. It was not until well into October that one dual-controlled Mosquito became available so that 'flying practice was a great rarity'. At the end of November it could still be pessimistically recorded in the Squadron ORB that, 'Training was carried out in the Mosquito.'

On 9th December, the Squadron transferred to No.100 Group and moved to West Raynham, 'All the crews were delighted, for it was clear that only operating as an integral part of Bomber Command could the Squadron have up-to-date information concerning heavy bomber activity, enemy tactics, and technical developments.' It had a difficult and unlucky start in the Group. Two days after the move the Squadron received its first operational aircraft. Two Mosquito Mk.IIs equipped with forward and backward looking AI Mk.IV, SERRATE equipment for homing on to the German Lichtenstein radar, and the navigational aid Gee. Special night shifts were worked by ground crews to get the aircraft ready for operations. 'It looks as though we will be getting some flying in between parades now!' one aircrew member caustically commented. On 14th January, the Squadron became operational and two crews were detailed for that night but no sorties took place as 'the aircraft weren't ready.'

On 20th January 1944, F/Ls Booth and Carpenter flew the Squadron's first sortie. It was uneventful. The following day one of the two aircraft detailed for 'ops' got bogged down on the airfield. In an effort to allow aircrews to gain experience of their new type of role, one inexperienced aircrew member was loaned to No.192 Squadron for a couple of nights, the second of which took him to Aachen 'where he made a fairly close acquaintance with some flak!'. On 27th January, three aircraft from the Squadron went with a large bomber raid on Berlin which 'raised morale considerably after 15 weeks of non-operational flying.' The following night F/Os Munro and Dickie Hurley scored the Squadron's first success when they destroyed an Me110 over Berlin. The Squadron lost its first crew when F/L Brachi and F/O Macleod failed to return. They had been giving 'fixes' right up to ditching but a search of the North Sea for them produced no result.

Lack of serviceable aircraft continued to be a problem. On 1st February, no aircraft were available for operations, a situation which improved four days later when four more Mosquitoes arrived. The Squadron was by now at full flying strength, eight of the 18 crews were now fully trained, and six of the eight had carried out operations over enemy territory. A second victory for the Squadron was obtained on 21st February when F/Os Knight and Doyle destroyed an Me110. Four days later brought a sad jolt to Squadron morale when both of the successful crews were lost. F/Os Munro and Hurley, with their aircraft suffering R/T failure, crashed three miles from West Raynham when they hit a tree and the aircraft burst into flames. F/Os Knight and Doyle, were forced to 'ditch' somewhere over the North Sea. F/O Knight's body was washed ashore at Ramsgate on 27th February.

The first three months of 1944 were to prove altogether frustrating. The weather interfered with training, and the aircraft, 'almost all of which were alleged to be tour-expired veterans from Fighter Command, developed engine trouble on so many occasions that, had the Squadron spirit not been particularly high, a feeling of despondency would have developed.' Four enemy aircraft were destroyed in the period but six experienced aircrews were lost. The Squadron ORB is highly critical:

2.3.44. Last night F/O Thomas and W/O Hayes taking off on an operational sortie on the short runway, had an engine cut just before they were airborne. The aircraft after traversing a certain amount of rough ground, came to rest in an almost whole condition. The only damage was the slightly wounded empennage due to the retraction of the rear wheel. This incident comes after a whole series of engine failures, and the aircrews have ceased to place any trust in the reliability of these old XXI engines. All the aircraft we have received from Fighter Command were in a very bad condition and it has been a thankless task trying to keep them serviceable.

The other two squadrons engaged in SERRATE operations have had exactly the same trouble, but we unfortunately have lost more crews than they have in the last two months. The aircrews, however, must be congratulated in refusing to be shaken by these mishaps, and the news, two days ago, that all the operational aircraft are going to be re-engined with new Merlin XXIIs is a just reward for their continuing fortitude and cheerfulness...

At the beginning of March improvements were forthcoming when, in fact, the aircraft were speedily re-engined with Rolls-Royce Merlin XXII engines. By the end of March the engine changes had been completed, and the destruction of a Ju88 by F/Ss Campbell and Phillips over Nuremburg (See Chapter Four) on Bomber Command's most disastrous night for losses (30/31st March 1944) began a successful four month-long period for the Squadron which resulted in the destruction of 31 enemy aircraft for the loss of three crews. June 1944 was the peak month. Eleven enemy aircraft were destroyed, four on the night of 7th/8th June, and six in July with no losses to the Squadron in either month. 'It was refreshing to note', records a Bomber Command report, [185] 'that victories were not falling to just a few individuals, the 31 aircraft being destroyed by 14 different crews.' F/Os W R Breithaupt (RCAF) and J A Kennedy were particularly successful shooting down a Ju88 to bring their personal total to four enemy aircraft destroyed and one damaged in five weeks:

4/5.6.44. F/Os W R Breithaupt (RCAF) and F/O J A Kennedy. Friesian Islands.2315-0220.

This crew obtained a forward-looking AI contact at maximum range and chased it for ten minutes and reducing it to 2,000 ft when they got a visual. Closed in to 150 yards and opened fire with a two-second burst setting the port engine on fire. The enemy aircraft was seen to be well alight and out of control. One Hun baled out and the enemy aircraft was seen to hit the sea and continue to burn. Claim one Ju88 destroyed.

This crew, sadly would fail to return from a sortie to Frankfurt the next September.

On the night of 27th/28th June, eight aircraft went to Northern France for what proved to be a very interesting night's work. Three combats took place and three enemy aircraft were destroyed. The first successful combat was by F/L Welfare and F/O Bellis who chased a contact flat out for ten minutes, closed to 200 ft, and shot down an Me410. The second was by F/L Howard and F/L Clay, who destroyed a Ju88. After the combat they sent out a 'Mayday' when their starboard engine caught fire, and their instruments and electrics became u/s. On landing at Manston a handful of WINDOW and pieces of the Ju88 were removed from one of their engines. The third crew, W/C Evans and F/O Perks, narrowly avoided a collision with an Fw190, which they pursued doggedly using their AI, and destroyed.

There was another one-engine Odyssey:

> 7/8.7.44. One Me110 destroyed by F/L Bridges and F/S Webb. This combat took place after a long chase, fire being opened at 100 yards. The enemy aircraft blew up with a terrific explosion right in front of the Mosquito which had pulled up to 140 Indicated Air Speed to prevent overshooting. The Mosquito pulled out to avoid flying debris which at low speed caused the Mosquito to stall and go into a spin. This was corrected but two other spins resulted during which flames from the starboard engine entered the cockpit through the door which had already been jettisoned preparatory to baling out. The Mosquito returned to Base, a journey of some 250 miles, on one engine and with its wheels partly down.

Other squadrons were experiencing difficulties and a Conference was held in the Station HQ at West Raynham. No.141 Squadron was lacking fully-trained crews; No.169 Squadron had too many unserviceable aircraft so, for the time being, No.239 Squadron would be 'called upon to carry a heavier portion of No.100 Group nightfighter effort than formerly.' (The squadron eventually flew the most Mosquito sorties in No.100 Group).

The weather interfered:

> 11.7.44. The weather has clamped down again and the prospects for tonight are anything but bright. This prospective inactivity, on top of a cancellation last night, imposes a great strain upon aircrew. There is no doubt that, within the limits of normal endurance, operational activity is at once both stimulant and opiate, so that, for short periods at least, confidence will spring from increased activity and, conversely, 'twitch' will diminish. It will be interesting to see how this theory works out during the next few weeks of intensive flying.

At the beginning of August things became depressingly difficult for the Squadron due to enemy jamming:

> ...which had begun to bother crews in June, and became rapidly worse. The next four months saw it reach such proportions that a maximum radar range of ten thousand feet was a rarity, and even the most experienced and successful crews returned from sortie after sortie with reports of jamming so intense that, as one navigator averred, 'it was flooding the tubes and spilling over into the cockpit'.

Disgust at the severe limitations now imposed on the radar equipment was almost equalled by envy of the consistent successes achieved by the fortunate squadrons, [Nos.85 and 157], equipped with AI Mk.X. From time to time the rumour that 'We're going to get it' spread through the Squadron, but there were to be many more weeks of AI Mk.IV frustration before the hope was to become reality.

In August only three enemy aircraft were destroyed although the percentage of completed sorties – 90.6% – was the highest yet recorded. The following three months were equally unsuccessful. Despite completed sorties always being well above 90% only a further six enemy aircraft were destroyed. Many LL Intruder patrols were flown but, 'the general opinion was that an occasional squirt at a truck or train was poor excitement by comparison with the full-blooded thrill of an AI chase terminating in the destruction of a Hun.'

A non-operational tragedy at the beginning of the month gives an insight into the conditions of the time:

> 3.8.44. A tragic accident at 1610. F/Os Norman Veale and R D Comyn stalled on landing from NFT and were killed. Their aircraft broke up and burst into flames immediately, giving potential rescuers no hope whatsoever.

> 7.8.44. F/O B A Leahy went as escort with the bodies of F/Os Veale and Comyn to Harpenden (Herts) where the funerals are to take place tomorrow. F/O Comyn, a Roman Catholic (RC), whose people live in Eire*, is being buried in the RC Church in Harpenden near the Church of England (C of E) Cemetery where F/O Veale will be laid to rest. S/L J S Booth and the Station Padre left by car at an early hour to attend the funeral at Harpenden.

> * Travel between the UK and Eire had been suspended on 1st April as a security precaution for D-Day. It was lifted a month after the funeral.

Technical difficulties diminished and at the end of August No.239 Squadron could show a Battle Order for combat of 11 crews. There were fewer 'early returns', seven out of 86 in the month. One crew returned after 20 minutes with controls 'unmanageable', and a second crew came back after two hours with a 'smouldering' AI Box – it had at one time actually burst into flames. The Squadron added yet another element to its role when, at the beginning of September six aircraft were available for Intruder operations; by December the Squadron was well into this type of work.

The press visited West Raynham:

> 2.11.44. Visit by Richard Dimbleby, from the BBC, and other journalists. They spent the evening observing the working of an operational station, dining in the Mess with the Station Commander and enjoying an inevitable 'noggin' in the Bar, and finally getting red-hot stories from the crews returning from the Dusseldorf raid. Unfortunately nobody returned on one wing, or minus both engines, but the precise efficiency of Flying Control, the unfailing accuracy of

incoming aircraft and the unassuming attitudes of the crews, were all insensibly transmuted into something gay and glamorous under the eager enthusiasms of those who trade in superlatives. The visit, in fact, was very successful.

At the end of December two crews (F/L Norfolk and F/S Moore: F/Ss Lowrey and Davie) were detailed to carry out the Squadron's first bombing operation. They carried out their sorties as planned each unloading two 500lb bombs, using Gee, over Duisburg. There was much interference with the radar over the target and there were, therefore, no AI contacts. The following night a similar raid on Osnabrück took place.

The end of the year also brought improved fortune with regard to equipment:

With unexpected suddenness the Squadron learned at the beginning of December that at long last it was to convert to AI Mk.Xs, which would be installed in Mosquito Mk.XXXs. Five crews were detached to Swannington to train with operational AI Mk. X crews, (they 'received an object lesson on one occasion when Nos. 85/157 Squadrons returned from the day's sorties with six enemy aircraft destroyed'): those remaining at West Raynham received instructions on the Mobile Trainer and with the Nav/Rad Conversion Flight in Wellingtons...the conversion was effected rapidly and efficiently, due largely to the thoroughness of the Conversion Flight personnel and the pertinacity of F/L Perks, who had become Nav/Rad Leader in November.

By January 7th the first Mosquito arrived, equipped with AI Mk.X, Monica, and Gee, and the first operation was flown on the 23rd...By this time, unfortunately the German reaction to Bomber Command's attacks was falling off rapidly, and it was generally admitted that 'joy' was hard to find even during a heavy raid. It is all the more creditable therefore, that during February four enemy aircraft were destroyed and three damaged, March saw four more accounted for, and, by April, when Luftwaffe air activity was almost non-existent, one enemy aircraft was destroyed and one damaged.[186]

Early in 1945, the Squadron undertook its first AI Mk.X raid on Kassel. It was a failure. One aircraft was detailed for this patrol but on switching on its radar, 'it became u/s almost immediately. F/L Cather and F/S Spicer carried on for about five minutes, changed fuses without effect, and so returned to Base.' After this initial set back, work with the AI Mk.X improved and in the following months it was used extensively near the German fighter beacons. The Squadron also participated in several No.100 Group 'Spoof' operations.

At the War's end only four members remained of the Squadron which had been formed at Ayr 20 months earlier. Of the others, apart from those posted, 16 were missing, 10 were killed, and four were PoWs. In the space of its short operational life the Squadron had flown 1,325 sorties and destroyed 54 enemy aircraft (+ one 'probable'), and damaged seven.

No. 515 Squadron

Like No.192 Squadron, No.515 Squadron was experienced in RCM when it came to No.100 Group and was not new to bomber support. The origin of the Squadron can be traced back to May 1942, when, at Tangmere, highly successful research tests were conducted with MOONSHINE equipment in a Boulton Paul Defiant aircraft flown by F/L E T Wilkins and TRE personnel. MOONSHINE was the RCM designed to give the impression to the enemy's early warning radar that a large force of aircraft was approaching when in fact it was a Defiant carrying the RCM equipment. As a result, the Defiant Flight was formed in June 1942, and attached to RAF Northolt, working under the direction of No.11 Group, Fighter Command. In the following September the Flight became No.515 Squadron and was to play a significant part in aerial RCM.

No.515 Squadron was posted to No. 100 Group on 15th December 1943, moved to Little Snoring and, the following month, W/C F F Lambert became its CO. Its function was debated at high level over a lengthy period. On 10th February 1944 the Deputy C-in-C, Bomber Command, Sir Robert Saundby wrote to the Air Ministry:

> The enemy has extended his Freya frequencies to 60 Mcs therefore No.515 Squadron (which had success in jamming on narrow band 8 Mcs) has now become less successful. This new enemy development had rendered MOONSHINE and MANDREL apparatus to be of little or no value.
>
> Now the Squadron can only be usefully employed in its present role for jamming the enemy Freya over a short stretch of coastline. This is now more effectively achieved by other means such as the concentrated use of WINDOW over the critical period. In the circumstances No.515 squadron, has had no operational task allotted for six months with a consequent all round deterioration, particularly as regards the morale of personnel. There is an urgent need for this Squadron to be given suitable employment without delay.

He recommended No.515 Squadron become a nightfighter squadron with special duties:

> The initial role envisaged for this Squadron is for it to attack enemy nightfighters whilst they are landing, or waiting to land, after their employment against our night bombers, a remunerative field which has not yet been exploited...The enemy is known to be using navigation lights whilst landing his nightfighters and should there be any delay in the provision of AI equipment it is considered non-AI Mosquitoes would meet with success in this type of operation for an interim period.[187]

Saundby suggested No. 515's MOONSHINE/MANDREL/CARPET role be abandoned and that the Squadron be re-equipped with Mosquitoes Mk VI for the new work. Three weeks later AVM Addison, AOC No. 100 Group, requested of the

No.515 Squadron. Left to right: LAC Geoff Sparrow (Engine Fitter), F/O Glen Graham, RCAF, (Pilot), and LAC Joe Gee (Airframe Fitter), in front of their De Havilland Mosquito at Little Snoring.

(Geoff Sparrow)

Air Ministry that 'a reply may be hastened', and, on 10th March, the Air Ministry agreed that No.515 Squadron could be re-equipped with Mosquito Mk.VI as 'an interim measure'. Two days later Addison added that, although the RCM commitments for the Squadron 'are, at present, under review', the new Mosquitoes 'may be employed in the nightfighter role suggested in your letter.' The Squadron's Mosquito Mk.VIs were not re-equipped with AI equipment, and the change of role saw all the air-gunners posted out, and navigators, together with further aircrews, posted in. Intensive training followed and the Squadron was ready for operations by the end of February.

In fact, operations began with Mosquitoes on 3rd March, when the destruction of an unidentified enemy twin-engined aircraft opened the No.100 Group account for No.515 Squadron. But still the Squadron's exact function was not clearly defined. Saundby thought the dilatoriness worthy of a 'hurry up' letter to the Air Ministry. He suggested this course of action on 6th April to ACM Harris, (a week after the disastrous Nuremburg Raid), 'I think it is most important to increase our fighting power against the German Nightfighter Force. Things are going very slowly at No.100 Group and...unless we do something drastic things will drift slowly along and we shall get nowhere.' This brought a rapid 'Agreed' from the C-in-C, Bomber Command. Official direction for No.515 Squadron to be employed for Intruder work over enemy airfields came from HQ Bomber Command to No.100 Group HQ on 9th April. The fitting of AI to the Squadron's aircraft was still 'under consideration'.

The Squadron undertook other tasks. On 12th May 1944, three of the Squadron's aircraft carried out successful anti-flak patrols of the Kiel Canal in support of minelaying aircraft by drawing fire from the gun positions towards themselves and

Vickers Wellington bomber used as a flying classroom for AI Mk.X training. The gun turret in the nose was replaced with an AI Mk.X radome. *(Crown Copyright)*

SERRATE equipment and aerials on a De Havilland Mosquito Mk.II. *(Crown Copyright)*

away from the minelaying aircraft. Then, on the night before D-Day, all Squadron aircraft were out on Ranger patrols, patrolling and bombing enemy airfields in France and strafing road, rail and canal traffic. Two crews were lost. The support given by the Squadron to the mining of the Dortmund Ems Canal by No.8 Group PFF has been classified as one of the most important minelaying operations of the War. Ten Mosquitoes from No. 515 Squadron patrolled the heavily defended canal area, and by drawing the fire away from the minelaying aircraft, or strafing the gun positions from very close range, silenced the opposition and enabled the mining of one of Germany's most important waterways to be achieved without loss. A congratulatory message was received from the C-in-C, Bomber Command, and the crews participating were subsequently decorated.

Occasionally crews finished in neutral territory. This happened to two from No.515 Squadron. On 30thSeptember 1944, S/L Morley, (Navigator, F/S Fidler), in Mosquito Mk VI No 440, and F/L Callard (Navigator, F/S Townsley), in Mosquito Mk.VI No. 993, flew to a forward base at St.Dizier, one aircraft carrying an extra passenger, (see Ted Harper's story in Chapter Seven). Both aircraft took off again at 1200 hrs on Day Ranger sorties to Munich, Linz and Vienna areas.

S/L Morley and F/S Fidler damaged, and probably destroyed, two aircraft at Holzkirchen Airfield, near Munich. After this attack they parted company with the other Mosquito and set course to return to Base. During their return trip they attacked a number of JU 86s parked on the perimeter of Munich (Neubiberg) Airfield, one of which they damaged. Between Konstanz and Zurich, at 200 ft, the Mosquito was hit by flak, and, with the aircraft losing height, S/L Morley feathered the port engine. Shortly after this, four Swiss Air Force Moraine fighters appeared and clearly indicated to the Mosquito crew that they must land at Dubendorf Airfield in Switzerland. Over the airfield, the Mosquito's starboard engine also failed and they made a crash landing.

Meanwhile, F/L Callard and F/S Townsley, continuing their sortie, attacked and destroyed two Dornier 24 Float Planes moored near the shore at Prien. They carried on to the Salzburg area and destroyed one Me 109G on the ground at Friedburg. With the windscreen of the aircraft covered with flies, thus obscuring his vision, Callard decided to return to Base. South of Munich, flying at zero feet, the starboard engine overheated and had to be 'feathered'. This made it difficult to gain sufficient height to cross the hills, and here again, this crew were surrounded by four Swiss Air Force Moraine fighters. They were escorted to Dubendorf where the Mosquito made a safe landing. Subsequently both crews escaped from their internment and returned to England.

Towards the end of 1944, AI Mk X was allocated to the Squadron and no sooner had the training for this equipment neared completion, when it was withdrawn and

A De Havilland Mosquito equipped with AI Mk.X (SCR 720). A Perspex radome on the nose covers the aerial scanner. *(Crown Copyright)*

replaced by ASH. On the last day of the year S/L Bennett scored the first victory with this new equipment.

On February 28th 1945, the Squadron was again directed to attack the flak on the Kiel Canal whilst No.5 Group were to lay mines. No.515 Squadron Mosquitoes strafed the flak and searchlights for 20 minutes until they had used up all their ammunition. The No.5 Group Markers were unable to find the Canal due to poor weather. The operation was repeated the following night and this time it was successful.

The work of the Squadron was varied and intensive:

...during its short history [in No.100 Group] the Squadron carried out night LL Intruder attacks as its basic efforts, followed by numerous anti-flak patrols, HL daylight Bomber escort, LL day and night Ranger patrols, target indicating and master bombing of aerodromes in all parts of enemy occupied territory. All new types of offensive duties have been welcomed and embarked upon with enthusiasm.

Latterly, when the airborne Hun became rather difficult to find, the fight was carried to their aerodromes. The Squadron provided a Master Bomber and a team of between four and six Mosquitoes, who marked with Target Indicators (TIs) and Incendiary Bombs the important aerodrome buildings for the fire bombs of Nos.169 and 141 Squadrons. Having marked, the Mosquitoes of No. 515 would sit over the enemy aerodromes and strafe any opposing flak. The raids were controlled throughout on VHF by the Master Bomber. A load of 2,000 lbs of bombs could be carried by each Mosquito, and a careful assortment of 500 lbs HE bombs with siren attachment, anti-personnel bombs, canisters of incendiary bombs and larger 250 lbs incendiary bombs were used. The target was usually marked with a green TI.

On some occasions the Squadron combined gun and bomb:

The idea of a concentrated attack with bombs and cannons against the enemy airfields was conceived by No.515 Squadron. On 13/14th April 12 Mosquitoes from the Squadron attacked Lubock/Blankensee aerodrome, and in spite of the poor weather over the target a highly successful raid was achieved. This operation heralded a series of attacks, thirteen of which were marked and controlled by No.515 Squadron.[188]

Frank Lindsay flew 35 sorties from Little Snoring. There were many incidents, he felt, which 'could be described as hair-raising, and which I would prefer to forget but there was one thing that happened which shows the skill of many of the crews at that time and was, in a way, very amusing':

On 10th July 1944, two aircraft took of from Little Snoring at 1510 hours for a daylight mission which took them over Northern Holland to Heligoland. The aircraft were crewed by S/L Mick Martin[189] (previously a Lancaster pilot on No. 617 Squadron) who had taken a major role in the attack on the Mohne and Sorpe Dams in May 1943. His navigator was F/O Smith. The other aircraft was flown by F/L Eric Llamie and I was the navigator.

We flew very low at 40 to 50 ft at an airspeed of 280 mph. and, on the way back over the North Sea our aircraft was leading the way. It was a lovely sunny day and to my surprise splashes began to appear on the fairly calm sea under our aircraft. It was fairly obvious to us someone was firing at us from behind and we took evasive action only to hear the Australian accent of Mick Martin saying, 'It's alright, Cobber, it's only me doing a spot of target practice!' We were flying at about 50 ft and he was firing his four 20mm cannons at the shadow of our aircraft on the waves! This gives some idea of the skill of S/L Martin who was one of the finest exponents of low-level flying, but it gave me a shock to see cannon traces flying past the underside of our aircraft only to find it was what would now be called 'Friendly Fire'.

Exposure to danger wasn't only confined to the air:

The Mosquito crews were transported between the crew room and dispersal sites in small trucks covered with canvas tops. Three or four crew members sat in the back and one sat next to the girl driver (the seat most favoured). On this occasion I was the quickest and managed to get in the seat next to Mary, a driver who came from Sheffield. Nearly all the aircraft at Little Snoring were Mosquitoes. No.515 Squadron also had an Avro Anson used mainly for transporting crews on leave, and for some secret radar practice for the new crews who had come from OTUs.

When Mosquitoes were taxying along the perimeter track the girls who drove the small trucks were able to drive under the end of the Mosquito wingtip, the trucks being about five feet high and the wingtip being about nine to ten feet from the ground. In this way they avoided having to drive on the grass which sometimes was ankle deep in mud and often rutted in winter.

On this particular night it was very dark when we were being driven from the aircraft after our 'op'. when we met an aircraft taxying towards us. Our WAAF driver drove on intending to drive under the green (starboard) light on the wingtip only for us to realise the light was coming straight at our windscreen. It was the Anson with a wingtip height of approximately four to five feet! A collision occurred with the propeller blade coming dangerously close to all the occupants in the truck. We learned that night it could be more dangerous on the ground than in the air!

On another occasion, also on the ground, Frank Lindsay and Eric Llamie dealt with a 'trespasser':

It was early in 1944 when we arrived at Little Snoring (having left 96 Squadron where we flew Beaufighters). The airfield was not quite finished and work on buildings on the airfield were being completed. The runways and perimeter tracks were laid so flying was taking place (this was mainly to get accustomed to the Mosquito after doing night 'ops' on Beaufighter Mk.VIs). The civilian workers used bicycles mainly to get about (petrol being too scarce) and many of them thought they had more right to be on the airfield than the aircraft.

Our Mosquito was coming in on approach to the runway to land, when a very large man on a bicycle came riding round the perimeter track and, without bothering to look to see if any aircraft were about, proceeded to cycle across the end of the runway we were about to land on. Eric said to me, 'I'll give this guy the fright of his life' and cut the engine revs down to make our approach as quiet as possible. At the last moment, as we were about 30 ft high and 100 yards from the cyclist crossing the runway end, Eric opened up the throttles causing a tremendous noise. The cyclist looked up, panicked and tried to put on speed to get out of the way. His foot slipped off the pedal and he nearly fell off his bicycle. There was really no danger though and we just flew over him to land on the runway. I doubt whether he cycled over the runway ends again without looking.

Aircraft recognition was sometimes a problem:

Between 5th and 12th August 1944, we were supporting Lancasters who were bombing the U-Boat pens at Bordeaux. On one of these raids a Lancaster was returning over the Bay of Biscay, having had an engine fire, and was coming

AI Mk.X Cathode Ray Tube indicator in De Havilland Mosquito cockpit. *(Crown Copyright)*

home on three engines. Two Mosquitoes were ordered by our CO, W/C Lambert to escort the Lancaster, which was travelling at 140 mph., until met by Spitfires who would take over somewhere over the Brest Peninsula. We were one of the Mosquitoes directed for the job and were flying round and about it at approximately 240 mph.

We were dismayed to see four single-engined fighters approaching us from the direction of the French Coast. They appeared to have large radial engines and I was sure they were Focke-Wulf 190s, which were the best fighters the Germans had at that time. We made a quick decision and Eric gave the word over the R/T to the other Mosquito. We would both turn 90 degrees and attack them head-on. As we did so they broke away and to our relief we could see the roundels and black and white 'task' markings like our own which were not visible from our head-on view. They were RAF Typhoons which looked like 190s from head-on with very large air intake under the propeller boss. It was only then I realised sweat was running from my flying helmet down the back of my neck.

Usually things happened so quickly in the air, one followed the excellent training we had been given and did what had to be done automatically...Although the War Years took a chunk out of our young lives, I feel pleased I was part of it. I wondered whether after all the training we were given I would be able to do what was needed when it came to actual war operations. Having successfully come through those days no task since then has worried me. I made many wonderful friends but sadly many of them went missing. I believe No.515 squadron lost 20 aircraft in May and June, 1944.

Bill Jones, a navigator, when attached to a heavy bomber squadron remembered that, at briefings, mention was often made that 'Aircraft of No.100 Group would be flying Special Duties during the Main Force attack', but was unaware what they were. After completing a tour, a brief interlude as a Navigation Instructor at an Advanced Flying Unit, in mid-February 1944, he found out by joining them. He was wanted immediately, 'no one knew why.' His introduction to the Group continued the mystery:

I arrived, cold and thirsty after my trip from Finningley, at Fakenham Railway Station on a cold, wet Norfolk evening. I was collected by a local Squadron vehicle driven by a WAAF who said she would take me to the camp. She told me I could not ask what the number of the Squadron was, or what aircraft were flown...she had instructions to drop me at the Officers Mess, and this she duly did.

I stood looking at the Nissen Hut and the two obvious extensions, when the door opened and the Mess Steward welcomed me in, stored my kit, and took me to the ante-room where a group of officers, including a W/C (Freddie Lambert) were stood around a double-sided fire drinking ale. They stared at me as if I had arrived from outer space. After I introduced myself, ale was produced and I at last established I had joined No.515 Squadron, and that it was non-operational, a state of affairs which lasted for some months.

After a period of hotel-type accommodation at Finningley the 25% of a Nissen Hut at No.6 Site in Little Snoring came as something of a shock but with true Welsh resilience, and Morgan's of Norwich Ale, I settled in.

The morning of 11th February dawned and I realised I was the only navigator on the Squadron (there was another but he was on leave) and, accompanied by a particularly pleasant fellow, F/L Josh Hoskin, I toured the airfield to find the airfield complement was some nine to ten 'clapped-out' Beaufighter Mk.2's, a couple of Oxfords, and a really ancient Anson. It was unbelievable, but Josh persuaded me to go on a familiarisation flight in a Beaufighter, so for about 90 minutes we toured the Norfolk landscape at reasonably low altitudes and it was the birth of the rather well-known team of Josh and Jonah.

Navigation was particularly difficult in the cramped conditions in the aircraft and a dearth of equipment added to the difficulties. 'We had to buy dividers and straight-edge rulers from local newsagents in Norwich and Fakenham'. Eventually the problems were overcome:

In early March a Mosquito Mk. II arrived on loan and by then we had a reasonable number of navigators to form crews. The navigators had generally come from OTU's, or from other squadrons where pilots had volunteered for this new type of work entitled 'Operational Low-Level Intruding by Night', with the promise that the aircraft would be the new Mk.VI Fighter/Bomber version of the Mosquito.

In the second week of April our Mosquito VI's began to arrive and, after a period of conversion, the Squadron was declared 'operational' and Josh and I flew to Manston to be briefed by No.605 Squadron staff who had some experience of night-intruding...We were sent off to attack the Airfield at St.Didier in France. Thus began a series of thrice-weekly operations that lasted until the beginning of October 1944.

There was always great talk of equipping our Mosquito VI's with AI but it never came about in my time...When AI Mk.X came into the Group several of us began studying the system but we were never given the opportunity to fly with it. We remained low-level intruders...We would navigate to the enemy airfield, orbit it, and hope the flying-control personnel would light the approaches if the airfield was quiet. Then we would take a swift turn down its runway, give a burst of cannon fire and drop the odd 500lb bomb. Then for about 40 minutes we would stand-off in the circuit. There was occasional light flak but this was rarely effective. The effect of our presence rather frustrated a take-off situation, and even more so it made the tired enemy pilot over-apprehensive as he returned to land from his long patrol. There were accidents at take-off and landing and we were gratified to receive pictures from the photo-reconnaisance boys at Benson showing the extent of crash landings etc. at the airfields we had covered.

We also enjoyed the odd 'Daylight Ranger' as a change from night intruding. We flew to Caen/Carpiquet soon after Caen had been liberated and accompanied G/C Sammy Hoare (now the Station Commander at Little Snoring), on a long intrusion into southern Germany including a visit to Munich. The G/C went on to Vienna but we attended an airfield at Inglestadt with some success.

We were sent on a long Ranger to Halborg in northern Denmark accompanied by S/L Mickey Martin who joined the Squadron from Group HQ. It was a long boring flight over miles and miles of North Sea but Mickey enlivened the proceedings by firing his guns over our starboard wing. This caused a minor panic until we realised it was all good, clean fun! When we got to Halborg the flying boats we had been after were gone!

Bill Jones graphically described an air-sea rescue of one of his Squadron:

In the summer of 1944 we were returning from Frankfurt when we heard a call on the listening-out frequency from one of our Squadron, F/L Joe Huggins, to the effect that he was on fire and had ordered his navigator, F/S Joe Cooper, to bale out. His best estimate of his position was that he was some 20 miles off the Dutch Coast level with Den Helder. We were not far away so we flew to his aid but saw nothing. We risked a climb to 7,000 ft to take a Gee fix but saw nothing. My pilot, Josh, and Joe Huggins had been sergeant-photographers in peacetime and had served together in India and Josh was determined to help. We did not know at the time that Joe Huggins had ditched near Lowestoft and had been picked up by the Royal Navy.

Soon after daybreak on the following day we set off to home on to our Gee fix of the previous day. It was a calm, beautiful day so we decided to institute what was called a 'square area' search. My pilot had never heard of this and my knowledge was limited to my Anson training days, but we made a bold effort for about an hour and must have driven the German radar operators to distraction. At times we were within a mile of the Dutch Coast and there was some desultory, depressed heavy flak, from the batteries in the Den Helder area.

It was approaching the time to leave but we decided to do a couple more legs at 5,000 ft and on the second we saw the dinghy. Amid great excitement we climbed to Gee fix the position and then climbed higher still to request Sector Control to fix us. We swiftly left the scene after a farewell wing-waggle to Joe Cooper and arrived back at Little Snoring at about 8am. Sector Control had told the Squadron that the dinghy had been sighted and all crews were at Dispersal. Our CO, W/C Freddie Lambert, had requested an Air/Sea Rescue launch but it was considered too dangerously near the Dutch Coast to risk a rescue and it was intended to report Joe's position on the international frequency for the Germans to collect him.

Freddie would have none of this and contacted the Royal Navy whom he knew had a Walrus flying boat. They were prepared to undertake the rescue providing they had an escort. Then Freddie uttered his famous words, 'How about 20 Mosquitoes?' We gave the Walrus a 90 miles start and then took off in ragged formation. Fortunately the Gee fix held and the Captain of the Walrus landed but cautioned us that only brief communication with us would be made as he needed all of his battery power to get off again. The message came, 'Cooper is well', and that was all. We returned to Base and Joe Cooper went to hospital suffering from sunburn!

P/O Chris Harrison, who had worked at Derby for Rolls-Royce, became a pilot in No.515 Squadron. His Navigator was F/S Mike Adams. Harrison recalled that when attacking the enemy airfields the Mosquito crews very rarely saw the enemy until very

SQUARE SEARCH

This was used for a systematic search of an area. The pilot estimated the visibility on his approach to the position where it was necessary to start his search. From previous experience he judged the distance that was required between the lines of search (called X below). Then the navigator had a busy few minutes as he calculated the compass headings for each leg, the ground speeds, and how long they would have to fly on each heading. When this was completed the search was carried out.

The table for the distances to be flown over the ground, or sea, is shown as follows:-

Leg	Distance
1	X
2	X
3	2X
4	2X
5	3X
6	3X

and so on.

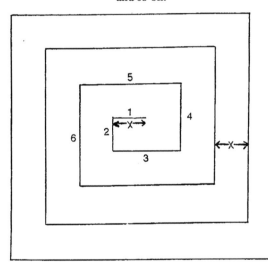

(From a sketch by Norman Mackenzie)

late, and then only when they lit a low-powered nose light, 'which looked like a glow-worm' as they came down the runway to land so that their own defences didn't fire at them:

> If the airfield was lit it meant they were using it, and I used to bomb and strafe the runway even if we couldn't see any enemy aircraft. When they were aware of our presence over the airfield, machine guns opened up and searchlights came on, sometimes before we had attacked them. At such a low altitude they could be lethal. During 1944 we lost 24 crews [the Squadron eventually had the highest loss rate amongst the Mosquito Squadrons in No.100 Group]. During this year

S/L Mick Martin, the Dambuster, came to us as a Flight Commander and we wondered if he had been sent by the Top Brass to find out why we had so many casualties. He thought three hours in a Mosquito was more tiring than six hours in a Lancaster and some of our sorties lasted five hours or more.

I liked the Mosquito. It was sometimes difficult to take off with, but once it was in the air it was extremely easy to fly; you could control it with your fingertips. It was very stable and had a good gun platform. Your navigator was close by you which was good for morale. The cockpit was warm, sometimes it was 90 degrees, and if you hadn't been resting before an op as you should have been you could find yourself at four or five in the morning over Germany trying to avoid dropping off to sleep! Baling out could be difficult. We did most of our 'ops' at about 2,000 ft and if you needed to jump – we did drills and the best I heard of was 10 seconds to get out of the aircraft – you didn't have a lot of time. The aircraft could climb at 160-170 mph and cruise at 260 mph.

One day I flew to Derby and, at about 1.30pm just as my old chums were going back to work, I probably established an alltime high-speed and low-altitude record going up Nightingale Road past Rolls-Royce. As frequently happens when you are doing something you are not supposed to be doing as I passed the factory one of my engines started to play up. It was the Constant-Speed Unit that was faulty. The aircraft vibrated very furiously and caused me some embarrassment.

As far as our armament was concerned we carried 600 rounds of 20mm cannon ammunition (we had four 20mm cannons), four .303 Browning machine guns with 2,000 rounds of ammunition. When you only had a few rounds of your ammunition left you would fire two or three rounds of 'tracer' bullets. So when you saw these coming out you knew you hadn't got much left. We used to fire both cannon and machine guns together. After all your cannon ammo had gone you still had quite a bit of .303 left. After the racket the cannons made (they really shook the aeroplane and slowed it down) when you were left with just the machine guns, the noise was considerably reduced, and it was almost as if you were using a peashooter by comparison.

Occasionally humour intruded. Peggy Frodin recollected a story her husband, F/L Les Frodin, a navigator in No. 515 Squadron, told her:

One day 'S' for Sugar had gone out on an operation from Little Snoring, but over the Channel the Pilot, 'Mac' Macready, didn't like the sound of one of the engines, so he turned back. Shortly afterwards it was obvious the engine was not going to see them home so they made an emergency crash landing at Stonehenge. My husband and Mac got out of the aircraft, and obeying orders, dashed away from the 'plane, expecting it to blow up any second. They hid behind one of the

Stonehenge Stones. After a few minutes nothing had happened so they peeped round the stone to look at the aircraft and saw two little lads helping themselves to bits and pieces for souvenirs! They shouted to the lads to get off and chased them away from it.

Peggy Frodin's husband undergoing exhaustive medical tests after complaining about getting a lot of headaches, to find that the eventual diagnosis was that he 'had been wearing his goggles too tight!' Her marriage could only have been in wartime. In the middle of the Service the air raid sirens sounded whereupon the Vicar said, 'Excuse me I have got to go and get my gas mask.' The congregation waited while he dashed back to the Vicarage, which was just behind the Church, and did so. The wedding then continued!

Harry Whitmill left training to be an accountant with Great Western Railway in October 1940, and, at the age of 19 years, joined the RAF. He became a pilot, eventually being posted to No.515 Squadron joining them at Heston, after serving in two other squadrons. Preferring squadron life to any other he turned down the opportunity to go to Canada as a flying instructor and came with the Squadron to Little Snoring. Like many others he believed in a talisman and always carried a small white plastic elephant for good luck when he went on operations.

On 9th April 1944, after a week in which the Squadron had spent its time repairing aircraft – the ground crews had been on continual night work for the whole week – seven sorties were planned for the night and F/O Harry Whitmill was to fly one of them. At 2253 hours, with F/O D L Biggs as his Navigator, he set off from Little Snoring in Mosquito NS 948 to support a Main Force raid on the goods yards at Lille. 'After becoming airborne' it is recorded, 'nothing was heard from this aircraft and it is missing. Cause unknown.' Both were later found to have been killed in action and were the first casualties sustained by No.515 Squadron during its time in No.100 Group. Whitmill's wife had been widowed after less than two months marriage.

F/O Kelvin Purdie (RNZAF), a Nav/Rad, found training for his AI work totalled thirteen airborne exercises:

> From learning to interpret the blip movement on the CRT's the next step was to carry out interceptions with a series of instructions to the pilot to bring him within visual range close up behind and just below the target aircraft – the 'identifying and Attacking' position.
>
> Then followed similar interceptions with the target aircraft taking evasive action, firstly in azimuth only, then altitude only, and finally in both azimuth and altitude. It was necessary to recognise the evasive action at the earliest possible stage to be able to follow without losing the blip off the CRT. Banking etc., by your own aircraft changed the dimensions of the blips and this had to be taken into account.

Regardless of the type of AI being used, it was up to the navigator/radar operator to quickly assess the relative position and movement of a target aircraft in order to give the pilot accurate instructions. The range and azimuth were immediately obvious from the dimensions of the blip but deciding on its course required a quick accurate assessment of the nature of the blip movement on the screen. For instance, a head-on approach by a target with a high closing speed called for quick reactions by both radar operator and pilot.

Purdie, having crewed up with a pilot, W/O Jack Flanagan who, like him, came from Christchurch, New Zealand, went to No.515 Squadron in January 1945. He had a 'spooky' introduction to his sleeping arrangements:

I remember I went into an eight bed dormitory at Little Snoring. There was a Belgian pilot in the corner writing a letter. 'Don't take that bed' he said, pointing to one of the vacant ones, 'the last three to sleep in that bed have all gone missing.' I wasn't taking any risks so I took another bed, but when we went back that night we found that our friend, Van, had taken it. Either he had not been warned or was not superstitious. Perhaps he should have been as he went missing a few weeks later. They took the bed away and destroyed it after that and left a gap where it had been.

The crew carried out their first operation on 20th February when they went to the Zuider Zee. The Squadron, Purdie found, had its own entry point on the Dutch Coast at a slight bulge in the coastline just north of a small town called Egmond. Apart from sighting two V2s in flight and experiencing tracer fire from the ground some distance in front of them the trip was uneventful. It was the policy of the Squadron to send crews on their second operations as soon as possible after the first, and Jack Flanagan and Kelvin Purdie found themselves experiencing some activity on the following night.:

The target for the heavy bombers was Bonn and we were to patrol two German airfields near Stuttgart in southern Germany. The ground forces were pushing up towards the Rhine at this stage so we made plans to fly over France to a landfall on the Rhine to keep our time over hostile territory to a minimum. We set course from Base at 1845 hours and headed south to the Channel and France. Navigation went according to plan and I was able to use Gee well into France. It was a clear, starry night and map-reading from then on was quite straightforward. I identified the bend in the Rhine near Karlsruhe and then it was a matter of setting course for the next landfall, 45 miles further on, a bend in the Enz River.

About 11 minutes later we reached this bend and set course for our first target, Saschenheim airfield. At this stage I was watching the radar screen closely and a few seconds later Jack called out that he could see the airfield. I also looked out and could see the clear, circular area with hangars standing out quite clearly from the surrounding countryside. It was a great boost to my confidence to have located this small grass airfield so far from Base.

We cruised around to gain confidence and then made some LL runs across the upwind and downwind ends of the airfield looking for radar contacts from planes landing, or taking off. There was no success and no other signs of activity so we headed for Malmsheim. Excitement mounted when we saw an illuminated flare path with two rows of red lights. We started our radar search and although the lights were doused immediately, continued searching for some time. When our one hour patrol was up we returned to the first airfield but there was still no activity.

Our orders had been 'no trains during the patrol' and of course there had been a number of trains travelling to and fro during the patrol. Now there were none to be seen but, cruising a little further afield, we saw the telltale trail of smoke. The railway line was running through a narrow valley and Jack proceeded to increase revs and boost before putting the aircraft into a shallow dive. My job at this stage was to call out the altitude at each one hundred feet so that, in his enthusiasm, Jack did not carry us down into the deck. I felt the plane react to the movement of the joystick and rudder bar as Jack lined up the train in the reflector sight and then heard the thumping of the four 20mm cannon as the firing button was pressed. Nothing happened for a brief moment and then I saw the shells exploding on the engine and waggons. On circling round we saw the train stationary with steam pouring from the engine.

We decided a further attack on this train was unwarranted so we went in search of another which we soon found. We repeated the process and raked the engine and carriages with a long burst of cannon fire. We had no sooner seen the strikes than a curtain of multi-coloured flak flew up at us from the nearby Saschenheim defences. Jack pulled the throttles wide open and dived still lower to within 200 ft of the ground. The ASI shot around to the 350 mph mark and we were soon out of range and unscathed. The flak had been an unpleasant experience although it should not have been. The ground defences obviously did not fire at every aircraft in the circuit unless it showed itself to be unfriendly! Needless to say after this unwonted opposition we headed for home.

When our pulses had settled down and the Rhine was behind us, we gradually relaxed while still maintaining a vigilant watch on our rear radar scanning screen. This had been our baptism in fire. We had fired at the Germans and they had fired at us. We had not been hit but had caused some damage and we were satisfied to have accomplished this much on our second operation. We returned to base about ten minutes after midnight having been airborne for five and a half hours.

Whilst in No.100 Group, No.515 Squadron destroyed 11 aircraft in the air, 18 on the ground, also damaging five on the ground. In addition, it destroyed and damaged much ground or water-based enemy transport such as locomotives, rolling stock, motor vehicles, barges and ships. The Squadron lost 21 aircraft and 41 aircrew during this period.

No.1692 Flight

Originally formed in late 1942 as the Radar Development Flight, this Unit was concerned with the development of airborne radar; it additionally trained some crews to home onto airborne jammers. This was probably the first attempt ever made to home onto transmitters carried in aircraft.

When, in June 1943, nine SERRATE equipped aircraft, complete with crews, arrived at Drem in Scotland from No.141 Squadron, to learn how to home onto airborne transmitters, no techniques had been evolved. S/L Motion and F/O Moy-Thomas, both of whom had served at TRE and FIU, had developed a method of AI and joined the Unit to train these crews. They also undertook the preliminary training in SERRATE of Nos.169 and 239 Squadrons which were then being formed.

The Drem Unit became No.1692 Flight. Its aircraft consisted, at this time, of three Bristol Beaufighters with 150cm radar, and five rather ancient Boulton Paul Defiants, which carried transmitters. At the beginning of November the establishment was increased when a further three Beaufighters, fitted with 60cm AI, arrived from No.141 Squadron to assist the training. Difficulty was experienced in maintaining the aircraft due to the shortage of ground crews, a problem which would persist for some time.

On 7th December 1943, No.1692 Flight was transferred to No.100 Group and moved to Little Snoring. The SERRATE training was now extended to include crews from OTUs as well as the three squadrons. The establishment was increased to eight Beaufighters. The Flight also did some experimental flying using Beaufighters, Mosquitoes and Ansons. During its time in the Group, No.1692 Flight would cover all types of AI instruction to No.100 Group fighter squadrons with the exception of PERFECTOS and SERRATE Mk. IV.

During April 1944, Mosquitoes were added to the Unit for conversion and advanced training. A third component of the Flight carried out refresher courses. The Unit moved to Great Massingham, dual-control Mosquitoes arriving in June. Due to the expansion in the work carried out the Flight's establishment was raised to that of a Bomber Command Training Unit comprising the three flights with W/C J Benson as CO. The following month 15 AI Mk.IV equipped Mosquitoes arrived. A Night Vision School was formed in August, and, in September, 'In order to cover the

ASH AI, a minature microwave radar, being manoeuvred into the nose of a De Havilland Mosquito. W/C Cordingly is standing to the immediate left of the mobile Hoist.

(N C Cordingly)

shortage of crews arriving from OTUs, a large number of pilots who had previously been flying heavy bombers were converted to Mosquitos and crewed with experienced radar operators from Fighter Command.' A Gunnery Flight was formed in October; also in this month ASH training was substituted for AI Mk.IV and SERRATE, which were not showing good results. Two squadrons in the Group had been equipped with ASH.

In January 1945, the first Wellington in which operators were to be converted and tested with AI Mk.X arrived; ASH Mosquitoes were substituted for those with AI Mk.IV only. A revised syllabus was introduced to supply qualified operational crews to the squadrons. Ground training was intensified by the addition of the AI MkX trainer and lectures; beam approach and bad weather training was also carried out. The increased workload of the Flight is indicated by the fact that 769 flying hours were completed in March 1945, compared with 217 in April 1944. A month before the War's end the first of the Unit's Mosquito Mk. XIXs with AI Mk.X fitted was delivered.

Footnotes – Chapter Six

123 Lecture. 'The Radio War' by AVM Addison, CB, CBE, at the Royal United Services Institute (RUSI), November 1946.

124 PRO AIR 14/2911. 'The Development and Activities of No. 100 (Bomber Support) Group'. Part 1.

125 PRO 25/777. No. 100 Group ORB. 1.1.44.

126 Op.cit. (124).

127 Ibid, pp. 5-6

128 Ibid. p.6.

129 PRO AIR 14/738. 'No.100 (BS) Group Operational Policy, p.57a', dated 12.12.44.

130 Ibid. p.6

131 Ibid. p.8

132 Ibid. p.9.

133 Ibid. p.10.

134 Op.cit (124), p.7.

135 Letter dated 8.7.44 from AOC, No.100 Group to C-in-C, Bomber Command. (Harris Archive, R A F Museum, Hendon).

136 Ibid.

137 Ibid.

138 Letter dated 10.7.44 from C-in-C, Bomber Command, to AOC No.100 Group. (Harris Archive, R A F Museum, Hendon).

139 When the fitting of AI Mk.X into No.100 Group fighters began there were insufficient to equip the whole fighter force. AI Mk.XV (also known as ASH) was available. This was an American 3cm AI originally intended for wing-fitting to single-engine fighters. Although not so elaborate as the AI Mk.X , and was also found to interfere with the magnetic compass on a Mosquito (a magnetron screen was developed to take care of this) it was expected to be better for bomber support operations than the AI Mk.IV, and it was decided to equip Nos. 23, 141, and 515 Squadrons. It was used on both high and low-level sorties with limited success. From over 1,000 high and low-level sorties flown between December 1944 and April 1945 there were only 100 suspicious contacts leading to 14 successful combats. (PRO AIR 14/2911: 'Development and Activities of No.100 (Bomber Support) Group, Pt.1, p.14)

140 Letter dated 1.11.44. from AOC, No 100 Group to C-in-C, Bomber Command, (Harris Archives, R A F Museum, Hendon).

141 Letter dated 9.12.44, from Deputy C-in-C, Bomber Command, Air Marshal Sir

Robert Saundby, KBE, CB, MC, DFC, AFC, to AOC, No. 100 Group.

142 Op.cit. (124), p.13.

143 Ibid.

144 Ibid., p.14.

145 The research and development unit of No.100 Group, the Bomber Support Development Unit (BSDU), at Foulsham, produced 40 PERFECTOS I sets (plus 48 in subsequent modifications), and 24 SERRATE IV, 9 and 21 in subsequent modifications).

146 Op.cit. (124), pp 12, 14/15.

147 'Report on German Nightfighter Defences' dated 16.11.44, by Dr. R V Jones, ADI (Science), Air Ministry. (Harris Archive Ref.H77. R A F Museum, Hendon).

148 Ibid.

149 PRO AIR 27/588: No.23 Squadron ORB.

150 Ibid.

151 Ibid.

152 Ibid.

153 Ibid.

154 Ibid.

155 Ibid.

156 PRO AIR 25/777. No.100 Group ORB.

157 From an article, 'Night Intruder' which first appeared in 'I'll Never Forget'. (Canadian Aviation Historical Society, 1977). Reproduced by permission of the author, George Stewart.

158 Op.cit(27)

159 PRO AIR 8/1161. CAS to C-in-C, Bomber Command, (date not shown).

160 AI Mk/X enabled the Mosquito radar operator to 'see' forward for up to ten miles with an 180 degrees coverage thus giving a much wider radar scan. When MONICA, the rearward-looking radar equipment was added to the Mosquito it gave the radar operator much improved radar 'vision'. 'Today (3.6.44) Mosquito VY-Y returned from Foulsham already fitted with MONICA, and it was found that it gave adequate warning of attack from behind of a range of 6,000 (or less). The instrument is not designed to indicate the whereabouts of a pursuing aircraft, merely its presence. It was found that indications from 45 degrees to port or starboard gave the best ranges. From dead astern the range was seriously reduced, in some cases to as little as 2,500 ft. However, it was felt that as most people would not be flying straight and level anyway, it was not too great a drawback.' (PRO AIR 27/706: No.85 Squadron ORB).

161 Ibid.

[162] Ibid.

[163] Ibid.

[164] PRO AIR 14/738: No 100 (BS) Group Operational Policy, dated 14.7.44.

[165] PRO AIR 14/738: 'Report prepared by Air Commodore Chisholm, SASO, No.100 Group, for C-in-C, Command Command, dated 8.8.44.

[166] Op.cit. (164).

[167] PRO AIR 27/706: No.85 Squadron ORB. All subsequent information concerning No.85 Squadron is taken from these records unless otherwise stated.

[168] The Luftwaffe clearly used 'decoy' nightfighers. John Whitehead (see Chapter Three) found out about them in 1943 whilst at the Air Ministry as CO of AI 4(a) Branch: 'A German nightfighter crew member PoW was interrogated and was quite open about the Germans' plan to bring in a 'decoy' system against our bombers. The plan was to send up a nightfighter with its navigation lights on. Whilst the bombers were focusing their attention on the 'lit-up' aircraft, the other enemy nightfighters would be vectored on to the bombers...I immediately 'phoned Vic Willis (also see Chapter Three) who briefed his crews. That very night one aircraft, I think it was a Wellington, was on a sortie when one of the crew reported that there was an aircraft with 'nav' lights on flying alongside them at a distance of about 300-400 metres. A general warning went out to all other Allied aircraft in the area. Some time later the rear gunner of the Wellington called out that he could see another aircraft behind. Just then another crew member reported tracer shells being fired over the wings of the Wellington. The pilot (I think it may have been Vic Willis himself), put the aircraft into a dive with the ASI at one point reading 360 mph. When the Wellington levelled out the rear gunner saw the German nightfighter which had followed them down vertically shoot past them hit the ground, and explode.'

[169] 'History of No.141 Squadron' by D F Aris. Unpublished MS (1991), 3 vols, (Deposited at the R A F Museum, Hendon).

[170] Ibid.

[171] PRO AIR 14/2911, 'Review of No.100 Group Operations', p.66.

[172] PRO AIR 27/970; No.141 Squadron ORB.

[173] See also AVM Addison's lengthy and detailed complaint regarding the quality of aircraft and equipment in the early stages of No.100 Group's existence contained in Chapter Four.

[174] Op. cit. (172); see also 'The Bostik Man' in Chapter Four.

[175] PRO AIR 25/777. No.100 Group ORB.

[176] Op.cit. (172).

[177] Ibid.

[178] 'No.157 Squadron History, 15th December 1941 to 16th August 1945'. Compiled by F/L R V Smythe and published by the Intelligence Section, R A F Swannington. (Date unknown).

[179] PRO AIR 27/104: No.157 Squadron ORB.

[180] See the entry for No.85 Squadron in this chapter. Also Chapter Four for the AOC No.100 Group's view. No.157 Squadron destroyed 37 V1s during its two-month detachment period.

[181] See 'Night Flyer' by Lewis Brandon DSO,DFC, (Crècy Publishing, 1961). Brandon was Benson's navigator/radar operator and describes in detail their operational experiences together.

[182] Jimmy Matthews was described to the author by Charles Clarke (qv), the Station Signals Officer at Swannington, as a 'very modest and unassuming chap, but a brilliant pilot.' They were colleagues at Fairey Aviation after the War where they formed two-thirds of a Swannington trio. Clarke was Avionics Manager and Matthews a test pilot. Gordon Slade, the Chief Test Pilot at Fairey Aviation, who had been Station Commander at Swannington. was the third.

[183] Op.cit. (179).

[184] PRO AIR 27/1094. No.169 Squadron ORB. All subsequent excerpts concerning the Squadron are taken from this document unless alternative sources are shown.

[185] PRO AIR 14/2911. 'The Development and Activities of No.100 (BS) Group'.

[186] Ibid.

[187] PRO AIR 14/738; 'No.100 (BS) Group Operational Policy'.

[188] PRO AIR 27/1981: No.515 Squadron ORB.

[189] This officer retired from the R A F in September 1974 as Air Marshal Sir Harold Martin.

Chapter Seven.

Ground Support – Airfields and RCM Units

The work of RAF ground personnel made a considerable contribution to the successful prosecution of the Air War. No.100 Group Ground Staff played their part at widely ranging geographical locations, where they undertook a variety of tasks. Experiences of some of the personnel who carried out this work are recorded below; these do not claim to be a comprehensive account of all the trades engaged, but the anecdotes of these few give some idea of the tasks undertaken.

(i) The Airfields

At the beginning of March every heart was gladdened by the news that all aircraft were to be re-engined with Merlin XXIIs. The change was made with amazing rapidity and efficiency, thanks to the unflagging enthusiasm of the ground staff, who worked from eight in the morning until ten at night for days on end in order to give the Squadron a fresh lease of life at the earliest possible moment.

Description of No.239 Squadron Ground Staff[190]

Most aircrews were appreciative of the supportive help given to them from the ground, 'We managed to keep flying as long as the ground staff were able to keep the elderly aircraft serviceable', observed No.515 Squadron Nav/Rad, Bill Jones, and an official report regarding No.223 Squadron was also complimentary:

A word should be said in praise of the ground crews. Very few of them had any experience of Liberator aircraft, no perfect tool kits, and because of the urgency of provisioning, aircraft that were far from new. Yet they never lost heart and, although the East of England turned out some of its most bitter Winter weather, they kept on trying and did exceptional things.[191]

Fitter (Airframes)

Bill Bridgman, a Londoner, was an LAC Fitter (Airframe) with No.515 Squadron joining them at Hunsdon. He recalled the transfer of the Squadron to No.100 Group where they were plucked from the comfortable 'happy haven of Hunsdon' and taken to 'an outlandish, apparently desolate spot' in North Norfolk, on a cold winter's day in December 1943. The move was viewed by many with great misgiving but these same critics came 'to regard the name of Little Snoring with reverence.' The cooperation between ground staff and aircrew was impressive:

> I was responsible for the airframe which included hydraulics, flying controls and the general state of the fuselage, wings and landing gear. There was a team for each aircraft consisting of a pilot, navigator, airframe fitter and engine fitter. The ancillary trades, as they were known (armourers, wireless mechanics, instrument people), were not allocated to particular aircraft. Myself and the engine fitter, Jimmy Kaylor, were expected by the pilot to go with him on airtests.

> The bond forged by this pattern of a combined aircrew and ground crew team was something special. Jimmy and myself would work on the aircraft during the day and then, in the evening, we would greet our aircrew, F/O Mike Macready, (Pilot), and P/O Leslie Frodin (Navigator), have a little chat and wish them good luck and see them off on to their night sortie. Jimmy and I would then go to the Flight hut and could wait for anything up to seven hours for the safe return of our charge. We were always delighted to welcome them back. Jimmy and I would have a brief chat with them about the aircraft's performance and any corrections would be noted and dealt with during the next day. The aircraft would then be 'put to bed' with engine covers on, its chocks (a chock was a wedge to prevent movement) put into place by the wheels and parked facing the wind with its pitot head (the instrument placed on the wing to register the airspeed) cover on. As ground crews we were all proud to have had the privilege of serving with the aircrews of World War Two. There was nothing worse for ground crews than to be told that the aircraft they had serviced earlier, and the men cheerfully waved off, would not be returning.

> We loved our job, but sometimes it wasn't all honey. Some mornings we would find our 'kite' covered in snow and our job was to remove this from the mainplane in a typical icy Norfolk wind before we could attempt our daily inspection. It was essential that the surfaces of the aircraft were scrupulously clean so that the pilot could obtain the highest possible speed from the aircraft. This meant we had to clean the aircraft regularly with a concoction known in the RAF as Gunk. This was a foul smelling liquid which wasn't exactly kind to one's hands. In fact my hands developed no less than 28 warts which survived two electrolytic treatments at Norwich Hospital, but were charmed away by an aged Norfolk character from one of the neighbouring villages for the cost of a pint of ale!

Fitter (Engines)

Geoff Sparrow was an LAC (Engines) also with No.515 Squadron. He helped to look after a Mosquito Mk.VI, 'G for George'. The pilot was a Canadian, F/O Glen Graham, and the Navigator F/L Atkinson. The Fitter (Airframes) was LAC Joe Gee. Coming back to camp after a visit to the pictures and a local pub (where he had been indulging freely) Geoff Sparrow was called upon to assist in the manhandling of an Oxford which could not be powered by its engines due to high winds. On reaching the aircraft:

I heard someone call for the brakes to be looked after, and, as I was near the door, I thought 'Great! a sit-down job.' I got into the cockpit, which had a cover over it so I had to rely on shouted instructions. I released the brakes and can't remember anything more. The next I knew I felt a hand shaking me. I immediately applied the brakes and was told it was pointless doing that. It seems the plane had been pushed down to the hangar (which was found to be full), and all the way back again, and lashed to iron stakes screwed into the ground to stabilise it against the wind. Fortunately for me and everybody else the brakes were not called for!

Sometimes he volunteered as a 'temporary' aircrew member:

I used to keep Glen company quite often, when it was possible, on air-tests as his Navigator had to combine his duties with that of Assistant Adjutant. One morning I asked Glen if I could fly with him but this time he surprised me by telling me he was going on Fighter Affiliation and asking if I still wanted to come. Not knowing what he meant I said I did.

On reaching the runway I noticed a USAAF Flying Fortress taking off. Glen informed me that this was the aircraft we had to look for. We climbed to 10,000 ft and located the Fortress. Switching on the camera gun, we went in hot pursuit attacking from the rear. I thought we would just go in, fire the camera gun and pull away but suddenly the Fort went into a steep evasive dive and then I realised that we were about to follow. The next thing I knew was that I was jammed into my seat unable to move because of the 'G' forces.

After chasing him for some time, we found ourselves approaching him from head-on although he was a little higher than us. As we got close the American changed course and dived straight at us. Glen pushed the control column forward and just managed to dive underneath as a huge shadow shot over our heads. He remarked that, 'The Yank is trying to kill us!' and thought it was time we returned to base – my sentiments entirely!

I was feeling sick by now and Glen told me to chew hard on some chewing-gum 'as he was going down quickly for lunch.' He put the aircraft into a steep dive from about 8,000 ft towards the airfield which seemed to be coming up towards us at an alarming rate and when we pulled out at 1,500 ft I felt as if I was going through the floor. On landing...I did not bother with lunch but cycled back to my hut and laid on the bed for a hour. Now I know what 'Fighter Affiliation' means!

He also took evasive action on the ground against an enemy intruder:

My aircraft having been on an 'op' I was refuelling it at 3am. The last Mosquito to return was coming into land when he suddenly opened up his engines and took off again. At this point all hell broke loose with tracer bullets flying in all directions. It seems a German raider had followed our aircraft in. Fortunately for them a detector device in the cockpit was still switched on and they had spotted the enemy aircraft and the pilot aborted his landing. The raider, realising he had been discovered, opened up with machine-gun fire onto the airfield. I straight away switched off the petrol hose, and, leaving the nozzle still in the tank, slid off the trailing edge and rolled beneath the plane until all went quiet. Then I finished refuelling.

It was thought the enemy aircraft, a Ju88, had dropped a canister onto the airfield. Next morning a special squad searched and found he had dropped 300 anti-personnel 'butterfly' bombs. Luckily all were found and there were no casualties...next morning I found several bullet holes in the tail of my aircraft. Luckily the Mosquito that had aborted its landing caught the German intruder as it crossed the coast on the way home and shot it down.

Acting as a navigator on the ground could be dangerous:

One particular night, a squadron of Halifax bombers was diverted to us because of bad weather and we had to get them parked on the other side of the airfield. As each plane landed we had to go out and guide it into a dispersal bay. On seeing the aircraft I had been allotted land, I set off on my bike for the end of the runway and found him waiting. Shining my blue-lensed torch up at him I set off down the perimeter track with the Halifax behind me. Suddenly I became aware of this huge shadow looming over me and a roar of engines. Fearing I was going to be run down I increased speed, one hand on the handlebars and the other trying to point my torch behind me. The faster I pedalled the faster the plane went. Eventually I swung into a layby hotly pursued by the Halifax. How the pilot managed to park in the bay at the speed he was travelling and without causing any damage was a miracle. When the Canadian pilot got out I asked him why he had followed me so closely and he told me that if he had not he would not have been able to see my torch.

On another occasion Geoff Sparrow was asked to fly the Oxford:

'G' for George was sent to Manston on one occasion to join a squadron there and gain some experience of a different type of operation to what they normally did. I was flown there for a week's detachment to look after it. At the end of the week I was picked up by the Oxford which was being flown by a F/S. I sat next to him and, on taking off, he surprised me by asking me to take over the controls while he looked at his maps.

I nervously took the controls and as gently as I could held the plane fairly steady. The pilot then looked at the compass situated above the centre of the windscreen and with a little guidance from him, I turned the aircraft on to its course. Then he told me to stick to this course and sat back and had a cigarette. I managed to do this until we reached Norfolk when he took over again saying he wanted to find a railway line as he was not sure where he was.

When he found the railway line he went down very low. We had the wing tips just above the embankments and were hopping over bridges. Whenever we approached a railway station he asked me to keep a sharp lookout for its name. This wasn't easy as the station names were only put on strips of paper for security reasons. Eventually I managed to read the name East Dereham (at the same time frightening the life out of a few passengers on the station by flying very low just above the station roof.) With this information the pilot knew our position, found the airfield, and landed.

Ken Thornton, was an LAC Engine Fitter on No.239 Squadron at West Raynham. Work began about 8am with a daily inspection on the Mosquitoes. 'Anything major, like engine changes was done by the Maintenance Unit in the next hangar, but we did everything else including airscrew changes.' He and his colleagues did a lot of night work:

Operations were 'on' about three to four nights each week and we were allowed a morning in bed after working all night. At first, when the aircraft returned we merely put the chocks in position and went to breakfast. Towards the end of 1944, an Air Ministry Instruction stated that, to avoid condensation forming in the fuel tanks, all aircraft should be refuelled as soon as they returned. This, in itself was no problem except on a few occasions, when with perhaps an icy wind blowing and holding a large torch, the petrol nozzle, and the tank cap key, matters were complicated for us by a Ju88 prowling about overhead. They attempted to drop anti-personnel 'Butterfly' bombs on or near the airfield.

My particular aircraft was HB-H and each morning I would inspect both engines for obvious signs of leakage or damage, top up the glycol tanks and also top up the oil tanks located on each wheel bay, and do any minor repairs. The riggers used to see to the tyre pressures, clean the perspex over the cockpit, and replace any missing rivets on the engine cowlings. Armourers would be busy on the 20 mm cannons. There were usually about four ground staff to each aircraft.

Cramped for Space!

Ground staff sometimes travelled in strange ways. On 30th September 1944 Ted Harper, an Engine Fitter in No. 515 Squadron flew in Mosquito PZ440 piloted by, S/L Henry Morley, to St. Dizier, in France from Little Snoring, sitting between the Navigator, Reg Fidler's, legs:

At St.Dizier I serviced both planes, wished them good luck (they were extending their trip to include a Day Ranger sortie from the airfield to the Munich area of south-east Germany), and went off to the town in my other operation, bartering coffee for other goods. Before going F/L Callard (pilot of the other Mosquito) handed his revolver to me saying 'You might need this!' I put the gun inside my coat making sure it was loaded.

St.Dizier was quite busy with plenty of French Freedom Fighters milling around. After some time I located a couple of likely places where I could use the coffee and exchanged it for lipsticks and perfume. Loaded up with these goods I made my way back to the airfield expecting to return to the UK in the manner in which I had come, ie between Reg Fidler's legs.

Neither aircraft returned to pick up Harper and he was flown back to England after a couple of days in a USAAF Liberator. The reason for the non-return of either aircraft is interesting. Both came down in neutral Switzerland, where all four aircrew were placed in internment from which they subsequently escaped. (The story of this sortie is described more fully in the previous Chapter).

Armourer

Don Aris, an LAC Armourer on No.141 Squadron, worked on the 'dead-beat' Mosquito Mk.II's supplied to the SERRATE Squadrons:

The Squadron entered a very unhappy period for all members, for the aircrew who had to try and operate these worn-out aircraft with the extra dangers of engine failures, and the ground crews who had to try and keep them serviceable. Those most affected amongst the latter were the engine fitters and radar mechanics.

I cannot remember the armament of these Mosquitoes giving any particular problems, except for the great difficulty of re-arming the four 20 mm Hispano cannons as access to the four ammunition boxes was very restricted. On the Mosquitoes used by No. 141 Squadron there were, of course, no nose 0.303 Browning machine guns as this space was taken up by the SERRATE and AI Mk.IV radar.

During the day four crews from each flight of No.141 Squadron carried out air-to-air firing. There was now at West Raynham No.1694 Target Towing Flight (it would later move to Great Massingham), which was equipped with Miles Martinet aircraft. These aircraft had a crew of two, the pilot, and a target or drogue operator. The latter was a non-aircrew aircraftsman who drew a daily flying pay allowance for his duties in the air.

The Martinet flew over the firing ranges out to sea, over The Wash, and let out a white drogue (similar in shape to an airfield 'windsock') on a long cable behind the Martinet. The winch for this cable was wind-driven by a four-bladed propeller mounted on the starboard side of the aircraft. The aircraft practising air-to-air firing would then fire at the drogue with its four cannons.

For this practice air-firing, ball, not HE, incendiary or armour-piercing 20 mm shells, would be used. Before loading these into the four ammunition boxes of the Mosquito, the noses of the 20 mm cannon shells would be dipped in paint, a different colour for each aircraft taking part in the practice. These colours would then show up on any recorded hits on the white drogue.

As an armourer I found it difficult, at first, to believe that the paint would remain on the shell after it had been fired but, of course, the nose of the shell when fired does not touch the inside of the barrel of the cannon. The various colours saved time and expense as a new drogue did not have to be used and then dropped over the airfield for each attacking aircraft.

Air-to-Air and Air-to-Ground firing practice gave a lot of extra work for the armourers as the non-ball ammunition had to be removed and ball ammunition loaded, and, after firing, the cannons had to be cleaned and checked, and reloaded with the HE, incendiaries, and semi-armour piercing shells used on operations.[192]

Station Signals Section

Vic Flowers, keen amateur radio man and Civilian Wireless Reservist, was quickly called up for wartime service in the RAF (he reported on 3rd September 1939). He spent his early service in France, being part of the Wireless Intelligence Screen until the evacuation of the BEF in June 1940. During this period, he and his colleagues, were self-supporting using commandeered farmhouses or similar buildings. On his return to the UK he was posted to No.80 (Signals) Wing, the ground-based RCM unit initially set up to combat Luftwaffe navigational radio beams.[193] He served on several No.80 Wing Outstations in the South of England being billeted with local people in villages close to these stations. He had been used to serving in independent units and , 'with experience of life on an operational squadron virtually nil', found himself transferred to North Creake in March 1944([North Creake acquired full station status the following month). 'Feeling like a fish out of water' he became the Sergeant in charge of Station Signals. Further disappointment came his way when he found that RCM, in which he had been involved for over four years, were no longer part of his duties. However, there was plenty to do.

Flowers found himself involved with all communications between the Control Tower and aircraft, landing systems, VHF Direction Finding (DF), and providing WOPs for the special operations:

Security was very strict and although I was working and living side by side with personnel attached to the RCM Sections, I was not supposed to know what they were doing, or if I did I was not supposed to discuss it! I shared a hut with a Sergeant Armourer, Sergeant Airframe Fitter, a Sergeant Storekeeper, plus an assortment of other trades so got to know what was going on, and during my off duty periods, had a look around the 'Hush-Hush' sections. At briefings for my WOPs we had to leave when times and frequencies were discussed for the RCM work...My sergeant Airframe Fitter friend was involved in helping to make a special device for distributing WINDOW... I spent some time with him at night in his workshop perfecting the unit which was a masterpiece of welded mild steel and moving parts.

One of my responsibilities was the VHF DF system, the receiver side of which was in a bullet and blast-proof hut located about a mile away from the camp, at Egmere. The building was unique because it was constructed entirely of hollow wooden panels all filled with shingle. It was strictly forbidden to bring cycles into the small compound in case they upset the very accurately calibrated sensing system. WOPs kept a 24 hour watch...I had a mobile signals vehicle which I used for transport. The aerials on the roof even in their 'minimum' position made it difficult to negotiate tree-lined roads.

I spent a long time at the section to gain as much knowledge of what was completely new equipment to me and gained the confidence of most of the lads, so much so that when a new operational channel was needed for the Control Tower, I decided, in order to gain experience, to do the job myself with backup from a couple of tradesmen from the section. Existing equipment could not be re-channelled so a complete installation was necessary with cables to be run from the equipment room to the control desk and to the roof for the aerial.

WOP/Mechanic

It will be obvious to all that in such highly technical activities as those undertaken by No.100 Group, maintenance, repair, and installation of radio and radar equipment was a significant occupation within the Group. Cedric Hall was a WOP/Mechanic originally with No.101 Squadron, later being transferred to No.214 Squadron:

My association with ABC commenced just after No.101 Squadron moved from Holme-on-Spalding in Yorkshire to a new airfield at Ludford Magna in 1943. We moved in before the station was completed. I had been in a Signals HQ and was a member of the Transmitter Station crew when I had the desire to join the Signals Section on the Squadron. I had been there only a few weeks when I was posted to a course on the ABC equipment at Defford. Our instructor was an American officer. He was a very amiable man and all of us on the Course liked him. When trained we all returned to Ludford Magna to join the Special Signals

Section...the Section was a very happy one and I wasn't pleased when I, and a close colleague, were posted to a similar section at Sculthorpe, where we joined No.214 Squadron at the beginning of 1944. If I remember correctly there were only three or four Fortresses on the Squadron at the time and there were a lot of Americans on the station. We weren't there long before we were posted to the Special Signals Section at Oulton.

I well remember the removal of the Squadron personnel in personnel carriers and the pleasure we experienced when we found our billets were in a very pleasant area between The Orangery at Blickling Hall and the main road. We were on the eastern side of the Hall and on the western side stood the 'Buckinghamshire Arms' where I eventually spent some very pleasant and convivial evenings. The Station turned out to be the happiest one during my time in the RAF. G/C Dickens was a thorough gentleman and there was a decided absence of 'bull' on the Camp. Regardless of that, or probably because of it, everyone worked well and I am sure it would have been considered a very efficient and successful station. We had access to the Lake in our off-duty periods. As the summer of 1944 was sunny and warm, many of us took advantage of the opportunity to go swimming.

Change of station brought new equipment:

The equipment in the planes was not ABC as it had been at Sculthorpe but JOSTLE. The transmitter was towed by a tractor to the dispersals on a converted bomb trolley together with a petrol electric set and a blower unit. We lowered the bomb doors and hoisted the transmitter into the aircraft after, of course, manoeuvring the trolley into position between the bomb doors. This is contrary to a description and photographs I have seen in an American publication about the Flying Fortresses in the USAAF, which depicts a transmitter hoisted on the rear of a vehicle from which it was lowered into a trench in the ground to enable it to be hoisted into the aircraft. As we had an American Liberator Squadron on the same airfield for a period, carrying out similar jamming exercises I assume the transmitter was installed in this manner.

I was never a 'gen' man on the science of radio and so I joined a group of three on one of the flights who worked mainly on the installation, testing, calibrating, and of course, removal of equipment where necessary. I am proud to say that on one occasion (during a bit of an emergency) I installed a transmitter by myself in one of our aircraft in the absence of any team mates. As JOSTLE operated on various frequencies the aircraft were fitted with trailing aerials, the released lengths of which were calibrated to the equipment. On flight tests the SO sometimes forgot to retract or rewind the aerial and often to our dismay an aerial would wind around the rear wheel on landing and we would be called out to fit a new one!

On one occasion Hall nearly went on an 'Op':

I recall one late afternoon when a request came for a mechanic to attend to the equipment of one particular aircraft just before 'take off'. I was the only mechanic available and thus had to pedal out as fast as I could on my bike, secretly praying that I would be able to put things right. I had only been in the aircraft for a few minutes when the engines started and the aircraft started to move forward from Dispersal. My pleas to the SO to inform the skipper that I was aboard came to no avail, and as we trundled along the perimeter track towards the end of the runway for take off, my first thought was how I would manage without an oxygen mask if the worst happened and I became airborne! The crew were just giving me a fright and subsequently let me out. I am sure I jumped over the tailplane in the propeller 'wash' in my anxiety to escape from the aircraft!

I was recalled from leave on another occasion and met the American officer who had first trained us. He told us about the threat of V2 rockets and that our equipment was to be used in an endeavour to put them off course. It was necessary in appreciating the seriousness of the situation to commit ourselves to secrecy. We in the Special Signals Section had been given advance warning of this threat. The idea was that one of our aircraft would be airborne over the North Sea, with fighter escort, each for a period of four hours, attempting to bend the radio waves which were supposed to be guiding each rocket. This was later found not to be the case.

The American Liberator Squadron also carried out these duties. I was on 'stand by' duty one night with one other member of the Section when a call came from them for attention to the equipment on one of their Liberators. Both the other 'duty' man and myself suddenly realised we had never driven a van although we had plenty of experience driving a tractor. Anyway I agreed to drive one of our vans to the other side of the Airfield. When I reached our Station Signals Section in the main Ops Block (halfway) I realised that I had driven the van with the handbrake on!

(ii) Ground-based RCM Units

The object of the exercise was to pick up, identify and break down the frequencies, and find the bearings of the Freya and Würzburg radar stations in Northern France.

Bert Moir, Ground-based WOP on PING-PONG duties

Ground-Based RCM for the Continental Offensive

It was anticipated that the Luftwaffe would make every effort to prevent the consolidation of the Allied Bridgehead in Normandy after D-Day. A number of enemy bombing and navigational aids, which had already been used in the War for attacks on the UK, were available for these attacks. As they could not be countered from the UK, mobile RCM units, Mobile Signals Units (MSUs), comprising of VHF jamming transmitters, receivers, and monitoring equipment, (together with W/T vehicles for communications channels), were formed. The first were landed in Normandy some ten days after D-Day and proceeded to pre-selected sites in the Bridgehead.

In addition, to assist in the jamming of the enemy fighter R/T Control, a high power (50 KW radiated) jammer was erected on the South Downs behind Brighton. When radiating south, this would have been capable of jamming the German fighter R/T communications over a large area of Northern France. In the event, the Luftwaffe did not make the expected response against the Bridgehead and little use was made of this equipment.

The opening of the Continental Offensive and the rapidity of the Allied advance, resulted in a progressive expansion of ground RCM stations for Bomber Support. The reduction of enemy long-range bomber attacks on the UK during the second half of 1944, allowed for a redistribution of available transmitters in the UK. To form a Bomber Support RCM organisation on the Continent a Main HQ was established, and eight radar jamming centres and six communications jamming centres (the MSUs mentioned above) were also formed. Until the end of hostilities operations, under the over-riding control of No.100 Group HQ, were carried out simultaneously from HQ, No.80 Wing (Main) at Schepdael (near Brussels), and HQ No.80 Wing (Rear) at Radlett in Hertfordshire.

Medium Frequency (MF) – Enemy Beacons

The growing weight of the Bomber Command offensive during 1944 had resulted in an expansion of enemy nightfighter defences, and an ever increasing use of its beacons as navigational aids/assembly points for its fighter force. The use of high-powered beacons for the transmission of running commentaries from the Fighter Control to fighters had first been noted in April 1944. Successful jamming of the alternative methods of communication caused the Luftwaffe to rely increasingly on this method to pass instructions to their nightfighters. This aid was countered by FIDGET action, whereby a modified Meacon transmitter radiated random automatic Morse on the exact frequency of the enemy beacon. Simultaneous to this the 'Y' Service Station, at Canterbury in Kent, working under the control of No.100 Group HQ, jammed the other enemy nightfighter communications. By the late Autumn of 1944, MEACON, MIMIC and FIDGET action had become the priority and changes were made in organisation to meet the increased workload:

In the UK

(i) A redistribution among the retained stations in No.80 Wing of the higher powered beacon transmitters was made available by the closing down of South Western and Southern areas of the UK.

(ii) A reorganisation of both layout and procedure in the Operations Room at the Radlett HQ of No.80 Wing (Rear) to enable both offensive and defensive action to be handled with a minimum of delay.

On the Continent

(iii) The establishment of an Operations Room at No.80 Wing HQ (Main) which controlled the MSUs deployed at intervals of approximately 60 to 100 miles along the battle front. Intelligence would be received from 'Y' Service sources, both in the UK and on the Continent, and from the Monitor Room at No.80 Wing (Main) HQ. Instructions to the sites were passed by landline or W/T and communication to No.100 Group HQ was maintained by teleprinter link, thus enabling the No. 80 Wing Liaison Officer at that HQ to coordinate the activities at both Main and Rear HQs and exercise an overriding control over operations.[194]

SPLASHER and FIXED BEACONS

These were used daily, mainly by the USAAF. These transmissions were continued at night until November 1944, to provide cover for the change of Bomber Command policy which, in view of the completion of the Gee programme, sanctioned the abandonment of MF beacons. These 'spoof' transmissions also provided cover for SPLASHER II (See below).

In September 1944, the complex SPLASHER system was modified to provide nine 'fixed' SPLASHER channels instead of the 27 which had previously operated to a scrambled schedule, thus releasing transmitters required for other commitments and freeing a number of MF channels. These nine channels were additional to the 13 Fixed Beacons already operative.

A continuous watch for any form of enemy interference to SPLASHER transmissions was maintained at a special Cathode Ray DF Station at Aldington and, where this was observed, warning of unreliability was provided by random mutilation of the callsign of the affected transmission.

SPLASHER II

SPLASHER II was instituted in April 1944 to provide alternative channels of communication for the OBOE system, since severe jamming was being experienced on the associated VHF channels in use at the time. Two transmitters were installed at Trimingham (Norfolk) and Worth (Dorset).

It was realised that, although these communication links were on a band remote from that normally employed for OBOE, the enemy would eventually appreciate the purpose of the transmissions. To complicate the application of enemy countermeasures the master transmissions were received by SPLASHER stations at Braintree and Templecombe and re-radiated on four different MF frequencies. This scheme was in operation till November 1944 when it was discontinued.

During the final stages of the European War RCM were taken against enemy nightfighter control which was using W/T in the HF band of frequencies. The 'Y' Service at Cheadle controlled DRUMSTICK, the measure designed to disrupt enemy HF W/T control channels in the 3-6 MHz band. Up to 20 transmitters were available in the UK for this RCM. When the monitoring service at Cheadle heard an enemy transmission within this band one of these transmitters would be tuned to it and the signal jammed, Cheadle taking care to check that the correct frequency was being jammed.

VHF MANDREL

In an effort to overcome the jamming of their early warning radar, the Germans increased the frequencies used on their equipment. The number of transmitters required made barrage jamming impracticable and, therefore the practice of spot jamming was adopted in late 1943. This entailed the tactical control of operations being taken over by local monitor sites at each No.80 Wing Outstation. It became the responsibility of the individual site to select the disposition of the jamming transmitters to give the most effective coverage possible. The fitting of the Outstations with the additional transmitters and monitoring equipment to cover the frequency band 69-220MHz was taking place when, with D-Day imminent, it was decided to concentrate GROUND MANDREL at two sites only, Dover and Ventnor (Isle of Wight). Information was later obtained from a PoW that both Kimmeridge (Dorset) and Ventnor Outstations, which were identified from bearings, had been most effective in jamming the Mammut long-range radar station on the Cherbourg Peninsular. After the collapse in Normandy, the Ventnor site became redundant and was moved to Hastings, the frequency coverage of this station and Dover being extended up to 600 MHz. As the Germans were driven out of France both of these stations became ineffective, and it was decided to convert them into mobile units. Eight Mobile

MANDREL stations were therefore built up. Each consisted of seven transmitters and aerials; they were transferred to the Continent where they could be deployed at intervals of approximately 30 miles along the Battle Front, as close to the front line as possible, to provide a Screen for Bomber Support with a frequency coverage from 20 to 600 MHz.

The first two of these units arrived on the Continent early in January 1945 and were followed at intervals by four others. The remaining two units were fitted with equipment of greater power but were not needed due to the rapid retreat of the enemy. Each station had autonomous jamming action owing to the difficulties of rapid communication, a general directive was given of the signals to be covered during specific times. Considerable care had to be exercised in this to avoid clashing with other Allied and enemy radar activities. The periods of activity were correlated with Bomber Command operations; the average number of signals covered each night was ten.

Disorganisation of the enemy radar system by Allied air and ground RCM, resulted in an introduction by the enemy in August 1944 of a small number of radar units of a new type in the 30 MHz band. In order to meet this new commitment six existing transmitters in the Eastern Area of the UK were adapted as Special MANDREL. Test flights made by No.192 Squadron showed effective jamming up to 200 miles was possible.

CIGAR

The battery of VHF jammers at Sizewell on the East Coast was used, in the autumn of 1944, to jam the German Fighter Benito traffic (38-42MHz), either by barrage or spot jamming, and so help the Bomber Command forces on their routes over the North Sea and the Dutch and Belgian coasts. The enemy nightfighter R/T was usually well jammed by airborne jammers, but on those occasions when any R/T could be recognised through this jamming, ground transmitters were immediately brought on.

Special Investigations

In order to obtain further information on certain enemy radio aids special watches were kept on the frequency bands of his new AI SN2 and on the Bernhardine navigational aid in the 30 MHz band. Mobile Watcher Stations toured the forward areas of Holland and Germany as close to the front line as possible. A number of signals were intercepted but identification proved difficult. A close watch on these frequencies was also maintained by stations in East Anglia.

GROUND GROCER

This RCM, against the use by the enemy of FuGe 202 (AI in the band 460-500 MHz) was operated from No.80 Wing Outstations at Dunwich and Walmer. Delivery was received of a high-powered American transmitter (TUBA) and this was temporarily installed at Sizewell, tests and training being carried out during operational periods. With the introduction of the new enemy AI SN2 operating on a lower frequency, the interception of FuGe 202 transmissions decreased steadily. By November 1944 they had ceased altogether and the GROUND GROCER Outstations were placed on Care and Maintenance.

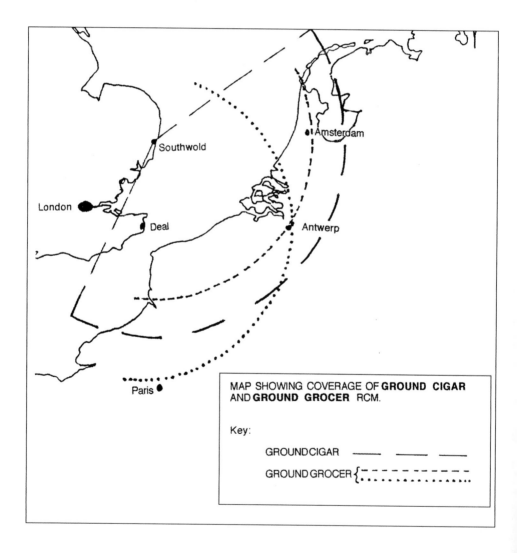

MAP SHOWING COVERAGE OF **GROUND CIGAR** AND **GROUND GROCER** RCM.

Key:

GROUND CIGAR ——— —— ——

GROUND GROCER {

Ottakar

German R/T alternating with beam-type signals on 31.2 and 32.1 MHz originating from the KNICKEBEIN K.3 Area, was first observed by East Coast Watcher Stations in December 1943. This use of K.3 Station (and possibly also K.5) as an aid to German nightfighters continued sporadically, for about three months, and was countered by the introduction in early January 1945 of RCM RAYON to jam the R/T Channel. For this purpose a high-powered transmitter at Mundesley using JOSTLE-type modulation was employed. Although the efficacy of this RCM was considered doubtful owing to the long range involved, evidence was forthcoming from PoW sources that some measure of success was obtained.[195]

No. 80 Wing (Main) HQ

Postal Clerk (with flexible duties!)

In 1944 Eric Reedman (he was to complete 35 years service in the RAF) was employed as a postal clerk with the initial No.80 Wing party which went to the Continent. During his wartime service he kept a diary:

> At Radlett we began the formation of the Advanced HQ for No.80 Wing, along with three supporting Mobile Signals Units (MSUs). After being kitted out with khaki battledress and extra equipment we were off to North Creake to be trained in 'invasion tactics'. A detachment of instructors from the Scots Guards were to train us in falling from the backs of lorries, unarmed combat, cliff scaling, making up field kitchens and, generally, how to cope. I don't know what it is about me, but if an instructor needed someone to demonstrate upon, I knew for sure his eye would rest upon me. So it was on one occasion at North Creake. 'You!', roared one of the instructors, 'The little man there with the glasses, come and stick your bayonet into my chest!' Well, I mean to say that's not cricket is it? Especially if he is unarmed.
>
> So I made a feeble attempt as if to charge at him but my heart really wasn't in it. The next thing I knew I found myself on my back, the instructor was holding the rifle, and the bayonet was touching my throat! I still don't know how it had happened, but it did!
>
> On completion of the course we returned once more to Radlett to be equipped with old vehicles which must have been in mothballs since the 1914-18 War. We stayed at Radlett while we prepared to become a self-contained mobile unit and for that period we were billeted upon the local civilian population.

Two weeks later we moved the short distance to Brickett Wood, near St. Albans. Tents were erected just outside the village, and this was to be a trial period for putting into practice what we had been taught at North Creake. Then we went on embarkation leave. Whilst at home my young nephew Keith remarked 'Well, it won't be for two weeks at least because Uncle Eric is on leave and they can't start without him!' He could have been right for when we returned to Brickett Wood after leave it was all systems 'Go!' and within two days we were packed and off to Old Sarum in Wiltshire.

This was to be our home until the Invasion began. Once inside the compound we were sealed in. No one was permitted to leave under any circumstances and compassionate leave was non-existent. Guards were stationed around the large tented area...we had a large NAAFI marquee which served as a bar, which was something. Well, everything really!

Whilst at Old Sarum our final water-proofing of the vehicles was completed, extensions to the exhaust pipes were fitted using flexible hoses which brought them up to the top of the vehicle cabs. Similar breather pipes were fitted to the carburettors so that the vehicles could be driven off the landing craft into about four to five feet of sea water and on up the beach.

When we had been there for two days, on the night of the 5th June 1944, we heard the distant rumblings of tanks and heavy transport vehicles making for the coast. Later the sky was darkened by the enormous number of aircraft and gliders carrying airborne troops. Two days after D-Day we left Old Sarum for Fareham in Hampshire where we carried out the final stages of water proofing the vehicles and boarded two LCTs at Gosport. We came under No.83 Group, and formed the No.80 Wing (Advanced) HQ Unit (comprising 13 vehicles). The CO was S/L Taylor. The MSUs with us were, I believe, Nos. 60 and 61. In total there were 110 personnel with 25 vehicles (mainly Crossleys).

After many delays in crossing the Channel we made a wet shod landing on Gold Beach about 100 yards from Omaha Beach in the early hours of the 16th June, and were amazed at the hundreds of boats and ships still in the vicinity.

Our trucks dropped off the ramps of the landing craft and, under their own power, made the journey safely up the beach. That is, with the exception of the newest 15 cwt truck being used by the CO, which tipped into an unseen shell crater and had to be towed out by a tractor of the Royal Engineers!

The cross-Channel trip had not been without incident:

The CO mentioned a collision during the night of the crossing concerning LCT 1070 (which I was on) when a large merchant vessel hit our landing ramp causing severe damage. Earlier the barrage balloon we were flying became entangled with that of another nearby vessel and had to be cast adrift.

Once the unit had landed:

We formed a convoy, and were directed by the RCAF Beachmaster to our rendezvous in the American Sector at Tour-en-Bessin. From the time we landed, there had been quite a lot of distant firing and aerial activity, but our area had been reasonably quiet. Our selected site at Tour-en-Bessin was next to an orchard. We positioned our vehicles around the field alongside the hedges. Slit trenches were dug.

I was given the job of lacing together two camouflaged nets on the high roof of a radio transmitter vehicle. The idea was that the nets would then hang down the van's sides, with branches etc, stuck in between them, hopefully believing we would blend into the hedgerows when seen from above. I found myself on my knees on the roof of the vehicle with head down, concentrating. I was making progress with roping the nets together when I heard the approaching roar of a fighter plane. Looking upwards into the setting sun I thought, 'Oh, its alright, its only a Spitfire.' Then it opened up and machine gunned right through the field! I leapt down towards the ditch but my toecaps caught in the tangled net. I pitched forward and down but my feet were firmly caught in the net and I slammed hard into the side of the vehicle, still upside down! I thought my ribs were broken with the force of the blow which winded me. There I hung until the attack was over making a mental note to brush up on my aircraft recognition!

Having been positioned in the orchard for three months the mobile Unit moved on with enthusiasm:

After the Allied breakthrough at Caen, we hit the road again, this time in a convoy which followed the 51st Highland Division through Caen itself, and many other towns and villages, crossing rivers over hastily erected Bailey Bridges, eventually arriving on the outskirts of Brussels where we had to stay for two days whilst the town was completely liberated.

After Brussels the Unit made its way to Wenduine, a village between Ostend and Blankenberge, where 'We made a tented camp on some tennis courts in this small seaside town. The next day our radio vans were fully operational.' Several weeks later, with the chillness of winter in the air, good fortune visited them when 'We took over an old pre-war TB hospital (recently vacated by the German Navy!)'. The move was blessed with an element of luck:

As we were led blindly to the Main Hospital gates, with the CO leading, we waited while an unsuccessful attempt was made to break the thin chain keeping the gates closed. As it was dark and raining by this time it was decided that we would effect an entrance by the rear gates which we did.

The following morning a bomb disposal team of Royal Engineers (REs) arrived to check for landmines and no less than 25 landmines were unearthed from the drive we originally had intended to use! In the process of the search a mine exploded and two RE's were killed. In addition, many of the toilets were found to be 'booby-trapped'. Later the Unit were to suffer casualties when some curious airmen searching for souvenirs at the former German fortification along the coast stepped on anti-personnel mines.

Soon after the Unit moved into its new quarters at Wenduine, Eric Reedman found himself in an unusual role for a postal clerk in No.80 Wing, escort for PoWs!:

...the Orderly Room received a telephone call from one of the radio receiver vans which was situated near a wood outside the town reporting they had seen German soldiers in the wood. The Senior Signals Officer, F/L Buckley, then detailed the Pay Accounts Corporal and myself to accompany him to search the woods. Later we collected two German prisoners. One was forty-plus, fearful and in a serious frame of mind; the other was twentyish and excitable. I don't know who was the most nervous, them or me. I was sitting on the tailboard but turned towards the front of the vehicle, covering them with my rifle. In the event of my having to use it I wouldn't have given the driver much chance of survival!

When we arrived back at HQ the Signals Officer tried to find a suitable safe room in which to place the captives until they could be collected by the army. He marched them from room to room so much that we thought he was giving them a conducted tour of the hospital! At last he found an escape-proof storeroom with a light but no windows. Into this he pushed the PoWs and placed a double guard on the door. Both of the Germans immediately relaxed and seemed glad it was all over.

The Marine Commandos used Wenduine as a practice ground for their assault on Walcheren Island [it was necessary to capture the Island in order to free the Scheldt Estuary thus making the port of Antwerp available for the delivery of much-needed Allied supplies]. I got to know them quite well and when they returned from the raid they shared with us the 'spoils of war' in the form of German Naval Rum which they had concealed in clean jerrycans on the journey back.

A few months later, we moved to the Chateau at Schepdael, on the outskirts of Brussels to form the No. 80 Wing (Main) HQ. Here we were joined by a great many arrivals from the No.80 Wing (Rear) HQ at Radlett.

On one of my daily visits to Brussels to collect the mail from the Army Post Office, I was driving a jeep along the main street when I saw my brother alight from a tram. I was amazed because the last I had heard of him he was in Italy. I yelled out his name and he stopped and managed to have a chat for about thirty minutes, and then we went our respective ways. I did not see him again until his wedding in 1946.

Ted Hardwick had been in the ATC, and joined the RAF at the age of 17 and 3/4. Failed for aircrew because he had long sight he became a wireless mechanic, working on transmitters, in No.80 Wing. After service in the Middle East and Italy he returned in February 1944 to the UK:

> At the time I lived in Acton in Middlesex and during clearance after disembarkation at Blackpool was asked where I would like to be posted. I said as close to home as possible and, whilst on disembarkation leave, received orders to report to Northolt, to a Polish Fighter Unit which was hardly a suitable place for No.80 Wing trained personnel. However, after a couple of weeks there I was called to Radlett who obliged with a 'cushy' posting to Hounslow Heath where the operation was radiating jumbled German on VHF to interfere with the Focke Wulf 'sneak' raids which were a feature of that period.

In June 1944 he found himself on the cliff-top Outstation at Hope Point , near Dover:

> The operations were really cloaked in secrecy...there were always plenty of TRE civvies around and one story circulated was that a US Mustang pilot had photographed vapour trails over The Hague which purported to be a V2 going out of control at the exact time of some transmissions.

At the end of the year he went to Europe:

> After a week in transit at Wenduine I was posted to HQ at the Chateau at Schepdael. I can see myself now sitting in the wagon with the link transmitter on a three-Watch system at the HQ. It was marvellous for Brussels which I got to know like the back of my hand. I had a quiet number which was, in the three-watch system, looking after this transmitter for the communications link with Radlett. There were two links, key and R/T and it was quite busy.

Ted Hardwick believed he made RAF History at the War's end:

> I can claim to be the first not just No.80 Wing member but indeed the first RAF person to enter Dunkirk when, on May 10th 1945, I entered the town, which was still occupied by the Germans.[196] The town had been bypassed by the advancing Allied armies in September 1944 in order that the Scheldt Estuary could be cleared thus allowing Antwerp to become a working port again to enable it to cope with the supplies needed by the Allied forces. I knew about the perimeter defences which enclosed the German garrison of some 15,000 men and hitch-hiked there to see what was going on.
>
> On arrival at the Bray end of the town I came to a road block manned by Lancashire Fusiliers and Royal Artillery soldiers who explained to me that the occupation of the town could not take place because of difficulties over minefields etc, and that discussions were going on in the town between the Royal Engineers and the German Command.

Out of the blue came a Toc-H service truck which was to supply the soldiers with tea and cakes. With the driver's agreement I jumped up into his cab. The barrier was lifted and into the town we went! I finished the day back in Poperinge, the Toc-H building which the Belgian population had looked after for over four years during the German occupation.

He also witnessed the retribution meted out to those deemed to have been collaborators:

Another interesting event at Wenduine was the return of the White Army Belgian Resistance workers who had been released from camps in Germany. On their return home to Wenduine they found that the collaborators who were responsible for them being caught were carrying on as normal. I have photographs of the collaborators' homes being stripped of furniture and belongings and set fire to in the streets. One of the collaborators was a cafe owner who had been supplying No.80 Wing personnel for some eight months. The Belgian police just stood by whilst all this was going on!

Mobile Signals Units (MSUs)

Frank Cooper joined the RAF in 1939 with a background in radio. After a lengthy spell in 'Y' Service, he was sent to the No. 80 Wing Outstation at Scole, in East Anglia, and was at a complete loss as to what his duties were:

I was a F/S when I went to Scole. I was NCO i/c. I didn't know what the hell they were doing there and felt such a fool. A Controller from Radlett came on asking to speak to the NCO i/c but I didn't know what he was talking about!

Cooper quickly learned. Later he found himself NCO-in-charge of No.50 MSU preparing at Sizewell, in Suffolk, for jamming duty on the Continent:

Our Unit had 24 personnel, five MT drivers and mechanics, one cook, three 'General Duties' airman, the rest being radio people. There were 12 trucks in all. The transmitter itself filled a Queen Mary truck and was being assembled ready for going abroad. A furniture type van was set up as a workshop and it must have been used as such for years judging by the assortment of radio parts and the lathe in it. When we were setting things up at Sizewell it was all done on sand. To save tripping over the cables we put them under the ground. We were given two days to move and couldn't get the damn things up. With it being so cold that winter they were frozen solid. We had to use cookers, heaters on the ground, to get them to shift! We were still using diathermy machines at Sizewell in 1944.

We went to Belgium in January 1945. We were spread out on various LCTs. The transmitter truck went on a separate one. We all went to Tilbury together. The chap in charge of the MT drove the transmitter truck. When we landed on

**Inside a mobile transmitter
Queen Mary vehicle.**
(Frank Cooper)

the beach on the other side, the captain of the LCT ordered him off but he refused as the truck was heavy and would sink so we went along a bit to some firmer ground.

Eventually we arrived at Wenduine. We were there for a few days until we moved to Leende, near Eindhoven. That's where we did most of the work. It was here we were told to modify the transmitter to radiate on 40-45 Mc/s instead of a fixed frequency. We had to find ways of modifying the transmitter and that took time. We debated how we could do this and one of the Unit, Corporal Furnace, came up with the idea of spinning a condenser between the lechers (special wires used for the purpose) . We tried with a couple of fixed plates to see if the frequency could be moved and found that it was possible. We found a suitable motor to use in the workshop but had no suitable materials for the plates and signalled our requirements to HQ. By 7am the next day a six by four feet sheet of quarter inch thick Duralium arrived. It took us several days to make and adjust the plates to give us the coverage. We were extremely pleased that we could create 'noise' over the 5 Mc/s bandwidth.

At this location we were next to a nunnery and the nuns used to do our washing and darning. I brought home an example of their darning. It was marvellous there until we had to move on.

My interest was in aerials. We spent a lot of time looking for a 'null'[197] where the signal is weaker. One day F/O Nicol and me spent a whole day driving about

Photo of Würzburg radar taken in May 1995 at a former German radar station which has been restored as a museum at Longues-sur-Mer, about ten miles from Bayeux, Normandy.

(Alan Mercer)

Würzburg radar at Wenduine, damaged after being attacked by Allied forces. *(Ted Hardwick)*

in a radius of ten miles and stopping at various points to find the 'null'. I think the idea was to prevent us interfering with our own forces. We never did find it. We created the jamming noise with what we called 'noise boxes'.

When VE-Day came we went over the border back into Belgium to see what we could buy. One evening three of us went back to this large village and we were having a drink when someone came in and said we ought to move out. There were groups of people standing around whispering. There were quite a few of us and we had taken a three tonner there. The locals were raiding the collaborators' houses and were throwing things out of the windows as we left this village. We actually ran over a bed!

Philip Colehan was with No.62 MSU at Wenduine:

One signals vehicle was placed right on the coast alongside massive concrete coastal fortifications...one November afternoon just as it was getting dusk, a German E-Boat came speeding along the coast shooting up military installations. We stood outside the cabin watching the 'fireworks' display with great interest, until the tracer bullets came whistling past, then we ducked for cover! We, and the signals vehicle were unscathed, but an ammunition ship further down the coast off Ostend was not so fortunate.

This MSU was engaged in trying to pick up signals from V2s; signallers were asked to send the Morse letter 'X' if they saw the launch of any of these weapons. As this arrangement brought no useful result No. 62 MSU was moved up closer to the enemy in the Ardennes, just behind the American front line and close to the German border:

We were near Malmedy in December 1944, in a deserted farmhouse. One morning an American liaison officer came to tell us the Germans had launched a counter-offensive. Nobody seemed concerned as it was assumed that the Germans were just about beaten. The liaison officer returned to say that the attack was coming our way and, as a non-combatant unit, we ought to move back.

We started to pack up and move out and then we saw, in the distance, German Tiger tanks moving menacingly towards us. We were rapidly making ourselves scarce when someone remembered that the safe had been left in the farmhouse. We backed up the lorry and Bert Downey ran into the farmhouse. Normally it took four people to carry the safe but Bert Downey, a Newfoundland lumberjack in civilian life, heaved it into the the back of the lorry and we went tearing off back to base. The attack by the Germans was Von Runstedt's 'push', which became known as 'The Battle of the Bulge'. We were well out of it. We lost the keys to the safe. Several weeks later, not knowing what to do with a safe we couldn't open, we quietly went down to Zeebrugge harbour one evening and dropped it into the sea!

Still trying to find locations close to where the V-2 rockets were being launched, in March 1945, the unit followed up the U S Army's capture of the bridge at Remagen by taking over Schloss Rheineck which overlooked it:

> The battle was still raging over the other side of the Rhine and there were remnants of the German Army behind us. It was eerie to be on duty in the castle's tower, which we had made our signals room, particularly at night. We lived on 'K' rations for several weeks, and life was bleak until we found the keys to the wine cellar!

Peter Giles served in the same unit as Philip Colehan. He was on the 'toughening up' course at North Creake which:

> ...was a pleasant change from watch-keeping. We practised firing several weapons, including the Twin-Browning anti-aircraft gun on a 'Stork' mounting. The guns would rear up in our inexperienced hands, so that after a twin stream of tracer was seen heading for Walsingham Church, the mounting was tied down to the horizontal. Our unit developed a strong team spirit , and one expects that the others did too...

In March 1945, Giles was transferred to No. 60 MSU which had earlier set up operations in a church tower at Vught, a village near Hertogenbosch, Holland, north of Eindhoven. A couple of weeks later he was sent to Kleve, just inside Germany and came across a piece of RCM history when he joined a detachment which had encamped beside the KNICKEBEIN transmitter from which the first signals had been traced back in 1940, which had led to the setting up of No. 80 Wing (which was now a part of No.100 Group).

George Morley, a WOP, had, since 1940, served at No. 80 Wing Outstations in the UK. He was also sent to Europe:

> We were told that we would be allowed over providing we did not get in the way of the 'fighting offensive' and would be used either to provide radio navigational aids for the Allied bombing forces, or for RCM jamming. In case of a vehicle breakdown whilst over there, we would be pushed aside. Originally expecting to go over to Europe in November 1944, we were delayed and given leave in December. Whilst on leave, for some unknown reason I received a telegram extending it until after Christmas.
>
> Early in January 1944, after a spell at RAF Hornchurch, we left Tilbury for Ostend with snow on the ground. Then we went on to Wenduine where we were billeted in the sanatorium which had been taken over by No. 80 Wing. It was so cold, a signal was sent asking for supplies of 'long Johns' (cold weather underwear). Before we left Wenduine, No.62 MSU joined us from the Ardennes (see above). There was a hole in one of the kitbags and they were accused of sticking a pencil into it to resemble a bullet hole. However, there was no doubt they had been in the 'battle' zone! We had been lucky to avoid it!

Eventually we settled in the town of Uden in Holland and set up our station. We were to provide navigational aids to the USAAF and jam particular frequencies with a magnetised steel tape called JOSTLE which sent out multiple tones. We had a control station in the town square with a main generator which supplied the station, the local cinema, and also, unknown to us, the local dentist. The latter fact was found out when we switched off the generator one day to save our oil only to receive a frantic plea from the dentist for the restoration of the electricity supply as he was in the middle of drilling the tooth of a patient! We made many friends amongst the Dutch people.

RCM from the UK

Prior to the D-Day landings careful investigation had been carried out to trace the enemy's coastal radar network closest to the likely invasion area. Particular attention was given to the mobile units. To assist in the solving of this problem Dr.Cockburn's staff at TRE had produced a special ground DF finder, PING PONG, which could measure the bearing of an enemy radar transmitter with great accuracy. (See Chapter Two for greater detail regarding PING-PONG). Equipment was set up on the south coast of the UK to provide 'fixes' on the enemy stations, the location of each being subsequently confirmed by photographic reconnaissance.

Bert Moir was a member of one of these ground sites:

I finished with No. 60 Group in early 1944 and joined a PING-PONG caravan on the Isle of Wight. The crew consisted of a corporal and five LACs and we worked a three-watch system, two on duty at a time. We were an extremely independent little unit owing allegiance to nobody although I am sure we were part of No.100 Group as we had B/100 on the side of our caravan. When I had been in No. 26 Group there had been a B/26 on our vehicles. As a result of our independence we slept in 'civvy' billets but were 'fed and watered' at RAF Ventnor...

The object of the exercise was to pick up, identify and breakdown the frequencies, and find the bearings of, the Freya and Würzburg radar stations in northern France. The unit was accommodated in a plywood cabin mounted on an anti-aircraft gun carriage which rotated through 360 degrees. This, and a large bearing indicator on a central column inside, enabled us to give a bearing up to 1/10th of a degree. Two handles mounted on this column rotated the whole affair. The aerial was similar to that used for GROUND GROCER but had two parts instead of the three parts on GROUND GROCER. A cross-bearing from another station to the east of us therefore, gave a very accurate position. How we broke the German signal down to its component parts escapes me now, but once it had been identified we had to monitor it at regular intervals.

Of course all this was leading up to D-Day so, every so often, we would be instructed to watch some particular enemy station and report when it went off the air. This usually meant that our aircraft had put it out of action.

At Ventnor we received an amazing example of the latest technology. This came in a box filled with electronic gadgets which I didn't understand. What I could see was a roll of aluminium-backed paper which ran slowly across the face of the thing. Over this was a brass wheel with three points on it. This rotated in the horizontal plane and, when a signal was picked up , a small electrical charge burned a tiny hole in the paper. These were collected daily and sent off to HQ. The frequencies could then be read off this to confirm what we had reported by telephone. So much for theory! In practice it developed a habit of setting itself on fire and what HQ made of all the charred paper is more than I can tell. However, its end was spectacular. I was in the cabin by myself (my mate was outside chatting up a Wren!) and I was luckily turned away from it when it blew up. My exit from the cabin must have been spectacular! I have no idea what caused it but the contents of a large electrolyte condenser were all over the walls, and my uniform! This was the last we saw of this device. TRE collected it and we heard no more about it.

With the advance of the Allied armies it was only a matter of time before we ran out of targets and, at the end of July 1944, we moved down to Coverack, in Cornwall, to cover the Cherbourg Peninsula and western France. We were billeted in a Nissen Hut in a farmyard which was part of a small army camp. This lot boasted the worst cook I have ever come across and no amount of pleading on our behalf could get our messing arrangements altered. There was a wicked but widely believed story that the cook had been part way through his training as a blacksmith when he was rejected for being too dirty, and then became a cook! Fortunately there again was a WRNS unit close by and we were grateful for their handouts.

Whilst we were there I cannot recall much activity probably because the German radar in northern France had already been taken care of. It's the daft things I remember. One day the farmer, in whose field we were set up, arrived and asked what our strange caravan was. At this time we had a mains leak and the whole chassis was only just live. You felt a small shock if you touched any metal. Anyway, I was outside telling the farmer that the whole thing was secret and could not be discussed, when his dog lifted his leg and urinated on the mudguard. The poor animal let out a scream and set of in the direction of Yorkshire at a speed that would have won a prize at White City Greyhound Track. We never saw either the farmer or his dog again!

Bomber Support Development Unit (BSDU)

The BSDU was formed on 10th April 1944, at Foulsham. Its role was to develop, test, and produce a wide variety of radar and radio equipment for No.100 Group. A small but very well equipped radio laboratory and workshop accommodated in 'The Houseboat' at Radlett, Hertfordshire, was transferred from No.80 Wing to the BSDU to carry out the larger development and production tasks. In December 1944, the Unit moved to Swanton Morley to be joined shortly afterwards by the BSDU Workshops which had also been at Radlett. The latter became known as the Radio Engineering Section. BSDU also had on its strength a Flight of nine Mosquitoes to carry out operational and non-operational trials relating to fighter equipment.

Alfred Jeffery, a Cornishman, had an early introduction to radio. 'When I was a very, very small child, my father would often sit me on his shoulders to look over the boundary hedge where Marconi's Poldhu Radio Station (from where Marconi sent the first Transatlantic signal in 1901) was situated. It adjoined our land and I watched the engineers high aloft adjusting aerials, and listened to the throb of the big engines, and the whine of generators. The sea breeze played tunefully through the maze of wires and insulators.' Electricity became Jeffery's schoolboy hobby and much later, as the result of 'Hitler's rude intervention into my life', he found himself in the RAF, ultimately being transferred to No.100 Group:

> In March 1944, Bernard Huntley and myself, both experienced electricians, together with two airframe fitters and one engine fitter, (we were all LACs), following our Route Form, arrived at a railway station a few miles from Foulsham in Norfolk. When we 'phoned for transport we were told to re-check as no personnel were expected. It so happened that a truck from Foulsham arrived to collect goods and we got a lift to the camp.
>
> At Station HQ (SHQ) we gave the Admin Officer a large sealed envelope which had been given to us on leaving No.21 OTU at Moreton-in-the-Marsh and he said, 'As there is no Unit at Foulsham of the description indicated by your papers, RAF Records will be contacted in the morning and you will be sent on to your correct destination.' As we were waiting for transport to take us for a late meal and accommodation an Admin Corporal came out to us and whispered, 'Don't take too much notice of what you have been told. With the set-up we have here they might be doing something he knows nothing about.'

Nothing happened for two to three days, then Jeffery and his colleagues were told that an officer would see them outside the SHQ at 10am the next day:

> More airframe and engine fitters had arrived, our number was now about twelve. We reported, and silently followed the officer and his F/S (who were quietly talking to each other) into empty workshop building. Having closed the door the

F/S chalked up the initials 'SD (RR) DU' (Special Duties, Radar and Radio, Development Unit) telling us to look at it, remember it, but not to ask what it meant, or mention it to other personnel, or in letters home. He then got a wet cloth and rubbed it out. The officer was a sincere and friendly man and spoke of the importance and urgency of our task which was to last about six to seven weeks, and that we should accept it as a challenge. We still didn't know what we were supposed to be doing.

Four airframe men were selected to go on a short course of special instruction, the remainder were to start work on the two Halifaxes which were in the big hangar. One electrician would be needed to disconnect the bomb gear, generators and fuel gauges. The other electrician would also go on this course...after a discussion Huntley went on the course. A few days later he came back. He said that he had not been able to make notes on the course for security reasons and would discuss things with me in one of the aircraft the next day.

Next morning, after we had gone over all he could remember, it became obvious that we were to help prepare aircraft for special RCM duties. We started by measuring out the position of the radio rooms and benches (the airframe people would build these), sealed up the bomb doors, and fixed several aerials and positions for scanners. We were working out the best position to fix a main electrical switchboard when there was a sharp knock on the door.

I opened it to find a stern looking F/L who told us he was the Engineering Officer. He added that he had come up to the aircraft 20 minutes before and had overheard what we had been talking about. He formed the view that we knew what we were talking about and asked us to make some rough drawings of what we thought was the best way of doing things so that work could proceed. After a couple of days with our work making rapid progress he seemed satisfied and left us alone to get on with it.

Then a complete electrical section arrived, with equipment and NCOs, and they were told that Huntley and myself were working under special instructions. We must be supported but not interfered with. Huntley and his helpers took on the AC and DC wiring system to the radio rooms and benches which were being rapidly built by the airframe men. My helper and I worked on the power supply up to and including the main switchboard. Large generators and alternators on each engine would supply 7,000 watts. All the old wiring was replaced. It was normal practice to test the work under airborne conditions but on this occasion it did not take place as the aircraft were ferried away when finished to other bases for the radar and radio equipment to be installed.

Work continued in April day and night. I generally started at 2-30pm and worked through with just brief meal breaks until 8-30am the following day. The fully-qualified and very capable electrician working with me started at 8am and finished about midnight. The main electrical supply panel was on the right hand side of the corridor and the only period when I could settle down undisturbed to concentrate on getting it wired up was between midnight and early morning.

Huntley sometimes worked the same period for the same reason, but his situation was different, working each day, as he did, with the radio and radar equipment specialists. These were dedicated, brilliant easy-to-work with men, who believed they were engaged in the RAF's scientific contribution to the overthrow of the Reich, and, more important at this time, the successful mainland Europe landing that was coming.

BSDU had quickly become quite a sizeable Unit with its own HQ, workshop buildings, plus draughtsmen and industrial photographic section. All work was carefully monitored with detailed drawings and photographs of how things were done.

The airframe fitters were jovial and energetic, all working 12 to 16 hours a day. There was an arrangement with the catering staff to provide a large urn of tea or cocoa at intervals during the night but there was no let up in the high-pitched whine of air-drills or the snap of riveting tools. Exhaustion was a problem, especially between 2am and dawn. There could be dizziness, tools just falling out of hands, and loss of balance. This was dangerous when working on top of stepladders. An especially hardworking Corporal devised the idea of laying on his back motionless for about five minutes on the cold concrete floor, and then jumping up smartly and pressing on. I tried it myself a few times and it worked!

The SOs being trained were spending two to three days at Foulsham, to familiarise themselves with the enhanced electrical system. They were introduced to Huntley and myself and we explained the 'full load' airborne test of the electrical supply so that they themselves could carry it out. It was necessary for them to spend more time with Huntley than myself, but why they decided to tell us much more than an outline of what they would be doing shortly was more than a surprise, but we decided to keep what they told us strictly to ourselves.

There were visits by important government officials and the AOC, AVM Addison, obviously pleased, came around and shook hands with many of us as it became evident that the work would be completed ahead of time. When the seven Halifax and Stirling aircraft left, those of us who had been working long hours were put on 'light duties'. Just after D-Day we were called together and thanked for the all the effort that got the job done. Afterwards all the others with the exception of Huntley and myself were posted away and we were taken over by BSDU. We retained the same position as previously, having support from the electrical section, with no questions, interference or camp duties, but we were now installing the enhanced electrical systems in Mosquitoes.

After VE-Day Alfred Jeffery was posted to India. Even there he was reminded of No.100 Group:

> The Viceroy, General Wavell, had provided a beautiful restroom for servicemen at his Palace in New Delhi. I made it my business to go there to read, write and rest. On the afternoon of Christmas Day about 12 of us, army and air force, were in there when General Wavell came in. When he spoke to me I told him I had only recently come to India and had been serving for the last two years in a unit under the command of AVM Addison. 'Addison?' he said, 'Addison is a close friend and we have much the same interests. I started to have an interest in radio because of Marconi. I visited his experimental station in Poldhu many times. I could see a big future for his developments from a military point of view.'

Footnotes – Chapter Seven

[190] PRO AIR 14/2911: 'The Development and Activities of No.100 (BS) Group', p.104.

[191] Ibid.

[192] 'The History of No.141 Squadron.' D F Aris (Vol.2, p.378).

[193] For the story of this Unit see 'Beam Benders, No.80 (Signals) Wing, 1940-45' by Laurie Brettingham (Midland Publishing, 1997).

[194] PRO AIR 14/2911, 'Development and Activities of No.100 (BS) Group: No.80 Wing' pp.4041

[195] PRO AIR 14/2911, 'The Development and Activities of No.100 (BS) Group 1943-45, part ii), pp41-44.

[196] A sad and tragic effect of this occupation occurred in the previous March when a small force of R A F bombers mistakenly bombed Calais (liberated six months previously) believing it to be the still German-occupied Dunkirk which was 23 miles away. There were 127 people killed. ('Dover Express' article dated 18.3.95.)

[197] Also known as 'cone of silence' this denotes a small area (resembling an inverted cone) extending upwards from a radio transmitter, within the limits of which signals are inaudible or blurred.

Chapter Eight.

'We Saw the Morning Break'
– A Summary

We saw the powers of darkness put to flight,
We saw the morning break.

(Printed on an invitation to a VE Day party at No.100 Group HQ, May 1945)

When the collapse of Germany in May 1945 brought an end to hostilities in Europe, the gradual adjustment to peacetime activities was demonstrated in No.100 Group by two, widely differing events. Firstly, during the euphoric atmosphere of the war's end, in a leisurely, almost recreational approach, permission was given for ground staff of the Unit to be taken by aircraft of the Group to look at towns and cities in Germany which had, particularly over the last three years of the European War, been the focal point of much Bomber Command operational activity. These trips became known somewhat flippantly as 'Cook's Tours' named after the Travel Agent Thomas Cook..

VE-Day Service at Bylaugh Hall (8th May 1945). AVM Addison is at the lectern; Air Commodore Chisholm, is standing on the grass to his right, by a WAAF, and Mrs Addison is seated.

(Maryse Addison)

Jack Philipson was an RAAF pilot on No.171 Squadron:

After the War finished we got permission to take ground crews over the Ruhr etc. to see the bomb damage. We were told to fly around 1000 ft over there...but between 100 ft to 300 ft was more likely! I did three trips.

First Trip. On the first occasion we took five ground crew from West Raynham taking a route which took us over Cap Gris Nez-Ypres-Brussels-Maastrict-Cologne-Neuss-Dusseldorf-Essen-Bochum-Duisberg-Krefeld-Gelsenkirchen-Dunkirk (5.40 hrs.)

Second Trip. The second time we took eight ground crew travelling over Margate-Dunkirk-Lille-Brussels-Remagen-Bonn-Cologne-Neuss-Antwerp-Ostend-Dover- Base (4.15 hrs.)

Third Trip. This time we took nine ground crew travelling Margate-Dunkirk-Aachen-Bonn-Cologne-Dusseldorf-Dortmund-Base. (4.40 hrs.)

On our second trip, when we were at Remagen, we nearly finished up in the Rhine! We had been following a river valley from the Maginot Line and saw all the concrete gun emplacements and tank traps. As we turned north up the Rhine we saw a large PoW camp in which there seemed to be thousands of Germans. We dived low across it at 30 ft and saw them all sitting there in the open with a tent here and there. This huge wire-fenced enclosure seemed to go for miles alongside the river. We kept low as the Rhine had cliffs along the west bank. On the right side were what seemed to be river flats and farms which, later on, gave way to another cliff. Both sides of the river were now about 200 yards apart but the gap was narrowing slowly as we flew along. We veered left and then started to turn right and bang in front of us was this 250 ft cliff too close to climb out, so round we went to the right. I eased up to level with the top of the cliff and stayed at that altitude flying along the cliff top to Bonn and then out over the plains to Cologne. The bomb aimer said the wingtip got a bit close to the water in the turn but you don't have much time to act travelling at 190 mph.

The ground crew, four of whom were jammed in the navigator's position at the front of the aircraft said it was like a ride on a roller coaster. The Sergeant in charge came and thanked me after we had landed. He said he knew we weren't supposed to be low-flying but said it was the best flight he had had in eight years in the RAF. He said to the blokes, and the one WAAF, 'You'll never get a better low-level than that so zip your lips!' We never heard a murmur from anyone but another couple of ground lads asked if I was doing another 'Cook's Tour'. I did one more, taking nine of them up on June 16th 1945.

George Jamieson, the only other Australian pilot in No.171 Squadron, also flew a couple of 'Cook's Tours':

> ...Four days after the European War finished we did two sightseeing trips to the Ruhr. The first was with just our crew and the second with lots of ground staff to show them round a bit. On the first trip we came back south of London. I saw St. Paul's Cathedral in the distance and made for it. I did a hard turn to starboard and circled the Cathedral. Then we went west over the City and finally headed for Base. We were a bit laid back and nobody seemed to care. Both my Navigator and Bomb aimer were Londoners.

Operation 'Post Mortem'

The second event, had greater significance as the frenzy of war gave way to peaceful contemplation. What had contributed to the Allied success? What could be learnt? It was a time for reflection, and No.100 Group joined in the debate. What effect had the Group's activities had on the enemy; how would the experiences be helpful in any future conflict? One way a contribution could be made, it was quickly decided, would be to investigate the German methods of operating their defence organisation of raid

No.100 Group senior officers visiting the Lufflotte-Reich HQ in the woods at Schleswig-Holstein as part of 'Operation Post Mortem'. AVM Addison is standing to the right of the signpost with W/C Tait on the extreme right. To the left of the signpost are G/C Tester and S/L Baillie.

(N C Cordingly)

reporting, and its method of control against Allied bomber attacks. Naturally enough a matter of particular interest to No.100 Group would be the effect of British RCM on this organisation and its equipment.

Thus the Air Ministry arranged 'Operation Post Mortem'[198], a detailed study of the German methods by British personnel. The terms of reference were:

> To investigate the German methods of operating their defence organisation of raid reporting and control against our bomber attacks, and in particular, to ascertain the effect of British RCM on this organisation, and on German Radar equipment.[199]

As a result of the Air Ministry Order, 59 RAF officers, and 72 other ranks, arrived at Schleswig and Grove airfields on 23rd June1945, and were dispersed to various radar and control stations

There were limits to what could be done. The German radar in Denmark was still largely operational at the cessation of hostilities and was the best location where 'Post Mortem' could take place, bearing in mind the resources available. It was impracticable to include in the Operation more than a limited part of the German defence organisation. The Exercise was confined to the Province of Schleswig-Holstein and Eastern Denmark. To ensure that conditions approximated as closely as possible to those under which the German air defence system operated during the war, the German radar stations and control organisation were manned throughout by German personnel whilst being observed by the British teams.

German radar in Denmark had not had to deal with heavy raids in the eighteen months before 'Post Mortem' and had never, therefore, experienced the full weight of Bomber Command RCM in the closing stages of the War. Thus the German ground radar crews there were very inexperienced. In a move indicative of the times, to ensure the security of these Luftwaffe personnel whilst 'Post Mortem' was in operation, instructions to protect their well-being were issued by the SHAEF Mission in Denmark.

In addition, selected staff officers, operations room personnel, radar operators and technicians from the HQs at Fighter Command, Nos. 60 and 100 Groups, assisted by British interpreters, studied the system and equipment in operation, with particular regard to the effectiveness of British RCM and the countermeasures employed by the Germans. The intention was to observe selected stations and control points of the ground organisation of the German air defence system in the designated area, which operated under simulated raid conditions provided by heavy bombers of Bomber Command, plus RCM aircraft from No. 100 Group. These series of 'raids' sometimes took place with, and sometimes without, RCM aircraft. As many types of RCM as possible were used, sometimes singly and sometimes collectively, in order to fully establish their effectiveness. The aircraft employed varied from 23 Mosquitoes to a mixed force of 331 aircraft. It was planned that 'Post Mortem' would take place during daylight hours in the period from 25th June to 7th July 1945, but, in fact, it finished two days earlier.

The Luftwaffe installations used were the Jagddivision Operations Room at Grove, a massive concrete building, 200 ft long, 100 ft wide and 60 ft high which was situated, carefully camouflaged, in a wood about one mile from Grove Airfield. This housed not only the Ops Room but also office accommodation for the entire Jagddivision HQ Staff. In addition, the three radar stations[200] at Star, Ringelnatter, and Faun, (plus seven associated reporting rooms), the Observer Corps Centre at Kolding, and two 'Y' Radar Observation Posts at Tamariske/Strohblume and Veilchen/Geissblatt were also used.

Most of the recently-beaten enemy's staff seemed willing to help:

> The great majority of the German personnel co-operated willingly and appeared
> eager to demonstrate the efficiency of their system. This was particularly so in the
> case of the higher ranks who seemed anxious to give evidence of their
> professional skills. The only exception was in the case of the Blitzmädel
> (equivalent to WAAF) in the Operations Room at Grove who appeared
> disgruntled and were probably responsible for certain delays and omissions in the
> passing of 'plots'.[201]

Despite bad weather which seriously delayed the flight plan, 11 of the 14 Exercises had been completed by 5th July. No.100 Group aircraft took part in seven. In Exercise Four, 20 of their aircraft formed a Mandrel Screen for the Main Force to fly through in an evaluation of that particular RCM; in Exercise Five this was repeated with additional aircraft providing PIPERACK, JOSTLE/ CARPET, and WINDOW. The subsequent five Exercises (six to ten), saw these various RCM again being employed either singly or in combination. It had been intended that fourteen Exercises should take place, but, in the event, the last two were cancelled.

As a result of the exercises the following general conclusions were formed:

(i) Tracking of Raids

The German air reporting system was obviously designed to give a good general picture of large scale raids and was not suitable for the accurate tracking of aircraft operating singly. On every Exercise when a main concentrated force of heavy bombers was employed the Grove plot gave a clear indication of its progress, except in the case of Exercise Ten when a change of direction of the Main Force was not immediately appreciated.

(ii) Long-Range Warning

The long-range warning provided by the German Radar varied greatly in the different Exercises. Where a normal high approach was used, adequate long-range warning was obtained, particularly by the Wasserman and Elefant equipments, but ranges in excess of 150 miles were very rare.

(iii) Value of Low Approach

The value of low approach (2000-3000 ft) was clearly demonstrated in most of the Exercises. In Exercise Two a main Bomber force approaching low was detected at a range of only 71 miles compared with a normal range of 143 miles when approaching high, and a Mosquito force was detected at 71 miles instead of 131 miles.

(iv) Effects of Mandrel Screen

(a) During 'Post Mortem' long-range radar equipments invariably gave excellent warning of the approach of the MANDREL aircraft approximately an hour and a half before H-Hour. The presence of the Screen was regarded by the Germans as a useful early indication of impending activity, but the Luftwaffe Chief Operations Officer stated that in operations he would have waited for indications of the approach of the Main Force before ordering fighters off the ground.

(b) In every case where the MANDREL Screen was used there were gaps in the jamming which enabled certain Radar equipments to pass sufficient information to Grove for an adequate assessment of the progress of the raid to be made. The power radiated from each jammer and the spacing of the jamming aircraft succeeded in preventing adequate plotting by Freya, Dreh Freya, and Mammut, but the efficiency of the Wasserman was only partially reduced and the Elefant was virtually unaffected throughout the Exercises.

(c) Although the MANDREL aircraft were fitted with MANDREL III apparatus capable of being tuned to the Elefant frequency, examination of the SOs logs suggests that no jammer was correctly tuned to the Elefant transmission. The failure of the Screen to provide effective cover against the Wasserman may be attributed to certain characteristics of this particular equipment, together with an increased power output which it had compared with the Mammut and Freya equipments.

(d) The reduction in early warning achieved by the MANDREL Screen during the Exercises was disappointing, but its presence added greatly to the difficulties of the German staff in assessing correctly the character of the raid.

(v) Effect of WINDOW

It was obvious that the use of WINDOW by the Allies had profoundly affected the whole of the German air reporting and control system. Close control methods of interception had been abandoned in favour of running commentary, and Radar equipments were used to plot the WINDOW areas in the hope that the position of the Main Force could be determined. Accurate estimation of numbers of aircraft proved virtually impossible and feint forces could easily be mistaken for Main Force attacks.[202]

As part of 'Post Mortem' a small technical team comprising of G/C Tester, (Deputy Director of Telecommunications); W/C Norman Cordingly, No.100 Group HQ (Radar); S/L George Baillie, No.100 Group HQ (BSDU); and Dr. Robert Cockburn, TRE; visited Schleswig Holstein during the period 27th May to 5th June 1945. During their duties the quartet interrogated three German senior technical officers. General-Major Boner (Chief Signals Officer, Luftflotte Reich), when asked about ABC and JOSTLE IV jamming, considered the former more effective than the latter; FIDGET MF jamming had very little effect on 'Big Screw' beacons but effectively interfered with a number of the 'Little Screw' installations. He thought CORONA was very effective for a short period but later the German aircrews were able to operate without serious interference. CORONA had been an RCM, first used in October 1943, whereby spurious information (eg false weather reports, 'test' calls, transmitted in the middle of operational instructions) was transmitted on the same frequency as the German Nightfighter Controller to the German nightfighters. The Germans tried to combat this Allied interference by using a woman to broadcast the instructions. AVM Addison wrote about this after the War:

> We had already anticipated this, it was another case of 'bathtub' inspiration, and was due to our habit of putting ourselves in the Germans' shoes and making guesses as to what we would do next if we were faced with the same awkward circumstances.
>
> Thus it came about that Barbara Pemberton (a 24 years-old WAAF officer from Borehamwood, in Hertfordshire), and her two colleagues were put under training some weeks before the need arose for their employment in this particular role. We chose more than one to make sure that there would be at least one on duty in the Ops Room on any night and so be ready to do battle against the expected Blitzm¬dchen. You can imagine the tension these girls were under during the weeks of waiting.
>
> I remember very well one night watching Barbara taking down the remarks that were being made by the German Controllers in competition with CORONA. I asked her to translate these messages to me. She came to one which

she refused to translate. I asked her 'Why?' She blushed deeply and replied, 'I don't want to tell you what this means, but if ever my chance comes the Germans wont find me so modest in answering them in their own vein!' A few nights later her chance did come, and the relief and tension on her part can only have been equalled by the surprise of the Germans when they found that their Fraulein was immediately taken to task. They must have thought that they would have at least one CORONA-free night.[203]

General-Major Boner also added that the meaconing of the German navigational beams, and KNICKEBEIN jamming by the RAF had, on the whole, been effective. He gave other interesting information:

German Air Force: the equivalent of No.192 Squadron

In 1944 the Luftwaffe set up an airborne search organisation similar to No.192 Squadron. The aircraft used for this role, flew with German bombers. The apparent lack of success of the airborne search organisation was due to the fact that they were unable to find a suitable aircraft to accommodate the operators and necessary equipment. An He177 was equipped but never widely used. Such aircraft as were used for airborne search work suffered very heavy losses. The enemy used a number of search aircraft to fly with our bomber stream over their own territory. They were well aware of the existence of No.192 Squadron and its function and, in some cases, were able to listen to our aircraft because they were able to pick up the radiation from our search receivers.

German Air Force: Intelligence Information on Radar Development in UK

The German Air Force appeared to lack Intelligence on the development of new radar apparatus in the UK, particularly airborne equipment. As far as this was concerned, the news of its existence was first obtained when equipment was taken from aircraft shot down. Later on, when the Wim sites (see below) were in operation, they very quickly recorded new signals on the 3 and 10 cm band. They had no knowledge of the use of AI until sets were taken from captured aircraft. They knew of our radar stations before the war but were not certain of the frequency bands employed until ground listening equipment was introduced.

Ground Radio Control of Rocket Projectiles

General-Major Boner confirmed the use of radio control in the early stages of the V2 operations but, because of the fear of jamming, this was soon abandoned. V1 radio launching control was also abandoned for the same reason. Homing devices in rockets were under consideration but were never used operationally.

Kapitän Leutnant (Lt.Cmdr.) Juergen Blomeyer was a German naval officer who was mainly concerned with the countermeasures against WINDOW and jamming of German naval equipments, such as the radar control of anti-aircraft installations used by the German Navy, and the radar control of heavy artillery for sea firing control and coastal watching services. His information led the panel to report the following:

(a) Noise jamming of Freya Stations

In the first instance, noise jamming of Freya stations was experienced and, as a result, the Germans resorted to frequency changing of the Freya installations. Freyas operating on 2.5 metres (125 Mc/s) were altered so that the transmitters could be switched to a frequency of 3.5 metres. At a later date an attempt was made to narrow down the beam of the stations. 'Long Lathe' came into vogue – this was a modification to the antenna system which employed 18 dipoles instead of 6.

At a later stage the Germans decided that it would be better to operate the Freya stations over a wide band of frequencies. Further anti-jamming trials, with Freya stations with vertically polarised aerials mounted on a frame which was capable of being elevated, were conducted. These trials were conducted with a Freya installation mounted on the peak of the Zugspitze mountain (10,000 ft high), near Garmisch in southern Germany. The results of these trials were found to be unsatisfactory, jamming was still present and the aerial structure was too flimsy – high winds on many occasions blew them down. Kapitän Leutnant Blomeyer also reported that attempts to alter the aerial polarisation were not effective against Allied jamming. Increases of frequency to avoid jamming were temporarily effective but caused serious loss of range performance of the equipment, because they did not resite this equipment.

(b) Würzburg Jamming

Trials were conducted at Schweinemunde to see whether Würzburg installations could be rendered free from jamming by WINDOW.

Würtzlaus. The German Navy started conducting anti-WINDOW trials two years before the RAF used WINDOW for the first time on Hamburg. Würtzlaus was the first anti-WINDOW device to be developed and consisted of a CW oscillator, the signals from which were injected into the receiver on nearly the same frequency as that of the transmitter (ie 580 Mc/s oscillator, 600 Mc/s transmitter). This experiment was not very effective so the next step was to use an oscillator on nearly the same frequency as the transmitter, with the result that the moving blip from an aircraft changed its phase with respect to that of the oscillator. The aircraft and WINDOW blips looked quite different. The difficulty with this system, it was stated, was to maintain the oscillator on the correct frequency and, for this reason, it was succeeded by a later device known as Tastlaus.

Tastlaus. produced (in early 1944) a similar effect of Wurtzlaus but had an oscillator working on the intermediate frequency. To test the efficacy of this new equipment the Germans conducted WINDOW trials and...it was possible to see the aircraft blip quite clearly. For DF purposes an AI Mk IV type of CRT was used.

The Nuremburg system which originally provided facilities for listening to the audible note set up by the noise of the aircraft propeller, was used by operators to listen to the Tastlaus or Wurtzlaus frequency. It was quite easy for them to differentiate between this noise and that of WINDOW, which produced a crackling noise.

Jamming of Würzburg by CARPET

Many attempts were made to change the frequency of Würzburg D in order to avoid CARPET jamming. A frequency shift from 50-60 cm was provided but it was found that this was an ineffective measure against CARPET II. It was noted that the shifting of the Würzburg frequency enabled the enemy to dodge to some extent the jamming from CARPET I and CARPET III.

Wim Search Equipment

This equipment was used extensively for listening to airborne radio and radar signals employed by the Main Force of Bomber Command. Such information assisted the enemy to plot the bomber stream.

Two Wim sites were situated at Glesborg, near Laen (north of Aarhus), and Tornby (north of Hjorring, Denmark). One particular receiver covered the 2.5 to 3 cm band and was successfully used to pick up ASH signals shortly after the equipment's first operational use by No.100 Group aircraft.

The use of Wim equipment for tracking H2S bombers was discussed in some detail. The Germans stated that they were soon well aware that crews had been instructed not to switch on the H2S before 5 degrees east. The Germans said quite categorically that they were still able to plot, however, because a few bombers always managed to have the equipment switched on throughout the whole of the journey to the target.

Early Warning of Invasion (D-Day)

An interesting statement was made by the Technical Officers of Luftflotte Reich who said that the German General Staff did not believe the radar reports of extensive shipping movements in the English Channel refusing to believe the information until visual reports had been received.

Visit to Grove Airfield Operations Room

Perhaps the most interesting feature of the Operations Room was its complexity. It is understood that in the early days of radar, optical projection was tried at Bawdsey and subsequently abandoned. The Germans, however, with their delight in complexity, designed a fantastic exhibition piece with enormous maps printed on transparent screens lining the walls of the Ops Room. The information displayed on the main screen was displayed optically – no less than 40 optical projectors were employed. Various symbols were used to denote the type of raid information. Below the optical projection set piece was to be seen the 'Royal Box' which was no doubt occupied by the Divisional Commander and his Staff, who endeavoured to direct his aircraft into the bomber stream. Such an Ops Room set-up asks for jamming and there is little doubt that a small amount of false information once thrown in, would be grossly magnified.

The enemy 'Y' service was 'exceptionally wide awake'. Their listening receivers were technically of great interest, and the German monitoring service quickly detected the use of ASH. Its airborne homing equipment appeared to be much more highly developed than the Allies, but where it did lag behind, both in the air and on the ground, was in its delay in introducing centimetre equipment, and using automatic scanning.[204]

Effectiveness of RCM

The aims of the RCM being employed during the early part of 1945 had been given by No.100 Group HQ in a paper dated 14th March 1945. They were:
(i)   To deny the enemy the use of GCI.
(ii) To deny the enemy early warning of raids.
(iii) To prevent the enemy obtaining a clear picture of operations over his territory.
(iv) To make things as difficult as possible for the enemy nightfighter attempting to carry out interception of the bombers.
(v)   To get enemy nightfighters airborne unnecessarily by means of 'Feint' attacks involving him in waste of effort and material and also 'conditioning' him to certain fighter deployments from the point of view of future targets.

The opinions of observers as to the extent to which these aims were achieved in 'Post Mortem' were summarised as follows:

(i) The combination of WINDOW and electronic jamming rendered the German close control methods useless.

(ii) The only completely successful method of reducing range of enemy early warning was by employing a low-approach. When a high-approach was used, the Germans obtained adequate long range warning since certain equipments, notably the Elefant and Wasserman, succeeding in penetrating the MANDREL Screen because all wavelengths were not jammed, or alternatively the intensity of jamming in certain areas was inadequate due to uneven distribution of the jamming aircraft.

(iii) The value of jamming tended to be reduced unless the strictest observance of radio silence was enforced, for example, early warning was invariably obtained by the German 'Y' Service from H2S and IFF transmissions. It cannot be over emphasised that any transmission of any kind from British aircraft immediately gave valuable information to the Germans.

(iv) During 'Post Mortem' the Germans succeeded in obtaining a fairly clear picture of the progress of the main attacking forces. This conclusion is qualified, however, by the fact that when carrying out operations over Germany at large, Bomber Command had far greater opportunities of exploiting fully, their diversionary tactics and RCM.

(v) There can be no doubt that the successful jamming of ground-to-air communications and AI, and the paralysis of all methods of close control, made the task of the German Nightfighter crews extremely difficult.

(vi) The 'Post Mortem' Exercises did not provide any opportunities for determining whether 'Feint' attacks involved the Germans in waste of effort and 'conditioned' them to certain Fighter deployments.[205]

Post Mortem Experience (1)

Leonard Lamerton (qv), the only civilian in a senior position at Bylaugh Hall, found himself in 1945 'made an honorary Flight Lieutenant'. He finished his wartime service with No.100 Group with what was, for him, an unforgettable and unique experience:

At the War's end I was on my way back to Southampton and when I got to Waterloo Station in London a message came over the public address system for me to return to No.100 Group H Q. I discovered a party was going to interrogate Luftwaffe officers regarding the efficiency of our RCM and I was to be the Secretary. We went to Schleswig-Holstein with Air Commodore Chisholm in charge. G/C Goodman, W/C Cordingly and W/C Donaldson were also in the party. I think there were about ten of us in all. When we landed and went to the hotel we found an extraordinary situation. The place was still being policed by a Panzer Grenadier Unit in their black uniforms! I went out in the evening with G/C Goodman and, as we walked along a German came up to us and asked, in English, if he could help us! It was like a dream.

It became more dreamlike later on when, the next morning, large cars, driven by Germans, arrived at the hotel to pick us up. Air Commodore Chisholm, G/C Goodman and myself went in the first car. I sat in the back wearing my new forage cap and trying to look important! We were driven at a fast speed along cobbled streets looking at our map. The German driver did not speak English and our German consisted of, 'Right', 'Left' and 'Straight on' but we eventually got to this clearing in a wood. The driver left us and we wondered what would happen next. He returned later and drove us further into the woods. We eventually came to a long, thin tent. Outside, in two rows, standing to attention were the senior officers of the Luftwaffe with their gold crosses and medals on display. We walked through them and went into the tent and sat down.

Then the rest of our party began to arrive and, through an interpreter, we began to ask the Luftwaffe officers questions. Right from the beginning we found the Germans were extraordinarily forthcoming. Over the next 14-16 days we interrogated many senior officers. Whilst we were there Admiral Dönitz, the current German leader following the death of Hitler, was arrested. An order was issued stating that all the German officers were not to wear their medals and so the only way you knew you were talking to a very senior German was because he had gold braid round his uniform. I interrogated one of them in his bedroom, and he looked rather frightened, I think. One of the junior officers told us they had been told to tell us everything because they thought that later we would be joining them in fighting the Russians.

Our group were to go to Flensburg airfield in Denmark. Our German driver refused to go as he was frightened what might happen to him so we had one of our own drivers. We drove through the German/Danish border where we saw the remnants of the German army marching in threes back into Germany without their arms. It was an astonishing sight. We had taken our own lunches to the airfield and when we ate we decided we would like a drink of water with the food. A German WAAF gave some to Chisholm but when we asked for some she told us the water was no good. She had not had the courage to refuse Chisholm! We made do with champagne which was produced from some place or the other!

Post Mortem Experience (2).

Jack Philipson remembered his 'Post-Mortem' flights:
    I did three 'Post Mortem' trips on July 3rd, 4th and 5th. The first was a jamming

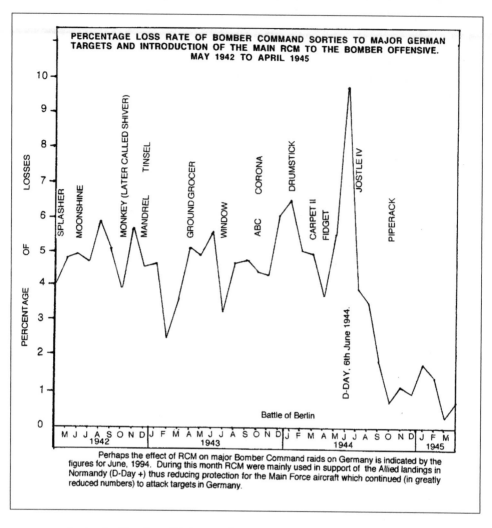

PERCENTAGE LOSS RATE OF BOMBER COMMAND SORTIES TO MAJOR GERMAN TARGETS AND INTRODUCTION OF THE MAIN RCM TO THE BOMBER OFFENSIVE. MAY 1942 TO APRIL 1945

Perhaps the effect of RCM on major Bomber Command raids on Germany is indicated by the figures for June, 1994. During this month RCM were mainly used in support of the Allied landings in Normandy (D-Day +) thus reducing protection for the Main Force aircraft which continued (in greatly reduced numbers) to attack targets in Germany.

exercise in the Flensburg/Kiel area; the second a 'Spoof' in the same area. The third was an attack on Flensburg. They had a camera obscura set up and you flashed your identification lamp as you passed over a ring of red lamps. This was a little unnerving as I had never flown close to the Main Force before and there were 250 Lancasters all around us. It was OK along the route, but over the target area with everybody wanting to get a good position, things were a bit hectic. It's no wonder a lot collided at night.

Clearly the Exercises were observational with emphasis more on a technical, rather than tactical, appraisal. Absent was the authenticity of an active and dangerous operation against a belligerent enemy and the genuine satisfaction which came from helping the Main Force. There was very limited scope in which to employ 'Spoof' operations. The non-participation of No.100 Group fighters who had so often turned predatory Luftwaffe nightfighters into prey was a significant omission. Therefore 'Post

Mortem' can only be seen as a partial indication of the influence of the Group on the Bomber Offensive.

Did No.100 Group carry out an effective and efficient job in supporting and protecting the Bombers in the air war over Europe? AVM Addison thought that, in the Group, Bomber Command had an instrument which could not only reduce losses but also boost the morale of its crews. 'Sometimes' he recalled, 'I used to go to the briefing of crews on a Main Force bomber station, and I was invariably impressed by the confidence shown in the No.100 Group support. The crews had the comforting feeling that they were being looked after...'[206] The C-in-C, Bomber Command, Air Chief Marshal Harris, and his staff were more than satisfied. At the War's end, Harris was quite complimentary. Acknowledging a report submitted to him by AVM Addison, he replied:

> Many thanks for sending me the 'Report on GAF Nightfighting from the Interrogation of Prisoners'. I have read it with very great interest and consider it most valuable and illuminating. It constitutes also a splendid testimonial to No.100 Group's fine aggressive spirit from those best situated to judge its devastating effects.[207]

No.100 Group was disbanded, two years after its formation, on 17th December 1945. It had been an original RAF wartime creation inasmuch as fighter and bomber squadrons served together for the first time in one Group. Overcoming early setbacks, such as being given worn out fighter aircraft, the Group developed rapidly, often employing new and imaginative scientific thoughts and operational tactics, and became well organised and administered.

There can be no doubt that during its existence, the Group's 'fine aggressive spirit' made a significant contribution to Bomber Command's attacks on the enemy. It destroyed and damaged many enemy ground installations, and its success against enemy aircraft was as follows:

In the Air.

Enemy aircraft	destroyed:	236	(plus 12 'probables')
	damaged:	64	

On the Ground.

Enemy aircraft	destroyed:	21
	damaged:	62

There can be no more telling epitaph to No.100 Group's operational life.

Footnotes – Chapter Eight

[198] PRO AIR 14/2778: 'Operation Post Mortem: Operation Order No.1., dated 18.6.45, issued by ACAS (Ops), Air Ministry.

[199] PRO AIR 20/4061: 'A Report on an Investigation of a Portion of the German Raid Reporting and Control Organisation, Part 1', para 3.

[200] Ibid. para 10.

At the War's end there were six basic types of German Ground Radar. 1] Freya 2] Würzburg-Riese 3] Wasserman 4] Mammut 5] Elefant-Russel 6] Jagdschloss, and the German Radar Sites were divided into three classes, First, Second and Third, the category of each being determined by the role that the individual site played in the 'Air Reporting Network':

Third Class Site was usually a single radar equipment which passed information direct to the First Class Site.

Second Class Site was responsible for constructing an 'Air Picture' from its own group of equipments, and for passing this 'picture' to its parent First Class Site.

First Class Site received air information from its Second Class Sites (usually 2 or 3 in number), or Third Class Sites (if any), and from its own radar equipments, passing the final picture up to the Central Command Post (the Jagddivision Operations Room at Grove). Normally the Site would also receive information from the Observer System.

[201] Ibid. para 21.

[202] Ibid. para 57.

[203] Addison Papers: Letter written by AVM Addison in March 1954.

[204] PRO AIR 14/2661: 'Report by the Technical Panel on a Mission to Schleswig Holstein Lufflotte Recich Signals, Radar, and RCM, by W/C Cordingly and S/L Baillie', dated 21.6.45.

[205] Ibid. paras 73-4.

[206] Addison Papers; Letter written by AVM Addison to unknown recipient, dated 15.5.66.

[207] Letter dated 9.6.45, from C-in-C, Bomber Command, (Air Chief Marshal Sir Arthur Harris, KCB,OBE, AFC, to AOC, No.100 Group, AVM Addison, CB, CBE).

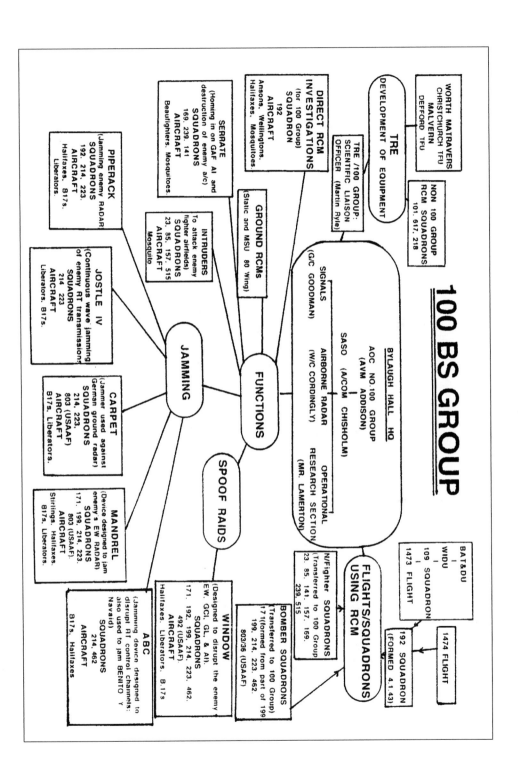

100 BS GROUP

BYLAUGH HALL   HQ

AOC   NO 100 GROUP
(AVM ADDISON)

SASO   (A/COM CHISHOLM)

SIGNALS
(G/C GOODMAN)

AIRBORNE RADAR
(W/C CORDINGLY)

OPERATIONAL
RESEARCH SECTION
(MR. LAMERTON)

FUNCTIONS

DEVELOPMENT OF EQUIPMENT

TRE

WORTH MATRAVERS
CHRISTCHURCH TFU
MALVERN
DEFFORD TFU

TRE /100 GROUP:
SCIENTIFIC LIAISON
OFFICER (Martin Ryle)

NON 100 GROUP
RCM SQUADRONS
101, 617, 218

**DIRECT RCM
INVESTIGATIONS**
(for 100 Group)
SQUADRON
192
AIRCRAFT
Ansons, Wellingtons,
Halifaxes, Mosquitoes.

SERRATE
(Homing in on GAF AI and
destruction of enemy a/c)
SQUADRONS
169, 239, 141
AIRCRAFT
Beaufighters, Mosquitoes.

GROUND RCMs
(Static and MSU 80 Wing)

INTRUDERS
To attack enemy
fighter airfields)
SQUADRONS
23, 85, 157, 515
AIRCRAFT
Mosquito

PIPERACK
(Jamming enemy RADAR)
SQUADRONS
192, 214, 223.
AIRCRAFT
Halifaxes, B17s,
Liberators.

JOSTLE IV
(Continuous wave jamming
of enemy RT transmissions)
SQUADRONS
214 223
AIRCRAFT
Liberators, B17s.

JAMMING

CARPET
(Jammer used against
German ground radar)
SQUADRONS
214, 223,
803 (USAAF)
AIRCRAFT
B17s, Liberators.

MANDREL
(Device designed to jam
enemy's EW RADAR)
SQUADRONS
171, 199, 214, 223.
803 (USAAF)
AIRCRAFT
Stirlings, Halifaxes,
B17s, Liberators.

SPOOF RAIDS

ABC
(Jamming device designed to
disrupt RT control channels;
also used to jam BENITO Y
Navaid)
SQUADRONS
214, 462
AIRCRAFT
B17s, Halifaxes

WINDOW
(Designed to disrupt the enemy
EW, GCI, GL, & AI)
SQUADRONS
171, 192, 199, 214, 223, 462,
492 (USAAF)
AIRCRAFT
Halifaxes, Liberators, B17s

BOMBER SQUADRONS
(Transferred to 100 Group)
171 (formed from part of 199,
199, 214, 223, 462
803/36 (USAAF)

N/Fighter SQUADRONS
(Transferred to 100 Group)
23, 85, 141, 157, 169,
239, 515.

**FLIGHTS/SQUADRONS
USING RCM**

BAT&DU

WIDU

109 SQUADRON

1473 FLIGHT

1474 FLIGHT

192 SQUADRON
(FORMED 4.1.43)

GLOSSARY OF TERMS

Abdullah: Airborne homer on to German early-warning radar stations.

AI: Airborne Interception.

Airborne Cigar: Jammer used against German VHF R/T Nightfighter control. (ABC) Was a development of Ground Cigar.

Airborne Grocer: Jammer used against German AI Lichtenstein; automatic scanning and re-transmission. Carried by Fortress and Mandrel-equipped aircraft. Modified to jam Würzburg radars. Developed from Ground Grocer.

Ash: AI Mk.XV. US 3cm design.

Bagful: Airborne automatic search and recording receiver.

Benito: German long-range navigational aid.

Boozer: RAF tail-warning receiver against German AI.

Carpet: Jammer used against German ground radar. Ground and airborne versions.

Coal Scuttle: Airborne D/F in the frequency band 1000-2000 Mc/s

Corona: RAF jammer used against HF R/T Control of German nightfighters. When the frequency had been identified, false instructions were broadcast to Luftwaffe nightfighter crews.

Dartboard: Originally called 'Light Up' this high-powered jammer, using a 800 kW transmitter (Aspidistra) at Crowborough in Sussex, was used against MF German nightfighter control transmissions from Stuttgart.

D/F: Direction Finding.

Dina: US version of Mandrel: later modified as Piperack (see below).

Drumstick: HF jammer used against Luftwaffe aircraft control.

Fidget: RCM against the Luftwaffe nightfighters who were controlled by the Big Screw high-powered MF beacons.

FIDO: Fog Investigation Dispersal Operation.

Flensburg: German airborne homer against Monica.

Freya: German early warning ground radar on 120 Mc/s. Was unable to establish height of aircraft; Würzburg (see below) was used for this purpose.

Gee: RAF medium-range aid to navigation.

GCI: Ground-controlled Interception.

H2S: RAF airborne blind-bombing and navigational aid.

HF: High Frequency.

IFF: Identification Friend or Foe.

Jostle IV: Airborne jammer used against German HF R/T nightfighter control.

Knickebein: Luftwaffe long-range aid to navigation where the approach beam was intersected by a cross beam over the target.

Lichtenstein: German nightfighter AI.

Mandrel: Jammer used against German early warning radar operating on 65-230 Mc/s. Ground and airborne versions.

Mc/s: Megacycles per second.

Meacon: The method of 'masking' a radio beacon or beam by automatic reception and re-radiation of its transmission on the same frequency.

MF: Medium Frequency.

Monica: RAF tail-warning radar against German AI.

Moonshine: Airborne responder triggered by German early warning radar and indicating to it a large formation of bomber aircraft.

Naxos: Airborne receiver enabling German nightfighters to home on to H2S transmissions.

Oboe: RAF ground-controlled radar used for blind-bombing. Operated from two stations (named Cat and Mouse), with a responder in the aircraft; the 'Cat' station controlled the range, and the 'Mouse' station indicated the bomb-release point.

Ottokar: German navigational aid for nightfighters. A modification of Knickebein.

Perfectos: Airborne homer on to German IFF.

Ping-Pong: Ground-controlled DF equipment used to locate enemy radar stations. Used in UK before D-Day to locate German radar stations in the invasion area.

Piperack: Airborne jammer against German AI, SN-2.

Rayon: RAF jammer against R/T channel of German 'Ottokar' nightfighter control.

R/T: Radio Telephony.

Serrate: Airborne equipment used for homing RAF fighters on to Luftwaffe nightfighter AI transmissions.

Shiver: Modified IFF jammer used against German radar controlled search-lights.

SN-2: German nightfigher AI. Modification of Lichtenstein.

Splasher: Homing aid for Allied bombers. No.80 Wing ground-controlled MF beacons, working in groups of four, employed frequency switching to prevent enemy interference.

Tinsel: Airborne jammers used against German HF Nightfighter R/T. The transmitter T 1154 was modified to produce noise-modulation from a microphone in the engine nacelle of the jamming aircraft. Special Tinsel was a high-powered ground version.

VHF: Very High Frequency.

Washtub: Use of BBC Transmitters at Droitwich (and later at Start Point, Devon) at selected times to counter German meaconing of MF beacons being used by the RAF.

Window: Metal foil dropped from raiding aircraft to confuse German radar. American version known as 'Chaff'.

W/T: Wireless Telegraphy.

Würzburg: German radar used to direct searchlights and anti-aircraft guns and, later, nightfighters, against raiding bombers.

Bibliography

Anthony, Arthur, *Lucky B-24*, (Janus Publishing, 1993).

Bartram, Len, *RAF Foulsham, 1942-47.*, privately published.

Bartram, Len, and Hambling, Merv, *RAF Oulton, 1940-47*, privately published.

Berry, Paul, *Airfield Heyday, The Daily Life Around Norfolk Airfields*, privately published, 1989.

Bowen, E G, *Radar Days*, Adam Hilger, 1987.

Bowman, M W, and Cushing. T, *Confounding the Reich*, Patrick Stephens, 1996.

Brandon, Lewis, *Night Flyer*, Goodall Publications. 1992, (Crecy Publishing).

Brettingham, Laurie, *Beam Benders, The History of No.80 (Signals) Wing, RAF 1940-45*, Midland Publishing, 1997.

Brookes, Andrew, *Bomber Squadron at War, (No.101 Squadron)*, Ian Allan,1983.

Callick, E B, *Metres to Microwaves*, Peter Peregrinus, 1990.

Carty, Pat, *Secret Squadrons of the Eighth*, Ian Allan, 1990.

Chisholm, Roderick, *Cover of Darkness*, Chatto and Windus, 1953.

Cordingly, Norman, *From a Cat's Whisker Beginning*, privately published, 1988.

Cordingly, Norman, *Time to Tell*, privately published, 1992.

Cordingly, Norman, *The Era of the Nocturnal Blip*, privately published, 1992.

Gunn, Peter, *RAF Great Massingham. A Norfolk Airfield at War, 1940-45*. Privately published.

Hanbury Brown, R, *A Personal Story of Early Days, Radio Astronomy and Quantum Optics*, Adam Hilger, 1991.

Harris, Sir Arthur T, *Bomber Offensive*, Collins, 1947.

Hutton, Stephen,*Squadron of Deception; the 36th Bomb Squadron in World War Two*, Bushwood Books, 1999.

Jones, Dr. R V, *Most Secret War*, Coronet Books, 1979.

Messenger, Charles, *Bomber Harris and the Strategic Bombing Offensive 1939-45*, Arms and Armour, 1984.

Middlebrook, Martin, and Everitt, Chris, *The Bomber Command War Diaries. An Operational Reference Book, 1939-45*, Midland Publishing, 1995.

Middlebrook, Martin, *The Nuremburg Raid*, Allen Lane, 1973.

Northrop, Joe, *Joe: The Autobiography of a Trenchard Brat*, Square One, 1993.

Peden, Murray, *A Thousand Shall Fall*, Canada's Wings Inc., 1979 (Stoddart Publishing).

Price, Alfred, I*nstrument of Darkness* , Wm Kimber, 1967.

Rawnsley, C F, and Wright, Robert, *Night Fighter*, Wm Collins, 1957.

Renaut, Michael, *Terror by Night*, Wm Kimber, 1982.

Richards, Dennis, *The Hardest Victory; RAF Bomber Command in the Second World War*, Coronet Books, 1995.

Saward, Dudley, *Bomber Harris*, Cassell, 1984,

Sykes, H C 'Bill', *The Forging of a Weapon*, SSAFA, 1989.

Streetley, Martin, *Confound and Destroy*, Macdonald and Janes, 1978.

Warren, Glyn, *The Endless Sky: Pershore and Defford*, privately published.

Watson-Watt, Sir Robert, *Three Steps to Victory*, Odham's Press, 1957.

Webster, Sir Charles, and Frankland, Noble, *The Strategic Air Offensive against Germany, 1939-45*, HMSO, 1961.

Index

Layout: Stephen M.L. Young (stephenmlyoung@aol.com)

Font: Adobe Garamond (11pt)

Copies of this book can be ordered via the Internet: www.librario.com

or from:

              Librario Publishing Ltd
              Brough House, Milton Brodie, Kinloss
              Moray IV36 2UA
              Tel /Fax No 01343 850 617